C000157772

CAR
GUIDE
2008

The facts
The figures
The knowledge

Published as Alle Auto's 2008, by Uitgeverij de Alk b.v.,
Alkmaar, The Netherlands, in November 2007,
This English edition, titled Haynes Car Guide 2008,
published by Haynes Publishing, in November 2007

A catalogue record for this book is available
from the British Library

ISBN 978 1 84425 455 2

Library of Congress catalog card no 2007931180

Produced by HSPublicity bv, Bodegraven, The
Netherlands Dutch editorial team: Henri Stolwijk,
Wim Otten, Niels van der Weiden, Celeste Rooswinkel,
Gwenda van Gorkum, Paul Spek, Charissa van Eijk,
Ellen de Vos, Kristian Spithout, Alma van Vliet

UK editorial team: Richard Dredge, Derek Smith, Lee Parsons

Published by Haynes Publishing, Sparkford,
Yeovil, Somerset BA22 7JJ, UK
Tel: 01963 442030 Fax: 01963 440001
Int.tel: +44 1963 442030 Int.fax: +44 1963 440001
E-mail: sales@haynes.co.uk
Website: www.haynes.co.uk

Haynes North America Inc., 861 Lawrence Drive,
Newbury Park, California 91320, USA

Printed and bound in Holland

Contents

The new car market shifts into overdrive

The car world is currently more active than ever, with an increasing number of fresh models being launched every month. Just a few years ago, the number of independent producers began shrinking due to mergers and takeovers. Today, that trend has reversed, and car makers are shedding many of their brands. Ford has already said farewell to Aston Martin and has put Land Rover and Jaguar up for sale (and may have already found a buyer). Meanwhile, DaimlerChrysler has split up, Mercedes, Maybach and Smart parting company with Dodge, Chrysler and Jeep.

BMW's Efficient Dynamics programme is typical of the efforts car manufacturers are putting into their products. The aim is to increase fuel efficiency while also reducing the weight of the vehicles.

In the meantime, Chinese and Indian carmakers are gaining ground, concentrating mainly on the growing car markets in Russia, India, Iran, Turkey, South Africa and China. Here is where the real competition will occur, where the big opportunities are waiting. In 2006, worldwide car sales rose by 20 per cent to 65 million cars, but in the United States, Western Europe and Japan the markets stayed steady with no growth overall between them.

Western producers are doing their utmost to bring inexpensive cars to market, competing to build a car that sells for under 5,000 dollars. This is only possible by bringing technically simple products to the market, built in low-wage countries. The cars that we in the West prefer to buy, are technically much more complex and equipped with many options, and are therefore are typically much more costly to build and hence to buy. Naturally, there are also some relatively inexpensive cars being built in Europe too, but they are primarily intended for the new markets. The average Chinese car buyer has much less to spend than his European counterpart.

However, while in China the race is on to put the nation on wheels, the goals are very different in more developed countries. While comfort is now essential if any car is to succeed, efficiency is also key. Lighter materials are beginning to be introduced, to improve agility while also cutting fuel consumption. New technologies are also being integrated into new models, to make them cleaner and more economical. Measures include stop/start systems, diesel particulate filters, low-resistance tyres and low-friction engines. There's still a long way to go though, before hydrogen fuel cells become viable, which is why for the foreseeable future we'll instead be moving to smaller, turbocharged internal combustion engines that offer much greater efficiencies without being significantly more costly to build or buy.

These developments mean that there is an enormous diversity of products to suit every taste, while the number of models will continue to grow. As editors of this handy reference, we are therefore faced with a great challenge – fitting it all into just 400 pages will prove quite a challenge! Still, we have compiled the most complete overview possible. By making intelligent choices, we can offer you as a reader an excellent insight into the current options available and the diversity of today's car market. We hope you enjoy reading it.

Henri Stolwijk

For the future, maybe?

Every year we see tantalising glimpses of what we may be able to buy in the future. Some of them are concepts that are initially displayed in a form barely different from what will reach the showroom. Sometimes we see a slick design study that's bound to be watered down for production so it makes economic sense. Then there are the projects that ambitious tiny outfits exhibit, in the hope of attracting enough interest for production to begin. Here are a few of these projects that have surfaced recently, some of which will sink without trace, and some of which you'll be able to buy. We'll leave you to work out which is which!

Artega GT

A car that has so far received few column inches but looks promising is the Artega GT. Styled by Henrik Fisker, the Artega was clearly inspired by all manner of existing sportscars from Porsche, Lotus and TVR – but it's none the worse for that. Artega makes the dubious claim that the car "breaks the mould", even though it's much like all manner of existing low-volume two-seaters. However, with great looks and an enticing technical specfication (mid-mounted VW-sourced 300bhp 3.6-litre V6), at least the car has a good chance of reaching production.

Assystem

The unfortunately named Assystem is one of the most bizarre motoring creations ever devised. With its four wheels in a diamond formation, the Assystem features an electric motor over the front wheel, while attached to the rear axle is a 60bhp Honda petrol engine. There's an 'augmented reality display'; a series of cameras that work out what's going on outside the car to help the driver avoid driving into things. Whatever happened to looking out of the windscreen?

© richarddredge.com

Audi Cross Quattro

Just like BMW, Audi is keen to enter as many market segments as possible, in a bid to expand production. In effect, this is Audi's take on the coupé-SUV market, which BMW is tackling with the X6. The transversely installed four-cylinder in-line TDI engine is a completely new development, developing 204bhp and 295lb ft of torque, giving sporty performance with surprising economy. Of course there's also Audi's famed quattro four-wheel drive system, mated to an S-Tronic dual-clutch gearbox.

BMW X6

The X6 that BMW unveiled at the 2007 Frankfurt motor show should make it to the showroom almost unchanged. This 'SUV-coupé' is intended to reinforce BMW's position in the upper market segments, and while it's clearly based on the X5, it has a completely different roof line and is more performance-oriented. BMW also unveiled a hybrid edition, the drive train developed in conjunction with Mercedes-Benz and General Motors and which will find its way into both the X5 and production versions of the X6.

Citroen C5 Airscape

A very important newcomer for Citroën is the new C5. The French brand chose not to unveil the new model at the 2007 Frankfurt show however, opting instead for a concept version of the new middle-segment car. The C5 Airscape is a four-seater convertible with a folding hard top, suggesting Citroën may enter a segment (the coupé-cabriolet) that it hasn't tried to sell in before. The 2.7-litre diesel engine is coupled to a start-stop system and uses regenerative braking to conserve fuel – and if the production car looks as good as the concept, it's bound to be a winner.

Ford Verve

New Edge Design is dead; Ford instead has a new aesthetic language called Kinetic Design. Models such as the Ford Mondeo, S-Max and Kuga were styled using this, and the next in line will be the new Fiesta. In order to provide a glimpse of how it will look, Ford has already revealed the Verve, with the production car being based on the Mazda2. Ford plans on making the new Fiesta a worldwide success; the new car will also be sold in the US, where small cars are booming business, as exemplified by the Mini.

Giugiaro Vadho

The Giugiaro Vadho concept, revealed at the 2007 Geneva Motor Show, is powered by a BMW-sourced V12 hydrogen engine. The concept is built on a one-off chassis, and is controlled by a pair of joysticks, rather than the more conventional steering wheel. The V12 sits next to the aircraft-style cockpit (which can't do much for weight distribution) and it's mated to a seven-speed SMG gearbox, which is also taken from the BMW parts bin. The red badge on the nose is Giugiaro's new corporate logo.

© richarddredge.com

Honda Accord

In America, the Honda Accord has already been replaced by a new model, and now it's Europe's turn to receive this mid-sized car with a new body. The new Accord will once again be available in saloon and estate versions, the latter being chosen as Honda's 2007 Frankfurt motor show concept. According to Honda, the Accord Sports Tourer Concept is more spacious than the current Accord model, and the production version will eventually be available with a much-improved diesel engine.

Lamborghini Reventon

Initially claimed to be limited to just 20 units, all of which were sold before the car was even unveiled, the Reventon is Lamborghini's most costly and powerful car ever. Weighing in at a cool one million euros, this hypercar packs 660bhp – but doesn't accelerate any quicker than the standard production Murciélago LP640, on which the car is based mechanically. If you're wondering where you've seen that styling before, the Reventon was inspired by the F-22 Raptor US fighter plane, with the new bodywork being constructed of carbon fibre.

Loremo

Just about everyone is trying to build a car that's usable yet capable of returning the fuel consumption of a moped. This French company may have come up with one of the most practical and novel answers yet, with a car that can seat four yet still use very little fuel. Hybrid and electric versions are being developed, but the key variants are two and three-cylinder turbodiesels, capable of taking the Loremo to as much as 120mph while also returning phenomenal economy thanks to low weight and a Cd of just 0.22.

Mercedes-Benz F700

Just to show that you don't need to have taste to be wealthy, Mercedes showed perhaps the most unattractive concept of the year at the 2007 Frankfurt motor show. However, while it's undeniably ugly, the F700 features some impressive technology. With a 1.8-litre engine, the F700 offers the space, comfort and performance of the current S350, but with the economy of an A-Class. So despite the F700 being able to achieve a limited maximum of 125mph, it's capable of returning up to 53mpg.

Mitsubishi Concept-cX

Mitsubishi hasn't enjoyed good times in recent years, but things have improved lately and this concept is a sign that there are good times ahead. A compact SUV in the tradition of the Suzuki SX4, the Concept-cX is based on the flexible platform Mitsubishi already uses for the Lancer and Outlander. The all-new diesel engine will replace the VW-sourced unit that Mitsubishi is currently having to buy in for the European market, while the nose continues the design theme already seen in the new Lancer.

Nissan Mixim

The Mixim concept is a compact vehicle for young drivers who are mostly engaged by their computer and the world via the internet. The driver sits centrally, while the steering wheel and controls are inspired by the interfaces so familiar to computer gamers. Powered by Nissan's 'Super Motor' electric motor/generator and using compact lithium-ion batteries, the Mixim has unusually rapid performance combined with a usefully extended range. One Super Motor powers the front axle and a second drives the rear axle, giving the Mixim all-wheel drive.

Opel Flextreme

Electric cars are the future, according to General Motors. The Opel Flextreme is a car the size of an Astra that can drive for nearly 35 miles with one battery charge. Then the efficient 1.3-litre diesel engine cuts in to charge the batteries, but not to power the wheels. Flextreme drivers can also charge their car's batteries by plugging the vehicle into a conventional power socket, and if a hitch should occur, GM has also made provision for storage of Segway human transporters.

Peugeot 308RCZ

It's not hard to see what inspired the RCZ; the TT has proved a huge hit for Audi and Peugeot clearly wants to emulate that. In a bid to increase fuel efficiency while also maximising agility, much of the RCZ is built of carbon fibre and aluminium, power being provided by a 1.6-litre THP turbocharged petrol engine developed from the unit normally found under the bonnet of the 207 GTi, but now with a maximum power output of 218 bhp. That's enough to give a top speed of 146mph, but with up to 42mpg.

Renault Laguna Coupé

Executive French cars have never done very well in the UK, with posh coupés performing especially poorly. That hasn't stopped Renault producing this two-door edition of the all-new Laguna though, with UK sales promised at some point in the future. Renault will release the Laguna coupé with a newly-developed V6 diesel engine, among others; this powerplant will also be used by Infiniti, Nissan's Lexus-rivalling luxury brand that will be launched in Western Europe in 2009.

Rinspeed eXasis

You can always rely on Rinspeed to devise something mad for the Geneva motor show, and this was the company's most recent effort. Called the eXasis, the concept featured a transparent plastic bodyshell, enabling its unusual running gear to be displayed to all. Up front is a two-cylinder 750cc turbocharged engine running on bioethanol, producing 150bhp. That's enough to give the car a top speed of over 130mph – with acceleration to match. Not much chance of seeing this one in the showrooms though!

Russo Baltique

Something that's unlikely to ever see production is the Russo Baltique, based on a Maybach floorpan and reviving a name last seen in 1915. Called the Impression, this mad contraption features rear wheel spats and suicide doors, but can allegedly top 195mph thanks to its 555bhp twin-turbo V12. As is par for the course, a company spokesman claimed that the car will go into production if there's enough demand. So it'll be remaining a one-off then, thanks to looks that only its mother could love, and a sky-high price tag.

Seat Tribu

The Belgian Luc Donckerwolke has been Seat's head of design since 2006. To give a glimpse of the direction in which the Spanish brand is heading, his team has come up with the Tribu, a sporty and compact SUV to take on established contenders such as the Land Rover Freelander and Honda CRV. Those trapezoidal headlamps, grille and air vents, plus the new grille-mesh design with elongated hexagons will provide the family look for Seats of the future; let's hope it isn't watered down at all.

© richarddredge.com

Stola

Like the Russo Baltique, this is another machine with Maybach running gear. This un-named concept from Italian coachbuilder Stola looks like an even more extreme edition of the Maybach Exelero, as that's the car that spawned this monster. Stola aims to offer "no more than 25 examples" of the car, but at this stage it seems pretty likely that this is yet another concept that won't ever get out of the starting blocks. One look at this and suddenly the Renault Avantime makes sense. Perhaps even the Ssangyong Rodius. Okay then, definitely not the Rodius.

Suzuki Kizashi

While many volume brands are developing ever smaller cars, the compact car specialist Suzuki has brought out this mid-sized sports hatch; completely new territory for the brand. That's because many current Suzuki owners are forced to leave the marque when they want to move into a bigger car; by building bigger vehicles, the company hopes to retain those customers. The Kizashi (Japanese for 'prelude') gives us a glimpse of Suzuki's future, with a production edition slated for some time after 2009.

Toyota iQ

With the iQ, Toyota proves that there is room for an even more compact car below the Aygo and Yaris; despite being just 2.97 metres long, there's still space for four people – although only three of these can be full-sized adults. The iQ wasn't designed in Japan, where small cars are a common sight on the streets, but in Toyota's design studio in France. An interesting detail: the instructions from the navigation system are projected onto a transparent piece of plexiglass on the dashboard.

Tramontana

One of the few oddball cars that's made several motor show outings is the Tramontana, from Spain. Now re-engineered with a carbon-fibre body tub, the Mercedes mid-mounted V12 remains. Once again the company is sitting on "numerous orders" and the first cars will be delivered to their owners "soon". Unfotunately there's still lots of development needed for this costly machine; the fit and finish of the display car makes the Lada Riva look like a coachbuilt luxury vehicle.

Volkswagen Up!

VW is also gambling on a small car; the Up! is 3.45 metres long, with a rear-engine layout, and as with the Toyota iQ, there's enough space for four people. The Up! concept, designed by a team overseen by Chief Designer of the Volkswagen Group, Walter de Silva, marks the debut of a new styling direction with simple features while retaining the instantly recognisable Volkswagen 'face'. At the rear is a tailgate section constructed entirely out of a transparent material, inset into the centre of which is a glowing Volkswagen roundel.

How the catalogue works

Due to space limitations, we can offer only each car's headline technical data in this book. However, there's a multitude of websites that offer massive amounts of facts and figures; here's the background to the various fields we've chosen.

Make and model designation
The model names are at the top of the tables. In some cases, two engine variants are included, separated by a slash. Usually the descriptions are limited to the basic versions with manual gearboxes; for hatchbacks, these are the three-door versions. In most cases we have chosen not to describe all available engines separately, but to spread them over several pages. Diesel engines, for example, are described with the estate cars.

Engine type
This is described as petrol or diesel, followed by the number of cylinders and the construction method. The standard construction method on the European market is the four-cylinder, in-line engine, so-called because four cylinders are placed in a single line on the crankshaft. This arrangement is also used for three, five and six-cylinder powerplants. Another popular configuration is the V, with two separate banks of cylinders that are placed at an angle to each other on the crankshaft. Volkswagen has a sort of combined line and V engine in which the cylinders are at so small an angle that they fit under one cylinder head. The Volkswagen W engines even have four banks of cylinders in a compact arrangement. The boxer engine (Porsche and Subaru) is an arrangement with two cylinder banks mounted horizontally opposite each other. Finally, there is a car on the market with a rotary engine, the Mazda RX-8.

Maximum power
The correct power specification is in kilowatts (kW). For those who are used to horsepower (hp) it's difficult to switch to kilowatts – but 400bhp sounds a lot more impressive than 298kW! For this reason, we have used both.

Maximum torque
Torque, expressed in pounds feet (lb ft), represents the turning force a motor can produce when the crankshaft turns. In simple terms, torque x rpm = power output. An engine with a lot of torque doesn't have to rev so much to get the car moving, making it quieter and more pleasant to drive. In very simple terms, the power output produces the top speed, while the torque provides acceleration.

Gears
There is constant pressure to make cars more economical and the gearbox plays a major role in this: a transmission with more gears means the engine doesn't have to run as fast and therefore operates more economically. Noise reduction is also a consideration, which is partly why the six-speed gearbox is gradually replacing five-speed units, just like the five-speed replaced the four-speed in the 1980s.

Automatic
In the case of the automatic, we're no longer just talking about an automatic with torque converter. Modern automatics have five ratios, or even seven (Mercedes) and eight (Lexus). In addition, there are increasingly more manual gearboxes with a clutch operated by a hydraulic pump. The continuous variable transmission (CVT), originally by Daf's van Doorne, has enjoyed something of a renaissance over the past decade, but there's a new pretender to the throne. Gradually gaining ground is Volkswagen's system, the DSG. This effectively consists of two half gearboxes, each with its own clutch so that the electronics can make the next gear 'ready' in advance, typically via steering wheel mounted paddle shifts.

Drive

Front-wheel drive is the norm for compact cars, but it has difficulty in handling outputs higher than 250bhp because it corrupts the steering. That's why large cars are fitted with rear-wheel or four-wheel drive; the latter isn't just for off-road cars because putting the power down effectively is key to making cars safer. That's why an increasing number of manufacturers are offering four-wheel drive as standard.

Brakes F/R (front/rear)

Most, if not all, cars have a power-assisted braking system with disc brakes in front. Often the rear brakes are solid discs, but there are still some drum brakes fitted in the case of smaller, cheaper cars. Ventilated or perforated discs are increasingly common though, with their channels to dissipate heat more efficiently.

Kerb weight

Most manufacturers give the kerb weight according to the European directive. This represents the car including all fluids, with a 90 percent full tank and 75 kilos of load. However, the weight is only an indication because it also depends on the version. Optional wheels, air-conditioning or roof rails add kilos. The vehicle registration weight will always differ from the manufacturer's specification.

Maximum towing weight

The maximum towing weight shows how heavy a caravan or trailer may be. The braked weight, indicating how much can be towed if the trailer is equipped with a braking installation, is always stated. The safest rule of thumb however is to tow no more than 85 per cent of the car's kerb weight.

Luggage storage capacity

This is stated in litres. It always gives the volume of the boot or, in the case of hatchbacks, the luggage space up to window level. For models with a fold-down rear seat or even removable seats, two figures are given. Some saloons also have fold-down rear seats.

Combined fuel consumption

Fuel consumption is measured according to the ECE standard. This is the combined fuel consumption: a combination of town driving and driving on the open road. Fuel consumption is given in litres per 100 kilometres, which can be converted to kilometres per litre (or miles per gallon). However, the ECE standard is a laboratory test that says little about the daily driving conditions. In practice, it is almost impossible to achieve the stated consumption.

EuroNCAP

A large number of European consumer organisations and governments are working together on the European New Car Assessment Programme (EuroNCAP). This involves more than just collision tests, but these collision tests have grown into the standard car safety test. Every manufacturer wants 'five stars' for their new model – and pays attention to that in the development phase.

Latest facelift

Sometimes a facelift is little more than a different grille or a different colour, but usually it also involves an improved engine and more extensive standard fittings. There is also a difference in model policy: European cars go on for a long time – often ten years or more – and are then replaced by something totally new. Sometimes there is a need for a facelift, even in the case of an evergreen like the Renault Twingo. The appearance of Japanese cars changes more quickly, but under the bonnet developments are more gradual.

Warranty

In the UK most manufacturers give a two-year general warranty, to which is added another year at dealership level. Some Asian manufacturers offer a five-year warranty.

Low-volume production cars

We've tried to include as many cars in this book as possible, but because the 2008 Car Guide started out as a Continental publication, the focus in the main pages is on cars that are available in mainland Europe. However, if there's one thing that marks out the British market, it's the diversity of small-volume manufacturers which produce niche models. To reflect this, in the following pages you can discover some of the great creations that we get to enjoy in Britain.

Conversion tables

Torque
1 Nm = 0.737 lb ft, 1 lb ft = 1.3568 Nm
Power
1 kW = 1.341 bhp, 1 bhp = 0.7457 kW
1 PS = 0.986 bhp, 1 bhp = 1.014 PS
Speed
1mph = 1.61km/h, 1km/h = 0.621mph
(62mph = 100km/h)

ARIEL ATOM

Engine type	Petrol, in-line 4
Displacement	1998cc
Max power	300bhp @ 8200rpm
Max torque	191lb ft @ 7150rpm
Gears	6-speed manual
Kerb weight	456kg
Consumption	N/A
0-62mph	3.4sec
Top speed	150mph
Notes	

Drivers' cars don't come much more focused than this; power to weight is everything.

© richarddredge.com

ASCARI KZ-1

Engine type	Petrol, V8
Displacement	4941cc
Max power	500bhp @ 7000rpm
Max torque	368lb ft @ 4500rpm
Gears	6-speed manual
Kerb weight	1330kg
Consumption	N/A
0-62mph	3.8sec
Top speed	200mph
Notes	

Hugely fast and very expensive, the KZ-1 uses the V8 from BMW's previous-generation M5.

BRISTOL BLENHEIM 3 / 3S

Engine type	Petrol V8
Displacement	5900cc
Max power	400bhp @ 5500rpm (est)
Max torque	390lb ft @ 4000rpm (est)
Gears	4-speed automatic
Kerb weight	1728kg
Consumption	N/A
0-62mph	6.3sec / 5.4sec
Top speed	150mph
Notes	

The Blenheim has been around since 1993, but its underpinnings are much older than that – and it shows. Not that Bristol's customers care of course...

BRISTOL FIGHTER

Engine type	Petrol, V10
Displacement	7996cc
Max power	386Kw (525bhp) @ 5600rpm
Max torque	525lb ft @ 3600rpm
Gears	6-speed manual
Kerb weight	1475kg
0-62mph	4.0sec
Top speed	210mph
Notes	

One of the most exclusive supercars around, Bristol offers even more extreme versions including the 1012bhp Fighter T, capable of a claimed 225mph.

© richarddredge.com

BROOKE DOUBLE R

Engine type	Petrol, in-line 4
Displacement	2261cc
Max power	260bhp @ 7500rpm
Max torque	200lb ft @ 6000rpm
Gears	5-speed manual
Kerb weight	550kg
0-62mph	3.2sec
Top speed	155mph
Notes	

This is what Brits do best: race cars for the road with the most advanced technology available.

CAPARO T1

Engine type	Petrol, V8
Displacement	2.4-litre
Max power	480bhp @ 10,500rpm
Max torque	N/A
Gears	6-speed sequential
Kerb weight	470kg
Consumption	N/A
0-62mph	2.5sec
Top speed	200mph
Notes	

With a power-to-weight ratio that's twice the Bugatti Veyron's, the T1 is set to take road cars to a new level.

CATERHAM SEVEN ROADSPORT 160

Engine type	Petrol, in-line 4
Displacement	1597cc
Max power	160bhp @ 7000rpm
Max torque	130lb ft @ 5000rpm
Gears	5-speed manual
Kerb weight	550kg
Consumption	N/A
0-62mph	4.9sec
Top speed	128mph
Notes	

The Roadsport 160 uses a VVC-equipped K-Series engine; the less powerful 125 and 150 editions use Ford's Sigma unit.

CATERHAM SEVEN SUPERLIGHT R400

Engine type	Petrol, in-line 4
Displacement	1999cc
Max power	210bhp @ 7600rpm
Max torque	150lb ft @ 6300rpm
Gears	6-speed manual
Kerb weight	500kg
Consumption	N/A
0-62mph	3.8sec
Top speed	140mph
Notes	

The Superlight takes adding lightness to a new level; anything that's comfort-focused is stripped out.

CATERHAM CSR 260

Engine type	Petrol in-line 4
Displacement	2261cc
Max power	260bhp @ 7500rpm
Max torque	200lb ft @ 6200rpm
Gears	5-speed manual
Kerb weight	550kg
0-62mph	3.1sec
Top speed	155mph
Notes	

The CSR features Cosworth-tuned Ford engines, along with independent rear suspension.

CONNAUGHT

Engine type	Petrol, V10, supercharged
Displacement	2.0 litres
Max power	300bhp @ 7000rpm
Max torque	274lb ft @ 3000rpm
Gears	5-speed manual
Kerb weight	950kg
Consumption	N/A
0-62mph	Under 5.0sec
Top speed	170mph
Notes	

Fascinating project from Wales, with bespoke V10 engine – plus there's a hybrid on the way.

ELFIN MS8 CLUBMAN

Engine type	Petrol, V8
Displacement	5.7 litres
Max power	329bhp
Max torque	343lb ft
Gears	6-speed manual
Kerb weight	900kg
Consumption	N/A
0-62mph	4.2sec
Top speed	186mph
Notes	

Elfin celebrates its 50th anniversary of car production this year, with each car hand-built to order.

FARBIO GTS

Engine type	Petrol, V6, supercharged
Displacement	3 litres
Max power	384bhp
Max torque	N/A
Gears	6-speed manual
Kerb weight	1066kg
Consumption	N/A
0-62mph	3.9sec
Top speed	175mph
Notes	

At last the Farboud GTS reaches the market, with a name change. Also available in normally aspirated form.

GRINNALL SCORPION

Engine type	Petrol, in-line 4
Displacement	1100cc
Max power	100bhp+
Gears	6-speed manual
Kerb weight	395kg
Consumption	40mpg
0-62mph	5.0sec
Top speed	130mph
Notes	

Established three-wheeler with a BMW 'bike engine; there's now a four-wheeler too, with Audi 1.8T power.

© richarddredge.com

GUMPERT APOLLO

Engine type	Petrol, V8
Displacement	4163cc
Max power	641bhp @ 6500rpm
Max torque	597lb ft @ 4500rpm
Gears	6-speed manual
Kerb weight	1200kg
Consumption	N/A
0-62mph	3.0sec
Top speed	224mph
Notes	

New arrival to an already overcrowded marketplace, using a twin-turbo Audi V8.

LONDON TAXIS INTERNATIONAL

Engine type	Turbodiesel, in-line 4
Displacement	2499cc
Max power	100bhp @ 4000rpm
Max torque	177lb ft @ 1800rpm
Gears	5-speed manual/auto
Kerb weight	1850kg
Consumption	35mpg
0-62mph	N/A
Top speed	81mph
Notes	

Following on from where the TXII left off, the TX4 features revised styling and more equipment.

MARCOS TSO GT2

Engine type	Petrol, V8
Displacement	5665cc
Max power	475bhp @ 6500rpm
Max torque	395lb ft @ 5500rpm
Gears	6-speed manual
Kerb weight	1150kg
0-62mph	4.0sec
Top speed	185mph
Notes	

As we went to press, Marcos went into administration – but such an illustrious name deserves to return.

MITSUBISHI i

Engine type	Petrol, in-line 3
Displacement	659cc
Max power	42kW (57bhp)
Max torque	62lb ft @ 3000rpm
Gears	4-speed auto
Kerb weight	900kg
Consumption	54.6mpg
0-62mph	N/A
Top speed	84mph
Notes	

Funky city car, available in limited numbers only.

PAGANI ZONDA F

Engine type	Petrol, V12
Displacement	7291cc
Max power	602bhp @ 6150rpm
Max torque	560lb ft @ 4000rpm
Gears	6
Kerb weight	1250kg
Consumption	20mpg
0-62mph	3.6sec
Top speed	216mph
Notes	

It came from nowhere and took on the big boys – winning in the process. Deeply impressive.

PERODUA KELISA

Engine type	Petrol, in-line 3
Displacement	989cc
Max power	40kW (55bhp) @ 5200rpm
Max torque	65lb ft @ 3600rpm
Gears	5-speed manual
Kerb weight	760kg
Consumption	55.4mpg
0-62mph	14.8sec
Top speed	88mph
Notes	

The cheapest new car in Britain started life as a Daihatsu Cuore. The EZi version comes with a 3-speed automatic transmission as standard.

PERODUA KENARI

Engine type Petrol, in-line 3
Displacement	989cc
Max power	43kW (58bhp) @ 6000rpm
Max torque	65lb ft @ 3600rpm
Gears	5-speed manual
Kerb weight	865kg
Consumption	50.4mpg
0-62mph	15.0sec
Top speed	87mph
Notes	

Formerly known as Daihatsu Move, also available
with a three-speed automatic transmission.

PERODUA MYVI

Engine type	Petrol in-line 4
Displacement	1298cc
Max power	63kW (86bhp) @ 6000rpm
Max torque	86lb ft @ 3200rpm
Gears	5-speed manual
Kerb weight	935kg
Consumption	48.7mpg
0-62mph	11.3sec
Top speed	106mph
Notes	

The Daihatsu Sirion's identical but cheaper twin.

PROTON SAVVY

Engine type Petrol in-line 4
Displacement	1149cc
Max power	55kW (75bhp) @ 5500rpm
Max torque	77lb ft @ 4250rpm
Gears	5-speed manual
Kerb weight	965kg
Consumption	49.6mpg
0-62mph	13.9sec
Top speed	99mph
Notes	

The Savvy was introduced in 2006, powered by a
Renault engine.

PROTON SATRIA NEO 1.6

Engine type	Petrol in-line 4
Displacement	1597cc
Max power	82kW (111bhp) @ 6000rpm
Max torque	109lb ft @ 4000rpm
Gears	5-speed manual
Kerb weight	1170kg
Consumption	42.8mpg
0-62mph	11.5sec
Top speed	118mph
Notes	

This all-new Satria, introduced in March 2007, is
also available with a more economical 1.3-litre
engine, offering 94bhp.

PROTON GEN2 1.6

Engine type	Petrol, in-line 4
Displacement	1597cc
Max power	110bhp @ 6000rpm
Max torque	109lb ft @ 4000rpm
Gears	5-speed manual
Kerb weight	1185kg
Consumption	39.2mpg
0-62mph	12.6sec
Top speed	118mph
Notes	

Five-door hatch revised in 2007; saloon on the way.
Looks dull but is great to drive thanks to Lotus.

VAUXHALL VXR8

Engine type	Petrol, V8
Displacement	5967cc
Max power	417bhp @ 6000rpm
Max torque	405lb ft @ 4400rpm
Gears	6-speed manual
Kerb weight	1831kg
Consumption	18.5mpg
0-62mph	4.9sec
Top speed	155mph
Notes	

A Holden Commodore with a Corvette engine.

WESTFIELD SEIGHT

Engine type	Petrol, in-line 4
Displacement	3950cc
Max power	200bhp @ 4750rpm
Max torque	235lb ft @ 2600rpm
Gears	5-speed manual
Kerb weight	680kg
Consumption	N/A
0-62mph	4.3sec
Top speed	140mph
Notes	

Based on the classic Seven shape that launched
Westfield into the big time, the SEight is a monster!

© richarddredge.com

WESTFIELD XI

Engine type	Petrol, in-line 4
Displacement	1275cc
Max power	65bhp @ 6000rpm
Max torque	72lb ft @ 3000rpm
Gears	4-speed manual
Kerb weight	1172kg
Consumption	40mpg
0-60mph	10.1sec
Top speed	120mph
Notes	

Classic kit now back in production using BMC A-
Series power.

ALFA ROMEO 147 1.6 / 2.0

engine type	: petrol, inline-4
displacement	: 1598 / 1970 cc
max. power	: 88 kW (120 bhp) / 110 kW (150 bhp)
@	: 6200 / 6300 rpm
max. torque	: 108/ 133 lb ft
@	: 4200 / 3800 rpm
gears	: 5
AT	: n.a.
drive	: FWD
brakes f/r	: vent. discs / discs
body type	: 3-, 5-dr. hatchback
l x w x h	: 4223 x 1729 x 1442 mm
wheelbase	: 2546 mm
turning circle	: 11,5 m
kerb weight	: 1175 / 1225 kg
towing weight	: 1300 kg
boot space	: 280 l – 1030 l
fuel capacity	: 60 l
consumption	: 34.4 / 31.7 mpg
acc. 0-62 mph	: 10.6 / 9.3 s
top speed	: 121 / 129 mph
EuroNCAP	: 3 stars
introduction	: October 2000
last revised in	: January 2005
warranty	: 2 years
miscellaneous	: Trendy Italian car, full of character. Rewarding driver because of excellent steering and responsive chassis. Basic version with 105 bhp 1.6 engine.

147 1.9 JTD 8V / 1.9 JTD 16V

engine type	: diesel, inline-4
displacement	: 1910 cc
max. power	: 88 kW (120 bhp) / 110 kW (150 bhp)
@	: 4000 rpm
max. torque	: 206 / 225 lb ft
@	: 2000 rpm
gears	: 5 / 6
kerb weight	: 1245 / 1265 kg
towing weight	: 1300 kg
consumption	: 48,7 mpg
acc. 0-60 mph	: 9.6 / 8.8 s
top speed	: 120 / 129 mph
miscellaneous	: 150 bhp Multijet diesel engine with lots of torque matches well with the 147. Excellent choice for hurried business people.

ALFA ROMEO 159 1.8 MPI / 1.9 JTS

engine type	: petrol, inline-4	kerb weight	: 1405 / 1455 kg
displacement	: 1796 / 1859 cc	towing weight	: 1400 / 1500 kg
max. power	: 103 kW (140 bhp) /	boot space	: 405 l
	118 kW (160 bhp)	fuel capacity	: 70 l
@	: 6300 / 6500 rpm	consumption	: n.a. / 32.5 mpg
max. torque	: 129 / 140 lb ft	acc. 0-62 mph	: 10.2 / 9.7 s
@	: 3800 / 4500 rpm	top speed	: 128 / 132 mph
gears	: 5 / 6	EuroNCAP	: 5 stars
AT	: n.a.	introduction	: October 2005
drive	: FWD	last revised in	: n.a.
brakes f/r	: vent. discs / discs	warranty	: 3 years
body type	: 4-dr. saloon	miscellaneous	: 1.8 mpi is the new entry level
l x w x h	: 4660 x 1828 x 1417 mm		engine for the 159 range. All
wheelbase	: 2700 mm		engines of saloon also available for
turning circle	: 11.1 m		Sportwagon.

159 2.2 JTS / 3.2 V6

engine type	: petrol, inline-4 / V6
displacement	: 2198 / 3195 cc
max. power	: 136 kW (185 bhp) /
	191kW (260 bhp)
@	: 6500 / 6200 rpm
max. torque	: 170 / 238 lb ft
@	: 4500 rpm
gears	: 6
kerb weight	: 1490 / 1740 kg
towing weight	: 1500 kg
consumption	: 30.1 / 24.6 mpg
acc. 0-60 mph	: 8.8 / 7.0 s
top speed	: 138 / 149 mph
miscellaneous	: 3.2 V6 engine in 159 comes
	standard with 4WD, which makes it a
	rather heavy car.

ALFA ROMEO 159 SPORTWAGON 1.9 JTDM 8V / 1.9 JTDM 16V

engine type	: diesel, inline-4	**kerb weight**	: 1560 kg
displacement	: 1910 cc	**towing weight**	: 1500 kg
max. power	: 110 kW (150 bhp)	**boot space**	: 445 l
@	: 4000 rpm	**fuel capacity**	: 70 l
max. torque	: 236 lb ft	**consumption**	: 46.3 mpg
@	: 2000 rpm	**acc. 0-62 mph**	: 9.6 s
gears	: 6	**top speed**	: 129 mph
AT	: n.a.	**EuroNCAP**	: 5 stars
drive	: FWD	**introduction**	: March 2006
brakes f/r	: vent. discs / discs	**last revised in**	: n.a.
body type	: 5-dr. stationwagon	**warranty**	: 2 years
l x w x h	: 4660 x 1828 x 1417 mm	**miscellaneous**	: The Sportwagon does not offer that much more interior space than the regular 159 model, but is nonetheless a very attractive car. Same diesel engines also available in saloon.
wheelbase	: 2700 mm		
turning circle	: 11.1 m		

159 SPORTWAGON 2.4 JTDM

engine type	: diesel, inline-5
displacement	: 2387 cc
max. power	: 154 kW (210 bhp)
@	: 4000 rpm
max. torque	: 295 lb ft
@	: 1500 rpm
gears	: 6
kerb weight	: 1655 kg
towing weight	: 1500 kg
consumption	: 40.4 mpg
acc. 0-60 mph	: 834 s
top speed	: 142 mph
miscellaneous	: Five-cylinder diesel engine now offers 10 bhp more. Maximum torque peaks at an engine speed which is 500 rpm lower than before. Four-wheel drive is optional.

ALFA ROMEO GT 2.0 JTS

engine type	: petrol, inline-4		kerb weight	: 1265 / 1295 kg
displacement	: 1970 cc		towing weight	: 1300 kg
max. power	: 122 kW (165 bhp)		boot space	: 320 l
@	: 6400 rpm		fuel capacity	: 63 l
max. torque	: 152 lb ft		consumption	: 32.5 mpg
@	: 3250 rpm		acc. 0-62 mph	: 8.7 s
gears	: 5		top speed	: 134 mph
AT	: -		EuroNCAP	: n.a.
drive	: FWD		introduction	: September 2003
brakes f/r	: vent. discs / discs		last revised in	: January 2007
body type	: 2-dr. coupe		warranty	: 2 years
l x w x h	: 4489 x 1763 x 1355 mm		miscellaneous	: The GT model was given a mild
wheelbase	: 2596 mm			facelift recently and remains part
turning circle	: 11.5 m			of the delivery programme next
				to the Brera.

GT 1.9 JTDM 16V

engine type	: diesel, inline-4
displacement	: 1910 cc
max. power	: 110 kW (150 bhp)
@	: 4000 rpm
max. torque	: 225 lb ft
@	: 2000 rpm
gears	: 6
kerb weight	: 1365 kg
towing weight	: 1300 kg
consumption	: 45.6 mpg
acc. 0-60 mph	: 9.6 s
top speed	: 130 mph
miscellaneous	: Sadly, the classic Alfa V6 is no longer with us.

ALFA ROMEO BRERA / SPIDER 2.2 JTS / 3.2 V6

engine type	: petrol, inline-4 / V6		kerb weight	: 1445 / 1605 kg
displacement	: 2198 / 3195 cc		towing weight	: 1450 / 1500 kg
max. power	: 136 kW (185 bhp) /		boot space	: 300 l
	191 kW (260 bhp)		fuel capacity	: 70 l
@	: 6500 / 6200 rpm		consumption	: 30.2 / 24.7 mpg
max. torque	: 170 / 238 lb ft		acc. 0-62 mph	: 9.4 / 11.5 s
@	: 4500 rpm		top speed	: 138 / 149 mph
gears	: 6		EuroNCAP	: n.a.
AT	: n.a.		introduction	: November 2005
drive	: FWD / 4WD		last revised in	: -
brakes f/r	: vent. discs / discs		warranty	: 2 years
body type	: 2-dr. coupe		miscellaneous	: What will it be: the quick but heavy
l x w x h	: 4413 x 1830 x 1372 mm			3.2 V6 or the 2.2 JTS which is not
wheelbase	: 2525 mm			as heavy and not as fast? A tough
turning circle	: 10.7 m			choice.

BRERA 2.4 JTDM

engine type	: diesel, inline-5
displacement	: 2387 cc
max. power	: 147 kW (200bhp)
@	: 4000 rpm
max. torque	: 295 lb ft
@	: 2000 rpm
gears	: 6
kerb weight	: 1600 kg
towing weight	: 1500 kg
consumption	: 41.7 mpg
acc. 0-60 mph	: 8.1 s
top speed	: 142 mph
miscellaneous	: Diesel engine sounds lovely and offers more torque than V6 petrol engine. A sporty yet economical version of the Brera.

ASTON MARTIN V8 VANTAGE

engine type	: petrol, V8		kerb weight	: 1570 kg
displacement	: 4280 cc		towing weight	: n.a.
max. power	: 283 kW (385 bhp)		boot space	: 300 l
@	: 7000 rpm		fuel capacity	: 77 l
max. torque	: 302 lb ft		consumption	: 20.3 mpg
@	: 5000 rpm		acc. 0-62 mph	: 5.0 s
gears	: 6		top speed	: 174 mph
AT	: optional 6-speed		EuroNCAP	: n.a.
drive	: RWD		introduction	: September 2005
brakes f/r	: vent. discs		last revised in	: -
body type	: 2-dr. coupe		warranty	: 2 years
l x w x h	: 4383 x 1866 x 1255 mm		miscellaneous	: The Vantage is the latest addition to
wheelbase	: 2600 mm			the Aston Martin range. The car
turning circle	: 11.1 m			is intended to compete with the
				Porsche 911 and Ferrari F430. A
				Volante version is in the making.

ASTON MARTIN DB9

`25`

engine type	: petrol, V12		**kerb weight**	: 1710 kg
displacement	: 5935 cc		**towing weight**	: n.a.
max. power	: 331 kW (450 bhp)		**boot space**	: 175 l
@	: 6000 rpm		**fuel capacity**	: 85 l
max. torque	: 420 lb ft		**consumption**	: 20.3 mpg
@	: 5000 rpm		**acc. 0-62 mph**	: 4.9 s
gears	: 6		**top speed**	: 186 mph
AT	: optional 6-speed		**EuroNCAP**	: n.a.
drive	: RWD		**introduction**	: July 2004
brakes f/r	: vent. discs		**last revised in**	: -
body type	: 2-dr. coupe		**warranty**	: 2 years
l x w x h	: 4710 x 1875 x 1318 mm		**miscellaneous**	: With its gorgeous lines, this car is
wheelbase	: 2740 mm			a serious contender for the title of
turning circle	: 11.5 m			Most Beautiful Car in this book.
				Performance fabulous too. Also
				available as Volante.

ASTON MARTIN DBS

engine type	: petrol, V12	kerb weight	: 1695 kg
displacement	: 5935 cc	towing weight	: n.v.t.
max. power	: 380 kW (510 bhp)	boot space	: n.b.
@	: 6500 rpm	fuel capacity	: 78 l
max. torque	: 420 lb ft	consumption	: n.b.
@	: 5750 rpm	acc. 0-62 mph	: 4.3 s
gears	: 6	top speed	: 191 mph
AT	: -	EuroNCAP	: n.b.
drive	: RWD	introduction	: September 2007
brakes f/r	: ceramic discs	last revised in	: n.v.t.
body type	: 2-dr. coupe	warranty	: 2 years
l x w x h	: 4721 x 1905 x 1280 mm	miscellaneous	: James Bond's company car
wheelbase	: 2740 mm		is now available for the rich
turning circle	: n.b.		and famous. It is based on the
			DB9.

AUDI A3 1.6 / 1.6 FSI

engine type	: petrol, inline-4
displacement	: 1595 / 1598 cc
max. power	: 75 kW (102 bhp) / 85 kW (115 bhp)
@	: 5600 / 6000 rpm
max. torque	: 109/ 114 lb ft
@	: 3800 / 4000 rpm
gears	: 5 / 6
AT	: -
drive	: FWD
brakes f/r	: vent. discs / discs
body type	: 3-dr. hatchback
l x w x h	: 4203 x 1765 x 1421 mm
wheelbase	: 2578 mm
turning circle	: 10.7 m

kerb weight	: 1205 / 1275 kg
towing weight	: 1200 kg
boot space	: 350 l – 1080 l
fuel capacity	: 55 l
consumption	: 40.5 / 43.8 mpg
acc. 0-62 mph	: 11.9 / 10.9 s
top speed	: 115 / 122 mph
EuroNCAP	: 4 stars
introduction	: June 2003
last revised in	: July 2005
warranty	: 2 years
miscellaneous	: New entry level Audi after the demise of the A2. Fairly sporty chassis. All petrol engines also available in A3 Sportback.

A3 1.8 TFSI / 2.0 TFSI

engine type	: petrol, inline-4
displacement	: 1781 / 1984 cc
max. power	: 118 kW (160 bhp) / 147 kW (200 bhp)
@	: n.a. / 5100 rpm
max. torque	: 184 / 206 lb ft
@	: n.a. / 1800 rpm
gears	: 6, optional 6-speed automatic
kerb weight	: n.a. / 1245 kg
towing weight	: n.a. / 1800 kg
consumption	: n.a. / 37.3 mpg
acc. 0-60 mph	: 8.2 / 6.9 s
top speed	: 137 / 147 mph
miscellaneous	: With the 2.0 TFSI engine under the bonnet, the A3 offers the performance of a VW Golf GTI, but in a rather less ostentatious suit.

A3 3.2 V6 / S3

engine type	: petrol, V6 / inline-4
displacement	: 3189 / 1984 cc
max. power	: 184 kW (250 bhp) / 195 kW (265 bhp)
@	: 6300 / 6000 rpm
max. torque	: 236 / 258 lb ft
@	: 2500 rpm
gears	: 6, optional 6-speed automatic
kerb weight	: 1495 kg / n.a.
towing weight	: 1600 kg / n.a.
consumption	: 26.8 / 31.0 mpg
acc. 0-60 mph	: 6,5 / 5.7 s
top speed	: 155 mph
miscellaneous	: The über-Audi A3. Rare beast because of high price.

AUDI A3 SPORTBACK 1.9 TDI

engine type	: diesel, inline-4	kerb weight	: 1335 kg
displacement	: 1896	towing weight	: 1700 kg
max. power	: 77 kW (105 bhp)	boot space	: 370 l – 1120 l
@	: 4000 rpm	fuel capacity	: 55 l
max. torque	: 184 lb ft	consumption	: 55.6 mpg
@	: 1900 rpm	acc. 0-62 mph	: 11.7 s
gears	: 5	top speed	: 116 mph
AT	: -	EuroNCAP	: n.a.
drive	: FWD	introduction	: September 2004
brakes f/r	: vent. discs / discs	last revised in	: -
body type	: 5-dr. hatchback	warranty	: 2 years
l x w x h	: 4286 x 1765 x 1423 mm	miscellaneous	: Sportback not just a 5-door A3
wheelbase	: 2578 mm		hatchback, but more of a
turning circle	: 10.7 m		stationwagon in appearance. All
			diesel engines also
			available in 3-door A3.

A3 SPORTBACK 2.0 TDI

engine type	: diesel, inline-4
displacement	: 1968 cc
max. power	: 103 kW (140 bhp)
@	: 4000 rpm
max. torque	: 236 lb ft
@	: 1750 rpm
gears	: 6, optional S-tronic
kerb weight	: 1380 kg
towing weight	: 1700 kg
consumption	: 51.6 mpg
acc. 0-60 mph	: 9.7 s
top speed	: 129 mph
miscellaneous	: Both 2.0 TDI versions also available with quattro 4WD.

AUDI A4 1.8 T

engine type	: petrol, inline-4		**kerb weight**	: 1410 kg
displacement	: 1796 cc		**towing weight**	: n.a.
max. power	: 118 kW (160 bhp)		**boot space**	: 480 l
@	: 5000 rpm		**fuel capacity**	: 65 l
max. torque	: 184 lb ft		**consumption**	: 39.8 mpg
@	: 1500 rpm		**acc. 0-62 mph**	: 8.6 s
gears	: 6		**top speed**	: 130 mph
AT	: optional CVT		**EuroNCAP**	: n.a.
drive	: FWD		**introduction**	: September 2007
brakes f/r	: vent. discs / discs		**last revised in**	: n.a.
body type	: 4-dr. saloon		**warranty**	: 2 years
l x w x h	: 4703 x 1826 x 1372 mm		**miscellaneous**	: Completely new car. Range of available engines still limited at this point, refer to Audi A5 for additional engine versions. The new A4 Avant will follow in due course.
wheelbase	: 2810 mm			
turning circle	: 11.4 m			

A4 2.0 TDI

engine type	: diesel, inline-4
displacement	: 1968 cc
max. power	: 105 kW (143 bhp)
@	: 4000 rpm
max. torque	: 236 lb ft
@	: 1750 rpm
gears	: 6, optional CVT
kerb weight	: n.a.
towing weight	: n.a.
consumption	: 51.4 mpg
acc. 0-60 mph	: 9.4 s
top speed	: 136 mph
miscellaneous	: Familiar name, but turbo diesel engine now features common-rail injection.

AUDI A4 AVANT 1.9 TDI / 2.0 TDI

engine type	: diesel, inline-4
displacement	: 1896 / 1968 cc
max. power	: 77 kW (105 bhp) /
	103 kW (140 bhp)
@	: 4000 rpm
max. torque	: 184 / 236 lb ft
@	: 1900 / 1750 rpm
gears	: 5 / 6
AT	: n.a.
drive	: FWD
brakes f/r	: vent. discs / discs
body type	: 5-dr. stationwagon
l x w x h	: 4586 x 1772 x 1427 mm
wheelbase	: 2648 mm
turning circle	: 11.1 m

kerb weight	: 1450 / 1490 kg
towing weight	: 1500 / 1600 kg
boot space	: 442 l – 1184 l
fuel capacity	: 70 l
consumption	: 49.8 / 48.9 mpg
acc. 0-62 mph	: 11.5 / 9.9 s
top speed	: 122 / 129 mph
EuroNCAP	: n.a.
introduction	: July 2001
last revised in	: November 2004
warranty	: 2 years
miscellaneous	: Avant is prettier than its saloon sibling, but load capacity is restricted. Also available with 170 bhp 2.0 TDI.

A4 AVANT 2.7 TDI / 3.0 TDI

engine type	: diesel, V6
displacement	: 2698 /2967 cc
max. power	: 132 kW (180 bhp) /
	150 kW (204 bhp)
@	: 3300 / 3500 rpm
max. torque	: 280 / 332 lb ft
@	: 1400 rpm
gears	: 6, optional CVT /
kerb weight	: 6, optional 6 speed automatic
towing weight	: 1600 / 1660 kg
consumption	: 1800 / 1800 kg
acc. 0-60 mph	: 41.7 / 37.8mpg
top speed	: 8.6 / 7.4 s
miscellaneous	: 139 / 144 mph
	: With an engine range that includes two 6-cylinder diesels, the A4 is popular in the car lease market. 2.7 TDI is latest diesel addition. All diesel engines also available in saloon.

AUDI A4 CABRIO 1.8 T / 2.0 T FSI

engine type	: petrol, inline-4
displacement	: 1781 / 1984 cc
max. power	: 120 kW (163 pk) /
@	147 kW (200 bhp)
max. torque	: 5700 / 5100 rpm
@	: 166 / 206 lb ft
gears	: 1950 / 1800 rpm
AT	: 5 / 6
drive	: optional CVT
brakes f/r	: FWD
body type	: vent. discs / discs
l x w x h	: 2-dr. convertible
wheelbase	: 4573 x 1777 x 1391 mm
turning circle	: 2650 mm
	: 11.1 m

kerb weight	: 1540 / 1600 kg
towing weight	: 1600 kg
boot space	: 315 l
fuel capacity	: 70 l
consumption	: 32.8 / 33.6 mpg
acc. 0-62 mph	: 9.4 / 8.2 s
top speed	: 135 /144 mph
EuroNCAP	: n.a.
introduction	: June 2006
last revised in	: -
warranty	: 2 years
miscellaneous	: Still a pretty convertible. Facelift includes upgraded engine range.

A4 CABRIO 3.2 FSI / S4

engine type	: petrol, V6 / V8
displacement	: 3123 / 4163 cc
max. power	: 188 kW (255 bhp) /
@	253 kW (344 pk)
max. torque	: 6500 / 7000 rpm
@	: 244 / 302 lb ft
gears	: 3250 / 3500 rpm
kerb weight	: 6, optional CVT / 6
towing weight	: 1695 / 1855 kg
consumption	: 1800 kg / n.a.
acc. 0-60 mph	: 25.7 / 20.6 mpg
top speed	: 6.8 / 5.9 s
miscellaneous	: 155 mph
	: For speed-hungry drivers who think even the S4 is not quick enough, the RS4 Cabriolet is the one to choose. We think the 3.2 FSI will do.

A4 CABRIO 2.0 TDI / 2.7 TDI

engine type	: diesel, inline-4 / V6
displacement	: 1968 / 2698 cc
max. power	: 103 kW (140 bhp) /
@	132 kW (180 pk)
max. torque	: 4000 / 3300 rpm
@	: 236 / 280 lb ft
gears	: 1750 / 1400 rpm
kerb weight	: 6
towing weight	: 1600 / 1745 kg
consumption	: 1800 kg
acc. 0-60 mph	: 43.5 / mpg
top speed	: 9.7 / 9.0 s
miscellaneous	: 132 / 138 mph
	: The A4 Cabriolet is available with a wide selection of diesel engines, including a 233 bhp 3.0 TDI. Particle filter standard equipment.

AUDI RS4

engine type	: petrol, V8	kerb weight	: 1650 kg
displacement	: 4163 cc	towing weight	: n.a.
max. power	: 309 kW (420 bhp)	boot space	: 460 l
@	: 7800 rpm	fuel capacity	: 66 l
max. torque	: 317 lb ft	consumption	: 21.2 mpg
@	: 5500 rpm	acc. 0-62 mph	: 4.8 s
gears	: 6	top speed	: 155 mph
AT	: n.a.	EuroNCAP	: 4 stars
drive	: 4WD	introduction	: October 2005
brakes f/r	: vent. discs	last revised in	: -
body type	: 4-dr. sedan	warranty	: 2 years
l x w x h	: 4589 x 1816 x 1415 mm	miscellaneous	: The hottest A4 around, for those
wheelbase	: 2648 mm		who find the S4 somewhat lacking
turning circle	: 11.5 m		in performance... Avant version of
			RS4 also available. First produc-
			tion V8 with direct fuel injection.

S4

engine type	: petrol, V8
displacement	: 4163 cc
max. power	: 253 kW (344 bhp)
@	: 7000 rpm
max. torque	: 302 lb ft
@	: 3500 rpm
gears	: 6
kerb weight	: 1635 kg
towing weight	: n.a.
consumption	: 21.3 mpg
acc. 0-60 mph	: 5.6 s
top speed	: 155 mph
miscellaneous	: Car not as fast as RS4, but
	nevertheless very potent. Avant and
	convertible versions available too.

AUDI A5 3.2 FSI / S5

engine type	: petrol, V6 / V8
displacement	: 3123 / 4163 cc
max. power	: 195 kW (265 bhp) / 260 kW (354 bhp)
@	: 6500 / 7000 rpm
max. torque	: 243 / 324 lb ft
@	: 3000 / 3500 rpm
gears	: - / 6
AT	: CVT / -
drive	: FWD / 4WD
brakes f/r	: vent. discs / discs; vent. discs f/r
body type	: 2-dr. coupe
l x w x h	: 4625 x 1854 x 1372 mm
wheelbase	: 2751 mm
turning circle	: 11.4 m

kerb weight	: 1495 / 1630 kg
towing weight	: 1800 / 2100 kg
boot space	: 455 l
fuel capacity	: 65 / 63 l
consumption	: 31.7 / 22.8 mpg
acc. 0-62 mph	: 6.6 / 5.1 s
top speed	: 155 mph
EuroNCAP	: n.a.
introduction	: March 2007
last revised in	: -
warranty	: 2 years
miscellaneous	: The A5 is essentially a coupe version of the new A4. A convertible and various 'light' engines will follow.

A5 2.7 TDI / 3.0 TDI

engine type	: diesel, V6
displacement	: 2698 / 2967 cc
max. power	: 140 kW (190 bhp) / 176 kW (240 bhp)
@	: 3500 / 4000 rpm
max. torque	: 295 / 368 lb ft
@	: 1400 / 1500 rpm
gears	: CVT / 6
kerb weight	: 1575 / 1610 kg
towing weight	: 1900 / 2000 kg
consumption	: 42.2 / 39.2 mpg
acc. 0-60 mph	: 7.6 / 5.9 s
top speed	: 144 / 155 mph
miscellaneous	: Familiar turbo diesel engines from Audi turn the A5 into a sensible choice.

AUDI A6 2.0 TFSI / 2.4

engine type	: petrol, inline-4 / V6	kerb weight	: 1520 / 1525 kg
displacement	: 1984 / 2393 cc	towing weight	: 1400 / 1500 kg
max. power	: 125 kW (170 bhp) / 130 kW (177 bhp)	boot space	: 546 l
		fuel capacity	: 70 l
@	: 6000 rpm	consumption	: 35.8 / 29.1 mpg
max. torque	: 206 / 170 lb ft	acc. 0-62 mph	: 8.4 / 8.9 s
@	: 1800 / 3000 rpm	top speed	: 141 / 143 mph
gears	: 6	EuroNCAP	: 5 stars
AT	: -	introduction	: April 2004
drive	: FWD	last revised in	: -
brakes f/r	: vent. discs / discs	warranty	: 2 years
body type	: 4-dr. saloon	miscellaneous	: The A6 looks the part, with a balanced design despite the prominent grille. Also available as Avant. For specifications of the 3.2 FSI and 4.2 FSI, refer to the Allroad Quattro.
l x w x h	: 4915 x 1855 x 1460 mm		
wheelbase	: 2845 mm		
turning circle	: 11.9 m		

A6 2.8 FSI / S6

engine type	: petrol, V6 / V10
displacement	: 2773 / 5204 cc
max. power	: 154 kW (210 bhp) / 320 kW (435 bhp)
@	: 5500 / 6800 rpm
max. torque	: 206 / 398 lb ft
@	: 3000 / 4000 rpm
gears	: 6 / 6-speed automatic
kerb weight	: 1540 / 1910 kg
towing weight	: 1600 kg / -
consumption	: 32.5 / 21.1 mpg
acc. 0-60 mph	: 7.9 / 5.2 s
top speed	: 151 / 155 mph
miscellaneous	: For its S6 model Audi borrowed the V10 from subsidiary Lamborghini. Also available is the RS6 model with 580 bhp on tap.

AUDI A6 AVANT 3.0 TDI QUATTRO

engine type	: diesel, V6	**kerb weight**	: 1805 kg
displacement	: 2967 cc	**towing weight**	: 1660 kg
max. power	: 165 kW (224 bhp)	**boot space**	: 565 l
@	: 4000 rpm	**fuel capacity**	: 80 l
max. torque	: 332 lb ft	**consumption**	: 35.0 mpg
@	: 1400 rpm	**acc. 0-62 mph**	: 7.3 s
gears	: 6	**top speed**	: 149 mph
AT	: optional 6-speed tiptronic	**EuroNCAP**	: 5 stars
drive	: 4WD	**introduction**	: April 2004
brakes f/r	: vent. discs / discs	**last revised in**	: -
body type	: 5-dr. stationwagon	**warranty**	: 2 years
l x w x h	: 4933 x 1855 x 1463 mm	**miscellaneous**	: Very potent diesel engine with 332
wheelbase	: 2845 mm		lb ft of torque. Thankfully, 4WD
turning circle	: 11.9 m		is standard fitment on cars with
			this engine. Engine also available
			in saloon.

A6 AVANT 2.0 TDI / 2.7 TDI

engine type	: diesel, inline-4 / V6
displacement	: 1968 / 2698 cc
max. power	: 103 kW (140 bhp) /
	132 kW (180 bhp)
@	: 4000 / 3300 rpm
max. torque	: 236 / 280 lb ft
@	: 1750 / 1400 rpm
gears	: 6
kerb weight	: 1610 / 1695 kg
towing weight	: 1800 / 1900 kg
consumption	: 46.5 / 40.5 mpg
acc. 0-60 mph	: 10.5 / 8.3 s
top speed	: 127 / 140 mph
miscellaneous	: 2.0 TDI is entry level diesel, 2.7 TDI
	the better choice however since it is
	almost as fast as the 3-litre but much
	cheaper. Engines also available in
	saloon.

AUDI A6 ALLROAD QUATTRO 3.2 FSI / 4.2 FSI

engine type	: petrol, V6 / V8	kerb weight	: 1760 / 1880 kg
displacement	: 3123 / 4163 cc	towing weight	: 2100 kg
max. power	: 188 kW (255 bhp) /	boot space	: 565 l
	257 kW (350 bhp)	fuel capacity	: 80 l
@	: 6500 / 6800 rpm	consumption	: 25.8 / 25.3 mpg
max. torque	: 243 / 325 lb ft	acc. 0-62 mph	: 7.2 / 6.3 s
@	: 3250 / 3500 rpm	top speed	: 150 mph
gears	: 6 / 6-speed tiptronic	EuroNCAP	: n.a.
AT	: optional 6-speed tiptronic / -	introduction	: March 2006
drive	: 4WD	last revised in	: -
brakes f/r	: vent. discs / discs	warranty	: 2 years
body type	: 5-dr. stationwagon	miscellaneous	: Offroad vehicle derived from A6
l x w x h	: 4934 x 1832 x 1519 mm		Avant. Good alternative for
wheelbase	: 2833 mm		traditional SUV.
turning circle	: 11.9 m		

ALLROAD QUATTRO 2.7 TDI / 3.0 TDI

engine type	: diesel, V6
displacement	: 2698 / 2967 cc
max. power	: 132 kW (180 bhp) /
	171 kW (233 bhp)
@	: 3300 / 4000 rpm
max. torque	: 280 / 332 lb ft
@	: 1400 rpm
gears	: 6-speed tiptronic
kerb weight	: 1875 / 1880 kg
towing weight	: 2100 kg
consumption	: 32.6 / 32.2 mpg
acc. 0-60 mph	: 9.3 / 7.8 s
top speed	: 134 / 143 mph
miscellaneous	: As it should be: both diesel engines
	feature a particle filter as standard.

AUDI A8 3.2 FSI / 4.2 FSI QUATTRO

engine type	: petrol, V6 / V8
displacement	: 3123 / 4163 cc
max. power	: 191 kW (260 bhp) / 257 kW (350 bhp)
@	: 6500 / 6800 rpm
max. torque	: 243 / 324 lb ft
@	: 3250 / 3500 rpm
gears	: 6 / n.a.
AT	: optional, CVT / 6-speed tiptronic
drive	: FWD / 4WD
brakes f/r	: vent. discs
body type	: 4-dr. saloon
l x w x h	: 5051 x 1894 x 1444 mm
wheelbase	: 2944 mm
turning circle	: 6.1 m

kerb weight	: 1690 / 1800 kg
towing weight	: 2100 / 2300 kg
boot space	: 500 l
fuel capacity	: 90 l
consumption	: 28.5 / 26 mpg
acc. 0-62 mph	: 7.7 / 6.1 s
top speed	: 155 mph
EuroNCAP	: n.a.
introduction	: November 2002
last revised in	: July 2005
warranty	: 3 years
miscellaneous	: 3.2 FSI frankly does not leave much to be desired. Direct fuel injection now on 4.2 V8 too. Wheelbase of A8 'Lang' version 130 mm longer.

A8 6.0 W12 / S8

engine type	: petrol, W12 / V10
displacement	: 5998 / 5204 cc
max. power	: 331 kW (450 bhp)
@	: 6200 / 7000 rpm
max. torque	: 427 / lb ft
@	: 4000 / 3500 rpm
gears	: 6-speed tiptronic
kerb weight	: 1960 / 1940 kg
towing weight	: 2300 kg
consumption	: 20 / 21.2 mpg
acc. 0-60 mph	: 5.1 s
top speed	: 155 mph
miscellaneous	: Stylish or sporty? Performance-wise you cannot go wrong with either of these, since they are equally fast.

A8 3.0 TDI / 4.2 TDI QUATTRO

engine type	: diesel, V6 / V8
displacement	: 2967 / 4134 cc
max. power	: 171 kW (233 bhp) / 240 kW (326 bhp)
@	: 4000 / 3750 rpm
max. torque	: 332 / 479 lb ft
@	: 1400 / 1600 rpm
gears	: 6-speed tiptronic
kerb weight	: 1830 / 1940 kg
towing weight	: 2300 kg
consumption	: 32.8 / 29.4 mpg
acc. 0-60 mph	: 7.8 / 5.9 s
top speed	: 151 / 155 mph
miscellaneous	: Fat diesel engines offer more torque than petrol versions. Diesel power hardly noticeable due to excellent noise insulation.

AUDI TT 2.0 T FSI

engine type	: petrol, inline-4		**kerb weight**	: 1260 kg
displacement	: 1984 cc		**towing weight**	: -
max. power	: 147 kW (200 bhp)		**boot space**	: 290 l
@	: 5100 rpm		**fuel capacity**	: 55 l
max. torque	: 206 lb ft		**consumption**	: 36.8 mpg
@	: 1800 rpm		**acc. 0-62 mph**	: 6.6 s
gears	: 6		**top speed**	: 149 mph
AT	: optional 6-speed S-Tronic		**EuroNCAP**	: n.a.
drive	: FWD		**introduction**	: June 2006
brakes f/r	: vent. discs / discs		**last revised in**	: -
body type	: 2-dr. coupe		**warranty**	: 2 years
l x w x h	: 4178 x 1842 x 1352 mm		**miscellaneous**	: Aluminium body reduces weight of new TT. Handsome and capable coupe. Diesel versions and Roadster soon to follow.
wheelbase	: 2468 mm			
turning circle	: 11.0 m			

TT 3.2 FSI QUATTRO

engine type	: petrol, V6
displacement	: 3189 cc
max. power	: 184 kW (250 bhp)
@	: 6300 rpm
max. torque	: 236 lb ft
@	: 2500 rpm
gears	: 6
kerb weight	: 1410 kg
towing weight	: n.a.
consumption	: 27.5 mpg
acc. 0-60 mph	: 5.9 s
top speed	: 155 mph
miscellaneous	: 4WD comes standard on the fastest TT, at the penalty of extra weight.

AUDI R8 4.2 FSI QUATTRO

engine type	: petrol, V8		**kerb weight**	: 1560 kg
displacement	: 4163 cc		**towing weight**	: -
max. power	: 309 kW (420 bhp)		**boot space**	: 190 l
@	: 7800 rpm		**fuel capacity**	: 75 l
max. torque	: 317 lb ft		**consumption**	: 19.3 mpg
@	: 4500 rpm		**acc. 0-62 mph**	: 4.6 s
gears	: 6		**top speed**	: 187 mph
AT	: optional R-Tronic		**EuroNCAP**	: n.a.
drive	: 4WD		**introduction**	: September 2006
brakes f/r	: vent. discs		**last revised in**	: -
body type	: 2-dr. coupe		**warranty**	: 2 years
l x w x h	: 4431 x 1904 x 1252 mm		**miscellaneous**	: Audi's own supercar makes do
wheelbase	: 2650 mm			with the engine from the RS4.
turning circle	: 11.8 m			Much, much cheaper than a
				Lamborghini Gallardo, but equally
				fast.

AUDI Q7 3.6 FSI / 4.2 FSI

engine type	: petrol, V6 / V8	kerb weight	: 2205 / 2240 kg
displacement	: 3597 / 4163 cc	towing weight	: 3500 kg
max. power	: 206 kW (280 bhp) / 257 kW (350 bhp)	boot space	: 330 l
		fuel capacity	: 100 l
@	: 6200 / 6800 rpm	consumption	: 22.2 / 20.8 mpg
max. torque	: 265 / 324 lb ft	acc. 0-62 mph	: 8.5 / 7.4 s
@	: 2500 / 3500 rpm	top speed	: 143 / 154 mph
gears	: -	EuroNCAP	: 4 stars
AT	: 6-speed	introduction	: September 2005
drive	: 4WD	last revised in	: -
brakes f/r	: vent. discs	warranty	: 2 years
body type	: 5-dr. SUV	miscellaneous	: Huge seven-seater SUV with adequate power under the bonnet. Not frugal, but fast and imposing.
l x w x h	: 5086 x 1983 x 1737 mm		
wheelbase	: 3002 mm		
turning circle	: 11.9 m		

Q7 3.0 TDI / 4.2 TDI

engine type	: diesel, V6 / V8
displacement	: 2967 / 4134 cc
max. power	: 171 kW (233 bhp) / 240 kW (326 bhp)
@	: 4000 / 3750 rpm
max. torque	: 368 / 560 lb ft
@	: 1750 / 1800 rpm
gears	: 6-speed automatic
kerb weight	: 2295 / 2420 kg
towing weight	: 3500 kg
consumption	: 27.2 / 25.4 mpg
acc. 0-60 mph	: 9.1 / 6.4 s
top speed	: 134 / 146 mph
miscellaneous	: Best of the range is the 4.2 TDI model with state-of-the-art injection technology.

BENTLEY CONTINENTAL GT

engine type	: petrol, W12	**kerb weight**	: 2385 kg
displacement	: 5998 cc	**towing weight**	: -
max. power	: 411 kW (552 bhp)	**boot space**	: 370 l
@	: 6100 rpm	**fuel capacity**	: 90 l
max. torque	: 479 lb ft	**consumption**	: 16.5 mpg
@	: 1600 rpm	**acc. 0-62 mph**	: 4.8 s
gears	: n.a.	**top speed**	: 198 mph
AT	: 6-speed tiptronic	**EuroNCAP**	: n.a.
drive	: 4WD	**introduction**	: September 2002
brakes f/r	: vent. discs	**last revised in**	: -
body type	: 2-dr. coupe	**warranty**	: 3 years
l x w x h	: 4807 x 1918 x 1390 mm	**miscellaneous**	: Extremely fast, relatively affordable 'supercar' with drivetrain from Volkswagen. Now also available as an open-topped car, dubbed GTC.
wheelbase	: 2745 mm		
turning circle	: 11.4 m		

BENTLEY CONTINENTAL FLYING SPUR

engine type	: petrol, W12		kerb weight	: 2500 kg
displacement	: 5998 cc		towing weight	: -
max. power	: 411 kW (552 bhp)		boot space	: 475 l
@	: 6100 rpm		fuel capacity	: 90 l
max. torque	: 479 lb ft		consumption	: 16 mpg
@	: 1600 rpm		acc. 0-62 mph	: 5.2 s
gears	: n.a.		top speed	: 195 mph
AT	: 6-speed tiptronic		EuroNCAP	: n.a.
drive	: 4WD		introduction	: February 2005
brakes f/r	: vent. discs		last revised in	: -
body type	: 4-dr. saloon		warranty	: 3 years
l x w x h	: 5307 x 2118 x 1479 mm		miscellaneous	: The fastest 4-door saloon in the
wheelbase	: 3065 mm			world, don't let its introvert
turning circle	: 11.8 m			appearance fool you.

BENTLEY ARNAGE R / T

engine type	: petrol, V8		**kerb weight**	: 2585 kg
displacement	: 6750 cc		**towing weight**	: -
max. power	: 298 kW (405 bhp) / 336 kW (457 bhp)		**boot space**	: 375 l
			fuel capacity	: 100 l
@	: 4000 / 4100 rpm		**consumption**	: 14.5 mpg
max. torque	: 645 / 738 lb ft		**acc. 0-62 mph**	: 6.3 / 5.8 s
@	: 3250 rpm		**top speed**	: 168 / 179 mph
gears	: n.a.		**EuroNCAP**	: n.a.
AT	: 4-speed automatic		**introduction**	: May 1998
drive	: RWD		**last revised in**	: June 2004
brakes f/r	: vent. discs		**warranty**	: 3 years
body type	: 4-dr. saloon		**miscellaneous**	: The ultimate Bentley. Very potent
l x w x h	: 5405 x 1930 x 1515 mm			car in angular disguise, ideally
wheelbase	: 3115 mm			suited for those who think Jaguars
turning circle	: 12.4 m			are ordinary.

BENTLEY AZURE

engine type	: petrol, V8	kerb weight	: 2695 kg
displacement	: 6750 cc	towing weight	: -
max. power	: 336 kW / 457 bhp	boot space	: 310 l
@	: 4100 rpm	fuel capacity	: 96 l
max. torque	: 738 lb ft	consumption	: n.a.
@	: 3250 rpm	acc. 0-62 mph	: 6.0 s
gears	: n.a.	top speed	: 179 mph
AT	: 4-speed automatic	EuroNCAP	: n.a.
drive	: RWD	introduction	: April 2006
brakes f/r	: vent. discs	last revised in	: -
body type	: 2-dr. convertible	warranty	: 3 years
l x w x h	: 5410 x 190 x 1485 mm	miscellaneous	: The finest convertible on today's
wheelbase	: 3115 mm		market. Unrivalled luxury and
turning circle	: n.a.		exclusivity, but very, very
			expensive.

BMW 116i / 118i

engine type	: petrol, inline-4	
displacement	: 1596 / 1995 cc	
max. power	: 90 kW (122 bhp) / 105 kW (143 bhp)	
@	: 6000 rpm	
max. torque	: 118 / 140 lb ft	
@	: 4250 / 4500 rpm	
gears	: 6	
AT	: optional 6-speed	
drive	: RWD	
brakes f/r	: vent. discs / discs	
body type	: 5-dr. hatchback	
l x w x h	: 4227 x 1751 x 1430 mm	
wheelbase	: 2660 mm	
turning circle	: 10.7 m	

kerb weight	: 1340 / 1350 kg
towing weight	: 1200 kg
boot space	: 330 l
fuel capacity	: 53 l
consumption	: 48.7 / 47.9 mpg
acc. 0-62 mph	: 10.0 / 8.8 s
top speed	: 127 / 130 mph
EuroNCAP	: 5 stars
introduction	: May 2004
last revised in	: March 2007
warranty	: 2 years
miscellaneous	: The upgraded 1-series benefits from a better overall fuel economy. The range includes a three-door model, but the above specifications apply to the five-door model.

120i / 130i

engine type	: petrol, inline-4 / -6
displacement	: 1995 / 2996 cc
max. power	: 125 kW (170 bhp) / 195 kW (265 bhp)
@	: 6700 / 6600 rpm
max. torque	: 155 / 232 lb ft
@	: 4250 / 2750 rpm
gears	: 6, optional 6-speed automatic
kerb weight	: 1375 / 1460 kg
towing weight	: 1200 kg
consumption	: 44.1 / 34.0 mpg
acc. 0-60 mph	: 7.8 / 6.1 s
top speed	: 139 / 155 mph
miscellaneous	: Flagship of the range is the 130i, but it costs almost as much as a 325i.

118d / 120d

engine type	: diesel, inline-4
displacement	: 1995 cc
max. power	: 105 kW (143 bhp) / 130 kW (177 bhp)
@	: 4000 rpm
max. torque	: 221 / 258 lb ft
@	: 2000 rpm
gears	: 6, optional 6-speed automatic
kerb weight	: 1395 / 1450 kg
towing weight	: 1200 kg
consumption	: 62.8 / 57.6 mpg
acc. 0-60 mph	: 9.0 / 7.6 s
top speed	: 130 / 142 mph
miscellaneous	: The best 1-series from an economical point of view. The 118d model in particular is extremely fuel-efficient.

BMW 135i COUPÉ

engine type	: petrol, inline-6	kerb weight	: 1560 kg
displacement	: 2979 cc	towing weight	: -
max. power	: 225 kW (306 bhp)	boot space	: 370 l
@	: 5800 rpm	fuel capacity	: 53 l
max. torque	: 295 lb ft	consumption	: 30.7 mpg
@	: 1300 rpm	acc. 0-62 mph	: 5.3 s
gears	: 6	top speed	: 155 mph
AT	: -	EuroNCAP	: n.a.
drive	: RWD	introduction	: November 2007
brakes f/r	: vent. discs	last revised in	: n.v.t.
body type	: 2-dr. coupe	warranty	: 2 years
l x w x h	: 4360 x 1748 x 1408 mm	miscellaneous	: BMW launched a coupe version
wheelbase	: 2660 mm		of the 1-series for the all-important
turning circle	: 10.7 m		market in the USA.

120d / 123d COUPÉ

engine type	: diesel, inline-4
displacement	: 1995 cc
max. power	: 130 kW (177 bhp) /
	150 kW (204 bhp)
@	: 4000 / 4400 rpm
max. torque	: 258 / 295 lb ft
@	: 1750 / 2000 rpm
gears	: 6, optional 6-speed automatic
kerb weight	: 1450 / 1495 kg
towing weight	: 1200 kg
consumption	: 58.9 / 54.3 mpg
acc. 0-60 mph	: 7.6 / 7.0 s
top speed	: 142 / 148 mph
miscellaneous	: The 123d is also available as
	a three-door or five-door hatchback.

BMW 318i / 320i

engine type	: petrol, inline-4
displacement	: 1995 cc
max. power	: 105 kW (143 bhp) / 125 kW (170 bhp)
@	: 6000 / 6700 rpm
max. torque	: 140 / 155 lb ft
@	: 4250 rpm
gears	: 6
AT	: optional 6-speed
drive	: RWD
brakes f/r	: vent. discs
body type	: 4-dr. saloon
l x w x h	: 4520 x 1817 x 1421 mm
wheelbase	: 2760 mm
turning circle	: 11.0 m

kerb weight	: 1435 / 1445 kg
towing weight	: 1400 / 1500 kg
boot space	: 460 l
fuel capacity	: 63 l
consumption	: 47.9 / 46.3 mpg
acc. 0-62 mph	: 9.1 / 8.2 s
top speed	: 130 / 142 mph
EuroNCAP	: 5 stars
introduction	: June 2005
last revised in	: -
warranty	: 2 years
miscellaneous	: Engines are more powerful and more economical than before. Refer to other model descriptions for rest of engine programme.

318d

engine type	: diesel, inline-4
displacement	: 1995 cc
max. power	: 105 kW (143 bhp)
@	: 4000 rpm
max. torque	: 221 lb ft
@	: 1750 rpm
gears	: 6, optional 6-speed automatic
kerb weight	: 1505 kg
towing weight	: 1600 kg
consumption	: 60.1 mpg
acc. 0-60 mph	: 9.3 s
top speed	: 130 mph
miscellaneous	: Entry-level diesel model is an attractive choice thanks to its lively yet frugal powerplant.

BMW 320d TOURING

engine type	: diesel, inline-4	kerb weight	: 1580 kg
displacement	: 1995 cc	towing weight	: 1600 kg
max. power	: 130 kW (177 bhp)	boot space	: 460 l
@	: 4000 rpm	fuel capacity	: 61 l
max. torque	: 258 lb ft	consumption	: 57.4 mpg
@	: 1750 rpm	acc. 0-62 mph	: 8.1 s
gears	: 6	top speed	: 142 mph
AT	: optional 6-speed	EuroNCAP	: 5 stars
drive	: RWD	introduction	: January 2006
brakes f/r	: vent. discs	last revised in	: -
body type	: 5-dr. stationwagon	warranty	: 2 years
l x w x h	: 4520 x 1817 x 1418 mm	miscellaneous	: When looks are more important in
wheelbase	: 2760 mm		a stationwagon than luggage
turning circle	: 11.0 m		space, Germans tend to speak of
			a 'Lifestylekombi'. The Touring ver-
			sion fits the description perfectly.

325d / 335d TOURING

engine type	: diesel, inline-6
displacement	: 2993 cc
max. power	: 145 kW (197 bhp) / 210 kW (286 bhp)
@	: 4000 / 4400 rpm
max. torque	: 295 / 428 lb ft
@	: 1300 / 1750 rpm
gears	: 6
kerb weight	: 1665 / 1720 kg
towing weight	: 1800 kg
consumption	: 47.1 / 41.5 mph
acc. 0-60 mph	: 7.6 / 6.3 s
top speed	: 145 / 155 mph
miscellaneous	: Also available as 330d. For specifications of this engine, refer to the 3-series convertible.

BMW 325i / 330i COUPÉ

engine type	: petrol, inline-6	kerb weight	: 1495 / 1545 kg
displacement	: 2497 / 2996 cc	towing weight	: 1600 / 1700 kg
max. power	: 160 kW (218 bhp) / 200 kW (272 bhp)	boot space	: 440 l
@	: 6500 / 6650 rpm	fuel capacity	: 63 l
max. torque	: 184 / 232 lb ft	consumption	: 33.6 / 32.1 mpg
@	: 2400 / 2750 rpm	acc. 0-62 mph	: 6.9 / 6.1 s
gears	: 6	top speed	: 153 / 155 mph
AT	: optional 6-speed	EuroNCAP	: n.a.
drive	: RWD	introduction	: September 2006
brakes f/r	: vent. discs	last revised in	: -
body type	: 2-dr. coupe	warranty	: 2 years
l x w x h	: 4580 x 1782 x 1395 mm	miscellaneous	: Also available as 320i, 335i,
wheelbase	: 2760 mm		330d and 335d.
turning circle	: 11.0 m		

M3

engine type	: petrol, V8
displacement	: 3999 cc
max. power	: 309 kW (420 bhp)
@	: 8300 rpm
max. torque	: 295 lb ft
@	: 3900 rpm
gears	: 6, optional 7-speed SMG
kerb weight	: 1655 kg
towing weight	: -
consumption	: 22.8 mpg
acc. 0-60 mph	: 4.8 s
top speed	: 155 mph
miscellaneous	: The M3 model started off with an in-line four-cylinder, followed by two straight sixes, but now there is a high-revving V8 under the bonnet to match its biggest rival, the Audi RS4.

BMW 335I CONVERTIBLE

engine type	: petrol, inline-6
displacement	: 2979 cc
max. power	: 225 kW (306 bhp)
@	: 5800 rpm
max. torque	: 295 lb ft
@	: 1300 rpm
gears	: 6
AT	: optional 6-speed automatic
drive	: RWD
brakes f/r	: vent. discs
body type	: 2-dr. convertible
l x w x h	: 4580 x 1782 x 1384 mm
wheelbase	: 2760 mm
turning circle	: 11.0 m

kerb weight	: 1810 kg
towing weight	: 1700 kg
boot space	: 210-350 l
fuel capacity	: 63 l
consumption	: 29.7 mpg
acc. 0-62 mph	: 5.8 s
top speed	: 155 mph
EuroNCAP	: n.a.
introduction	: May 2007
last revised in	: -
warranty	: 2 jaar
miscellaneous	: Convertible with a retractable hardtop is a first for BMW. The open-topped version is identical to the Coupe in every other respect.

330D CONVERTIBLE

engine type	: diesel, inline-6
displacement	: 2993 cc
max. power	: 170 kW (231 bhp)
@	: 4000 rpm
max. torque	: 368 lb ft
@	: 1750 rpm
gears	: 6, optional 6-speed automatic
kerb weight	: 1825 kg
towing weight	: 1800 kg
consumption	: 41.5 mpg
acc. 0-60 mph	: 7.0 s
top speed	: 152 mph
miscellaneous	: A diesel engine in a convertible: unheard of a decade ago, but nowadays an accepted combination.

BMW 523I SEDAN

engine type	: petrol, inline-6
displacement	: 2497 cc
max. power	: 140 kW (190 bhp)
@	: 6100 rpm
max. torque	: 177 lb ft
@	: 3500 rpm
gears	: 6
AT	: optional 6-speed
drive	: RWD
brakes f/r	: vent. discs
body type	: 4-dr. saloon
l x w x h	: 4841 x 1846 x 1468 mm
wheelbase	: 2888 mm
turning circle	: 11.4 m
kerb weight	: 1535 / 1575 kg
towing weight	: 1600 kg
boot space	: 520 l
fuel capacity	: 70 l
consumption	: 38.7 mpg
acc. 0-62 mph	: 8.2 s
top speed	: 147 mph
EuroNCAP	: 4 stars
introduction	: July 2003
last revised in	: March 2007
warranty	: 2 years
miscellaneous	: Like the 1-series, the 5-series was upgraded with caution. Small changes make it much more economical however.

525i / 540i SEDAN

engine type	: petrol, inline-6 / V8
displacement	: 2996 / 4000 cc
max. power	: 160 kW (218 bhp) / 225 kW (306 bhp)
@	: 6100 / 6300 rpm
max. torque	: 199 / 288 lb ft
@	: 2400 / 3500 rpm
gears	: 6, optional 6-speed automatic
kerb weight	: 1585 / 1725 kg
towing weight	: 1800 / 2000 kg
consumption	: 38.2 / 26.9 mpg
acc. 0-60 mph	: 7.1 / 6.1 s
top speed	: 154 / 155 mph
miscellaneous	: The 530i and 550i are identical to the 6-series from a technical perspective. Refer to the 6-series for specifications. All engines on this page are also available in the Touring model (and vice versa).

BMW 520d / 525d TOURING

engine type	: diesel, inline-4 / -6	kerb weight	: 1675 / 1735 kg
displacement	: 1995 / 2497 cc	towing weight	: 1800 / 2000 kg
max. power	: 130 kW (177 bhp) / 145 kW (197 bhp)	boot space	: 500 l
@	: 4000 / 3750 rpm	fuel capacity	: 70 l
max. torque	: 258 / 295 lb ft	consumption	: 53.3 / 44.1 mpg
@	: 1750 / 1300 rpm	acc. 0-62 mph	: 8.9 / 7.8 s
gears	: 6	top speed	: 139 / 144 mph
AT	: optional 6-speed	EuroNCAP	: 4 stars
drive	: RWD	introduction	: March 2004
brakes f/r	: vent. discs	last revised in	: March 2007
body type	: 5-dr. stationwagon	warranty	: 2 years
l x w x h	: 4843 x 1846 x 1491	miscellaneous	: For a car this big, the 520 model
wheelbase	: 2886 mm		is particularly fuel-efficient. The
turning circle	: 11.4 m		same engine can be specified in
			the saloon as well.

530d / 535d TOURING

engine type	: diesel, inline-6
displacement	: 2993 cc
max. power	: 173 kW (235 bhp) /
	210 kW (286 bhp)
@	: 4000 / 4400 rpm
max. torque	: 369 / 428 lb ft
@	: 1750 rpm
gears	: 6 / 6-speed automatic
kerb weight	: 1735 / 1835 kg
towing weight	: 2000 kg
consumption	: 42.8 / 40.9 mpg
acc. 0-60 mph	: 6.9 / 6.5 s
top speed	: 152 / 155 mph
miscellaneous	: The 535d is an expendable com-
	modity but not to be sneezed at.
	The car is so good that BMW
	deemed it wise to offer its engine in
	the 6-series too.

BMW 630i / 650i COUPÉ

engine type	: petrol, inline-6 / V8
displacement	: 2996 / 4800 cc
max. power	: 190 kW (258 bhp) / 270 kW (367 bhp)
@	: 6600 / 6100 rpm
max. torque	: 221 / 362 lb ft
@	: 2500 / 3600 rpm
gears	: 6
AT	: optional 6-speed
drive	: RWD
brakes f/r	: vent. discs
body type	: 2-dr. coupe
l x w x h	: 4820 x 1855 x 1373 mm
wheelbase	: 2780 mm
turning circle	: 11.4 m

kerb weight	: 1465 / 1590 kg
towing weight	: -
boot space	: 450 l
fuel capacity	: 70 l
consumption	: 31.4 / 23.7 mpg
acc. 0-62 mph	: 6.5 / 5.4 s
top speed	: 155 mph
EuroNCAP	: n.a.
introduction	: September 2003
last revised in	: -
warranty	: 2 years
miscellaneous	: Of bold design, this splendid coupe is a real headturner. Both engines also available in beautiful convertible.

BMW M5

engine type	: petrol, V10	kerb weight	: 1685 kg
displacement	: 4999 cc	towing weight	: -
max. power	: 373 kW (507 bhp)	boot space	: 520 l
@	: 7750 rpm	fuel capacity	: 70 l
max. torque	: 384 lb ft	consumption	: 19.1 mpg
@	: 6100 rpm	acc. 0-62 mph	: 4.7 s
gears	: 7-speed SMG	top speed	: 155 mph
AT	: -	EuroNCAP	: 4 stars
drive	: RWD	introduction	: August 2004
brakes f/r	: vent. discs	last revised in	: -
body type	: 4-dr. saloon	warranty	: 2 years
l x w x h	: 4855 x 1846 x 1469 mm	miscellaneous	: The M5 is a Formula I car for the
wheelbase	: 2889 mm		road, it even has a launch control
turning circle	: 11.4 m		system. State-of-the-art technol-
			ogy.

M6

engine type	: petrol, V10
displacement	: 4999cc
max. power	: 373 kW (507 bhp)
@	: 7750 rpm
max. torque	: 384 lb ft
@	: 6100 rpm
gears	: 7-speed SMG
kerb weight	: 1685 kg
towing weight	: n.a.
consumption	: 19.1 mpg
acc. 0-60 mph	: 4.6 s
top speed	: 155 mph
miscellaneous	: The M6 has one of the most
	expensive car roofs in the world,
	made of carbonfibre for reduced
	weight and lower centre of gravity.
	Marginally faster than M5.

BMW 730i / 740i

engine type	: petrol, inline-6 / V8
displacement	: 2996 / 4000 cc
max. power	: 190 kW (258 bhp) / 225 kW (306 bhp)
@	: 6600 / 6300 rpm
max. torque	: 222 / 288 lb ft
@	: 2500 / 3500 rpm
gears	: 6-speed automatic
AT	: n.a.
drive	: RWD
brakes f/r	: vent. discs
body type	: 4-dr. saloon
l x w x h	: 5039 x 1902 x 1491 mm
wheelbase	: 2990 mm
turning circle	: 12.1 m

kerb weight	: 1780 / 1870 kg
towing weight	: 2000 / 2100 kg
boot space	: 500 l
fuel capacity	: 88 l
consumption	: 28 / 25.2 mpg
acc. 0-62 mph	: 7.8 / 6.6 s
top speed	: 152 / 155 mph
EuroNCAP	: n.a.
introduction	: November 2001
last revised in	: March 2005
warranty	: 2 years
miscellaneous	: It took a facelift for this model to become distinctive again. I-Drive system still difficult to master. All engine variants also available in long-wheelbase version, as is the 730d.

750i / 760i

engine type	: petrol, V8 / V12
displacement	: 4798 / 5972 cc
max. power	: 270 kW (367 bhp) / 327 kW (445 bhp)
@	: 6300 / 6000 rpm
max. torque	: 362 / 442 / lb ft
@	: 3400 / 3950 rpm
gears	: 6-speed automatic
kerb weight	: 1885 / 2080 kg
towing weight	: 2100 kg
consumption	: 24 / 21.2 mpg
acc. 0-60 mph	: 5.9 / 5.5 s
top speed	: 155 mph
miscellaneous	: Limousine that makes life difficult for A6 W12, Phaeton and S600. For well-heeled and sporty people who are not worried by its fuel consumption.

BMW 730d / 745d

engine type	: diesel, inline-6 / V8
displacement	: 2993 / 4423 cc
max. power	: 170 kW (231 bhp) / 242 kW (330 bhp)
@	: 4000 rpm
max. torque	: 383 / 553 lb ft
@	: 2000 / 1750 rpm
gears	: 6-speed automatic
kerb weight	: 1875 / 2015 kg
towing weight	: 2100 kg
consumption	: 34.4 / mpg
acc. 0-60 mph	: 7.8 / 6.6 s
top speed	: 148 / 155 mph
miscellaneous	: Two diesel-engined models that make petrol versions redundant. 745d offers more power and torque than rivals from Audi and Mercedes-Benz. Astonishingly powerful, yet relatively frugal.

BMW X3 2.5SI

engine type	: petrol, inline-6	kerb weight	: 1730 / 1805 kg
displacement	: 2497 cc	towing weight	: 1600 / 1800 kg
max. power	: 160 kW (218 bhp)	boot space	: 480 l
@	: 6500 rpm	fuel capacity	: 67 l
max. torque	: 184 lb ft	consumption	: 28.5 mpg
@	: 2750 rpm	acc. 0-62 mph	: 8.5 s
gears	: 6	top speed	: 130 mph
AT	: optional 5-speed automatic	EuroNCAP	: n.a.
drive	: 4WD	introduction	: September 2003
brakes f/r	: vent. discs	last revised in	: September 2006
body type	: 5-dr. SUV	warranty	: 2 years
l x w x h	: 4569 x 1853 x 1674 mm	miscellaneous	: BMW X3 benefits from facelift. Still
wheelbase	: 2795 mm		not a very capable SUV off-road,
turning circle	: 11.7 m		but its on-road driving characteris-
			tics are among the best.

X3 2.0D

engine type	: diesel, inline-4
displacement	: 1995 cc
max. power	: 130 kW (177 bhp)
@	: 4000 rpm
max. torque	: 258 lb ft
@	: 1750 rpm
gears	: 6, optional 6-speed automatic
kerb weight	: 1815 kg
towing weight	: 1700 kg
consumption	: 43.5 mpg
acc. 0-60 mph	: 8.9 s
top speed	: 128 mph
miscellaneous	: Also available as 3.0si, 3.0d and
	3.0sd. Refer to the BMW X5 on the
	next page for specifications of these
	engines.

BMW X5 3.0si / 4.8i

engine type	: petrol, inline-6 / V8
displacement	: 2996 / 4799 cc
max. power	: 200 kW (272 bhp) / 261 kW (355 bhp)
@	: 6650 / 6300 rpm
max. torque	: 232 / 350 lb ft
@	: 2750 / 3400 rpm
gears	: -
AT	: 6-speed automatic
drive	: 4WD
brakes f/r	: vent. discs
body type	: 5-dr. SUV
l x w x h	: 4854 x 1933 x 1776 mm
wheelbase	: 2933 mm
turning circle	: 12.8 m

kerb weight	: 2075 / 2180 kg
towing weight	: 2700 kg
boot space	: 620 l
fuel capacity	: 85 l
consumption	: 25.9 / 22.6 mpg
acc. 0-62 mph	: 8.1 / 6.5 s
top speed	: 140 / 150 mph
EuroNCAP	: n.a.
introduction	: January 2007
last revised in	: -
warranty	: 2 years
miscellaneous	: BMW decided to make the X5 bigger and has thus widened the gap with the X3. Also available as 7-seater. Engines both more powerful and more economical.

X5 3.0D / 3.0SD

engine type	: diesel, inline-6
displacement	: 2993 cc
max. power	: 173 kW (235 bhp) / 210 kW (286 bhp)
@	: 4000 / 4400 rpm
max. torque	: 383 / 427 lb ft
@	: 2000 / 1750 rpm
gears	: 6-speed automatic
kerb weight	: 2150 / 2185 kg
towing weight	: 2700 kg
consumption	: 32.5 / 34.4
acc. 0-60 mph	: 8.1 / 7.0 s
top speed	: 134 / 146 mph
miscellaneous	: 3.0d version is the most economical choice of the range. It is every bit as capable as the 3.0si and offers best value as a company car.

BMW Z4 2.0i / 2.5i

engine type	: petrol, inline-4 / inline-6	kerb weight	: 1195 / 1225 kg
displacement	: 1995 / 2497 cc	towing weight	: -
max. power	: 110 kW (150 bhp) / 130 kW (177 bhp)	boot space	: 260 l
@	: 6200 / 5800 rpm	fuel capacity	: 55 l
max. torque	: 148 / 170 lb ft	consumption	: 37.7 / 34.4 mpg
@	: 3600 / 3500 rpm	acc. 0-62 mph	: 8.2 / 7.7 s
gears	: 6	top speed	: 137 / 142 mph
AT	: optional 6-speed	EuroNCAP	: 4 stars
drive	: RWD	introduction	: March 2003
brakes f/r	: vent. discs	last revised in	: October 2005
body type	: 2-dr. convertible	warranty	: 2 years
l x w x h	: 4091 x 1781 x 1299 mm	miscellaneous	: Roadster was given a technical
wheelbase	: 2495 mm		and optical makeover. Also available
turning circle	: 9.8 m		as 2.5si with 218 bhp.

Z4 3.0Si / M

engine type	: inline-6
displacement	: 2996 / 3246 cc
max. power	: 195 kW (265 bhp) / 252 kW (343 bhp)
@	: 6600 / 7900
max. torque	: 232 / 269 lb ft
@	: 2750 / 4900 rpm
gears	: 6, optional 6-speed automatic
kerb weight	: 1285 / 1385 kg
towing weight	: -
consumption	: 32.8 / 23.3 mpg
acc. 0-60 mph	: 5.7 / 5.0 s
top speed	: 155 mph
miscellaneous	: M-badge and coupe body are latest additions to the Z4 range Handsome coupe only available with these two petrol engines.

BUGATTI VEYRON 16.4

engine type	: petrol, W16		**kerb weight**	: 1888 kg
displacement	: 7993 cc		**towing weight**	: -
max. power	: 736 kW (1.001 bhp)		**boot space**	: n.a.
@	: 6000 rpm		**fuel capacity**	: 100 l
max. torque	: 922 lb ft		**consumption**	: 11.8 mpg
@	: 2200 rpm		**acc. 0-62 mph**	: 2.5 s
gears	: -		**top speed**	: 253 mph
AT	: 7-speed seq.		**EuroNCAP**	: n.a.
drive	: 4WD		**introduction**	: August 2005
brakes f/r	: vent. discs		**last revised in**	: -
body type	: 2-dr. coupe		**warranty**	: 2 years
l x w x h	: 4462 x 1998 x 1204 mm		**miscellaneous**	: After years of postponement due to development problems, the first batch of Veyrons has finally taken to the road. Remarkable car in every respect, but unattainable for nearly everyone on earth.
wheelbase	: 2710 mm			
turning circle	: 11.6 m			

CADILLAC BLS 2.0T / 2.8 T V6

engine type	: petrol, inline-4 / V6	kerb weight	: 10.9 m
displacement	: 1988 / 2792 cc	towing weight	: 1450 / 1560 kg
max. power	: 131 kW (175 bhp) /	boot space	: n.a.
	186 kW (255 bhp)	fuel capacity	: 425 l
@	: 5500 rpm	consumption	: 58 l
max. torque	: 195 / 258 lb ft	acc. 0-62 mph	: 37.2 / 27.7 mpg
@	: 2500 / 2000 rpm	top speed	: 8.7 / 6.9 s
gears	: 5 / 6	EuroNCAP	: 137 / 155 mph
AT	: optional 5-speed automatic / option-	introduction	: n.a.
drive	al 6-speed automatic	last revised in	: September 2005
brakes f/r	: FWD	warranty	: 3 years
body type	: vent. discs / discs	miscellaneous	: Cadillac BLS is built alongside
l x w x h	: 4-dr. saloon		technically identical Saab 9-3.
wheelbase	: 4679 x 1762 x 1449 mm		Striking appearance is strongpoint,
turning circle	: 2675 mm		but small dealer network is not.
			Also available as 2.0 T with
			210 bhp.

BLS 1.9 D

engine type	: diesel, inline-4
displacement	: 1910 cc
max. power	: 110 kW (150 bhp)
@	: 4000 rpm
max. torque	: 236 lb ft
@	: 2000 rpm
gears	: 6, optional 6-speed automatic
kerb weight	: 1510 kg
towing weight	: n.a.
consumption	: 46.3 mpg
acc. 0-60 mph	: 9.8 s
top speed	: 131 mph
miscellaneous	: First diesel-engined car from Cadillac, apart from the disastrous V8 in the Seventies. Diesel engine already familiar from Saab and Vauxhall however.

CADILLAC CTS 2.8 / 3.6

engine type	: petrol, V6
displacement	: 2792 / 3564 cc
max. power	: 155 kW (211 bhp) / 229 kW (311 bhp)
@	: 6500 / 6300 rpm
max. torque	: 194 / 273 lb ft
@	: 3200 / 5200 rpm
gears	: 6
AT	: optional 6-speed
drive	: RWD
brakes f/r	: vent. discs / discs
body type	: 4-dr. saloon
l x w x h	: 4860 x 1842 x 1464 mm
wheelbase	: 2880 mm
turning circle	: n.a.

kerb weight	: 1700 / 1750 kg
towing weight	: n.a.
boot space	: 385 l
fuel capacity	: 68 l
consumption	: n.a.
acc. 0-62 mph	: n.a.
top speed	: n.a.
EuroNCAP	: n.a.
introduction	: December 2007
last revised in	: -
warranty	: 3 years
miscellaneous	: Much-improved CTS is second attempt to put Cadillac on the map in Europe. The 3.6 is also available with four-wheel drive.

CTS 2.9 D

engine type	: diesel, V6
displacement	: 2900 cc
max. power	: 184 kW (250 bhp)
@	: n.a.
max. torque	: 406 lb ft
@	: 2000 rpm
gears	: 6
kerb weight	: n.a.
towing weight	: n.a.
consumption	: n.a.
acc. 0-60 mph	: n.a.
top speed	: n.a.
miscellaneous	: The growing popularity of diesel engines in the USA makes it financially more feasible to market a diesel version in Europe too, but it will not be launched before 2009.

CADILLAC STS 3.6 / 4.6

engine type	: petrol, V6 / V8	kerb weight	: 1782 / 1825 kg
displacement	: 3564 / 4565 cc	towing weight	: 1928 kg
max. power	: 189 kW (257 bhp) /	boot space	: 464 l
	239 kW (325 bhp)	fuel capacity	: 66 l
@	: 6500 / 6400 rpm	consumption	: 22.9 / 19.7 mpg
max. torque	: 252 / 315 lb ft	acc. 0-62 mph	: 7.4 / 6.2 s
@	: 3200 / 4400 rpm	top speed	: 142 / 155 mph
gears	: -	EuroNCAP	: n.a.
AT	: 5-speed automatic	introduction	: February 2005
drive	: RWD	last revised in	: -
brakes f/r	: vent. discs	warranty	: 3 years
body type	: 4-dr. saloon	miscellaneous	: Not your average billowing ship
l x w x h	: 4985 x 1845 x 1465 mm		from America this time. Much bet-
wheelbase	: 2957 mm		ter car than preceding model, for
turning circle	: 11.5 m		the discerning buyer. V8 version
			available with AWD.

STS-V

engine type	: petrol, V8
displacement	: 4371cc
max. power	: 328 kW (446 bhp)
@	: 6400 rpm
max. torque	: 430 lb ft
@	: 3600 rpm
gears	: 6-speed automatic
kerb weight	: 1950 kg
towing weight	: -
consumption	: n.a.
acc. 0-60 mph	: < 5 s
top speed	: > 155 mph
miscellaneous	: Heavyweight, but more nimble
	thanks to big supercharged V8.
	Finetuning at the Nürburgring paid
	off. Nice alternative if you think the
	M5 and E55 AMG are ordinary.

CADILLAC XLR

engine type	: petrol, V8		**kerb weight**	: 1655 kg
displacement	: 4565 cc		**towing weight**	: -
max. power	: 239 kW (325 bhp)		**boot space**	: 125 - 330 l
@	: 6400 rpm		**fuel capacity**	: 68 l
max. torque	: 315 lb ft		**consumption**	: 13.2 mpg
@	: 4400 rpm		**acc. 0-62 mph**	: 5.9 s
gears	: -		**top speed**	: 155 mph
AT	: 5-speed automatic		**EuroNCAP**	: n.a.
drive	: RWD		**introduction**	: January 2003
brakes f/r	: vent. discs		**last revised in**	: -
body type	: 2-dr. convertible		**warranty**	: 3 years
l x w x h	: 4515 x 1835 x 1280 mm		**miscellaneous**	: Aggressively styled and luxuriously
wheelbase	: 2685 mm			appointed coupe-convertible.
turning circle	: 11.9 m			Sales disappointing however
				because of hefty price. Top-of-the-
				range model is the 446 bhp XLR-V.

CADILLAC SRX 3.6 V6 / 4.6 V8

engine type	: petrol, V6	kerb weight	: 1996 / 2051 kg
displacement	: 2792 / 3564 cc	towing weight	: 2268 kg
max. power	: 158 kW (215 bhp) /	boot space	: 240 / 1970 l
	189 kW (257 bhp)	fuel capacity	: 76 l
@	: 7000 / 6200 rpm	consumption	: 19.2 / 20.2 mpg
max. torque	: 194 / 251 lb ft	acc. 0-62 mph	: 8.1 / 7.4 s
@	: 3000 / 3200 rpm	top speed	: 125 / 140 mph
gears	: 6	EuroNCAP	: n.a.
AT	: optional 5-speed automatic	introduction	: October 2004
drive	: 4WD	last revised in	: -
brakes f/r	: vent. discs	warranty	: 3 years
body type	: 5-dr. SUV	miscellaneous	: For those who are torn between a
l x w x h	: 4950 x 1845 x 1721 mm		stationwagon and a SUV. Good
wheelbase	: 2880 mm		alternative for X5 and XC90. V8
turning circle	: 10.8 m		engine sounds great.

CADILLAC ESCALADE

engine type	: petrol, V8	**kerb weight**	: 2609 kg
displacement	: 6162 cc	**towing weight**	: 3100 kg
max. power	: 301 kW (409 bhp)	**boot space**	: 479-3084 l
@	: 5700 rpm	**fuel capacity**	: 98 l
max. torque	: 416 lb ft	**consumption**	: 17.4 mpg
@	: 4300 rpm	**acc. 0-62 mph**	: 6.8 s
gears	: -	**top speed**	: 106 mph
AT	: 6-speed	**EuroNCAP**	: n.a.
drive	: 4WD	**introduction**	: May 2006
brakes f/r	: vent. discs	**last revised in**	: -
body type	: 5-dr. SUV	**warranty**	: 3 years
l x w x h	: 5151 x 2008 x 1887 mm	**miscellaneous**	: Impressive car, but too big
wheelbase	: 2946 mm		for our roads. It can carry
turning circle	: 11.9 m		as much as eight people.

CHEVROLET MATIZ 0.8 / 1.0

engine type	: petrol, inline-3	kerb weight	: 770 kg
displacement	: 796 / 995 cc	towing weight	: -
max. power	: 38 kW (51 bhp) / 48 kW (65 bhp)	boot space	: 170 l
@	: 6000 / 5400 rpm	fuel capacity	: 35 l
max. torque	: 53 / 67 lb ft	consumption	: 54.3 / 50.4 mpg
@	: 4400 / 4200 rpm	acc. 0-62 mph	: 18.2 / 14.1 s
gears	: 5	top speed	: 90 / 97 mph
AT	: -	EuroNCAP	: 3 stars
drive	: FWD	introduction	: May 2005
brakes f/r	: discs / drum brakes	last revised in	: -
body type	: 3-dr. hatchback	warranty	: 3 years
l x w x h	: 3495 x 1495 x 1500 mm	miscellaneous	: Practical, cute little car. Chevrolet
wheelbase	: 2345 mm		name normally not associated with
turning circle	: 9.2 m		this type of car, but all Daewoo
			models are now badged as
			Chevrolets in Europe.

CHEVROLET AVEO 1.2 / 1.4

engine type	: petrol, inline-4		**kerb weight**	: n.a.
displacement	: 1148 / 1399 cc		**towing weight**	: n.a.
max. power	: 62 kW (84 bhp) / 73 kW (98 bhp)		**boot space**	: 220 l
@	: n.a.		**fuel capacity**	: n.a.
max. torque	: n.a.		**consumption**	: n.a.
@	: n.a.		**acc. 0-62 mph**	: n.a.
gears	: 5		**top speed**	: n.a.
AT	: -		**EuroNCAP**	: n.a.
drive	: FWD		**introduction**	: January 2005
brakes f/r	: vent. discs / discs		**last revised in**	: March 2008
body type	: 5-dr. hatchback		**warranty**	: 3 years
l x w x h	: 3920 x 1680 x 1510 mm		**miscellaneous**	: Facelift now spells the end for
wheelbase	: 2480 mm			the Kalos nomenclature on the tail
turning circle	: n.a.			of the hatchback model too. The
				four-door Aveo (see below) is
				available only with the 1.4 engine.

CHEVROLET LACETTI 1.4 / 1.6

engine type	: petrol, inline-4	kerb weight	: 1170 / 1195 kg
displacement	: 1399 / 1598 cc	towing weight	: 1200 kg
max. power	: 68 kW (92 bhp) / 80 kW (109 bhp)	boot space	: 275 l
@	: 6000 / 5800 rpm	fuel capacity	: 60 l
max. torque	: 97 / 110 lb ft	consumption	: 39.2 / 39.7 mpg
@	: 3600 / 4000 rpm	acc. 0-62 mph	: 11.6 / 10.7 s
gears	: 5	top speed	: 109 / 116 mph
AT	: - / optional 4-speed	EuroNCAP	: n.a.
drive	: FWD	introduction	: January 2005
brakes f/r	: vent. discs / discs	last revised in	: -
body type	: 5-dr. hatchback	warranty	: 3 years
l x w x h	: 4295 x 1725 x 1445 mm	miscellaneous	: Unpretentious but proper hatch-
wheelbase	: 2600 mm		back. A fair performer at a reason-
turning circle	: 10.4 m		able price. Also available with a 1.8
			petrol engine. Refer to the saloon
			version of the Lacetti for details.

LACETTI 2.0 TCDI

engine type	: diesel, inline-4
displacement	: 1991 cc
max. power	: 89 kW (121 bhp)
@	: 3800 rpm
max. torque	: 206 lb ft
@	: 2000 rpm
gears	: 5
kerb weight	: 1280 kg
towing weight	: 1000 kg
consumption	: 49.6 mpg
acc. 0-60 mph	: 9.8 s
top speed	: 116 mph
miscellaneous	: Modern diesel engine may
	help to boost Lacetti sales.

CHEVROLET LACETTI SALOON 1.6 / 1.8

engine type	: petrol, inline-4		**kerb weight**	: 1180 / 1210 kg
displacement	: 1598 / 1799cc		**towing weight**	: 1200 kg
max. power	: 80 kW (109 bhp) / 90 kW (122 bhp)		**boot space**	: 405 l
@	: 6000 rpm		**fuel capacity**	: 60 l
max. torque	: 110 / 119 lb ft		**consumption**	: 40 / 37.8 mpg
@	: 3400 / 4000 rpm		**acc. 0-62 mph**	: 12.4 / 11.0 s
gears	: 5		**top speed**	: 116 / 121 mph
AT	: - / optional 4-speed automatic		**EuroNCAP**	: n.a.
drive	: FWD		**introduction**	: January 2005
brakes f/r	: vent. discs / discs		**last revised in**	: -
body type	: 4-dr. saloon		**warranty**	: 3 years
l x w x h	: 4500 x 1725 x 1440 mm		**miscellaneous**	: Also available with 94 bhp
wheelbase	: 2600 mm			1.4 engine. Old acquaintance from
turning circle	: 10.4 m			Daewoo, with minor changes only.
				Proper family car, but stationwagon
				offers even more space.

CHEVROLET EPICA 2.0 VCDI

engine type	: diesel, inline-4	kerb weight	: 1560 kg
displacement	: 1991 cc	towing weight	: 1700 kg
max. power	: 110 kW (150 bhp)	boot space	: 480 l
@	: 4000 rpm	fuel capacity	: 65 l
max. torque	: 236 lb ft	consumption	: 46.3 mpg
@	: 2000 rpm	acc. 0-62 mph	: 9.7 s
gears	: 5	top speed	: 124 mph
AT	: optional 5-speed	EuroNCAP	: n.a.
drive	: FWD	introduction	: July 2006
brakes f/r	: vent. discs / discs	last revised in	: -
body type	: 4-dr. saloon	warranty	: 3 years
l x w x h	: 4805 x 1810 x 1450 mm	miscellaneous	: With a diesel-powered version of
wheelbase	: 2700 mm		the Epica, Chevrolet lives up to its
turning circle	: 10.8 m		earlier promise. Automatic trans-
			mission suits the car best.

EPICA 2.0 / 2.5

engine type	: petrol, inline-6
displacement	: 1993 / 2492 cc
max. power	: 105 kW (143 bhp) /
	115 kW (156 bhp)
@	: 6400 / 5800 rpm
max. torque	: 144 / 175 lb ft
@	: 4600 / 4000 rpm
gears	: 5 / 5-speed automatic
kerb weight	: 1460 kg
towing weight	: 1700 kg
consumption	: 34.4 / 30.4 mpg
acc. 0-60 mph	: 9.9 s
top speed	: 129 / 130 mph
miscellaneous	: Both six-cylinder engines are not that powerful, but they are extremely quiet.

CHEVROLET HHR

engine type	: petrol, inline-4	kerb weight	: 1431 / 1455 kg
displacement	: 2189 / 2384 cc	towing weight	: n.a.
max. power	: 111 kW (152 bhp) / 130 kW (177 bhp)	boot space	: 674 l
		fuel capacity	: 65 l
@	: 5600 / 6200 rpm	consumption	: 32.1 / 31.7 mpg
max. torque	: 155 / 168 lb ft	acc. 0-62 mph	: n.a.
@	: 4000 / 5000 rpm	top speed	: n.a.
gears	: 5	EuroNCAP	: n.a.
AT	: optional 4-speed	introduction	: June 2007
drive	: FWD	last revised in	: -
brakes f/r	: vent. discs / drums	warranty	: 3 years
body type	: 5-dr. MPV	miscellaneous	: Already available in America, but now introduced in Europe as a successor to the Tacuma. Looks like a Chrysler PT Cruiser.
l x w x h	: 4475 x 1757 x 1657 mm		
wheelbase	: 2628 mm		
turning circle	: 11.0 m		

CHEVROLET CAPTIVA 2.4 / 3.2

engine type	: petrol, inline-4 / V6	kerb weight	: 1760 / 1780 kg
displacement	: 2405 / 3195 cc	towing weight	: 1500 / 1700 kg
max. power	: 100 kW (136 bhp) /	boot space	: 465 - 1165 l
	169 kW (230 bhp)	fuel capacity	: 60 l
@	: 5000 / 6600 rpm	consumption	: 31.2 / 24.7 mpg
max. torque	: 156 / 214 lb ft	acc. 0-62 mph	: 13.5 / 10.5 s
@	: 4000 / 3600 rpm	top speed	: 109 / 115 mph
gears	: 5	EuroNCAP	: n.a.
AT	: - / optional 5-speed automatic	introduction	: June 2005
drive	: FWD	last revised in	: -
brakes f/r	: vent. discs / discs	warranty	: 3 years
body type	: 5-dr. SUV	miscellaneous	: Nice SUV. Captiva platform used
l x w x h	: 4635 x 1850 x 1720 mm		for Opel Antara too. 2.4 version
wheelbase	: 2705 mm		also
turning circle	: 11.4 m		available with 4WD.

CAPTIVA 2.0D

engine type	: diesel, inline-4
displacement	: 1991 cc
max. power	: 110 kW (150 bhp)
@	: 4000 rpm
max. torque	: 229 lb ft
@	: 2000 rpm
gears	: 5, optional 5-speed automatic
kerb weight	: 1795 kg
towing weight	: 2000 kg
consumption	: 38.4 mpg
acc. 0-60 mph	: 12.5 s
top speed	: 109 mph
miscellaneous	: Powerful diesel-engined version probably bestseller of Captiva range. Rightly so, since it is quicker and more economical than its two petrol-engined siblings.

CHRYSLER PT CRUISER 1.6 / 2.4

engine type	: petrol, inline-4
displacement	: 1598 / 2429 cc
max. power	: 85 kW (116 bhp) /
	105 kW (143 bhp)
@	: 6300 / 5200 rpm
max. torque	: 116 / 158 lb ft
@	: 6300 / 5200 rpm
gears	: 5
AT	: - / optional 4-speed automatic
drive	: FWD
brakes f/r	: vent. discs / discs
body type	: 5-dr. MPV
l x w x h	: 4288 x 1704 x 1601 mm
wheelbase	: 2616 mm
turning circle	: 11.6 m

kerb weight	: 1341 / 1410 kg
towing weight	: 1000 kg
boot space	: 521 - 2150 l
fuel capacity	: 57 l
consumption	: 36.8 / 30.1 mpg
acc. 0-62 mph	: 13.5 / 12.2 s
top speed	: 109 / 121 mph
EuroNCAP	: n.a.
introduction	: Summer 2000
last revised in	: Autumn 2005
warranty	: 2 years
miscellaneous	: Still genuinely retro-looking car, despite recent facelift. Also available as convertible. Replacement soon to follow.

PT CRUISER 2.4 TURBO

engine type	: petrol, inline-4
displacement	: 2429 cc
max. power	: 164 kW (223 bhp)
@	: 5100 rpm
max. torque	: 245 lb ft
@	: 3950 rpm
gears	: 5
kerb weight	: 1480 kg
towing weight	: 1000 kg
consumption	: 28.9 mpg
acc. 0-60 mph	: 7.5 s
top speed	: 124 mph
miscellaneous	: Reasonably quick car, but chassis is not entirely up to the job. Turbo engine endows soft-topped version with fine cruising characteristics.

PT CRUISER 2.2 CRD

engine type	: diesel, inline-4
displacement	: 2148 cc
max. power	: 89 kW (121 bhp)
@	: 4200 rpm
max. torque	: 221 lb ft
@	: 1600 rpm
gears	: 5
kerb weight	: 1485 kg
towing weight	: 1000 kg
consumption	: 47.2 mpg
acc. 0-60 mph	: 12.1 s
top speed	: 133 mph
miscellaneous	: Models destined for Europe are built in Austria. Diesel engine supplied by Mercedes-Benz available only in Europe.

CHRYSLER SEBRING 2.0

engine type	: petrol, inline-4	kerb weight	: 1555 / 1585 kg
displacement	: 1998 / 2360 cc	towing weight	: 900 kg
max. power	: 115 kW (154 bhp) /	boot space	: 441 l
	124 kW (167 bhp)	fuel capacity	: 63 l
@	: 6400 / 6000 rpm	consumption	: 36.2 / 31.7 mpg
max. torque	: 140 / 162 lb ft	acc. 0-62 mph	: 11.1 / 11.3 s
@	: 5100 / 4500 rpm	top speed	: 118 / 124 mph
gears	: 5 / -	EuroNCAP	: n.a.
AT	: - / 4-speed	introduction	: September 2006
drive	: FWD	last revised in	: -
brakes f/r	: vent. discs / discs	warranty	: 3 years
body type	: 4-dr. saloon	miscellaneous	: Chrysler does not go to all lengths
l x w x h	: 4850 x 1843 x 1497 mm		anymore to promote the big
wheelbase	: 2765 mm		Sebring models with V6 power.
turning circle	: 11.1 m		Impressive audio system with
			MP3-harddisk is a bonus.

SEBRING 2.0 CRD

engine type	: diesel, inline-4
displacement	: 1968 cc
max. power	: 103 kW (138 bhp)
@	: 4000 rpm
max. torque	: 229 lb ft
@	: 1750 rpm
gears	: 6
kerb weight	: 1555 kg
towing weight	: 1000 kg
consumption	: 45.6 mpg
acc. 0-60 mph	: 12.0 s
top speed	: 126 mph
miscellaneous	: The diesel engine is supplied
	by Volkswagen.

CHRYSLER CROSSFIRE 3.2 V6 / SRT-6 AUTO

engine type	: petrol, V6	**kerb weight**	: 1352 / 1455 kg
displacement	: 3199 cc	**towing weight**	: -
max. power	: 160 kW (218 bhp) / 246 kW (330 bhp)	**boot space**	: 215 l / roadster 190 l
		fuel capacity	: 60 l
@	: 5700 / 6100 rpm	**consumption**	: 27.2 / 25.7 mpg
max. torque	: 229 / 310 lb ft	**acc. 0-62 mph**	: 6.5 / 5.0 s
@	: 3000 / 3500 rpm	**top speed**	: 155 mph
gears	: -	**EuroNCAP**	: n.a.
AT	: 5-speed automatic	**introduction**	: Late 2003, roadster summer 2004
drive	: RWD	**last revised in**	: -
brakes f/r	: vent. discs / discs	**warranty**	: 2 years
body type	: 2-dr. coupe	**miscellaneous**	: Drivetrain borrowed from previous Mercedes-Benz SLK, in a striking body with a charisma all of its own. Crossfire model stands out in the crowd.
l x w x h	: 4058 x 1766 x 1307 mm		
wheelbase	: 2400 mm		
turning circle	: 10.3 m		

CHRYSLER 300 C 2.7L V6 / C 3.5L V6

engine type	: petrol, V6
displacement	: 2736 / 3518 cc
max. power	: 142 kW (193 bhp) /
	183 kW (249 bhp)
@	: 6400 rpm
max. torque	: 192 / 250 lb ft
@	: 4000 / 3800 rpm
gears	: -
AT	: 4-speed automatic
drive	: RWD
brakes f/r	: vent. discs
body type	: 4-dr. saloon
l x w x h	: 4999 x 1881 x 1483 mm
wheelbase	: 3048 mm
turning circle	: 11.9 m

kerb weight	: 1810 / 1824 kg
towing weight	: 1500 / 1725 kg
boot space	: 442 l
fuel capacity	: 68 l
consumption	: 26.3 / 25.5 mpg
acc. 0-62 mph	: 11.1 / 9.2 s
top speed	: 129 / 136 mph
EuroNCAP	: n.a.
introduction	: Summer 2004
last revised in	: -
warranty	: 2 years
miscellaneous	: For managers who dare to be different, but car has a lot to offer. Also available with 5.7-litre V8.

300 C 3.0 CRD

engine type	: diesel, V6
displacement	: 2987 cc
max. power	: 160 kW (218 bhp)
@	: 3800 rpm
max. torque	: 376 lb ft
@	: 1600 rpm
gears	: 5-speed automatic
kerb weight	: 1916 kg
towing weight	: n.a.
consumption	: 34.6 mpg
acc. 0-60 mph	: 7.6 s
top speed	: 143 mph
miscellaneous	: Diesel-engined version is serious business for Chrysler. Modern engine the same as in Mercedes-Benz E-class.

CHRYSLER 300 C TOURING 5.7 HEMI

engine type	: petrol, V8
displacement	: 5654 cc
max. power	: 254 kW (340 bhp)
@	: 5000 rpm
max. torque	: 387 lb ft
@	: 4000 rpm
gears	: -
AT	: 5-speed automatic
drive	: RWD
brakes f/r	: vent. discs
body type	: 5-dr. stationwagon
l x w x h	: 4999 x 1881 x 1481 mm
wheelbase	: 3048 mm
turning circle	: 11.9 m

kerb weight	: 1947 kg
towing weight	: 1725 kg
boot space	: 630 – 1602 l
fuel capacity	: 71 l
consumption	: 22.6 mpg
acc. 0-62 mph	: 6.4 s
top speed	: 155 mph
EuroNCAP	: n.a.
introduction	: Summer 2004
last revised in	: -
warranty	: 2 years
miscellaneous	: Other engines available, but this is the real thing. The word 'Hemi' has an iconic ring to it in the States. Spectacular V8 sound.

300 C TOURING SRT-8

engine type	: petrol, V8
displacement	: 6059 cc
max. power	: 317 kW (431 bhp)
@	: 6000 rpm
max. torque	: 420 lb ft
@	: 4800 rpm
gears	: 5-speed automatic
kerb weight	: 1725 kg
towing weight	: -
consumption	: 20.3 mpg
acc. 0-60 mph	: 5.0 s
top speed	: 165 mph
miscellaneous	: SRT-8 model is flagship of 300 C range, with an even bigger Hemi engine under the bonnet.

CHRYSLER VOYAGER 2.4l / 3.3l V6 AUTO

engine type	: petrol, inline-4 / V6	kerb weight	: 1805 / 1850 kg
displacement	: 2429 / 3301 cc	towing weight	: 1600 kg
max. power	: 105 kW (144 bhp) /	boot space	: 660 - 3460 l
	128 kW (174 bhp)	fuel capacity	: 75 l
@	: 5200 / 5100 rpm	consumption	: 28.5 / 22.1 mpg
max. torque	: 161 / 205 lb ft	acc. 0-62 mph	: 12.4 / 11.9 s
@	: 4000 rpm	top speed	: 114 / 111 mph
gears	: 5 / n.a.	EuroNCAP	: n.a.
AT	: n.a. / 4-speed automatic	introduction	: November 2001
drive	: FWD	last revised in	: Spring 2004
brakes f/r	: vent. discs / discs	warranty	: 2 years
body type	: 5-dr. MPV	miscellaneous	: Very successful model, this first
l x w x h	: 4808 x 1997 x 1803 mm		American people carrier. Very
wheelbase	: 2878 mm		big, with clever Stow&Go seating
turning circle	: 12.0 m		arrangement. Wheelbase of Grand
			Voyager another 288 millimetres
			longer.

VOYAGER 2.5 CRD / 2.8 CRD LX

engine type	: diesel, inline-4
displacement	: 2499 / 2776 cc
max. power	: 105 kW (143 bhp) /
	110 kW (150 bhp)
@	: 4000 / 3800 rpm
max. torque	: 251 / 265 lb ft
@	: 2000 / 1800 rpm
gears	: 5
kerb weight	: 1925 / 1915 kg
towing weight	: 1600 kg
consumption	: 35.5 / 33.7mpg
acc. 0-60 mph	: 12.9 /11.9 s
top speed	: 115 / 112 mph
miscellaneous	: Voyager and Grand Voyager share
	a somewhat European look, but
	build quality is not up to European
	standards.

CITROËN C1 1.0

engine type	: petrol, inline-3	kerb weight	: 765 kg
displacement	: 998 cc	towing weight	: -
max. power	: 50 kW (68 bhp)	boot space	: 139 - 712 l
@	: 6000 rpm	fuel capacity	: 35 l
max. torque	: 69 lb ft	consumption	: 61.4 mpg
@	: 3600 rpm	acc. 0-62 mph	: 13.7 s
gears	: 5	top speed	: 98 mph
AT	: n.a.	EuroNCAP	: n.a.
drive	: FWD	introduction	: May 2005
brakes f/r	: vent. discs / drum brakes	last revised in	: -
body type	: 3, 5-dr. hatchback	warranty	: 2 years
l x w x h	: 3435 x 1630 x 1465 mm	miscellaneous	: One of three models that are trip-
wheelbase	: 2350 mm		lets: Citroën C1, Peugeot 107 and
turning circle	: 9.5 m		Toyota Aygo. Also available with
			5-door body.

C1 1.4 HDI

engine type	: diesel, inline-4
displacement	: 1398 cc
max. power	: 40 kW (55 bhp)
@	: 4000 rpm
max. torque	: 96 lb ft
@	: 1750 rpm
gears	: 5
kerb weight	: 880 kg
towing weight	: -
consumption	: 68.9 mpg
acc. 0-60 mph	: 15.6 s
top speed	: 96 mph
miscellaneous	: With the 1.4 HDI engine, the C1 is an even more economical car to drive.

CITROËN C2 1.1 / 1.4

engine type	: petrol, inline-4	kerb weight	: 931 / 965 kg
displacement	: 1124 / 1361 cc	towing weight	: 520 / 530 kg
max. power	: 44 kW (61 bhp) / 54 kW (75 bhp)	boot space	: 193 l
@	: 5500 / 5400 rpm	fuel capacity	: 41 l
max. torque	: 69 / 87 lb ft	consumption	: 48.7 / 47.0 mpg
@	: 3300 rpm	acc. 0-62 mph	: 14.4 / 12.2 s
gears	: 5	top speed	: 98 / 105 mph
AT	: n.a. / optional Sensodrive	EuroNCAP	: 4 stars
drive	: FWD	introduction	: August 2003
brakes f/r	: discs / drums	last revised in	: -
body type	: 3-dr. hatchback	warranty	: 2 years
l x w x h	: 3666 x 1461 x 1659 mm	miscellaneous	: Smart little brother of the C3. Also
wheelbase	: 2315 mm		available with 1.4 HDI diesel
turning circle	: 9.6 m		engine. Refer to Citroën C3 for
			diesel engine specifications.

C2 VTS

engine type	: petrol, inline-4
displacement	: 1587 cc
max. power	: 90 kW (125 bhp)
@	: 6500 rpm
max. torque	: 105 lb ft
@	: 3750 rpm
gears	: 5
kerb weight	: 1059 kg
towing weight	: 620 kg
consumption	: 40.9 mpg
acc. 0-60 mph	: 8.9 s
top speed	: 126 mph
miscellaneous	: The real successor to the Saxo VTS. The range also includes the 1.6 VTR with a 110 bhp engine and Sensodrive transmission.

CITROEN C3 1.4 / 1.4 16V

engine type	: petrol, inline-4
displacement	: 1360 cc
max. power	: 54 kW (75 bhp) / 65 kW (90 bhp)
@	: 5400 / 5250 rpm
max. torque	: 87 / 98 lb ft
@	: 3400 / 3250 rpm
gears	: 5
AT	: n.a. / Sensodrive
drive	: FWD
brakes f/r	: discs / drums
body type	: 5-dr. hatchback
l x w x h	: 3850 x 1667 x 1519 mm
wheelbase	: 2460 mm
turning circle	: 11.3 m

kerb weight	: 989 / 1026 kg
towing weight	: 1160 kg
boot space	: 305 l
fuel capacity	: 47 l
consumption	: 46.3 / 49.6
acc. 0-62 mph	: 12.4 / 13.0 s
top speed	: 104 / 110 mph
EuroNCAP	: 4 stars
introduction	: Spring 2002
last revised in	: Autumn 2005
warranty	: 2 years
miscellaneous	: The 1.4 model is also available in a version which runs on natural gas. Alternative versions are the 1.1 (60 bhp) and 1.6 (110 bhp), plus the XT-R which resembles a sports utility vehicle.

C3 1.4 HDI

engine type	: diesel, inline-4
displacement	: 1398 cc
max. power	: 50 kW (70 bhp)
@	: 4000 rpm
max. torque	: 118 lb ft
@	: 2000 rpm
gears	: 5
kerb weight	: 1023 kg
towing weight	: 1160 kg
consumption	: 64.2 mpg
acc. 0-60 mph	: 14.8 s
top speed	: 101 mph
miscellaneous	: By far the most frugal C3 model. An alternative option is the 1.6 HDi, with either a 90 bhp or 110 bhp diesel engine.

CITROËN C3 PLURIEL 1.4 / 1.6 16V

engine type	: petrol, inline-4	kerb weight	: 1128 / 1175 kg
displacement	: 1361 / 1587 cc	towing weight	: 850 kg
max. power	: 54 kW (75 bhp) / 80 kW (110 bhp)	boot space	: 267 l
@	: 5400 / 5750 rpm	fuel capacity	: 47 l
max. torque	: 87 / 108 lb ft	consumption	: 41.5 / 42.2 mpg
@	: 3300 / 4000 rpm	acc. 0-62 mph	: 13.9 / 11.6 s
gears	: 5	top speed	: 99 / 117 mph
AT	: - / optional SensoDrive	EuroNCAP	: 4 stars
drive	: FWD	introduction	: Spring 2003
brakes f/r	: vent. discs / drum brakes	last revised in	: -
body type	: 2-dr. convertible	warranty	: 2 years
l x w x h	: 3934 x 1700 x 1559 mm	miscellaneous	: Nice roof construction, but Pluriel
wheelbase	: 2460 mm		is not free from rattles. With the
turning circle	: 10.1 m		roof closed and a driving speed of
			over 75 mph, the wind noise is
			deafening. Therefore better suited
			for the city.

CITROËN C4 1.4 16V / 1.6 16V

engine type	: petrol, inline-4	kerb weight	: 1157 / 1175 kg
displacement	: 1361 / 1587cc	towing weight	: 1561 / 1511 kg
max. power	: 65 kW (90 bhp) / 80 kW (110 bhp)	boot space	: 320 - 1023 l
@	: 5250 / 5800 rpm	fuel capacity	: 60 l
max. torque	: 98 / 108 lb ft	consumption	: 44.1 / 39.8 mpg
@	: 3300 / 4000 rpm	acc. 0-62 mph	: 14.2 / 11.9 s
gears	: 5	top speed	: 113 / 121 mph
AT	: - / optional 4-speed	EuroNCAP	: 5 stars
drive	: FWD	introduction	: Autumn 2004
brakes f/r	: vent. discs / discs	last revised in	: -
body type	: 5-dr. hatchback	warranty	: 2 years
l x w x h	: 4260 x 1773 x 1471 mm	miscellaneous	: Good-looking car, pitched against VW Golf. Citroën full of élan again. Non-revolving steering wheel centre and perfume device are very special.
wheelbase	: 2608 mm		
turning circle	: 10.8 m		

C4 1.6HDI 90 / 2.0 HDIF 138

engine type	: diesel, inline-4
displacement	: 1560 / 1997 cc
max. power	: 66 kW (92 bhp) / 100 kW (138 bhp)
@	: 4000 rpm
max. torque	: 159 / 236 lb ft
@	: 1750 / 2000 rpm
gears	: 5 / 6
kerb weight	: 1232 / 1356 kg
towing weight	: 1636 / 1811 kg
consumption	: 60.1 / 51.4 mpg
acc. 0-60 mph	: 13.9 / 10.5 s
top speed	: 112 /125 mph
miscellaneous	: 1.6 HDI engine with 110 bhp also available. The larger diesel engine is equipped with a particle filter.

CITROËN C4 COUPE 2.0 16V 138 / 180 pk

engine type	: petrol, inline-4	**kerb weight**	: 1254 / 1312 kg
displacement	: 1997cc	**towing weight**	: 1611 / 1401 kg
max. power	: 100 kW (138 bhp) /	**boot space**	: 314 l
	130 kW (180 bhp)	**fuel capacity**	: 60 l
@	: 6000 / 7000 rpm	**consumption**	: 37.2 / 33.6 mpg
max. torque	: 148 / 149 lb ft	**acc. 0-62 mph**	: 10.1 / 8.9 s
@	: 4100 / 4750 rpm	**top speed**	: 129 / 141 mph
gears	: 5	**EuroNCAP**	: 5 stars
AT	: -	**introduction**	: Autumn 2004
drive	: FWD	**last revised in**	: -
brakes f/r	: vent. discs / discs	**warranty**	: 2 years
body type	: 3-dr. hatchback	**miscellaneous**	: Coupe with exciting looks. Same
l x w x h	: 4273 x 1769 x 1456 mm		engine range as saloon, except for
wheelbase	: 2608 mm		the 180 bhp VTS which is mounted
turning circle	: 10.8 m		exclusively in the Coupe.

CITROËN C5 1.8 16V / 2.0 16V

85

engine type	: petrol, inline-4
displacement	: 1749 / 1997 cc
max. power	: 85 kW (117 bhp) / 104 kW (143 bhp)
@	: 5500 / 6000 rpm
max. torque	: 125 / 148 lb ft
@	: 4000 rpm
gears	: 5
AT	: - / optional 4-speed
drive	: FWD
brakes f/r	: vent. discs / discs
body type	: 5-dr. hatchback
l x w x h	: 4618 x 1770 x 1476 mm
wheelbase	: 2750 mm
turning circle	: 11.8 m

kerb weight	: 1290 / 1320 kg
towing weight	: 1300 / 1500 kg
boot space	: 455 - 1310 l
fuel capacity	: 66 l
consumption	: 37.2 / 35.3 mpg
acc. 0-62 mph	: 12.1 / 10.1 s
top speed	: 125 / 131 mph
EuroNCAP	: 4 stars
introduction	: March 2001
last revised in	: Autumn 2004
warranty	: 2 years
miscellaneous	: Front has gained most from recent facelift, rear of car somewhat cluttered. Fortunately, the stationwagon is as beautiful as ever.

C5 3.0 V6

engine type	: petrol, V6
displacement	: 2946 cc
max. power	: 152 kW (210 bhp)
@	: 6000 rpm
max. torque	: 215 lb ft
@	: 3750 rpm
gears	: 5, optional 4-speed automatic
kerb weight	: 1480 kg
towing weight	: 1600 kg
consumption	: 28.2 mpg
acc. 0-60 mph	: 8.2 s
top speed	: 143 mph
miscellaneous	: Lovely grand tourer. In the C5, Paris is just around the corner. Suspension system defies convention, but is unmatched.

CITROËN C5 BREAK 1.6 HDIF 16V / 2.0 HDIF 16V

engine type	: petrol, inline-4	kerb weight	: 1585 kg
displacement	: 1596 / 1997 cc	towing weight	: 1600 kg
max. power	: 80 kW (110 bhp) / 104 kW (143 bhp)	boot space	: 563 - 1658 l
@	: 4000 rpm	fuel capacity	: 68 l
max. torque	: 125 / 148 lb ft	consumption	: 51.4 / 47.1 mpg
@	: 4000 rpm	acc. 0-62 mph	: 11.5 / 10.1 s
gears	: 5 / 6	top speed	: 116 / 125 mph
AT	: optional 4-speed automatic	EuroNCAP	: 4 stars
drive	: FWD	introduction	: Summer 2001
brakes f/r	: vent. discs / discs	last revised in	: Autumn 2004
body type	: 5-dr. stationwagon	warranty	: 2 years
l x w x h	: 4839 x 1780 x 1511 mm	miscellaneous	: Infinitely big baggage space.
wheelbase	: 2750 mm		Pleasant, modern diesel engines
turning circle	: 11.8 m		with particle filter, also available
			in saloon.

C5 BREAK 2.2 HDI 16V

engine type	: diesel, inline-4
displacement	: 2179 cc
max. power	: 125 kW (173 bhp)
@	: 4000 rpm
max. torque	: 273 lb ft
@	: 1500 rpm
gears	: 6
kerb weight	: 1585 kg
towing weight	: 1600 kg
consumption	: 45.8 mpg
acc. 0-60 mph	: 8.2 s
top speed	: 135 mph
miscellaneous	: With this model, Citroën joins the horsepower race in the diesel-engined business car segment.

CITROEN C6 3.0i V6

engine type	: petrol, V6		kerb weight	: 1791 kg
displacement	: 2946 cc		towing weight	: 1700 kg
max. power	: 155 kW (215 bhp)		boot space	: 421 l
@	: 6000 rpm		fuel capacity	: 72 l
max. torque	: 214 lb ft		consumption	: 25.2 / 32.5 mpg
@	: 3750 rpm		acc. 0-62 mph	: 9.4 s
gears	: -		top speed	: 143 mph
AT	: 6-speed		EuroNCAP	: 5 stars
drive	: FWD		introduction	: Autumn 2005
brakes f/r	: vent. discs		last revised in	: -
body type	: 4-dr. saloon		warranty	: 2 years
l x w x h	: 4908 x 1860 x 1464 mm		miscellaneous	: Unconventional design and
wheelbase	: 2900 mm			suspension system should win
turning circle	: 12.4 m			customers over, for the C6 is more
				expensive than similar offerings from
				Mercedes-Benz and BMW.

C6 2.2 HDiF / 2.7 HDiF V6

engine type	: diesel, V6
displacement	: 2720 cc
max. power	: 150 kW (204 bhp)
@	: 4000 rpm
max. torque	: 325 lb ft
@	: 1900 rpm
gears	: 6-speed automatic
kerb weight	: 1846 kg
towing weight	: 1700 kg
consumption	: 32.5 mpg
acc. 0-60 mph	: 8.9 s
top speed	: 143 mph
miscellaneous	: Best buy: refined diesel version of V6 engine is quicker and zuiniger is dan de benzine-V6.

CITROËN C-CROSSER 2.2 HDI

engine type	: diesel, inline-4	kerb weight	: 1747 kg
displacement	: 2178 cc	towing weight	: 2000 kg
max. power	: 115 kW (156 bhp)	boot space	: 184 l
@	: 4000 rpm	fuel capacity	: 60 l
max. torque	: 280 lb ft	consumption	: 39.2 mpg
@	: 2000 rpm	acc. 0-62 mph	: 9.9 s
gears	: 6	top speed	: 124 mph
AT	: -	EuroNCAP	: n.a.
drive	: 4WD	introduction	: July 2007
brakes f/r	: vent. discs / discs	last revised in	: -
body type	: 5-dr. SUV	warranty	: 2 years
l x w x h	: 4646 x 1806 x 1713 mm	miscellaneous	: Citroën C-Crosser, built by
wheelbase	: 2670 mm		Mitsubishi, is an Outlander in
turning circle	: 10.6 m		disguise. Peugeot buildsa version
			of its own.

CITROËN BERLINGO 1.4 / 1.6 16V

engine type	: petrol, inline-4
displacement	: 1361 / 1587cc
max. power	: 55 kW (75 bhp) / 80 kW (110 bhp)
@	: 5500 / 5800 rpm
max. torque	: 89 / 108 lb ft
@	: 3300 / 4000 rpm
gears	: 5
AT	: -
drive	: FWD
brakes f/r	: vent. discs / drum brakes
body type	: 5-dr. MPV
l x w x h	: 4137 x 1724 x 1810 mm
wheelbase	: 2696 mm
turning circle	: 11.1 m

kerb weight	: 1163 / 1226 kg
towing weight	: 900 / 1100 kg
boot space	: 625 - 2800 l
fuel capacity	: 55 l
consumption	: 38.2 / 37.7 mpg
acc. 0-62 mph	: 17.5 / 13.1 s
top speed	: 94 / 106 mph
EuroNCAP	: n.a.
introduction	: January 1997
last revised in	: September 2002
warranty	: 2 years
miscellaneous	: The sensible choice. A lot of space for this kind of money.

BERLINGO 1.6 HDI 75 / 90

engine type	: diesel, inline-4
displacement	: 1560 cc
max. power	: 55 kW (75 bhp) / 66 kW (92 bhp)
@	: 4000 rpm
max. torque	: 125 / 168 lb ft
@	: 1750 / 1900 rpm
gears	: 5
kerb weight	: 1244 / 1215 kg
towing weight	: 1100 kg
consumption	: 52.3 mpg
acc. 0-60 mph	: 15.4 / 12.9 s
top speed	: 93 / 99 mph
miscellaneous	: More horsepower is tempting, but costs a great deal more. Not recommended really in a budget car like the Berlingo.

CITROËN XSARA PICASSO 1.6 16V / 2.0 16V

engine type	: petrol, inline-4	kerb weight	: 1243 kg
displacement	: 1587 cc	towing weight	: 1200 kg
max. power	: 80 kW (110 bhp)	boot space	: 550 l
@	: 6000 rpm	fuel capacity	: 55 l
max. torque	: 108 lb ft	consumption	: 38.7 mpg
@	: 4000 rpm	acc. 0-62 mph	: 11.4 s
gears	: 5	top speed	: 112 mph
AT	: n.a.	EuroNCAP	: 4 stars
drive	: FWD	introduction	: January 2000
brakes f/r	: vent. discs / drums	last revised in	: March 2004
body type	: 5-dr. MPV	warranty	: 2 years
l x w x h	: 4275 x 1751 x 1635 mm	miscellaneous	: Proven Xsara Picasso still part of
wheelbase	: 2760 mm		model range as a cheap mid-sized
turning circle	: 11.5 m		MPV alternative. Do not look any
			further if you are looking for interior
			space on a budget.

XSARA PICASSO 1.6 HDI / 1.6 HDIF

engine type	: diesel, inline-4
displacement	: 1560 cc
max. power	: 66 kW (92 bhp) / 80 kW (110 bhp)
@	: 4000 rpm
max. torque	: 159 / 192 lb ft
@	: 1750 rpm
gears	: 5
kerb weight	: 1265 / 1293 kg
towing weight	: 1300 kg
consumption	: 55.4 mpg
acc. 0-60 mph	: 12.1 / 10.8 s
top speed	: 109 / 114 mph
miscellaneous	: HDiF version is equipped with
	a diesel particle filter.

CITROËN C4 PICASSO 1.8 16V / 2.0 16V

engine type	: petrol, inline-4
displacement	: 1749 / 1997 cc
max. power	: 92 kW (127 bhp) / 104 kW (143 bhp)
@	: 6000 rpm
max. torque	: 125 / 148 lb ft
@	: 3750 / 4000 rpm
gears	: 5 / 6
AT	: - / optional 4-speed
drive	: FWD
brakes f/r	: vent. discs / discs
body type	: 5-dr. MPV
l x w x h	: 4590 x 1830 x 1660 mm
wheelbase	: 2728 mm
turning circle	: 11.8 m

kerb weight	: 1510 / 1560 kg
towing weight	: 1500 kg
boot space	: 208 – 1951 l
fuel capacity	: 60 l
consumption	: 35.3 mpg
acc. 0-62 mph	: 11.9 / 11.5 s
top speed	: 115 / 121 mph
EuroNCAP	: n.a.
introduction	: September 2006
last revised in	: -
warranty	: 2 years
miscellaneous	: The new C4 Picasso boasts seven seats, but a 5-seater version will make its appearance later.

C4 PICASSO 1.6 HDIF 16V / 2.0 HDIF 16V

engine type	: diesel, inline-4
displacement	: 1560 / 1997 cc
max. power	: 80 kW (110 bhp) / 100 kW (138 bhp)
@	: 4000 rpm
max. torque	: 177 / 199 lb ft
@	: 1750 / 2000 rpm
gears	: 5 / 6
kerb weight	: 1530 / 1620 kg
towing weight	: 1180 / 1500 kg
consumption	: 47.9 / 46.3 mpg
acc. 0-60 mph	: 12.7 / 12.5 s
top speed	: 112 / 121 mph
miscellaneous	: Biggest diesel version sports a sequential gearbox. Extra interior space is an added advantage of this box, which is also mounted in the two-litre petrol version.

CITROËN C8 2.0 16V / 2.0 HDIF 16V

engine type	: petrol / diesel, inline-4	**kerb weight**	: 1606 / 1718 kg
displacement	: 1997 cc	**towing weight**	: 1700 / 1850 kg
max. power	: 104 kW (143 bhp) /	**boot space**	: 480 - 2948 l
	100 kW (138 bhp)	**fuel capacity**	: 80 l
@	: 6000 / 4000 rpm	**consumption**	: 31.4 / 40.9 mpg
max. torque	: 148 / 221 lb ft	**acc. 0-62 mph**	: 11.6 / 12.9 s
@	: 4100 / 2000 rpm	**top speed**	: 117 / 112 mph
gears	: 5 / 6	**EuroNCAP**	: n.a.
AT	: optional 4-speed / -	**introduction**	: May 2002
drive	: FWD	**last revised in**	: -
brakes f/r	: vent. discs / discs	**warranty**	: 2 years
body type	: 5-dr. MPV	**miscellaneous**	: Also available as HDiF with 110
l x w x h	: 4726 x 1854 x 1752 mm		bhp
wheelbase	: 2823 mm		and automatic transmission. It
turning circle	: 10.9 m		looks like Citroën is gradually
			budging out of the segment of the
			large MPV's.

CORVETTE C6

engine type	: petrol, V8
displacement	: 5967 cc
max. power	: 297 kW (404 bhp)
@	: 6000 rpm
max. torque	: 416 lb ft
@	: 4400 rpm
gears	: 6
AT	: optional 4-speed
drive	: RWD
brakes f/r	: vent. discs
body type	: 2-dr. coupe
l x w x h	: 4435 x 1845 x 1245 mm
wheelbase	: 2685 mm
turning circle	: 12.0 m
kerb weight	: 1492 kg
towing weight	: -
boot space	: 635 l
fuel capacity	: 68 l
consumption	: 21.7 mpg
acc. 0-62 mph	: 4.3 s
top speed	: 186 mph
EuroNCAP	: n.a.
introduction	: January 2005
last revised in	: -
warranty	: 3 years
miscellaneous	: The Corvette is to the USA what the Porsche 911 is to Germany. Capable and good alternative for European sportscars. Also available as Convertible.

Z06

engine type	: petrol, V8
displacement	: 7011 cc
max. power	: 377 kW (512 bhp)
@	: 6300 rpm
max. torque	: 470 lb ft
@	: 4800 rpm
gears	: 6
kerb weight	: 1393 kg
towing weight	: -
consumption	: 19.3 mpg
acc. 0-60 mph	: 7.6 s
top speed	: 143 mph
miscellaneous	: Fastest Corvette in history, born at the Nürburgring. But it is rumoured that an even more powerful version is already on its way.

DACIA LOGAN MCV 1.4 / 1.6

engine type	: petrol, inline-4	kerb weight	: 1165 kg
displacement	: 1390 / 1598 cc	towing weight	: 1300 kg
max. power	: 55 kW (75 bhp) / 64 kW (87 bhp)	boot space	: 700 l
@	: 5500 rpm	fuel capacity	: 50 l
max. torque	: 83 / 94 lb ft	consumption	: 37.2 / 36.2 mpg
@	: 3000 rpm	acc. 0-62 mph	: 15.6 / 13.4 s
gears	: 5	top speed	: 96 / 104 mph
AT	: n.a.	EuroNCAP	: 3 stars
drive	: FWD	introduction	: March 2007
brakes f/r	: discs / drums	last revised in	: -
body type	: 5-dr. stationwagon	warranty	: 2 years
l x w x h	: 4450 x 1735 x 1640 mm	miscellaneous	: Very cheap and spacious stationwagon is a sales hit and comes with the option of 7 seats. Specifications refer to the 5-seater MCV version.
wheelbase	: 2905 mm		
turning circle	: 11.3 m		

LOGAN MCV 1.5 dCi

engine type	: diesel, inline-4
displacement	: 1461 cc
max. power	: 50 kW (68 bhp)
@	: 4000 rpm
max. torque	: 118 lb ft
@	: 1700 rpm
gears	: 5
kerb weight	: 1205 kg
towing weight	: 1300 kg
consumption	: 58.9 mpg
acc. 0-60 mph	: 17.7 s
top speed	: 93 mph
miscellaneous	: The original saloon version of the Logan only plays a minor role in total Dacia sales now. It is also available with a 105 bhp 1.6 16V petrol engine.

DAIHATSU CUORE

engine type	: petrol, inline-3		**kerb weight**	: 695 kg
displacement	: 989 cc		**towing weight**	: 600 kg
max. power	: 43 kW (58 bhp)		**boot space**	: 157 - 826 l
@	: 6000 rpm		**fuel capacity**	: 36 l
max. torque	: 67 lb ft		**consumption**	: 58.9 mpg
@	: 4000 rpm		**acc. 0-62 mph**	: 12.8 s
gears	: 5		**top speed**	: 99 mph
AT	: optional 4-speed automatic		**EuroNCAP**	: n.a.
drive	: FWD		**introduction**	: April 2003
brakes f/r	: vent. discs / drum brakes		**last revised in**	: Autumn 2005
body type	: 3, 5-dr. hatchback		**warranty**	: 3 years
l x w x h	: 3410 x 1475 x 1500 mm		**miscellaneous**	: Cute car, but interior space
wheelbase	: 2345 mm			is inferior to that of other small
turning circle	: 8.4 m			cars.

DAIHATSU TREVIS

engine type	: petrol, inline-3
displacement	: 989 cc
max. power	: 43 kW (58 bhp)
@	: 6000 rpm
max. torque	: 67 lb ft
@	: 4000 rpm
gears	: 5
kerb weight	: 790 kg
towing weight	: n.a.
consumption	: 57.6 mpg
acc. 0-60 mph	: n.a.
top speed	: n.a.
miscellaneous	: Well-equipped but expensive variant of Cuore.

DAIHATSU SIRION 2 1.0 / 1.3

engine type	: petrol, inline-3 / inline 4	**kerb weight**	: 890 / 940 kg
displacement	: 989 / 1298 cc	**towing weight**	: 750 / 1000 kg
max. power	: 51 kW (71 bhp) / 64 kW (87 bhp)	**boot space**	: 225 l
@	: 6000 rpm	**fuel capacity**	: 40 l
max. torque	: 69 / 88 lb ft	**consumption**	: 56.5 / 48.7 mpg
@	: 3600 / 3200 rpm	**acc. 0-62 mph**	: 13.9 / 11.0 s
gears	: 5	**top speed**	: 99 / 106 mph
AT	: optional 4-speed automatic	**EuroNCAP**	: n.a.
drive	: FWD	**introduction**	: January 2005
brakes f/r	: vent. discs / drum brakes	**last revised in**	: -
body type	: 5-dr. hatchback	**warranty**	: 3 years
l x w x h	: 3600 x 1665 x 1550 mm	**miscellaneous**	: New design copied from Cuore
wheelbase	: 2430 mm		and YRV. Sirion 2 more tailored
turning circle	: 8.6 m		to European taste than previous
			model.

DAIHATSU MATERIA 1.5

engine type	: petrol, inline-4	**kerb weight**	: 1010 kg
displacement	: 1495 cc	**towing weight**	: 1000 kg
max. power	: 76 kW (102 bhp)	**boot space**	: 290-360 l
@	: 6000 rpm	**fuel capacity**	: 40 l
max. torque	: 97 lb ft	**consumption**	: 39.2 mpg
@	: 4400 rpm	**acc. 0-62 mph**	: 10.8 s
gears	: 5	**top speed**	: 106 mph
AT	: optional 4-speed	**EuroNCAP**	: n.a.
drive	: FWD	**introduction**	: December 2006
brakes f/r	: discs / drums	**last revised in**	: -
body type	: 5-dr. MPV	**warranty**	: 3 years
l x w x h	: 3800 x 1690 x 1635 mm	**miscellaneous**	: Boxy MPV-model is an eye-catch-
wheelbase	: 2540 mm		ing alternative to a Vauxhall Meriva
turning circle	: 9.8 m		or Nissan Note. Four-wheel drive
			is an option.

DAIHATSU TERIOS

engine type	: petrol, inline 4	kerb weight	: 1140 kg
displacement	: 1495 cc	towing weight	: 1350 kg
max. power	: 77 kW (105 bhp)	boot space	: 380 l
@	: 6000 rpm	fuel capacity	: 50 l
max. torque	: 103 lb ft	consumption	: 35.8 mpg
@	: 3600 / 3200 rpm	acc. 0-62 mph	: 12.4 s
gears	: 5	top speed	: 99 mph
AT	: -	EuroNCAP	: n.a.
drive	: FWD	introduction	: April 2006
brakes f/r	: vent. discs / drum brakes	last revised in	: -
body type	: 5-dr. SUV	warranty	: 3 years
l x w x h	: 4055 x 1695 x 1690 mm	miscellaneous	: 4WD is an option, but not really
wheelbase	: 2580 mm		necessary for normal road use.
turning circle	: 9.8 m		More mature car than predecessor.

DAIHATSU COPEN

engine type	: petrol, inline 4		**kerb weight**	: 825 kg
displacement	: 1298 cc		**towing weight**	: -
max. power	: 64 kW (87 bhp)		**boot space**	: 210 l
@	: 6000 rpm		**fuel capacity**	: 40 l
max. torque	: 74 lb ft		**consumption**	: 44.1 mpg
@	: 4400 rpm		**acc. 0-62 mph**	: n.a.
gears	: 5		**top speed**	: 106 mph
AT	: -		**EuroNCAP**	: n.a.
drive	: FWD		**introduction**	: Late 2004
brakes f/r	: vent. discs / drum brakes		**last revised in**	: Autumn 2005
body type	: 2-dr. convertible		**warranty**	: 3 years
l x w x h	: 3395 x 1475 x 1245 mm		**miscellaneous**	: Now available with a bigger petrol
wheelbase	: 2225 mm			engine. Not very practical, but still
turning circle	: n.a.			great fun.

DAIMLER SUPER EIGHT

engine type	: petrol, V8	kerb weight	: 1665 kg
displacement	: 4196 cc	towing weight	: 1900 kg
max. power	: 298 kW (400 bhp)	boot space	: 470 l
@	: 6100 rpm	fuel capacity	: 85 l
max. torque	: 408 lb ft	consumption	: 23.3 mpg
@	: 3500 rpm	acc. 0-62 mph	: 5.3 s
gears	: n.a.	top speed	: 155 mph
AT	: 6-speed	EuroNCAP	: n.a.
drive	: RWD	introduction	: November 2005
brakes f/r	: vent. discs	last revised in	: July 2007
body type	: 4-dr. saloon	warranty	: 3 jaar
l x w x h	: 5216 x 1898 x 1448 mm	miscellaneous	: Deluxe version of the Jaguar XJ. Received a facelift together with the Jag.
wheelbase	: 3159 mm		
turning circle	: 12.0 m		

DODGE CALIBER 1.8 / 2.0

engine type	: petrol, inline-4	**kerb weight**	: 1295 / 1335 kg
displacement	: 178 / 1998c	**towing weight**	: 1200 kg
max. power	: 110 kW (150 bhp) / 115 kW (156 bhp)	**boot space**	: 525 l
@	: 6500 / 6300 rpm	**fuel capacity**	: 51 l
max. torque	: 124 / 140 lb ft	**consumption**	: 38.9 / 35.0 mpg
@	: 5200 / 5100 rpm	**acc. 0-62 mph**	: 12.8 / 11.8 s
gears	: 5 / -	**top speed**	: 118 / 124 mph
AT	: - / optional CVT	**EuroNCAP**	: n.a.
drive	: FWD	**introduction**	: June 2006
brakes f/r	: vent. discs / discs	**last revised in**	: -
body type	: 5-dr. hatchback	**warranty**	: 3 years
l x w x h	: 4415 x 1800 x 1535 mm	**miscellaneous**	: The Caliber is the car that has to put
wheelbase	: 2635 mm		Dodge back on the map in Europe.
turning circle	: 10.8 m		

CALIBER 2.0 CRD

engine type	: diesel, inline-4
displacement	: 1968 cc
max. power	: 103 kW (140 bhp)
@	: 4000 rpm
max. torque	: 236 lb ft
@	: 2500 rpm
gears	: 6
kerb weight	: 1400 kg
towing weight	: 1200 kg
consumption	: 47.1 mpg
acc. 0-60 mph	: 9.3 s
top speed	: 115 mph
miscellaneous	: With its original design and low price, its future looks promising.

DODGE AVENGER 2.0

engine type	: petrol, inline-4	kerb weight	: 1480 kg
displacement	: 1998 cc	towing weight	: 1000 kg
max. power	: 115 kW (154 bhp)	boot space	: 438 l
@	: 6300 rpm	fuel capacity	: 63 l
max. torque	: 140 lb ft	consumption	: 36.2 mpg
@	: 5100 rpm	acc. 0-62 mph	: 10.8 s
gears	: 5	top speed	: 124 mph
AT	: -	EuroNCAP	: n.a.
drive	: FWD	introduction	: September 2006
brakes f/r	: vent. discs / discs	last revised in	: -
body type	: 4-dr. saloon	warranty	: 3 years
l x w x h	: 4850 x 1843 x 1497 mm	miscellaneous	: The Avenger shares its technical
wheelbase	: 2765 mm		lay-out with the Chrysler Sebring,
turning circle	: 11.1 m		but the Dodge is a bit lighter,
			quicker and cheaper.

AVENGER 2.0 CRD

engine type	: diesel, inline-4
displacement	: 1968 cc
max. power	: 103 kW (138 bhp)
@	: 4000 rpm
max. torque	: 229 lb ft
@	: 1750 rpm
gears	: 6
kerb weight	: 1560 kg
towing weight	: 1000 kg
consumption	: 45.6 mpg
acc. 0-60 mph	: 10.5 s
top speed	: 124 mph
miscellaneous	: The diesel engine is supplied by Volkswagen.

DODGE NITRO 3.7 V6

engine type	: petrol, V6	**kerb weight**	: 1875 kg
displacement	: 3700 cc	**towing weight**	: 3500 kg
max. power	: 151 kW (203 bhp)	**boot space**	: 369 l
@	: 6000 rpm	**fuel capacity**	: 74 l
max. torque	: 232 lb ft	**consumption**	: 23.3 mpg
@	: 4000 rpm	**acc. 0-62 mph**	: 10.3 s
gears	: -	**top speed**	: 118 mph
AT	: 4-speed	**EuroNCAP**	: n.a.
drive	: 4WD	**introduction**	: June 2007
brakes f/r	: vent. discs / discs	**last revised in**	: -
body type	: 5-dr. SUV	**warranty**	: 3 years
l x w x h	: 4584 x 1856 x 1773 mm	**miscellaneous**	: Wild and uncivilized looking SUV, but good-natured and full of character. Striking alternative to a Kia Sorento or Jeep Cherokee.
wheelbase	: 2763 mm		
turning circle	: 11.1 m		

NITRO 2.8 CRD

engine type	: diesel, inline-4
displacement	: 2768 cc
max. power	: 130 kW (174 bhp)
@	: 3800 rpm
max. torque	: 302 lb ft
@	: 2000 rpm
gears	: 6, optional 5-speed automatic
kerb weight	: 1940 kg
towing weight	: 2000 kg
consumption	: 32.8 mpg
acc. 0-60 mph	: 11.5 s
top speed	: 112 mph
miscellaneous	: You get more torque if you opt for the automatic transmission, in which case the maximum towable weight rises to 3500 kg.

DODGE VIPER SRT-10

engine type	: petrol, V10	kerb weight	: n.a.
displacement	: 8354 cc	towing weight	: -
max. power	: 447 kW (600 bhp)	boot space	: 415 l
@	: 6100 rpm	fuel capacity	: n.a.
max. torque	: 560 lb ft	consumption	: n.a.
@	: 4100 rpm	acc. 0-62 mph	: <4.0 s
gears	: 6	top speed	: >200 mph
AT	: n.a.	EuroNCAP	: n.a.
drive	: RWD	introduction	: August 2005
brakes f/r	: vent. discs	last revised in	: February 2007
body type	: 2-dr. convertible / coupe	warranty	: 3 years
l x w x h	: 4459 x 1911 x 1210 mm	miscellaneous	: The megalomaniac SRT-10 is
wheelbase	: 2510 mm		an even more brutal car now.
turning circle	: 12.4 m		Available as GTS (Coupe) and
			Roadster.

DONKERVOORT D8 150 / 180

engine type	: petrol, inline-4
displacement	: 1781 cc
max. power	: 110 kW (150 bhp) / 132 kW (180 bhp)
@	: 5700 / 5500 rpm
max. torque	: 155 /173 lb ft
@	: 2000 / 1950 rpm
gears	: 5
AT	: -
drive	: RWD
brakes f/r	: vent. discs / discs
body type	: 2-dr. convertible
l x w x h	: 3410 x 1730 x 1100 mm
wheelbase	: 2300 mm
turning circle	: 8.0 m

kerb weight	: 630 kg
towing weight	: -
boot space	: 100 l
fuel capacity	: 40 l
consumption	: 31.5 mpg
acc. 0-62 mph	: 6.0 / 5.0 s
top speed	: 124 / 131 mph
EuroNCAP	: n.a.
introduction	: January 2003
last revised in	: -
warranty	: 2 years
miscellaneous	: A terrific car that offers bike-like driving sensations. Far from cheap, but depreciation is low. Also available with 210 bhp and 270 bhp engines.

FERRARI F430

engine type	: petrol, V8	kerb weight	: 1450 kg
displacement	: 4308 cc	towing weight	: -
max. power	: 360 kW (490 bhp)	boot space	: 250 l
@	: 8500 rpm	fuel capacity	: 95 l
max. torque	: 343 lb ft	consumption	: 15.4 mpg
@	: 5250 rpm	acc. 0-62 mph	: 4.0 s
gears	: 6	top speed	: 196 mph
AT	: -	EuroNCAP	: n.a
drive	: RWD	introduction	: October 2004
brakes f/r	: vent. discs	last revised in	: -
body type	: 2-dr. coupe	warranty	: 2 years
l x w x h	: 4512 x 1923 x 1214 mm	miscellaneous	: Unmistakably a Ferrari. Worthy
wheelbase	: 2600 mm		replacement for the 360 Modena.
turning circle	: 10.8 m		Also F1 version available with
			sequential gearshift.

FERRARI 599 GTB FIORANO

engine type	: petrol, V12	kerb weight	: 1690 kg
displacement	: 5999 cc	towing weight	: -
max. power	: 456 kW (620 bhp)	boot space	: 320 l
@	: 7600 rpm	fuel capacity	: 105 l
max. torque	: 448 lb ft	consumption	: 21.3 mpg
@	: 5600 rpm	acc. 0-62 mph	: 3.7 s
gears	: 6	top speed	: 205 mph
AT	: optional seq. gearbox	EuroNCAP	: n.a.
drive	: RWD	introduction	: January 2006
brakes f/r	: vent. discs	last revised in	: -
body type	: 2-dr. coupe	warranty	: 2 years
l x w x h	: 4665 x 1962 x 1336 mm	miscellaneous	: Successor to the 575 M Maranello,
wheelbase	: 2750 mm		but a better car in every respect.
turning circle	: n.a.		Cluttered design takes some get-
			ting used to.

FERRARI 612 SCAGLIETTI

engine type	: petrol, V12	kerb weight	: 1840 kg
displacement	: 5748 cc	towing weight	: -
max. power	: 397 kW (540 bhp)	boot space	: 240 l
@	: 7250 rpm	fuel capacity	: 108 l
max. torque	: 434 lb ft	consumption	: 13.6 mpg
@	: 5250 rpm	acc. 0-62 mph	: 4.2 s
gears	: 6	top speed	: 199 mph
AT	: optional seq. gearbox	EuroNCAP	: n.a.
drive	: RWD	introduction	: April 2004
brakes f/r	: vent. discs	last revised in	: -
body type	: 2-dr. coupe	warranty	: 2 years
l x w x h	: 4902 x 1957 x 1344 mm	miscellaneous	: Larger, lighter, more spacious and
wheelbase	: 2950 mm		more powerful than predecessor
turning circle	: 12.0 m		456 M GT. Not your average
			Ferrari, though, but different in
			many ways.

FIAT 500 1.2 / 1.4

engine type	: petrol, inline-4
displacement	: 1242 / 1368 cc
max. power	: 51 kW (69 bhp) / 74 kW (100 bhp)
@	: 5500 / 6000 rpm
max. torque	: 75 / 97 lb ft
@	: 3000 / 4250 rpm
gears	: 5 / 6
AT	: optional 5-speed
drive	: FWD
brakes f/r	: vent. discs / drums
body type	: 3-dr. hatchback
l x w x h	: 3546 x 1627 x 1488 mm
wheelbase	: 2300 mm
turning circle	: 9.2 m

kerb weight	: 865 / 930 kg
towing weight	: -
boot space	: 185 l
fuel capacity	: 35 l
consumption	: 55.4 / 44.8 mpg
acc. 0-62 mph	: 12.9 / 10.5 s
top speed	: 100 / 115 mph
EuroNCAP	: 5 stars
introduction	: November 2007
last revised in	: -
warranty	: 2 years
miscellaneous	: The new 500 is like an iPod on wheels. The cute looks, low price and endless list of options should help to turn this retro-looking city car into a smashing sales hit.

500 1.3 MULTIJET

engine type	: diesel, inline-4
displacement	: 1248 cc
max. power	: 55 kW (75 bhp)
@	: 4000 rpm
max. torque	: 107 lb ft
@	: 1500 rpm
gears	: 5
kerb weight	: 980 kg
towing weight	: -
consumption	: 67.3 mpg
acc. 0-60 mph	: 12.5 s
top speed	: 103 mph
miscellaneous	: A Fiat 500 as a company car? It could well be, thanks to a diesel-powered model version.

FIAT PANDA 1.1 / 1.2

engine type	: petrol, inline-4	kerb weight	: 815 / 835 kg
displacement	: 1108 / 1242 cc	towing weight	: 800 kg
max. power	: 40 kW (54 bhp) / 44 kW (60 bhp)	boot space	: 206 – 775 l
@	: 5000 rpm	fuel capacity	: 35 l
max. torque	: 65 / 75 lb ft	consumption	: 49.6 / 50.4 mpg
@	: 2750 / 2500 rpm	acc. 0-62 mph	: 15.0 / 14.0 s
gears	: 5	top speed	: 93 / 96 mph
AT	: - / optional CVT	EuroNCAP	: 3 stars
drive	: FWD	introduction	: Autumn 2003
brakes f/r	: discs / drum brakes	last revised in	: -
body type	: 5-dr. hatchback	warranty	: 2 years
l x w x h	: 3538 x 1589 x 1540 mm	miscellaneous	: The Panda is proof of what Fiat
wheelbase	: 2299 mm		does best: building small cars.
turning circle	: 9.1 m		

PANDA 1.3 MULTIJET DYNAMIC

engine type	: diesel, inline-4
displacement	: 1248 cc
max. power	: 51 kW (bhp)
@	: 4000 rpm
max. torque	: 107 lb ft
@	: 1500 rpm
gears	: 5
kerb weight	: 910 kg
towing weight	: 900 kg
consumption	: 65.7 mpg
acc. 0-60 mph	: 13.0 s
top speed	: 99 mph
miscellaneous	: 1.3 diesel is the best engine in the Panda line-up: quiet, powerful and economical.

FIAT PANDA 4X4 CLIMBING

engine type	: petrol, inline-4		**kerb weight**	: 955 kg
displacement	: 1242 cc		**towing weight**	: 800 kg
max. power	: 44 kW (60 bhp)		**boot space**	: 206 l
@	: 5000 rpm		**fuel capacity**	: 30 l
max. torque	: 75 lb ft		**consumption**	: 43 mpg
@	: 2500 rpm		**acc. 0-62 mph**	: 20.0 s
gears	: 5		**top speed**	: 90 mph
AT	: -		**EuroNCAP**	: 3 stars
drive	: 4WD		**introduction**	: September 2004
brakes f/r	: vent. discs / discs		**last revised in**	: -
body type	: 5-dr. hatchback		**warranty**	: 2 years
l x w x h	: 3574 x 1605 x 1632 mm		**miscellaneous**	: Capable offroader, but less
wheelbase	: 2305 mm			suited as a city car. Sturdy looks.
turning circle	: 9.6 m			

PANDA 4X4 CROSS

engine type	: diesel, inline-4
displacement	: 1248 cc
max. power	: 51 kW (bhp)
@	: 4000 rpm
max. torque	: 107 lb ft
@	: 1500 rpm
gears	: 5
kerb weight	: 1065 kg
towing weight	: 900 kg
consumption	: 53.5 mpg
acc. 0-60 mph	: 18.0 s
top speed	: 93 mph
miscellaneous	: Not very quick either, but more powerful and better looking than the Climbing. More expensive too.

FIAT PUNTO 1.2

engine type	: petrol, inline-4	kerb weight	: 895 / 935 kg
displacement	: 1242 cc	towing weight	: 1000 kg
max. power	: 44 kW (60 bhp)	boot space	: 264 - 1080 l
@	: 5000 rpm	fuel capacity	: 47 l
max. torque	: 75 lb ft	consumption	: 50.4 mpg
@	: 2500 rpm	acc. 0-62 mph	: 14.3 s
gears	: 5	top speed	: 96 mph
AT	: -	EuroNCAP	: 4 stars
drive	: FWD	introduction	: September 1999
brakes f/r	: discs / drum brakes	last revised in	: Summer 2003
body type	: 3-, 5-dr. hatchback	warranty	: 2 years
l x w x h	: 3840 x 1660 x 1480 mm	miscellaneous	: The previous Punto is still in
wheelbase	: 2460 mm		production and serves as a
turning circle	: 10.5 m		cheaper alternative for the Grande
			Punto.

FIAT GRANDE PUNTO 1.2 / 1.4

engine type	: petrol, inline-4
displacement	: 1242 / 1368 cc
max. power	: 48 kW (65 bhp) / 57 kW (77 bhp)
@	: 5500 / 6000 rpm
max. torque	: 76 / 85 lb ft
@	: 3000 rpm
gears	: 5
AT	: optional 5-speed
drive	: FWD
brakes f/r	: vent. discs / drums
body type	: 3- / 5-dr. hatchback
l x w x h	: 4030 x 1687 x 1490 mm
wheelbase	: 2510 mm
turning circle	: 10.0 m

kerb weight	: 1015 / 1025 kg
towing weight	: 900 / 1000 kg
boot space	: 275 l
fuel capacity	: 45 l
consumption	: 47.9 mpg
acc. 0-62 mph	: 14.5 / 13.2 s
top speed	: 96 / 103 mph
EuroNCAP	: 5 stars
introduction	: September 2005
last revised in	: -
warranty	: 2 years
miscellaneous	: Much bigger than its predecessor and endowed with a striking design. Very modern small car.

GRANDE PUNTO 1.4 / 1.4 T-JET

engine type	: petrol, inline-4
displacement	: 1368 cc
max. power	: 70 kW (95 bhp) / 88 kW (120 bhp)
@	: 6000 / 5000 rpm
max. torque	: 92 / 152 lb ft
@	: 4500 / 2000 rpm
gears	: 5
kerb weight	: 1035 / 1155 kg
towing weight	: 1000 kg
consumption	: 47.1 / 42.8 mpg
acc. 0-60 mph	: 11.4 / 8.9 s
top speed	: 111 / 121 mph
miscellaneous	: The T-Jet badge denotes turbo power under the bonnet. A 150 bhp strong model and sporty Abarth Grande Punto with 180 bhp will follow.

GRANDE PUNTO 1.3 / 1.9 MULTIJET

engine type	: diesel, inline-4
displacement	: 1248 / 1910 cc
max. power	: 55kW (75 bhp) / 96 kW (130 bhp)
@	: 4000 rpm
max. torque	: 140/ 206 lb ft
@	: 1750 / 2000 rpm
gears	: 6
kerb weight	: 1105 / 1180 kg
towing weight	: 1000 kg
consumption	: 62.8 / 48.7 mpg
acc. 0-60 mph	: 13.6 / 9.5 s
top speed	: 103 / 124 mph
miscellaneous	: Choices, choices: the 1.3 diesel unit is also available with 90 bhp and the 1.9 also with 120 bhp.

FIAT BRAVO 1.4 / 1.4 T-JET

engine type	: petrol, inline-4		kerb weight	: 1205 / 1250 kg
displacement	: 1368 cc		towing weight	: 1000 / 1300 kg
max. power	: 66 kW (90 bhp) / 110 kW (150 bhp)		boot space	: 400 l
@	: 5500 rpm		fuel capacity	: 58 l
max. torque	: 94 / 152 lb ft		consumption	: 42.2 / 39.8 mpg
@	: 4500 / 2250 rpm		acc. 0-62 mph	: 12.5 / 8.5 s
gears	: 5 / 6		top speed	: 111 / 131 mph
AT	: -		EuroNCAP	: 5 stars
drive	: FWD		introduction	: March 2007
brakes f/r	: vent. discs / discs		last revised in	: -
body type	: 5-dr. hatchback		warranty	: 2 years
l x w x h	: 4336 x 1792 x 1498 mm		miscellaneous	: Fiat has high hopes for the new
wheelbase	: 2600 mm			Bravo model which replaces the
turning circle	: 10.4 m			Stilo. Its price tag positions it in
				between the European and
				Asian competition.

BRAVO 1.9 MULTIJET 8V / 16V

engine type	: diesel, inline-4
displacement	: 1910 cc
max. power	: 88 kW (120 bhp) / 110 kW (150 bhp)
@	: 4000 rpm
max. torque	: 188 / 225 lb ft
@	: 2000 rpm
gears	: 5 / 6
kerb weight	: 1320 / 1360 kg
towing weight	: 1300 kg
consumption	: 53.3 / 50.4 mpg
acc. 0-60 mph	: 10.5 / 9.0 s
top speed	: 120 / 130 mph
miscellaneous	: Familiar diesel engines from Fiat are used in the Bravo too.

FIAT CROMA 1.8 / 2.2

engine type	: petrol, inline-4		**kerb weight**	: 1430 / 1485 kg
displacement	: 1796 / 2198 cc		**towing weight**	: 1500 kg
max. power	: 103 kW (140 bhp) /		**boot space**	: 500 – 1620 l
	108 kW (147 bhp)		**fuel capacity**	: 62 l
@	: 6300 / 5800 rpm		**consumption**	: 38.2 / 32.8 mpg
max. torque	: 129 / 150 lb ft		**acc. 0-62 mph**	: 10.2 / 10.1 s
@	: 3800 / 4000 rpm		**top speed**	: 128 / 131 mph
gears	: 5		**EuroNCAP**	: n.a.
AT	: - / optional 5-speed automatic		**introduction**	: -
drive	: FWD		**last revised in**	: June 2005
brakes f/r	: vent. discs / discs		**warranty**	: 2 years
body type	: 5-dr. stationwagon		**miscellaneous**	: Ambitious re-entry of Italian car
l x w x h	: 4756 x 1775 x 1597 mm			manufacturer in medium-sized car
wheelbase	: 2700 mm			segment. Unconventional design.
turning circle	: 10.9 m			Spacious interior and fine driving
				characteristics should bring more
				customers.

CROMA 1.9 / 2.4 JTD

engine type	: diesel, inline-4 / inline-5
displacement	: 1910 / 2387cc
max. power	: 110 kW (150 bhp) / 147 kW (200 bhp)
@	: 4000 rpm
max. torque	: 236 / 295 lb ft
@	: 2000 rpm
gears	: 6 / 6-speed automatic
kerb weight	: 1505 / 1625 kg
towing weight	: 1500 kg
consumption	: 46.3 / 35.3 mpg
acc. 0-60 mph	: 9.6 / 8.5 s
top speed	: 131 / 134 mph
miscellaneous	: Excellent diesel engines should promote sales of the Croma as a business car. Also available with 120 bhp 1.9 JTD diesel engine.

FIAT DOBLÒ 1.4

engine type	: petrol, inline-4
displacement	: 1242 / 1596 cc
max. power	: 44 kW (65 bhp) / 74 kW (100 bhp)
@	: 5500 / 4000 rpm
max. torque	: 75 / 148 lb ft
@	: 3500 / 1500 rpm
gears	: 5
AT	: -
drive	: FWD
brakes f/r	: discs / drum brakes
body type	: 5-dr. MPV
l x w x h	: 4159 x 1714 x 1810 mm
wheelbase	: 2566 mm
turning circle	: 10.5 m

kerb weight	: 1195 / 1250 kg
towing weight	: 1100 kg
boot space	: 750 - 3000 l
fuel capacity	: 60 l
consumption	: 38.3 / 44.9 mpg
acc. 0-62 mph	: 18.9 / 12.4 s
top speed	: 88 / 104 mph
EuroNCAP	: 3 stars
introduction	: Late 2001
last revised in	: -
warranty	: 2 years
miscellaneous	: More of a van than MPV, but an excellent alternative for people who think twice when buying a car.

DOBLÒ 1.3 JTD / 1.9 JTD

engine type	: diesel, inline-4
displacement	: 1248 / 1910 cc
max. power	: 55 kW (75 bhp) / 77 kW (105 bhp)
@	: 4000 rpm
max. torque	: 148 / 155 lb ft
@	: 1750 / 2000 rpm
gears	: 5
kerb weight	: 1285 / 1295 kg
towing weight	: 1100 / 1100 kg
consumption	: 51.4 / 48.7 mpg
acc. 0-60 mph	: 16.1 / 12.4 s
top speed	: 97 / 102 mph
miscellaneous	: Angular design results in ample interior space. Hard-pressed drivers opt for the 105 bhp version.

FIAT SEDICI 1.6 16V

engine type	: petrol, inline-4
displacement	: 1242 / 1596 cc
max. power	: 44 kW (65 bhp) / 74 kW (100 bhp)
@	: 5500 / 4000 rpm
max. torque	: 75 / 148 lb ft
@	: 3500 / 1500 rpm
gears	: 5
AT	: -
drive	: FWD
brakes f/r	: discs / drum brakes
body type	: 5-dr. MPV
l x w x h	: 4159 x 1714 x 1810 mm
wheelbase	: 2566 mm
turning circle	: 10.5 m
kerb weight	: 1195 / 1250 kg
towing weight	: 1100 kg
boot space	: 750 - 3000 l
fuel capacity	: 60 l
consumption	: 38.3 / 44.9 mpg
acc. 0-62 mph	: 18.9 / 12.4 s
top speed	: 88 / 104 mph
EuroNCAP	: 3 stars
introduction	: Late 2001
last revised in	: -
warranty	: 2 years
miscellaneous	: Fiat's Sedici was built in association with Suzuki. 4WD always comes as standard.

SEDICI 1.9 MULTIJET 8V

engine type	: diesel, inline-4
displacement	: 1248 / 1910 cc
max. power	: 55 kW (75 bhp) / 88 kW (120 bhp)
@	: 4000 rpm
max. torque	: 148 / 155 lb ft
@	: 1750 / 2000 rpm
gears	: 5
kerb weight	: 1285 / 1295 kg
towing weight	: 1100 / 1100 kg
consumption	: 51.4 / 48.7 mpg
acc. 0-60 mph	: 16.1 / 12.4 s
top speed	: 97 / 102 mph
miscellaneous	: Opt for the powerful diesel engine if you plan to use the Sedici in rough terrain.

FIAT IDEA 1.4 8V / 1.4 16V

engine type	: petrol, inline-4
displacement	: 1368 / 1368 cc
max. power	: 57 kW (77 bhp) / 70 kW (95 bhp)
@	: 6000 / 5800 rpm
max. torque	: 85 / 94 lb ft
@	: 3000 / 4500 rpm
gears	: 5 / 6
AT	: optional CVT
drive	: FWD
brakes f/r	: discs / drum brakes
body type	: 5-dr. MPV
l x w x h	: 3930 x 1658 x 1660 mm
wheelbase	: 2508 mm
turning circle	: 10.4 m

kerb weight	: 1155 / 1155 kg
towing weight	: 1000 kg
boot space	: 320 - 1420 l
fuel capacity	: 47 l
consumption	: 46.3 / 43.5 mpg
acc. 0-62 mph	: 13.5 / 11.5 s
top speed	: 101 / 109 mph
EuroNCAP	: n.a.
introduction	: Autumn 2003
last revised in	: Autumn 2005
warranty	: 2 years
miscellaneous	: Hardly a big seller, despite its taut design, pleasant driving behaviour, extensive equipment and competitive price.

IDEA 1.3 16V MULTI. / 1.9 JTD MULTIJET

engine type	: diesel, inline-4
displacement	: 1248 / 1910 cc
max. power	: 51 kW (70 bhp) / 74 kW (100 bhp)
@	: 4000 rpm
max. torque	: 148 / 155 lb ft
@	: 1750 rpm
gears	: 5
kerb weight	: 1200 / 1275 kg
towing weight	: 1000 / 1100 kg
consumption	: 56.3 / 52.2 mpg
acc. 0-60 mph	: 15.4 / 11.5 s
top speed	: 99 / 112 mph
miscellaneous	: Performance of smallest version far from disappointing, but 1.9 Multijet does everything just a tiny bit better.

FIAT ULYSSE 2.0 MULTIJET 120 / 136

engine type	: petrol, inline-4
displacement	: 1997 cc
max. power	: 88 kW (120 bhp) / 100 kW (136 bhp)
@	: 4000 rpm
max. torque	: 221 / 251 lb ft
@	: 2000 rpm
gears	: 6
AT	: -
drive	: FWD
brakes f/r	: vent. discs / discs
body type	: 5-dr. MPV
l x w x h	: 4719 x 1863 x 1752 mm
wheelbase	: 2823 mm
turning circle	: 10.9 m

kerb weight	: 1711 / 175 kg
towing weight	: 1800 / 1850 kg
boot space	: 324 – 2948 l
fuel capacity	: 80 l
consumption	: 41.6 / 40.4 mpg
acc. 0-62 mph	: 12.9 / 11.4 s
top speed	: 112 / 118 mph
EuroNCAP	: 5 stars
introduction	: Autumn 2002
last revised in	: -
warranty	: 2 years
miscellaneous	: Car is now available with diesel engines only, including a 107 bhp 2.0 JTD combined with automatic transmission.

FORD KA

engine type	: petrol, inline-4	kerb weight	: 894 kg
displacement	: 1297 cc	towing weight	: -
max. power	: 51 kW (70 bhp)	boot space	: 186 l
@	: 5500 rpm	fuel capacity	: 40 l
max. torque	: 78 lb ft	consumption	: 45.6 mpg
@	: 3000 rpm	acc. 0-62 mph	: 13.7 s
gears	: 5	top speed	: 104 mph
AT	: n.a.	EuroNCAP	: 3 stars
drive	: FWD	introduction	: December 1997
brakes f/r	: vent. discs / drums	last revised in	: -
body type	: 3-dr. hatchback	warranty	: 2 years
l x w x h	: 3620 x 1639 x 1385 mm	miscellaneous	: Already a decade on the market
wheelbase	: 2448 mm		and even older from a technical
turning circle	: 9.9 m		point of view. Still a popular cheap
			choice. Its successor is at hand
			which shares its platform with the
			new Fiat 500.

SPORTKA

engine type	: petrol, inline-4
displacement	: 1597 cc
max. power	: 70 kW (95 bhp)
@	: 5500 rpm
max. torque	: 99 lb ft
@	: 4250 rpm
gears	: 5
kerb weight	: 944 kg
towing weight	: n.a.
consumption	: 37.2 mpg
acc. 0-60 mph	: 9.7 s
top speed	: 108 mph
miscellaneous	: Sportka delivers more driving fun per pound than most, thanks to its finely-tuned chassis.

FORD FIESTA 1.3 8V / 1.4 16V

engine type	: petrol, inline-4
displacement	: 1297 / 1388 cc
max. power	: 51 kW (70 bhp) / 59 kW (80 bhp)
@	: 5600 / 5700 rpm
max. torque	: 78 / 91 lb ft
@	: 2600 / 3500 rpm
gears	: 5
AT	: - / optional 5-speed automatic
drive	: FWD
brakes f/r	: vent. discs / drum brakes
body type	: 3-, 5-dr. hatchback
l x w x h	: 3916 x 1683 x 1430 mm
wheelbase	: 2486 mm
turning circle	: 9.8 m

kerb weight	: 1120 / 1105 kg
towing weight	: 800 / 900 kg
boot space	: 268 – 945 l
fuel capacity	: 45 l
consumption	: 45.8 / 44.3 mpg
acc. 0-62 mph	: 17.3 / 13.2 s
top speed	: 99 / 103 mph
EuroNCAP	: 4 stars
introduction	: Summer 2002
last revised in	: Late 2005
warranty	: 2 years
miscellaneous	: Model celebrated its 30th birthday in 2006. Looks fresh again after facelift. Also available with 100 bhp 1.6 petrol engine.

FIESTA ST

engine type	: petrol, inline-4
displacement	: 1999 cc
max. power	: 110 kW (150 bhp)
@	: 6000 rpm
max. torque	: 190 lb ft
@	: 4500 rpm
gears	: 5
kerb weight	: 1137 kg
towing weight	: -
consumption	: 38.3 mpg
acc. 0-60 mph	: 8.4 s
top speed	: 129 mph
miscellaneous	: Big engine for such a small car, but chassis is up to the job.

FORD FUSION 1.4 16V / 1.6 16V

engine type	: petrol, inline-4		kerb weight	: 1134 / 1171 kg
displacement	: 1388 / 1596 cc		towing weight	: 900 kg
max. power	: 58 kW (80 bhp) / 74 kW (100 bhp)		boot space	: 337 – 1175 l
@	: 5700 / 6000 rpm		fuel capacity	: 45 l
max. torque	: 92 / 108 lb ft		consumption	: 43 / 42.3 mpg
@	: 3500 / 4000 rpm		acc. 0-62 mph	: 14.0 / 11.1 s
gears	: 5		top speed	: 98 / 109 mph
AT	: optional 4-speed automatic		EuroNCAP	: n.a.
drive	: FWD		introduction	: Autumn 2002
brakes f/r	: vent. discs / drum brakes		last revised in	: Autumn 2005
body type	: 5-dr. hatchback		warranty	: 2 years
l x w x h	: 4020 x 1721 x 1498 mm		miscellaneous	: Fusion is a crossover, according
wheelbase	: 2486 mm			to Ford, but the car's interior has
turning circle	: 9.8 m			no added flexibility. It is simply a
				Fiesta with more interior space and
				higher seating position.

FUSION 1.4 TDCI / 1.6 16V TDCI

engine type	: diesel, inline-4
displacement	: 1399 / 1560 cc
max. power	: 50 kW (68 bhp) / 66 kW (90 bhp)
@	: 4000 rpm
max. torque	: 118 / 156 lb ft
@	: 2000 / 1750 rpm
gears	: 5
kerb weight	: 1192 / 1200 kg
towing weight	: 750 kg
consumption	: 62.8 / 62.8 mpg
acc. 0-60 mph	: 16.3 / 12.9 s
top speed	: 98 / 109 mph
miscellaneous	: Also available with 90 bhp
	1.6 diesel engine.

FORD FOCUS 1.4 16V / 1.6 16V

engine type	: petrol, inline-4	kerb weight	: 1147 / 1127 kg
displacement	: 1388 / 1596 cc	towing weight	: 700 / 1200 kg
max. power	: 59 kW (80 bhp) / 74 kW (100 bhp)	boot space	: 385 l
@	: 5700 / 6000 rpm	fuel capacity	: 55 l
max. torque	: 91 / 110 lb ft	consumption	: 42.8 / 42.2 mpg
@	: 3500 / 4000 rpm	acc. 0-62 mph	: 14.1 / 11.9 s
gears	: 5	top speed	: 102 / 112 mph
AT	: optional 4-speed	EuroNCAP	: 5 stars
drive	: FWD	introduction	: December 2005
brakes f/r	: vent. discs / drums	last revised in	: October 2007
body type	: 3- / 5-dr. hatchback	warranty	: 2 years
l x w x h	: 4342 x 1840 x 1797 mm	miscellaneous	: The entire Focus range will receive a facelift, starting with the hatchback model. All other available engines are listed under the other Focus models.
wheelbase	: 2640 mm		
turning circle	: 10.4 m		

FOCUS ST

engine type	: petrol, inline-5
displacement	: 2522 cc
max. power	: 166 kW (225 bhp)
@	: 6100 rpm
max. torque	: 236 lb ft
@	: 1600 rpm
gears	: 6
kerb weight	: 1362 kg
towing weight	: n.a.
consumption	: 30.4 mpg
acc. 0-60 mph	: 6.8 s
top speed	: 152 mph
miscellaneous	: The top-of-the-range Focus borrows its capable five-cylinder from Volvo.

FORD FOCUS ESTATE 1.6 TDCI / 1.8 TDCI

engine type	: diesel, inline-4	kerb weight	: 1286 / 1426 kg
displacement	: 1560 / 1800 cc	towing weight	: 1300 / 1500 kg
max. power	: 81 kW (109 bhp) / 85 kW (115 bhp)	boot space	: 482 – 1525 l
@	: 4000 / 3700 rpm	fuel capacity	: 53 l
max. torque	: 177 / 206 lb ft	consumption	: 60.4 / 53.5 mpg
@	: 1750 / 1900 rpm	acc. 0-62 mph	: 11.2 / 10.9 s
gears	: 5	top speed	: 117 / 119 mph
AT	: CVT / -	EuroNCAP	: 5 stars
drive	: FWD	introduction	: Spring 2005
brakes f/r	: vent. discs / discs	last revised in	: -
body type	: 5-dr. stationwagon	warranty	: 2 years
l x w x h	: 4475 x 1840 x 1501 mm	miscellaneous	: Ford platform also used for
wheelbase	: 2640 mm		estate and saloon variants (see
turning circle	: 10.4 m		below). Refer to Focus and Focus
			C-Max listings for specifications of
			available petrol engines. Also
			available with 90 bhp 1.6 TDCi
			diesel engine.

FOCUS ESTATE 2.0 TDCI

engine type	: diesel, inline-4
displacement	: 1999 cc
max. power	: 100 kW (136 bhp)
@	: 4000 rpm
max. torque	: 236 lb ft
@	: 2000 rpm
gears	: 5
kerb weight	: 1429 kg
towing weight	: 1300 kg
consumption	: 50.4 mpg
acc. 0-60 mph	: 9.5 s
top speed	: 126 mph
miscellaneous	: The Focus Estate is popular as a lease car, not in the least because of the strong diesel engines available.

FORD C-MAX 1.8 16V FLEXIFUEL

engine type	: petrol / E85, inline-4		**kerb weight**	: 1309 kg
displacement	: 1798 cc		**towing weight**	: 1200 kg
max. power	: 92 kW (123 bhp)		**boot space**	: 550 l
@	: 6000 rpm		**fuel capacity**	: 55 l
max. torque	: 122 lb ft		**consumption**	: 39.2 mpg
@	: 4000 rpm		**acc. 0-62 mph**	: 10.8 s
gears	: 5		**top speed**	: 121 mph
AT	: -		**EuroNCAP**	: 4 stars
drive	: FWD		**introduction**	: September 2003
brakes f/r	: vent. discs / discs		**last revised in**	: May 2007
body type	: 5-dr. MPV		**warranty**	: 2 years
l x w x h	: 4333 x 1825 x 1595 mm		**miscellaneous**	: Can run on bioethanol and petrol.
wheelbase	: 2640 mm			Specifications apply to engine
turning circle	: 10.7 m			running on petrol. The rest of the
				engine programme is identical to
				that of the Ford Focus.

FORD FOCUS CC 1.6 16V / 2.0 16V

engine type	: petrol, inline-4
displacement	: 1596 / 1999 cc
max. power	: 74 kW (100 bhp) / 107 kW (145 bhp)
@	: 5500 / 6000 rpm
max. torque	: 110 / 136 lb ft
@	: 4000 / 4500 rpm
gears	: 5
AT	: -
drive	: FWD
brakes f/r	: vent. discs / discs
body type	: 2-dr. convertible
l x w x h	: 4509 x 1834 x 1456 mm
wheelbase	: 2640 mm
turning circle	: 10.4 m

kerb weight	: 1413 / 1465 kg
towing weight	: 1000 / 1350 kg
boot space	: 248 – 534 l
fuel capacity	: 55 l
consumption	: 39.8 / 37.7 mpg
acc. 0-62 mph	: 13.6 / 10.3 s
top speed	: 114 / 130 mph
EuroNCAP	: n.a.
introduction	: Late 2006
last revised in	: -
warranty	: 2 years
miscellaneous	: Fords rival to the VW Eos and Vauxhall Astra Twin Top. Folding roof type construction makes it a rather long car.

FORD FOCUS CC 2.0 TDCI

engine type	: diesel, inline-4
displacement	: 1999 cc
max. power	: 100 kW (136 bhp)
@	: 4000 rpm
max. torque	: 236 lb ft
@	: 2000 rpm
gears	: 6
kerb weight	: 1548 kg
towing weight	: -
consumption	: 47.9 mpg
acc. 0-60 mph	: 10.3 s
top speed	: 128 mph
miscellaneous	: Convertibles are more and more being used for business. For this reason, the Focus CC is also available with diesel power.

FORD KUGA

engine type	: petrol, inline-4
displacement	: 1999 cc
max. power	: 100 kW (136 bhp)
@	: 4000 rpm
max. torque	: 236 lb ft
@	: 2000 rpm
gears	: 5
AT	: n.a.
drive	: FWD / 4WD
brakes f/r	: vent. discs / discs
body type	: 5-dr. SUV
l x w x h	: n.a.
wheelbase	: 2640 mm
turning circle	: n.a.

kerb weight	: n.a.
towing weight	: n.a.
boot space	: n.a.
fuel capacity	: 55 l
consumption	: n.a.
acc. 0-62 mph	: n.a.
top speed	: n.a.
EuroNCAP	: n.a.
introduction	: December 2007
last revised in	: n.a.
warranty	: 2 years
miscellaneous	: For the time being, the new Kuga is available with only one engine option. But interested parties can choose between front-wheel drive and four-wheel drive.

FORD MONDEO 1.6 / 2.0

engine type	: petrol, inline-4	kerb weight	: 1437 / 1479 kg
displacement	: 1596 / 1999 cc	towing weight	: 900 / 1500 kg
max. power	: 92 kW (122 bhp) / 107 kW (145 bhp)	boot space	: 493 l
@	: 6300 / 6000 rpm	fuel capacity	: 70 l
max. torque	: 118 / 136 lb ft	consumption	: 38.2 / 35.8 mpg
@	: 4100 / 4500 rpm	acc. 0-62 mph	: 12.3 / 9.9 s
gears	: 5	top speed	: 121 / 130 mph
AT	: -	EuroNCAP	: n.a.
drive	: voorwielen	introduction	: June 2007
brakes f/r	: vent. discs / discs	last revised in	: -
body type	: 4-dr. saloon	warranty	: 2 years
l x w x h	: 4844 x 1886 x 1500 mm	miscellaneous	: New Mondeo also available in
wheelbase	: 2850 mm		five-door hatchback and Wagon
turning circle	: 11.4 m		version. Refer to the Mondeo
			Wagon entry for diesel engine
			specs.

MONDEO 2.3 / 2.5

engine type	: petrol, inline-4 / -5
displacement	: 2261 / 2521 cc
max. power	: 118 kW (161 bhp) / 162 kW (220 pk)
@	: 6500 / 5000 rpm
max. torque	: 154 / 236 lb ft
@	: 4000 / 1500 rpm
gears	: 6-speed automatic / 6
kerb weight	: 1543 / 1569 kg
towing weight	: 1400 / 1800 kg
consumption	: 30.4 mpg
acc. 0-60 mph	: 10.5 / 7.5 s
top speed	: 129 / 152 mph
miscellaneous	: Ford Group creates synergy:
	2.3 engine is supplied by Mazda,
	2.5 unit by Volvo.

FORD MONDEO ESTATE 1.8 TDCI

engine type	: diesel, inline-4
displacement	: 1753 cc
max. power	: 92 kW (125 bhp)
@	: 3700 rpm
max. torque	: 251 lb ft
@	: 1800 rpm
gears	: 6
AT	: -
drive	: FWD
brakes f/r	: vent. discs / discs
body type	: 5-dr. stationwagon
l x w x h	: 4830 x 1886 x 1512 mm
wheelbase	: 2850 mm
turning circle	: 11.4 m

kerb weight	: 1567 kg
towing weight	: 1600 kg
boot space	: 494 l
fuel capacity	: 70 l
consumption	: 47.9 mpg
acc. 0-62 mph	: 10.9 s
top speed	: 121 mph
EuroNCAP	: n.a.
introduction	: June 2007
last revised in	: -
warranty	: 2 years
miscellaneous	: Wagon is the bestseller in the Mondeo range. The estate model is also available with the petrol engines as described under the saloon entry.

MONDEO 2.0 TDCI

engine type	: diesel, inline-4
displacement	: 1997 cc
max. power	: 103 kW (140 bhp)
@	: 4000 rpm
max. torque	: 251 lb ft
@	: 1750 rpm
gears	: 6
kerb weight	: 1578 kg
towing weight	: 1800 kg
consumption	: 47.9 mpg
acc. 0-60 mph	: 9.8 s
top speed	: 127 mph
miscellaneous	: With the optional automatic transmission installed, the TDCi engine delivers 130 bhp instead of 140 bhp.

FORD TOURNEO CONNECT 1.8

engine type	: petrol, inline-4		**kerb weight**	: 1420 kg
displacement	: 1796 cc		**towing weight**	: 1000 kg
max. power	: 85 kW (115 bhp)		**boot space**	: 1200 – 3200 l
@	: 5750 rpm		**fuel capacity**	: 60 l
max. torque	: 118 lb ft		**consumption**	: 34.2 mpg
@	: 4400 rpm		**acc. 0-62 mph**	: 12.7 s
gears	: 5		**top speed**	: 103 mph
AT	: -		**EuroNCAP**	: n.a.
drive	: FWD		**introduction**	: 2002
brakes f/r	: vent. discs / discs		**last revised in**	: -
body type	: 5-dr. MPV		**warranty**	: 2 years
l x w x h	: 4278 x 1795 x 1814 mm		**miscellaneous**	: Looks like a van with extra
wheelbase	: 2664 mm			sideglazing. Not very popular.
turning circle	: 11.0 m			

TOURNEO CONNECT 1.8 TDCI

engine type	: diesel, inline-4
displacement	: 1753 cc
max. power	: 66 kW (90 bhp)
@	: 4000 rpm
max. torque	: 162 lb ft
@	: 1750 rpm
gears	: 6
kerb weight	: 1485 kg
towing weight	: 1000 kg
consumption	: 43.6 mpg
acc. 0-60 mph	: 16.3 s
top speed	: 96 mph
miscellaneous	: Tourneo Connect faces tough opposition from Fiat Doblò and Renault Kangoo.

FORD GALAXY 2.0 16V

engine type	: petrol, inline-4	kerb weight	: 1697 kg
displacement	: 1999 cc	towing weight	: 1100 kg
max. power	: 107 kW (145 bhp)	boot space	: 308 – 2325 l
@	: 6000 rpm	fuel capacity	: 70 l
max. torque	: 140 lb ft	consumption	: 34.4 mpg
@	: 4500 rpm	acc. 0-62 mph	: 11.2 s
gears	: 5	top speed	: 121 mph
AT	: optional 4-speed	EuroNCAP	: n.a.
drive	: FWD	introduction	: May 2006
brakes f/r	: vent. discs / discs	last revised in	: -
body type	: 5-dr. MPV	warranty	: 2 years
l x w x h	: 4731 x 1812 x 1429 mm	miscellaneous	: New Galaxy was entirely developed
wheelbase	: 2754 mm		by Ford, without the help of VW.
turning circle	: 11.6 m		Biggest Ford model is a bit more
			practical than its stablemate, the
			S-Max.

GALAXY 2.0 TDCI

engine type	: diesel, inline-4
displacement	: 1999 cc
max. power	: 103 kW (140 bhp)
@	: 4000 rpm
max. torque	: 251 lb ft
@	: 1750 rpm
gears	: 6
kerb weight	: 1806 kg
towing weight	: 1700 kg
consumption	: 43.5 mpg
acc. 0-60 mph	: 10.5 s
top speed	: 120 mph
miscellaneous	: Less powerful diesel engines are
	also available.

FORD S-MAX 2.0 16V / 2.5

engine type	: petrol, inline-4 / inline-5
displacement	: 1999 / 2522 cc
max. power	: 107 kW (145 bhp) /
	162 kW (210 bhp)
@	: 6000 / 5000 rpm
max. torque	: 140 / 239 lb ft
@	: 4500 / 1500 rpm
gears	: 5 / 6
AT	: -
drive	: FWD
brakes f/r	: vent. discs / discs
body type	: 5-dr. MPV
l x w x h	: 4768 x 1884 x 1658 mm
wheelbase	: 2850 mm
turning circle	: 11.6 m

kerb weight	: 1605 / 1681 kg
towing weight	: 1100 / 1700 kg
boot space	: 285 – 2000 l
fuel capacity	: 70 l
consumption	: 34.9 / 30.1 mpg
acc. 0-62 mph	: 10.9 / 7.9 s
top speed	: 143 mph
EuroNCAP	: n.a.
introduction	: Spring 2006
last revised in	: -
warranty	: 2 years
miscellaneous	: 2.5-litre engine stems from Focus ST and transforms S-Max into one of the fastest MPVs on the market.

S-MAX 2.0 TDCI

engine type	: diesel, inline-4
displacement	: 1999 cc
max. power	: 103 kW (140 bhp)
@	: 4000 rpm
max. torque	: 236 lb ft
@	: 1750 rpm
gears	: 6
kerb weight	: 1743 kg
towing weight	: 1700 kg
consumption	: 44.1 mpg
acc. 0-60 mph	: 10.2 s
top speed	: 122 mph
miscellaneous	: A particle filter is standard on this diesel engine.

HONDA JAZZ 1.2 / 1.4

engine type	: petrol, inline-4		**kerb weight**	: 815 / 835 kg
displacement	: 1246 / 1339 kg		**towing weight**	: 800 kg
max. power	: 57 kW (78 bhp) / 61 kW (83 bhp)		**boot space**	: 206 - 775
@	: 6000 / 5700 rpm		**fuel capacity**	: 35 l
max. torque	: 82 / 88 lb ft		**consumption**	: 51.6 / 48.9 mpg
@	: 2800 rpm		**acc. 0-62 mph**	: 13.7 / 12.0 s
gears	: 5		**top speed**	: 106 mph
AT	: optional CVT		**EuroNCAP**	: 4 stars
drive	: FWD		**introduction**	: Autumn 2001
brakes f/r	: vent. discs / discs		**last revised in**	: Autumn 2004
body type	: 5-dr. hatchback		**warranty**	: 2 years
l x w x h	: 3830 x 1675 x 1525 mm		**miscellaneous**	: Car of the Year in Japan.
wheelbase	: 2450 mm			Good-looking, spacious model,
turning circle	: 9.4 m			merits more recognition because
				of its fine qualities. Diesel power
				not available.

HONDA CIVIC 1.4 / 1.8

engine type	: petrol, inline-4	kerb weight	: 1140 / 1165 kg
displacement	: 1339 / 1798 cc	towing weight	: 1200 / 1400 kg
max. power	: 61 kW (83 bhp) / 103 kW (140 bhp)	boot space	: 415 – 485 l
@	: 5700 / 6300 rpm	fuel capacity	: 50 l
max. torque	: 88 / 128 lb ft	consumption	: 47.9 / 44.1 mpg
@	: 2800 / 4300 rpm	acc. 0-62 mph	: 14.2 / 8.6 s
gears	: 6	top speed	: 106 / 127 mph
AT	: optional 6-speed automatic	EuroNCAP	: n.a.
drive	: FWD	introduction	: Autumn 2005
brakes f/r	: vent. discs / discs	last revised in	: -
body type	: 5-dr. hatchback	warranty	: 2 years
l x w x h	: 4250 x 1760 x 1460 mm	miscellaneous	: New Civic, hopefully more
wheelbase	: 2635 mm		successful than previous model.
turning circle	: 11.0 m		Much more striking appearance.
			1.8 petrol engine has low fuel
			consumption. 3-door Type-S also
			available. Range topper is Civic
			Type-R, with 200 bhp engine.

CIVIC 2.2 i-CTDi

engine type	: diesel, inline-4
displacement	: 2204 cc
max. power	: 103 kW (140 bhp)
@	: 4000 rpm
max. torque	: 251 lb ft
@	: 2000 rpm
gears	: 6
kerb weight	: 1310 kg
towing weight	: 1500 kg
consumption	: 62.8 / 62.8 mpg
acc. 0-60 mph	: 8.4 s
top speed	: 127 mph
miscellaneous	: More frugal type, but almost as quick as 1.8. Probably the best choice.

HONDA CIVIC HYBRID

engine type	: petrol, inline-4 + electrical engine		**kerb weight**	: 1268 kg
displacement	: 1339 cc		**towing weight**	: -
max. power	: 85 kW (115 bhp)		**boot space**	: 350 l
@	: 6000 rpm		**fuel capacity**	: 50 l
max. torque	: 166 lb ft		**consumption**	: 61.4 mpg
@	: 4600 rpm		**acc. 0-62 mph**	: 12.1 s
gears	: -		**top speed**	: 115 mph
AT	: CVT		**EuroNCAP**	: n.a.
drive	: FWD		**introduction**	: March 2006
brakes f/r	: vent. discs / discs		**last revised in**	: -
body type	: 4-dr. sedan		**warranty**	: 3 years
l x w x h	: 4545 x 1750 x 1430 mm		**miscellaneous**	: Honda chose to install the advanced technology in this rather conventional looking saloon, not in the trendy Civic hatchback. Nice alternative to the more expensive Toyota Prius.
wheelbase	: 2700 mm			
turning circle	: 10.8 m			

CIVIC TYPE R

engine type	: petrol, inline-4
displacement	: 1998 cc
max. power	: 148 kW (201 bhp)
@	: 7800 rpm
max. torque	: 142 lb ft
@	: 5600 rpm
gears	: 6
kerb weight	: 1324 kg
towing weight	: -
consumption	: 31.0 mpg
acc. 0-60 mph	: 6.6 s
top speed	: 146 mph
miscellaneous	: The high-revving and very fast Type-R is quite the opposite of the 'green' Civic Hybrid.

HONDA ACCORD 2.0i / 2.4i

engine type	: petrol, inline-4	kerb weight	: 1293 / 1356 kg
displacement	: 1998 / 2398 cc	towing weight	: 1500 kg
max. power	: 114 kW (155 bhp) /	boot space	: 459 l
	141 kW (190 bhp)	fuel capacity	: 65 l
@	: 6000 / 6800 rpm	consumption	: 38.2 / 31.4 mpg
max. torque	: 140 / 164 lb ft	acc. 0-62 mph	: 9.6 / 7.9 s
@	: 4500 rpm	top speed	: 137 / 141 mph
gears	: 5 / 6	EuroNCAP	: 4 stars
AT	: optional 5-speed automatic	introduction	: Autumn 2002
drive	: FWD	last revised in	: Autumn 2002
brakes f/r	: vent. discs / discs	warranty	: 2 years
body type	: 4-dr. saloon	miscellaneous	: Modern car with excellent build
l x w x h	: 4665 x 1760 x 1445 mm		quality. Rather limited model range
wheelbase	: 2680 mm		hinders sales. Stationcar has
turning circle	: 10.8 m		striking profile.

ACCORD 2.2 i-CTDi

engine type	: diesel, inline-4
displacement	: 2204 cc
max. power	: 103 kW (140 bhp)
@	: 4000 rpm
max. torque	: 251 lb ft
@	: 2000 rpm
gears	: 5
kerb weight	: 1545 kg
towing weight	: 1500 kg
consumption	: 51.4 mpg
acc. 0-60 mph	: 9.8 s
top speed	: 132 mph
miscellaneous	: It took some time for Honda to develop its own diesel engine, but it was worth the wait. One of the best diesel engines in its class.

HONDA LEGEND

engine type	: petrol, V6		kerb weight	: 1864 kg
displacement	: 3471 cc		towing weight	: 1600 kg
max. power	: 217 kW (295 bhp)		boot space	: 452 l
@	: 6200 rpm		fuel capacity	: 73 l
max. torque	: 259 lb ft		consumption	: 23.7 mpg
@	: 5000 rpm		acc. 0-62 mph	: 7.3 s
gears	: -		top speed	: 155 mph
AT	: 5-speed		EuroNCAP	: n.a.
drive	: 4WD		introduction	: July 2006
brakes f/r	: vent. discs / discs		last revised in	: -
body type	: 4-dr. saloon		warranty	: 3 years
l x w x h	: 4955 x 1845 x 1450 mm		miscellaneous	: Modern yet impersonal Japanese
wheelbase	: 2800 mm			business limousine. The price is
turning circle	: 11.6 m			rather high.

HONDA S2000

engine type	: petrol, inline-4	kerb weight	: 1220 kg
displacement	: 1997 cc	towing weight	: -
max. power	: 177 kW (240 bhp)	boot space	: 143 l
@	: 8300 rpm	fuel capacity	: 50 l
max. torque	: 153 lb ft	consumption	: 28.2 mpg
@	: 7500 rpm	acc. 0-62 mph	: 6.2 s
gears	: 6	top speed	: 150 mph
AT	: -	EuroNCAP	: n.a
drive	: RWD	introduction	: Spring 1999
brakes f/r	: vent. discs / discs	last revised in	: Spring 2004
body type	: 2-dr. convertible	warranty	: 3 years
l x w x h	: 4135 x 1750 x 1285 mm	miscellaneous	: Concept car SSM first shown in
wheelbase	: 2405 mm		1995, but resulting S2000 has a
turning circle	: 9.5 m		timeless design. Excellent driver's
			car with high-revving power unit.
			Now better than ever, following
			its second facelift.

HONDA FR-V 1.8

engine type	: petrol, inline-4	**kerb weight**	: 1394 kg
displacement	: 1798 cc	**towing weight**	: 1500 kg
max. power	: 103 kW (140 bhp)	**boot space**	: 439 l
@	: 6300 rpm	**fuel capacity**	: 58 l
max. torque	: 128 lb ft	**consumption**	: 37.7 mpg
@	: 4300 rpm	**acc. 0-62 mph**	: 10.6 s
gears	: 6	**top speed**	: 118 mph
AT	: optional 5-speed	**EuroNCAP**	: 4 stars
drive	: FWD	**introduction**	: July 2004
brakes f/r	: vent. discs / discs	**last revised in**	: September 2006
body type	: 5-dr. MPV	**warranty**	: 3 years
l x w x h	: 4285 x 1810 x 1610 mm	**miscellaneous**	: Compact MPV with sufficient width
wheelbase	: 2685 mm		to accommodate three people in
turning circle	: 10.5 m		the front row.

FR-V 2.2 i-CDTi

engine type	: diesel, inline-4
displacement	: 2204 cc
max. power	: 103 kW (140 bhp)
@	: 4000 rpm
max. torque	: 251 lb ft
@	: 2000 rpm
gears	: 6
kerb weight	: 1543 kg
towing weight	: 1500 kg
consumption	: 44.8 mpg
acc. 0-60 mph	: 10.1 s
top speed	: 118 mph
miscellaneous	: Seating arrangement is ideally suited for families with four children, because one of them can sit in the front row.

HONDA CR-V 2.0

engine type	: petrol, inline-4		kerb weight	: n.a.
displacement	: 1998 cc		towing weight	: 1600 kg
max. power	: 110 kW (150 bhp)		boot space	: 527 – 1568 l
@	: 6200 rpm		fuel capacity	: 58 l
max. torque	: 140 lb ft		consumption	: 34.9 mpg
@	: 4200 rpm		acc. 0-62 mph	: 10.2 s
gears	: 6		top speed	: n.a.
AT	: n.a.		EuroNCAP	: n.a.
drive	: 4WD		introduction	: September 2006
brakes f/r	: vent. discs / discs		last revised in	: -
body type	: 5-dr. SUV		warranty	: 3 years
l x w x h	: 4635 x 1785 x 1710 mm		miscellaneous	: New CR-V is an SUV rather than an offroader.
wheelbase	: 2630 mm			
turning circle	: n.a.			

CR-V 2.2 i-CDTi

engine type	: diesel, inline-4
displacement	: 2204 cc
max. power	: 103 kW (140 bhp)
@	: 4000 rpm
max. torque	: 251 lb ft
@	: 2000 rpm
gears	: 6
kerb weight	: n.a.
towing weight	: 2000 kg
consumption	: 43.5 mpg
acc. 0-60 mph	: 12.2 s
top speed	: n.a.
miscellaneous	: CR-V is a much more interesting proposition thanks to Honda's own diesel engine.

HUMMER H3

engine type	: petrol, inline-5		**kerb weight**	: 2269 kg
displacement	: 3653 cc		**towing weight**	: 2000 kg
max. power	: 180 kW (245 bhp)		**boot space**	: 835 l
@	: 5600 rpm		**fuel capacity**	: 87 l
max. torque	: 242 lb ft		**consumption**	: 20.5 mpg
@	: 4600 rpm		**acc. 0-62 mph**	: n.a.
gears	: 5		**top speed**	: 99 mph
AT	: optional 4-speed automatic		**EuroNCAP**	: n.a.
drive	: 4WD		**introduction**	: July 2005
brakes f/r	: vent. discs / discs		**last revised in**	: March 2007
body type	: 5-dr. terreinauto		**warranty**	: 3 years
l x w x h	: 4782 x 1989 x 1872 mm		**miscellaneous**	: The Hummer H3 received
wheelbase	: 2841 mm			a bigger engine. A diesel version
turning circle	: 11.3 m			is on its way.

HUMMER H2

engine type	: petrol, V8	kerb weight	: 2980 kg
displacement	: 5965 cc	towing weight	: 3182 kg
max. power	: 239 kW (325 bhp)	boot space	: 1132 – 2452 l
@	: 5200 rpm	fuel capacity	: 121 l
max. torque	: 365 lb ft	consumption	: n.a.
@	: 4000 rpm	acc. 0-62 mph	: < 10 s
gears	: -	top speed	: > 105 mph
AT	: 4-speed automatic	EuroNCAP	: n.a.
drive	: 4WD	introduction	: Summer 2004
brakes f/r	: vent. discs / discs	last revised in	: -
body type	: 5-dr. SUV	warranty	: 3 years
l x w x h	: 4821 x 2063 x 2080 mm	miscellaneous	: 'Smaller' H2 is in fact both higher
wheelbase	: 3119 mm		and longer than original Hummer
turning circle	: 13.5 m		and weighs about the same. Model
			variation with small, open load
			platform called H2 SUT.

HYUNDAI AMICA 1.1I

engine type	: petrol, inline-4	**kerb weight**	: 859 kg
displacement	: 1086 cc	**towing weight**	: 700 kg
max. power	: 47 kW (65 bhp)	**boot space**	: 220 - 889 l
@	: 5500 rpm	**fuel capacity**	: 35 l
max. torque	: 72 lb ft	**consumption**	: 52.3 mpg
@	: 3000 rpm	**acc. 0-62 mph**	: 15.8 s
gears	: 5	**top speed**	: 91 mph
AT	: optional 4-speed automatic	**EuroNCAP**	: 3 stars
drive	: FWD	**introduction**	: June 2003
brakes f/r	: discs / drum brakes	**last revised in**	: September 2005
body type	: 5-dr. hatchback	**warranty**	: 3 years
l x w x h	: 3565 x 1525 x 1570 mm	**miscellaneous**	: Much better-looking than original
wheelbase	: 2380 mm		Atos launched in 1997. One of the
turning circle	: 9.8 m		cheapest cars on today's market.

HYUNDAI GETZ 1.1 / 1.4

engine type	: petrol, inline-4
displacement	: 1086 / 1399 cc
max. power	: 48 kW (65 bhp) / 70 kW (95 bhp)
@	: 5500 / 6000 rpm
max. torque	: 73 / 92 lb ft
@	: 3200 / 3200 rpm
gears	: 5
AT	: - / optional 4-speed automatic
drive	: FWD
brakes f/r	: vent. discs / drum brakes
body type	: 3-, 5-dr. hatchback
l x w x h	: 3810 x 1665 x 1490 mm
wheelbase	: 2455 mm
turning circle	: 10.0 m

kerb weight	: 976 / 1025 kg
towing weight	: 700 / 1000 kg
boot space	: 254 - 977 l
fuel capacity	: 45 l
consumption	: 51.4 / 47.1 mpg
acc. 0-62 mph	: 15.6 / 11.2 s
top speed	: 93 / 106 mph
EuroNCAP	: n.a.
introduction	: July 2002
last revised in	: -
warranty	: 2 years
miscellaneous	: Hyundai called in the help of Italian designers. The outcome is very pleasing, with European looks.

GETZ 1.6

engine type	: petrol, inline-4
displacement	: 1599 cc
max. power	: 77 kW (105 bhp)
@	: 5800 rpm
max. torque	: 106 lb ft
@	: 3000 rpm
gears	: 5
kerb weight	: 1027 kg
towing weight	: 1100 kg
consumption	: 47.3 mpg
acc. 0-60 mph	: 9.6 s
top speed	: 112 mph
miscellaneous	: 1.6 engine endows Getz with performance characteristics of a small GTI. Direct steering response, fine chassis. All in all, a surprising package.

GETZ 1.5 CRDi

engine type	: diesel, inline-4
displacement	: 1493 cc
max. power	: 65 kW (88 bhp)
@	: 5800 rpm
max. torque	: 159 lb ft
@	: 1900 rpm
gears	: 5
kerb weight	: 1112 kg
towing weight	: 1100 kg
consumption	: 62.8 mpg
acc. 0-60 mph	: 12.1 s
top speed	: 106 mph
miscellaneous	: Diesel version is most economical Getz of all.

HYUNDAI ACCENT 1.4 / 1.6

engine type	: petrol, inline-4
displacement	: 1399 / 1599 cc
max. power	: 70 kW (95 bhp) / 82 kW (112 bhp)
@	: 6000 rpm
max. torque	: 92 / 108 lb ft
@	: 4700 / 4500 rpm
gears	: 5
AT	: -
drive	: FWD
brakes f/r	: vent. discs / drum brakes
body type	: 3-dr. hatchback/4-dr. saloon
l x w x h	: 4045 x 1695 x 1470 mm
wheelbase	: 2500 mm
turning circle	: 10.1 m

kerb weight	: 1055 kg
towing weight	: 1100 kg
boot space	: n.a.
fuel capacity	: 45 l
consumption	: 45.6 / 44.3 mpg
acc. 0-62 mph	: 12.3 / 10.2 s
top speed	: 110 / 118 mph
EuroNCAP	: n.a.
introduction	: May 2006
last revised in	: -
warranty	: 3 years
miscellaneous	: 'Interim' model until the arrival of the new Accent. Cheap and uncomplicated. Specifications apply to 3-dr. hatchback.

HYUNDAI MATRIX 1.6i / 1.8i

engine type	: petrol, inline-4
displacement	: 1599 / 1795 cc
max. power	: 76 kW (103 bhp) / 89 kW (121 bhp)
@	: 5800 / 6000 rpm
max. torque	: 104 / 119 lb ft
@	: 4500 / 4500 rpm
gears	: 5
AT	: optional 4-speed automatic
drive	: FWD
brakes f/r	: vent. discs / drum brakes
body type	: 5-dr. MPV
l x w x h	: 4025 x 1740 x 1635 mm
wheelbase	: 2600 mm
turning circle	: 10.4 m

kerb weight	: 1223 / 1270 kg
towing weight	: 1300 kg
boot space	: 354 – 1284 l
fuel capacity	: 55 l
consumption	: 39.8 / 34 mpg
acc. 0-62 mph	: 12.7 / 11.3 s
top speed	: 106 / 114 mph
EuroNCAP	: n.a.
introduction	: July 2001
last revised in	: August 2005
warranty	: 3 years
miscellaneous	: Originally styled mini-MPV by Pininfarina. With a longer lease of life again, thanks to minor facelift.

MATRIX 1.5 CRDi VGT

engine type	: diesel, inline-4
displacement	: 1493 cc
max. power	: 75 kW (102 bhp)
@	: 4000 rpm
max. torque	: 141 lb ft
@	: 2000 rpm
gears	: 5
kerb weight	: 1280 kg
towing weight	: 1300 kg
consumption	: 52.3 mpg
acc. 0-60 mph	: 14.3 s
top speed	: 99 mph
miscellaneous	: Matrix more interesting now with new 4-cylinder diesel engine.

HYUNDAI i30 1.4 / 1.6

engine type	: petrol, inline-4	kerb weight	: 1268 kg
displacement	: 1396 / 1591 cc	towing weight	: 1200 kg
max. power	: 80 kW (107 bhp) / 90 kW (120 bhp)	boot space	: 340 l
@	: 6200 rpm	fuel capacity	: 53 l
max. torque	: 101 / 114 lb ft	consumption	: 46.3 / 45.5 mpg
@	: 5000 / 4200 rpm	acc. 0-62 mph	: 12.6 / 11.1 s
gears	: 5	top speed	: 116 / 119 mph
AT	: - / optional 4-speed automatic	EuroNCAP	: n.a.
drive	: FWD	introduction	: June 2007
brakes f/r	: vent. discs / discs	last revised in	: n.v.t.
body type	: 5-dr. hatchback	warranty	: 3 years
l x w x h	: 4245 x 1775 x 1480 mm	miscellaneous	: Medium-sized Korean car is identical to the Kia Cee'd. Refer to Crosswagon entry for diesel specifications.
wheelbase	: 2650 mm		
turning circle	: n.a.		

i30 2.0

engine type	: petrol, inline-4
displacement	: 1975 cc
max. power	: 105 kW (140 bhp)
@	: 6000 rpm
max. torque	: 137 lb ft
@	: 4600 rpm
gears	: 5, optional 4-speed automatic
kerb weight	: 1327 kg
towing weight	: 1500 kg
consumption	: 39.8 mpg
acc. 0-60 mph	: 10.6 s
top speed	: 127 mph
miscellaneous	: The most potent i30 up till now, but a more spicy edition is in the offing.

HYUNDAI I30 CROSSWAGON 1.6 CRDI

engine type	: diesel, inline-4	kerb weight	: 1333 kg
displacement	: 1582 cc	towing weight	: 1400 kg
max. power	: 85 kW (113 bhp)	boot space	: 415 l
@	: 4000 rpm	fuel capacity	: 53 l
max. torque	: 188 lb ft	consumption	: 60.1 mpg
@	: 1900 tpm	acc. 0-62 mph	: 11.9 s
gears	: 5	top speed	: 117 mph
AT	: optional 4-speed	EuroNCAP	: n.a.
drive	: FWD	introduction	: December 2007
brakes f/r	: vent. discs / discs	last revised in	: -
body type	: 5-dr. stationwagon	warranty	: 3 years
l x w x h	: 4475 x 1775 x 1530 mm	miscellaneous	: A petrol-engined estate version of the i30 is also part of the model range. Refer to saloon version of i30 for details.
wheelbase	: 2700 mm		
turning circle	: 10.3 m		

I30 CROSSWAGON 2.0 CRDI

engine type	: diesel, inline-4
displacement	: 1991 cc
max. power	: 103 kW (138 bhp)
@	: 3800 rpm
max. torque	: 224 lb ft
@	: 1800 rpm
gears	: 6
kerb weight	: 1381 kg
towing weight	: 1500 kg
consumption	: 51.4 mpg
acc. 0-60 mph	: 10.7 s
top speed	: 127 mph
miscellaneous	: A diesel particle filter is standard on this engine.

HYUNDAI COUPÉ 2.0 / 2.7 V6

engine type	: petrol, inline-4 / V6
displacement	: 1975 / 2656 cc
max. power	: 105 kW (143 bhp) / 123 kW (167 bhp)
@	: 4500 / 4000 rpm
max. torque	: 137 / 181 lb ft
@	: 4500 / 4000 rpm
gears	: 5 / 6
AT	: - / optional 4-speed automatic
drive	: FWD
brakes f/r	: vent. discs / discs
body type	: 3-dr. coupe
l x w x h	: 4395 x 1760 x 1330 mm
wheelbase	: 2530 mm
turning circle	: 10.9 m

kerb weight	: 1255 / 1308 kg
towing weight	: 1400 kg
boot space	: 418 l
fuel capacity	: 55 l
consumption	: 35.3 / 28.5 mpg
acc. 0-62 mph	: 9.1 / 8.2 s
top speed	: 129 / 137 mph
EuroNCAP	: n.a.
introduction	: September 2001
last revised in	: November 2004
warranty	: 3 years
miscellaneous	: Korean sportscars are thin on the ground, but here we have one. Rather stern face after facelift.

HYUNDAI SONATA 2.0I / 2.4I

engine type	: petrol, inline-4	kerb weight	: 1448 / 1438 kg
displacement	: 1998 / 2359 cc	towing weight	: 1700 kg
max. power	: 106 kW (145 bhp) /	boot space	: 523 l
	119 kW (161 bhp)	fuel capacity	: 70 l
@	: 6000 / 5800 rpm	consumption	: 35.3 / 34.2 mpg
max. torque	: 139 / 162 lb ft	acc. 0-62 mph	: 10.5 / 8.9 s
@	: 4250 / 4250 rpm	top speed	: 127 / 132 mph
gears	: 5	EuroNCAP	: n.a.
AT	: optional 4-speed automatic	introduction	: September 2004
drive	: FWD	last revised in	: -
brakes f/r	: vent. discs / discs	warranty	: 3 years
body type	: 4-dr. sedan	miscellaneous	: Good alternative for other, more
l x w x h	: 4800 x 1832 x 1475 mm		customary business saloons.
wheelbase	: 2730 mm		Well-built car with severe looks.
turning circle	: 10.9 m		Also available with 3.3-litre V6
			engine.

SONATA 2.0 CRDI

engine type	: diesel, inline-4
displacement	: 1991 cc
max. power	: 103 kW (140 bhp)
@	: 4000 rpm
max. torque	: 224 lb ft
@	: 1800 rpm
gears	: 6
kerb weight	: 1566 kg
towing weight	: 1700 kg
consumption	: 46.3 mpg
acc. 0-60 mph	: 10.7 s
top speed	: 126 mph
miscellaneous	: Diesel engine should bring
	more customers.

HYUNDAI GRANDEUR 3.3 V6

engine type	: petrol, V6	kerb weight	: 1664 kg
displacement	: 3342 cc	towing weight	: 1800 kg
max. power	: 173 kW (235 bhp)	boot space	: 469 l
@	: 6000 rpm	fuel capacity	: 75 l
max. torque	: 224 lb ft	consumption	: 27.8 mpg
@	: 3500 rpm	acc. 0-62 mph	: 7.8 s
gears	: -	top speed	: 147 mph
AT	: 5-speed automatic	EuroNCAP	: n.a.
drive	: FWD	introduction	: Autumn 2005
brakes f/r	: vent. discs / discs	last revised in	: -
body type	: 4-dr. sedan	warranty	: 3 years
l x w x h	: 4895 x 1845 x 1490 mm	miscellaneous	: Successor to XG model. Car
wheelbase	: 2780 mm		deserves to be successful.
turning circle	: 11.4 m		

HYUNDAI TUCSON 2.0i CVVT / 2.7i V6

engine type	: petrol, inline-4 / V6
displacement	: 1975 / 2656 cc
max. power	: 105 kW (143 bhp) /
	129 kW (175 bhp)
@	: 6000 rpm
max. torque	: 136 / 178 lb ft
@	: 4500 / 4000 rpm
gears	: 5
AT	: optional 4-speed automatic
drive	: FWD
brakes f/r	: vent. discs / discs
body type	: 5-dr. SUV
l x w x h	: 4325 x 1830 x 1730 mm
wheelbase	: 2630 mm
turning circle	: 10.8 m

kerb weight	: 1600 kg
towing weight	: 1400 - 4WD 1600 kg
boot space	: 644 - 1856 l
fuel capacity	: 65 l
consumption	: 35.3 / 28.2 mpg
acc. 0-62 mph	: 10.4 / 10.5 s
top speed	: 108 / 112 mph
EuroNCAP	: n.a.
introduction	: March 2004
last revised in	: September 2005
warranty	: 3 years
miscellaneous	: Highly successful model for ambitious Korean car manufacturer.

TUCSON 2.0 CRDI VGT

engine type	: diesel, inline-4
displacement	: 1991 cc
max. power	: 103 kW (140 bhp)
@	: 4000 rpm
max. torque	: 225 lb ft
@	: 1800 rpm
gears	: 6
kerb weight	: 1660 kg
towing weight	: 1600 kg
consumption	: 39.8 mpg
acc. 0-60 mph	: 12.0 s
top speed	: 110 mph
miscellaneous	: Diesel-powered Tucson available with 2WD and 4WD.

HYUNDAI SANTA FE 2.7 V6

engine type	: petrol, V6	kerb weight	: 1645 kg
displacement	: 2656 cc	towing weight	: 2000 kg
max. power	: 139 kW (189 bhp)	boot space	: 969 l
@	: 6000 rpm	fuel capacity	: 75 l
max. torque	: 183 lb ft	consumption	: 26.6 mpg
@	: 3500 rpm	acc. 0-62 mph	: 10.0 s
gears	: 5	top speed	: 111 mph
AT	: optional 4-speed automatic	EuroNCAP	: n.a.
drive	: FWD	introduction	: January 2006
brakes f/r	: vent. discs / discs	last revised in	: -
body type	: 5-dr. SUV	warranty	: 3 years
l x w x h	: 4675 x 1890 x 1725 mm	miscellaneous	: New Santa Fe positioned higher in the market to widen the gap with the Tucson. 2.7 also available with 4WD.
wheelbase	: 2700 mm		
turning circle	: 10.9 m		

SANTA FE 2.2 CRDi

engine type	: diesel, inline-4
displacement	: 2188 cc
max. power	: 110 kW (150 bhp)
@	: 4000 rpm
max. torque	: 247 lb ft
@	: 1800 rpm
gears	: 5
kerb weight	: 1718 kg
towing weight	: 2200 kg
consumption	: 38.7 mpg
acc. 0-60 mph	: 11.3 s
top speed	: 111 mph
miscellaneous	: Modern 2.2 diesel engine will soon find its way to other Hyundai models too.

HYUNDAI TRAJET 2.0 / 2.7 V6

engine type	: petrol, inline-4 / V6	kerb weight	: 1712 / 1752 kg
displacement	: 1997 / 2656 cc	towing weight	: 1800 / 1950 kg
max. power	: 103 kW (140 bhp) /	boot space	: 523 – 1801 l
	127 kW (173 bhp)	fuel capacity	: 65 / 75 l
@	: 5800 / 6000 rpm	consumption	: 33.5 / 24.9 mpg
max. torque	: 136 / 181 lb ft	acc. 0-62 mph	: 13.1 / 11.5 s
@	: 4600 / 4000 rpm	top speed	: 114 / 119 mph
gears	: 5 / -	EuroNCAP	: 3 stars
AT	: optional 4-speed automatic /	introduction	: February 2000
	4-speed automatic	last revised in	: April 2004
drive	: FWD	warranty	: 3 years
brakes f/r	: vent. discs / discs	miscellaneous	: Spacious and affordable, but on
body type	: 5-dr. MPV		the market for some time now.
l x w x h	: 4695 x 1840 x 1760 mm		Exterior, choice of materials and
wheelbase	: 2830 mm		build quality have improved since
turning circle	: 11.3 m		latest facelift.

INVICTA S1

engine type	: petrol, V8		kerb weight	: 1100 kg
displacement	: 4601 cc		towing weight	: -
max. power	: 239 kW (325 bhp)		boot space	: n.a.
@	: 5900 rpm		fuel capacity	: 100 l
max. torque	: 300 lb ft		consumption	: 25.1 mpg
@	: 4800 rpm		acc. 0-62 mph	: 5.0 s
gears	: 5		top speed	: 170 mph
AT	: -		EuroNCAP	: n.a.
drive	: RWD		introduction	: n.a.
brakes f/r	: vent. discs		last revised in	: -
body type	: 2-dr. coupe		warranty	: n.a.
l x w x h	: 4400 x 2000 x 1225 mm		miscellaneous	: Revival of illustrious British car
wheelbase	: 2500 mm			make dating back to the 1930s.
turning circle	: 11.5 m			Voluptuous carbonfibre body with
				big V8 from Ford Mustang
				underneath. Luxuriously appointed
				and very fast.

JAGUAR X-TYPE 2.5 V6 / 3.0 V6

engine type	: petrol, V6
displacement	: 2495 / 2967 cc
max. power	: 145 kW (194 bhp) / 172 kW (231 bhp)
@	: 6800 rpm
max. torque	: 180 / 209 lb ft
@	: 3000 rpm
gears	: 5
AT	: optional 5-speed
drive	: 4WD
brakes f/r	: vent. discs
body type	: 4-dr. saloon
l x w x h	: 4672 x 1789 x 1392 mm
wheelbase	: 2710 mm
turning circle	: 10.8 m

kerb weight	: 1555 kg
towing weight	: 1500 kg
boot space	: 452 l
fuel capacity	: 62 l
consumption	: 29.5 / 27.3 mpg
acc. 0-62 mph	: 8.3 / 7.0 s
top speed	: 140 / 144 mph
EuroNCAP	: 4 stars
introduction	: May 2001
last revised in	: June 2007
warranty	: 3 years
miscellaneous	: Model based on previous Ford Mondeo platform did not live up to its expectations. Now fully equipped at an interesting price.

X-TYPE 2.0D / 2.2D

engine type	: diesel, inline-4
displacement	: 1998 / 2198 cc
max. power	: 96 kW (128 bhp) / 113 kW (152 bhp)
@	: 3800 / 3500 rpm
max. torque	: 244 / 270 lb ft
@	: 1800 rpm
gears	: 5 / 6
kerb weight	: 1502 kg
towing weight	: 1500 kg
consumption	: 49.1 / 47.1 mpg
acc. 0-60 mph	: 9.9 / 9.1 s
top speed	: 125 / 137 mph
miscellaneous	: Diesel particle filter standard in all diesel versions. Full range of engines available for estate version as well.

JAGUAR XF 3.0 V6

engine type	: petrol, V6		**kerb weight**	: 1679 kg
displacement	: 2967 cc		**towing weight**	: 1850 kg
max. power	: 175 kW (240 bhp)		**boot space**	: 540 l
@	: 6800 rpm		**fuel capacity**	: 70 l
max. torque	: 216 lb ft		**consumption**	: 26.8 mpg
@	: 4100 rpm		**acc. 0-62 mph**	: 8.3 s
gears	: -		**top speed**	: 148 mph
AT	: 6-speed		**EuroNCAP**	: n.a.
drive	: RWD		**introduction**	: April 2008
brakes f/r	: vent. discs		**last revised in**	: n.a.
body type	: 4-dr. saloon		**warranty**	: 3 years
l x w x h	: 4961 x 1877 x 1460 mm		**miscellaneous**	: The XF replaces the S-type. With
wheelbase	: 2909 mm			modern looks but a drive train
turning circle	: 11.5 m			which stems from its predecessor.
				Also available with a 4.2-litre V8
				engine of either 298 or 416 bhp.

XF 2.7D

engine type	: diesel, V6
displacement	: 2720 c
max. power	: 152 kW (207 bhp)
@	: 4000 rpm
max. torque	: 320 lb ft
@	: 1500 rpm
gears	: 6-speed automatic
kerb weight	: 1771 kg
towing weight	: 1850 kg
consumption	: 37.6 mpg
acc. 0-60 mph	: 8.2 s
top speed	: 143 mph
miscellaneous	: Familiar diesel engine should help to win over customers in the company car market.

JAGUAR XJ6 3.0 / XJR

engine type	: petrol, V6
displacement	: 2967 / 3555 cc
max. power	: 179 kW (240 bhp) /
	196 kW (262 bhp)
@	: 6800 /3250 rpm
max. torque	: 221 / 247 lb ft
@	: 4100 / 4200 rpm
gears	: -
AT	: 6-speed automatic
drive	: RWD
brakes f/r	: vent. discs
body type	: 4-dr. saloon
l x w x h	: 5090 x 1860 x 1448 mm
wheelbase	: 3035 mm
turning circle	: 11.7 m

kerb weight	: 1545 / 1615 kg
towing weight	: 1900 kg
boot space	: 470 l
fuel capacity	: 85 l
consumption	: 27 / 26.8 mpg
acc. 0-62 mph	: 8.1 / 7.6 s
top speed	: 145 / 150 mph
EuroNCAP	: n.a.
introduction	: February 2003
last revised in	: -
warranty	: 3 years
miscellaneous	: Car exudes distinctive air, but styling is rather conservative. All-aluminium body reduces weight and enhances driving characteristics. Better performer than S-type. Also available in LWB-version, nearly 5 inches longer.

XJ6 2.7D

engine type	: diesel, V6
displacement	: 2722 cc
max. power	: 152 kW (204 bhp)
@	: 4000 rpm
max. torque	: 321 lb ft
@	: 1900 rpm
gears	: 6-speed automatic
kerb weight	: 1659 kg
towing weight	: 1900 kg
consumption	: 35.0 mpg
acc. 0-60 mph	: 8.2 s
top speed	: 141 mph
miscellaneous	: The XJ will have to make do without the V8 diesel engine from the Range Rover.

JAGUAR XK 3.5 / 4.2

engine type	: petrol, V8
displacement	: 3555 / 4196 cc
max. power	: 190 kW (258 bhp) / 219 kW (300 bhp)
@	: 6250 / 6000 rpm
max. torque	: 246 / 310 lb ft
@	: 4200 / 4100 rpm
gears	: -
AT	: 6-speed
drive	: RWD
brakes f/r	: vent. discs
body type	: 2-dr. coupe / convertible
l x w x h	: 4791 x 1892 x 1322 mm
wheelbase	: 2752 mm
turning circle	: 11.0 m

kerb weight	: 1595 kg
towing weight	: -
boot space	: 300 l
fuel capacity	: 75 l
consumption	: 25.0 mpg
acc. 0-62 mph	: 7.6 / 6.2 s
top speed	: 151 / 155 mph
EuroNCAP	: n.b.
introduction	: April 2006
last revised in	: n.v.t.
warranty	: 3 years
miscellaneous	: The XK is the successor to the XK8. Its gorgeous aluminium body hides A 2+2 seating arrangement. A convertible is also available.

XKR

engine type	: petrol, V8
displacement	: 4196 cc
max. power	: 306 kW (420 bhp)
@	: 6250 rpm
max. torque	: 413 lb ft
@	: 4000 rpm
gears	: 6-speed automatic
kerb weight	: 1665 kg
towing weight	: -
consumption	: 22.9 mpg
acc. 0-60 mph	: 5.2 s
top speed	: 155 mph
miscellaneous	: Flagship of the model range.

JEEP COMPASS 2.4

engine type	: petrol, inline-4	kerb weight	: 1435 kg
displacement	: 2359 cc	towing weight	: 1500 kg
max. power	: 125 kW (168 bhp)	boot space	: 334 l
@	: 6000 rpm	fuel capacity	: 51 l
max. torque	: 162 lb ft	consumption	: 32.5 mpg
@	: 4500 rpm	acc. 0-62 mph	: 10.7 s
gears	: 5	top speed	: 112 mph
AT	: optional CVT	EuroNCAP	: n.a.
drive	: 4WD	introduction	: January 2007
brakes f/r	: vent. discs / discs	last revised in	: -
body type	: 5-dr. hatchback	warranty	: 2 years
l x w x h	: 4405 x 1760 x 1632 mm	miscellaneous	: A turning point in the history
wheelbase	: 2635 mm		of Jeep: the Compass is a
turning circle	: 10.8 m		sports utility vehicle rather than
			an off-roader.

PATRIOT 2.0 CRD

engine type	: diesel, inline-4
displacement	: 1968 cc
max. power	: 103 kW (138 bhp)
@	: 4000 rpm
max. torque	: 229 lb ft
@	: 1750 rpm
gears	: 6
kerb weight	: 1610 kg
towing weight	: 1500 kg
consumption	: 43.5 mpg
acc. 0-60 mph	: 11.0 s
top speed	: 117 mph
miscellaneous	: The Compass and Patriot share the same technology but are clothed in different bodies. The Patriot is available with the 2.4 unit from the Compass, which in turn can be specified with a 2.0 CRD diesel engine too.

JEEP WRANGLER 3.8 V6

engine type	: petrol, V6	kerb weight	: 1705 kg
displacement	: 3778 cc	towing weight	: 2000 kg
max. power	: 144 kW (196 bhp)	boot space	: 485 l
@	: 5000 rpm	fuel capacity	: 70 l
max. torque	: 232 lb ft	consumption	: 24.4 mpg
@	: 4000 rpm	acc. 0-62 mph	: 11.2 s
gears	: 6	top speed	: 112 mph
AT	: optional 4-speed	EuroNCAP	: n.a.
drive	: 4WD	introduction	: March 2007
brakes f/r	: vent. discs / discs	last revised in	: -
body type	: 2-dr. SUV	warranty	: 2 years
l x w x h	: 4223 x 1873 x 1800 mm	miscellaneous	: The Wrangler is now also available with a four-door body, adding 50 centimeters to the total length. This version is called Unlimited.
wheelbase	: 2424 mm		
turning circle	: 10.4 m		

WRANGLER 2.8 CRD

engine type	: diesel, inline-4
displacement	: 2777 cc
max. power	: 130 kW (174 bhp)
@	: 3800 rpm
max. torque	: 302 lb ft
@	: 2000 rpm
gears	: 6, optional 5-speed automatic
kerb weight	: 1780 kg
towing weight	: 2000 kg
consumption	: 28.5 mpg
acc. 0-60 mph	: 10.1 s
top speed	: 112 mph
miscellaneous	: Diesel engine from Italian manufacturer VM is used in several models of Dodge, Jeep and Chrysler.

JEEP CHEROKEE 2.8 CRD

engine type	: diesel, inline-4	kerb weight	: 1940 kg
displacement	: 2768 cc	towing weight	: 2000 kg
max. power	: 130 kW (174 bhp)	boot space	: 369 l
@	: 3800 rpm	fuel capacity	: 74 l
max. torque	: 174 lb ft	consumption	: 32.8 mpg
@	: 2000 rpm	acc. 0-62 mph	: 11.5 s
gears	: 6	top speed	: 112 mph
AT	: optional 5-speed	EuroNCAP	: n.a.
drive	: 4WD	introduction	: October 2007
brakes f/r	: vent. discs / discs	last revised in	: -
body type	: 5-dr. SUV	warranty	: 3 years
l x w x h	: 4584 x 1856 x 1773 mm	miscellaneous	: Identical to the Dodge Nitro
wheelbase	: 2763 mm		from a technical point of view.
turning circle	: 11.1 m		Turn to that Dodge for details
			of the 3.7 V6.

JEEP GRAND CHEROKEE 4.7 V8 / 5.7 V8

engine type	: petrol, V8	kerb weight	: 2110 / 2150 kg
displacement	: 4700 / 5654 cc	towing weight	: 3360 kg
max. power	: 170 kW (231 bhp) /	boot space	: 978 - 1908 l
	240 kW (326 bhp)	fuel capacity	: 79 l
@	: 4500 / 5000 rpm	consumption	: 19 / 18.3 mpg
max. torque	: 302 / 369 lb ft	acc. 0-62 mph	: 8.8 / 7.1 s
@	: 3600 / 4000 rpm	top speed	: 124 / 129 mph
gears	: -	EuroNCAP	: n.a.
AT	: 5-speed automatic	introduction	: March 2005
drive	: 4WD	last revised in	: -
brakes f/r	: vent. discs / discs	warranty	: 2 years
body type	: 5-dr. SUV	miscellaneous	: With a big HEMI V8 engine under
l x w x h	: 4750 x 2149 x 1740 mm		the bonnet, even this heavyweight
wheelbase	: 2780 mm		turns into an agile performer.
turning circle	: 11.2 m		Not the best on-road behaviour
			though, but it really shines off road.
			Also available with a 218 bhp
			strong 3.0-litre diesel engine from
			Mercedes-Benz.

GRAND CHEROKEE SRT-8

engine type	: petrol, V8
displacement	: 6059 cc
max. power	: 313 kW (426 bhp)
@	: 6000 rpm
max. torque	: 420 lb ft
@	: 4600 rpm
gears	: 5-speed automatic
kerb weight	: 2220 kg
towing weight	: n.a.
consumption	: 17.2 mpg
acc. 0-60 mph	: 5.0 s
top speed	: 152 mph
miscellaneous	: Almost as capable as a Porsche Cayenne Turbo, but rather less costly.

JEEP COMMANDER 3.0 CRD

engine type	: diesel, V6	**kerb weight**	: 2315 kg
displacement	: 2987 cc	**towing weight**	: 3500 kg
max. power	: 160 kW (218 bhp)	**boot space**	: 212 - 1940 l
@	: 4000 rpm	**fuel capacity**	: 77 l
max. torque	: 376 lb ft	**consumption**	: 26.2 mpg
@	: 1600 rpm	**acc. 0-62 mph**	: 9.0 s
gears	: n.a.	**top speed**	: 118 mph
AT	: 5-speed automatic	**EuroNCAP**	: n.a.
drive	: 4WD	**introduction**	: Spring 2006
brakes f/r	: vent. discs / discs	**last revised in**	: -
body type	: 5-dr. SUV	**warranty**	: 2 years
l x w x h	: 4787 x 1900 x 1826 mm	**miscellaneous**	: Also available with 4.7 V8 and
wheelbase	: 2780 mm		5.7 V8 engines. Bigger and tougher
turning circle	: 11.8 m		than Grand Cherokee.

JMC LANDWIND 2.0 L / 2.4 L

engine type	: petrol, inline-4	kerb weight	: 1750 kg
displacement	: 1997 / 2351 cc	towing weight	: 2380 kg
max. power	: 84 kW (115 bhp) / 92 kW (125 bhp)	boot space	: n.a.
@	: 5500 / 5200 rpm	fuel capacity	: n.a.
max. torque	: 120 / 144 lb ft	consumption	: 33.4 / 31.5 mpg
@	: 3500 / 3000 rpm	acc. 0-62 mph	: n.a.
gears	: 5	top speed	: 99 / 109 mph
AT	: -	EuroNCAP	: -
drive	: 4WD	introduction	: Summer 2005
brakes f/r	: n.a.	last revised in	: -
body type	: 5-dr. SUV	warranty	: 2 years
l x w x h	: 4745 x 1800 x 1750 mm	miscellaneous	: Biggest petrol version also available with 4WD. Sales of Landwind suffer from its alleged poor crashworthiness in German crash tests.
wheelbase	: 2760 mm		
turning circle	: 11.6 m		

JMC LANDWIND 2.8 T

engine type	: diesel, inline-4
displacement	: 2771 cc
max. power	: 68 kW (92 bhp)
@	: 3600 rpm
max. torque	: 155 lb ft
@	: 2300 rpm
gears	: 5
kerb weight	: 1830 kg
towing weight	: 2265 kg
consumption	: 40.5 mpg
acc. 0-60 mph	: n.a.
top speed	: 90 mph
miscellaneous	: With an old and sluggish engine under the bonnet, the diesel-powered Landwind can hardly keep up with modern-day traffic.

KIA PICANTO 1.0

engine type	: petrol, inline-4	kerb weight	: 836 kg
displacement	: 999 cc	towing weight	: 700 kg
max. power	: 45 kW (61 bhp)	boot space	: 157 - 882 l
@	: 5600 rpm	fuel capacity	: 35 l
max. torque	: 64 lb ft	consumption	: 55.4 mpg
@	: 2800 rpm	acc. 0-62 mph	: 16.4 s
gears	: 5	top speed	: 93 mph
AT	: -	EuroNCAP	: n.a.
drive	: FWD	introduction	: February 2004
brakes f/r	: vent. discs / drum brakes	last revised in	: -
body type	: 5-dr. hatchback	warranty	: 3 years
l x w x h	: 3495 x 1595 x 1480 mm	miscellaneous	: Kind of a Korean Fiat Panda and
wheelbase	: 2370 mm		like its Italian rival very successful.
turning circle	: 9.2 m		Looks best in bright colours. Also
			available with 65 bhp 1.1 petrol
			engine and 4-speed automatic
			transmission.

PICANTO 1.1 CRDI VGT

engine type	: diesel, inline-3
displacement	: 1120 cc
max. power	: 55 kW (75 bhp)
@	: 4000 rpm
max. torque	: 113 lb ft
@	: 1900 rpm
gears	: 5
kerb weight	: 945 kg
towing weight	: 700 kg
consumption	: 64.5 mpg
acc. 0-60 mph	: n.a.
top speed	: 101 mph
miscellaneous	: Quick and economical car.

KIA RIO 1.4 / 1.6

engine type	: petrol, inline-4	**kerb weight**	: 1154 / 1175 kg
displacement	: 1399 / 1599 cc	**towing weight**	: 1100 kg
max. power	: 71 kW (97 bhp) / 82 kW (112 bhp)	**boot space**	: 272 - 1107 l
@	: 6000 rpm	**fuel capacity**	: 45 l
max. torque	: 92 / 108 lb ft	**consumption**	: 44.8 / 43.6 mpg
@	: 4700 / 4500 rpm	**acc. 0-62 mph**	: 12.3 / 10.2 s
gears	: 5	**top speed**	: 110 / 117 mph
AT	: - / optional 4-speed	**EuroNCAP**	: n.a.
drive	: FWD	**introduction**	: Autumn 2005
brakes f/r	: vent. discs / discs	**last revised in**	: -
body type	: 5-dr. hatchback	**warranty**	: 3 years
l x w x h	: 3990 x 1695 x 1470 mm	**miscellaneous**	: New edition is totally different from previous Rio model. Well-built hatchback with European styling cues.
wheelbase	: 2500 mm		
turning circle	: 10.1 m		

RIO 1.5 CRDi

engine type	: diesel, inline-4
displacement	: 1493 cc
max. power	: 81 kW (110 bhp)
@	: 4000 rpm
max. torque	: 173 lb ft
@	: 1900 rpm
gears	: 5
kerb weight	: 1221 kg
towing weight	: 1636 / 1811 kg
consumption	: 60.1 mpg
acc. 0-60 mph	: 11.5 s
top speed	: 110 mph
miscellaneous	: Fine diesel engine.

KIA CERATO 1.6 16V / 2.0 CVVT

engine type	: petrol, inline-4
displacement	: 1599 / 1975 cc
max. power	: 77 kW (105 bhp) / 105 kW (143 bhp)
@	: 5800 / 6000 rpm
max. torque	: 105 / 138 lb ft
@	: 4500 rpm
gears	: 5
AT	: - / optional 4-speed
drive	: FWD
brakes f/r	: vent. discs / discs
body type	: 5-dr. hatchback
l x w x h	: 4480 x 1735 x 1470 mm
wheelbase	: 2610 mm
turning circle	: 10.1 m

kerb weight	: 1153 / 1220 kg
towing weight	: 1200 / 1400 kg
boot space	: 345 - 1494 l
fuel capacity	: 55 l
consumption	: 40.4 / 37.7 mpg
acc. 0-62 mph	: 11 / 9 s
top speed	: 115 / 129 mph
EuroNCAP	: n.a.
introduction	: April 2004
last revised in	: -
warranty	: 3 years
miscellaneous	: Car with European looks and fine driving characteristics. Deserves more success. Also available as 4-door saloon.

CERATO 1.6 CRDi VGT

engine type	: diesel, inline-4
displacement	: 1582 cc
max. power	: 85 kW (115 bhp)
@	: 4000 rpm
max. torque	: 174 lb ft
@	: 2000 rpm
gears	: 5
kerb weight	: 1254 kg
towing weight	: 1200 kg
consumption	: 57.6 mpg
acc. 0-60 mph	: n.a.
top speed	: 107 mph
miscellaneous	: New diesel engine makes its first appearance in the Cerato.

KIA CEE'D 1.4 / 1.6

engine type	: petrol, inline-4
displacement	: 1396 / 1591 cc
max. power	: 80 kW (104 bhp) / 90 kW (120 bhp)
@	: 6200 rpm
max. torque	: 101 / 114 lb ft
@	: 5000 / 4200 rpm
gears	: 5
AT	: - / optional 4-speed automatic
drive	: FWD
brakes f/r	: vent. discs / discs
body type	: 5-dr. hatchback
l x w x h	: 4240 x 1790 x 1480 mm
wheelbase	: 2650 mm
turning circle	: 10.3 m

kerb weight	: 1163 kg
towing weight	: 1200 kg
boot space	: 340 l
fuel capacity	: 53 l
consumption	: 46.3 / 44.1 mpg
acc. 0-62 mph	: 11.6 / 10.8 s
top speed	: 116 / 119 mph
EuroNCAP	: n.a.
introduction	: February 2007
last revised in	: -
warranty	: 5 years
miscellaneous	: Proper medium-sized model from Kia with an attractive price. Also available with diesel power, as described under the Sporty Wagon entry on the next page.

CEE'D 2.0

engine type	: petrol, inline-4
displacement	: 1975 cc
max. power	: 105 kW (140 bhp)
@	: 6000 rpm
max. torque	: 137 lb ft
@	: 4600 rpm
gears	: 5, optional 4-speed automatic
kerb weight	: 1241 kg
towing weight	: 1500 kg
consumption	: 39.8 mpg
acc. 0-60 mph	: 10.4 s
top speed	: 127 mph
miscellaneous	: Kia plans a more potent range-topping version, just like Hyundai does with twin brother i30.

KIA CEE'D SPORTY WAGON 1.6 CRDI

engine type	: diesel, inline-4	kerb weight	: 1319 kg
displacement	: 1582 cc	towing weight	: 1400 kg
max. power	: 85 kW (113 bhp)	boot space	: 534 l
@	: 4000 rpm	fuel capacity	: 53 l
max. torque	: 188 lb ft	consumption	: 60.1 mpg
@	: 1900 rpm	acc. 0-62 mph	: 11.6 s
gears	: 5	top speed	: 117 mph
AT	: -	EuroNCAP	: n.a.
drive	: FWD	introduction	: September 2007
brakes f/r	: vent. discs / discs	last revised in	: -
body type	: 5-dr. stationwagon	warranty	: 3 years
l x w x h	: 4470 x 1790 x 1490 mm	miscellaneous	: At a small charge, Kia turns the
wheelbase	: 2650 mm		Cee'd into an estate. Also available
turning circle	: n.a.		with a 1.6 or 2.0 petrol engine.

PRO_CEE'D 2.0

engine type	: petrol, inline-4
displacement	: 1975 cc
max. power	: 105 kW (143 bhp)
@	: 6000 rpm
max. torque	: 137 lb ft
@	: 4600 rpm
gears	: 5, optional 4-speed AT
kerb weight	: n.a.
towing weight	: n.a.
consumption	: 39.8 mpg
acc. 0-60 mph	: 10.4 s
top speed	: 127 mph
miscellaneous	: Three-door hatchback is based on the Cee'd and identical under-neath.

KIA MAGENTIS 2.0 / 2.7 V6

engine type	: petrol, inline-4 / V6
displacement	: 1998 / 2656 cc
max. power	: 106 kW (145 bhp) / 138 kW (188 bhp)
@	: 6000 rpm
max. torque	: 139 / 182 lb ft
@	: 4250 / 4000 rpm
gears	: 5 / -
AT	: - / optional 4-speed automatic
drive	: FWD
brakes f/r	: vent. discs / discs
body type	: 4-dr. saloon
l x w x h	: 4735 x 1805 x 1480 mm
wheelbase	: 2720 mm
turning circle	: 10.8 m

kerb weight	: 1383 / 1465 kg
towing weight	: 1700 kg
boot space	: 420 l
fuel capacity	: 62 l
consumption	: 36.7 / 30.7 mpg
acc. 0-62 mph	: 10.2 / 9.1 s
top speed	: 129 / 137 mph
EuroNCAP	: n.a.
introduction	: February 2006
last revised in	: -
warranty	: 3 years
miscellaneous	: New Magentis shares DNA with Hyundai Sonata. Much better-looking than predecessor.

MAGENTIS 2.0 CRDI

engine type	: diesel, inline-4
displacement	: 1991 cc
max. power	: 103 kW (140 bhp)
@	: 4000 rpm
max. torque	: 224 lb ft
@	: 1800 rpm
gears	: 6, optional 4-speed automatic
kerb weight	: 1500 kg
towing weight	: 1700 kg
consumption	: 47.1 mpg
acc. 0-60 mph	: n.a.
top speed	: 125 mph
miscellaneous	: Diesel engine already familiar from Hyundai, but upgraded recently with a turbo with variable geometry.

KIA CARENS 2.0

engine type	: petrol, inline-4	kerb weight	: 1563 kg
displacement	: 1997 cc	towing weight	: n.a.
max. power	: 106 kW (144 bhp)	boot space	: 400 – 2106 l
@	: 6000 rpm	fuel capacity	: 62 l
max. torque	: 139 lb ft	consumption	: 29.7 mpg
@	: 4250 rpm	acc. 0-62 mph	: 10.8 s
gears	: 5	top speed	: 118 mph
AT	: optional 5-speed	EuroNCAP	: n.a.
drive	: FWD	introduction	: August 2006
brakes f/r	: vent. discs / discs	last revised in	: -
body type	: 5-dr. MPV	warranty	: 3 years
l x w x h	: 4545 x 1820 x 1650 mm	miscellaneous	: Carens now available as a 7-seat-
wheelbase	: 2700 mm		er. Not a very innovative car, but it
turning circle	: 10.8 m		offers good value for money.

CARENS 2.0 CRDi

engine type	: diesel, inline-4
displacement	: 1991 cc
max. power	: 99 kW (135 bhp)
@	: 4000 rpm
max. torque	: 225 lb ft
@	: 1800 rpm
gears	: 6, optional 4-speed automatic
kerb weight	: 1619 kg
towing weight	: n.a.
consumption	: 42.8 mpg
acc. 0-60 mph	: 10.8 s
top speed	: 116 mph
miscellaneous	: Carens model range also includes a
	diesel-powered version, an engine
	we are already familiar with.

KIA SEDONA 2.7 V6

engine type	: petrol, V6	kerb weight	: 1924 kg
displacement	: 2656 cc	towing weight	: 2000 kg
max. power	: 139 kW (189 bhp)	boot space	: 364 l
@	: 6000 rpm	fuel capacity	: 80 l
max. torque	: 184 lb ft	consumption	: 26.5 mpg
@	: 4000 rpm	acc. 0-62 mph	: n.a.
gears	: 5	top speed	: 117 mph
AT	: optional 4-speed	EuroNCAP	: n.a.
drive	: FWD	introduction	: May 2006
brakes f/r	: vent. discs / drum brakes	last revised in	: -
body type	: 5-dr. MPV	warranty	: 3 years
l x w x h	: 4810 x 1985 x 1815 mm	miscellaneous	: Updated Sedona positioned higher in the market now, in order to make room for the new Carens.
wheelbase	: 2890 mm		
turning circle	: 11.0 m		

SEDONA 2.9 CRDi VGT

engine type	: diesel, inline-4
displacement	: 2902 cc
max. power	: 136 kW (185 bhp)
@	: 3800 rpm
max. torque	: 253 lb ft
@	: 2000 rpm
gears	: 5, optional 5-speed automatic
kerb weight	: 2068 kg
towing weight	: 2000 kg
consumption	: 36.4 mpg
acc. 0-60 mph	: n.a.
top speed	: 122 mph
miscellaneous	: Diesel-engined version still most economical choice, as with previous Sedona. But frankly, it is also the best of the range.

KIA SPORTAGE 2.0 / 2.7 V6

engine type	: petrol, inline-4 / V6
displacement	: 1998 / 2656 cc
max. power	: 104 kW (141 bhp) / 129 kW (179 bhp)
@	: 6000 rpm
max. torque	: 136 / 178 lb ft
@	: 4500 / 4000 rpm
gears	: 5 / -
AT	: optional 4-speed automatic / 4-speed automatic
drive	: FWD, optional 4WD
brakes f/r	: vent. discs / discs
body type	: 5-dr. SUV
l x w x h	: 4350 x 1800 x 1700 mm
wheelbase	: 2630 mm
turning circle	: 10.8 m

kerb weight	: 1442 / 1570 kg
towing weight	: 1400 / 1600 kg
boot space	: 667 - 1886 l
fuel capacity	: 58 / 65 l
consumption	: 34.4 / 28.2 mpg
acc. 0-62 mph	: 10.4 / 10.5 s
top speed	: 112 / 104 mph
EuroNCAP	: n.a.
introduction	: September 2004
last revised in	: -
warranty	: 3 years
miscellaneous	: Twin brother of Hyundai Tucson and just as successful. Another Kia hit after the Sorento.

159 2.2 JTS / 3.2 V6

engine type	: diesel, inline-4
displacement	: 1991 cc
max. power	: 103 kW (140 bhp)
@	: 4000 rpm
max. torque	: 224 lb ft
@	: 1800 rpm
gears	: 6
kerb weight	: 1565 kg
towing weight	: 1400 kg
consumption	: 39.8 mpg
acc. 0-60 mph	: 12.0 s
top speed	: 104 mph
miscellaneous	: Diesel version now boasts more horsepower.

KIA SORENTO 3.3 V6

engine type	: petrol, V6		kerb weight	: 1886 kg
displacement	: 3342 cc		towing weight	: 3500 kg
max. power	: 182 kW (248 bhp)		boot space	: 486 l
@	: 6000 rpm		fuel capacity	: 80 l
max. torque	: 226 lb ft		consumption	: 26.2 mpg
@	: 4500 rpm		acc. 0-62 mph	: 9.2 s
gears	: -		top speed	: 118 mph
AT	: 5-speed		EuroNCAP	: 4 stars
drive	: 4WD		introduction	: May 2002
brakes f/r	: vent. discs / discs		last revised in	: January 2007
body type	: 5-dr. SUV		warranty	: 3 years
l x w x h	: 4590 x 1885 x 1725 mm		miscellaneous	: Still a strong proposition in
wheelbase	: 2710 mm			a crowded market segment.
turning circle	: 11.1 m			However, regarding looks and
				dynamic properties it can no lon-
				ger match its opponents.

SORENTO 2.5 CRDi

engine type	: diesel, inline-4
displacement	: 2497 cc
max. power	: 125 kW (168 bhp)
@	: 3800 rpm
max. torque	: 289 lb ft
@	: 2000 rpm
gears	: 5, optional 5-speed AT
kerb weight	: 1965 kg
towing weight	: 3000 kg
consumption	: 32.8 mpg
acc. 0-60 mph	: 12.0 s
top speed	: 113 mph
miscellaneous	: It was this car that put Kia on the map. In its heydays delivery times ran up to more than one year.

KOENIGSEGG CCX

engine type	: petrol, V8		**kerb weight**	: 1180 kg
displacement	: 4700 cc		**towing weight**	: -
max. power	: 600 kW (816 bhp)		**boot space**	: 120 l
@	: 6900 rpm		**fuel capacity**	: 70 l
max. torque	: 678 lb ft		**consumption**	: 16.7 mpg
@	: 5700 rpm		**acc. 0-62 mph**	: 3.2 s
gears	: 6		**top speed**	: > 245 mph
AT	: -		**EuroNCAP**	: n.a.
drive	: RWD		**introduction**	: May 2004
brakes f/r	: vent. discs		**last revised in**	: March 2006
body type	: 2-dr. coupe		**warranty**	: n.a.
l x w x h	: 4293 x 1996 x 1120 mm		**miscellaneous**	: American legislation forced Koenigsegg to adapt its CCR model, resulting in CCX. Less expensive alternative to Bugatti Veyron.
wheelbase	: 2660 mm			
turning circle	: 11.0 m			

LADA KALINA

engine type	: petrol, inline-4	kerb weight	: 1050 kg
displacement	: 1596 cc	towing weight	: 900 kg
max. power	: 60 kW (81 bhp)	boot space	: 260 l
@	: 5200 rpm	fuel capacity	: 43 l
max. torque	: 90 lb ft	consumption	: 39.8 mpg
@	: 2500 rpm	acc. 0-62 mph	: 13.0 s
gears	: 5	top speed	: 102 mph
AT	: -	EuroNCAP	: n.a.
drive	: FWD	introduction	: January 2007
brakes f/r	: vent. discs / drums	last revised in	: -
body type	: 5-dr. hatchback	warranty	: 2 years
l x w x h	: 3850 x 1700 x 1500 mm	miscellaneous	: Lada makes a comeback with the
wheelbase	: 2470 mm		good-looking Kalina. Car rivals
turning circle	: 10.4 m		with the Dacia Logan, but must
			do without ABS braking. Also
			available as four-door saloon.
			Stationwagon will follow.

LADA 110 8V / 16V

engine type	: petrol, inline-4
displacement	: 1499 cc
max. power	: 59 kW (80 bhp) / 66 kW (90 bhp)
@	: 5200 / 5000 rpm
max. torque	: 89 / 97 lb ft
@	: 3000 / 3700 rpm
gears	: 5
AT	: -
drive	: FWD
brakes f/r	: vent. discs / drum brakes
body type	: 4-dr. saloon / 5-dr. stationwagon
l x w x h	: 4265 x 1680 x 1420 mm
wheelbase	: 2492 mm
turning circle	: 11.0 m

kerb weight	: 995 / 1015 kg
towing weight	: 1000 kg
boot space	: 415 - 1270 l
fuel capacity	: 43 l
consumption	: 38.9 / 38.3 mpg
acc. 0-62 mph	: 14 / 12 s
top speed	: 104 / 115 mph
EuroNCAP	: n.a.
introduction	: October 1999
last revised in	: -
warranty	: 2 years
miscellaneous	: Sales very disappointing. Car almost as rare as a Ferrari. Also available as a stationwagon, called 111.

112 16V

engine type	: petrol, inline-4
displacement	: 1499 cc
max. power	: 67 kW (90 bhp)
@	: 5600 rpm
max. torque	: 97 lb ft
@	: 3700 rpm
gears	: 5
kerb weight	: 1060 kg
towing weight	: 1000 kg
consumption	: 38.3 mpg
acc. 0-60 mph	: n.a.
top speed	: 115 mph
miscellaneous	: Hatchback version of Lada 110, also available with 80 bhp 8V engine. 16V versions have power steering.

LADA NIVA

engine type	: petrol, inline-4
displacement	: 1690 cc
max. power	: 60 kW (82 bhp)
@	: 5000 rpm
max. torque	: 95 lb ft
@	: 4000 rpm
gears	: 5
AT	: -
drive	: 4WD
brakes f/r	: vent. discs / drum brakes
body type	: 3-dr. SUV
l x w x h	: 3720 x 1680 x 1640 mm
wheelbase	: 2200 mm
turning circle	: 11.0 m

kerb weight	: 1210 kg
towing weight	: 1500 kg
boot space	: 265 - 982 l
fuel capacity	: 45 l
consumption	: 24.9 mpg
acc. 0-62 mph	: 19.0 s
top speed	: 85 mph
EuroNCAP	: n.a.
introduction	: 1977
last revised in	: -
warranty	: 2 years
miscellaneous	: A prehistoric but durable and charismatic car with offroad capability. Old bone-shaker that approaches cult car status.

LAMBORGHINI GALLARDO / SUPERLEGGERA

engine type	: petrol, V10	kerb weight	: 1430 / 1330 kg
displacement	: 4961 cc	towing weight	: -
max. power	: 382 kW (520 bhp) /	boot space	: 110 l
	390 kW (530 bhp)	fuel capacity	: 90 l
@	: 8000 rpm	consumption	: 14.5 mpg
max. torque	: 520 lb ft	acc. 0-62 mph	: 4.0 / 3.8 s
@	: 4250 rpm	top speed	: 197 mph
gears	: 6 / -	EuroNCAP	: n.a.
AT	: optional / 6-speed seq.	introduction	: January 2004
drive	: 4WD	last revised in	: -
brakes f/r	: vent. discs	warranty	: 2 years
body type	: 2-dr. coupe	miscellaneous	: The Superleggera is a new,
l x w x h	: 4300 x 1900 x 1165 mm		stripped-down version of the
wheelbase	: 2560 mm		Gallardo for the performance-ori-
turning circle	: 11.5 m		ented driver. The 'basic' model is
			also available with a softtop.

LAMBORGHINI MURCIÉLAGO LP640

engine type	: petrol, V12		**kerb weight**	: 1665 kg
displacement	: 6496 cc		**towing weight**	: -
max. power	: 471 kW (640 bhp)		**boot space**	: 140 l
@	: 8000 rpm		**fuel capacity**	: 100 l
max. torque	: 487 lb ft		**consumption**	: 13.2 mpg
@	: 6000 rpm		**acc. 0-62 mph**	: 3.4 s
gears	: 6		**top speed**	: 210 mph
AT	: optional 6-speed seq.		**EuroNCAP**	: n.a.
drive	: 4WD		**introduction**	: September 2006
brakes f/r	: vent. discs		**last revised in**	: n.v.t.
body type	: 2-dr. coupe		**warranty**	: 2 years
l x w x h	: 4610 x 2058 x 1135 mm		**miscellaneous**	: The only Murciélago model listed
wheelbase	: 2665 mm			is he high-spec LP 640, but it is
turning circle	: 12.6 m			also available in Roadster form.

LANCIA YPSILON 1.4 8V / 1.4 16V

engine type	: petrol, inline-4	kerb weight	: 945 / 955 kg
displacement	: 1368 cc	towing weight	: 900 kg
max. power	: 56 kW (77 bhp) / 70 kW (95 bhp)	boot space	: 215 l
@	: 6000 / 5800 rpm	fuel capacity	: 47 l
max. torque	: 83 / 94 lb ft	consumption	: 51.6 / 42.8 mpg
@	: 3750 / 4500 rpm	acc. 0-62 mph	: 13.5 / 10.9 s
gears	: 5 / 6	top speed	: 104 / 109 mph
AT	: - / 6-speed DFN	EuroNCAP	: n.a.
drive	: FWD	introduction	: October 2003
brakes f/r	: discs / drums	last revised in	: December 2006
body type	: 3-dr. hatchback	warranty	: 2 years
l x w x h	: 3810 x 1704 x 1530 mm	miscellaneous	: Stylish city car received new front.
wheelbase	: 2388 mm		There is also a version with a 60
turning circle	: 9.8 m		bhp strong 1.2 petrol engine. 'DFN'
			is a semi-automatic transmission
			which does without a clutch.

YPSILON 1.3 MULTIJET 16V

engine type	: diesel, inline-4
displacement	: 1251 cc
max. power	: 66 kW (90 bhp)
@	: 4000 rpm
max. torque	: 148 lb ft
@	: 1750 rpm
gears	: 6
kerb weight	: 1020 kg
towing weight	: 900 kg
consumption	: 62.8 mpg
acc. 0-60 mph	: 11.0 s
top speed	: 109 mph
miscellaneous	: Lancia has chosen to equip the Ypsilon with one of the stronger diesel units on hand.

LANCIA MUSA 1.3 / 1.9 MULTIJET

engine type	: diesel, inline-4
displacement	: 1248 / 1910 cc
max. power	: 66 kW (90 bhp) / 74 kW (100 bhp)
@	: 4000 rpm
max. torque	: 148 / 192 lb ft
@	: 1750 rpm
gears	: 5
AT	: optional 5-speed seq. / -
drive	: FWD
brakes f/r	: vent. discs / drums
body type	: 5-dr. MPV
l x w x h	: 4010 x 1698 x 1688 mm
wheelbase	: 2508 mm
turning circle	: 10.4 m

kerb weight	: 1175 / 1250 kg
towing weight	: 1000 / 1100 kg
boot space	: 390 l
fuel capacity	: 47 l
consumption	: 57.6 / 51.4 mpg
acc. 0-62 mph	: 12.2 / 11.5 s
top speed	: 108 / 111 mph
EuroNCAP	: n.a.
introduction	: June 2004
last revised in	: September 2007
warranty	: 2 years
miscellaneous	: This deluxe interpretation of the Fiat Idea received a recent upgrade. Like the Ypsilon, it is available with two-tone paintwork.

MUSA 1.4 8V / 1.4 16V

engine type	: petrol, inline-4
displacement	: 1368 cc
max. power	: 57 kW (77 bhp) / 70 kW (95 bhp)
@	: 6000 / 5800 rpm
max. torque	: 85 / 94 lb ft
@	: 3000 / 4500 rpm
gears	: 5
kerb weight	: 1130 kg
towing weight	: 1000 kg
consumption	: 45.6 / 42.8 mpg
acc. 0-60 mph	: 13.5 / 11.5 s
top speed	: 101 / 109 mph
miscellaneous	: As an option the 16V engine can be combined with a robotized transmission.

LANCIA THESIS 2.4 20V / 2.0 TURBO 20V

engine type	: petrol, inline-5	kerb weight	: 1755 / 1770 kg
displacement	: 2446 / 1998 cc	towing weight	: 1500 kg
max. power	: 125 kW (170 bhp) /	boot space	: 400 l
	136 kW (185 bhp)	fuel capacity	: 75 l
@	: 6000 / 5500 rpm	consumption	: 25.9 mpg
max. torque	: 167 / 227 lb ft	acc. 0-62 mph	: 9.5 / 8.9 s
@	: 3500 / 2200 rpm	top speed	: 135 / 139 mph
gears	: 6	EuroNCAP	: n.a.
AT	: optional 5-speed / -	introduction	: June 2002
drive	: FWD	last revised in	: -
brakes f/r	: vent. discs	warranty	: 2 years
body type	: 4-dr. saloon	miscellaneous	: The Thesis remains a rare sight on
l x w x h	: 4888 x 1830 x 1470 mm		our roads. Both the 3.0 V6 and 3.2
wheelbase	: 2803 mm		V6 version are no longer available.
turning circle	: 12.2 m		

THESIS 2.4 MULTIJET 20V

engine type	: diesel, inline-5
displacement	: 2387 cc
max. power	: 136 kW (185 bhp)
@	: 4000 rpm
max. torque	: 243 Nm
@	: 1750 rpm
gears	: 5-speed automatic
kerb weight	: 1795 kg
towing weight	: 1500 kg
consumption	: 32.1 mpg
acc. 0-60 mph	: 9.7 s
top speed	: 138 mph
miscellaneous	: The diesel engine in the Thesis is equipped with a particle filter and comes with an automatic transmission.

LANCIA PHEDRA 2.0 JTD 120 / 136

engine type	: petrol, inline-4
displacement	: 1997 / 2179 cc
max. power	: 79 kW (108 bhp) / 94 kW (128 bhp)
@	: 4000 rpm
max. torque	: 199 / 232 lb ft
@	: 1750 / 2000 rpm
gears	: 5
AT	: -
drive	: FWD
brakes f/r	: vent. discs / discs
body type	: 5-dr. MPV
l x w x h	: 4750 x 1863 x 1752 mm
wheelbase	: 2823 mm
turning circle	: 10.9 m

kerb weight	: 1660 / 1710 kg
towing weight	: 1850 / 1850 kg
boot space	: 324 – 2948 l
fuel capacity	: 80 l
consumption	: 39.4 / 38.3 mpg
acc. 0-62 mph	: 13.4 / 12.6 s
top speed	: 108 / 113 mph
EuroNCAP	: 5 stars
introduction	: June 2002
last revised in	: -
warranty	: 2 years
miscellaneous	: MPV with style, grace and space. Far more stylish than C8, 807 and Ulysse sister models.

LAND ROVER FREELANDER I6

engine type	: petrol, inline-6
displacement	: 3192 cc
max. power	: 171 kW (233 bhp)
@	: 6300 rpm
max. torque	: 234 lb ft
@	: 3200 rpm
gears	: -
AT	: 6-speed
drive	: 4WD
brakes f/r	: vent. discs
body type	: 5-dr. SUV
l x w x h	: 4500 x 1910 x 1740 mm
wheelbase	: 2660 mm
turning circle	: n.a.

kerb weight	: 1770 kg
towing weight	: 2000 kg
boot space	: 755 l
fuel capacity	: 59 l
consumption	: 25.2 mpg
acc. 0-62 mph	: 8.9 s
top speed	: 124 mph
EuroNCAP	: 5 stars
introduction	: December 2006
last revised in	: -
warranty	: 3 years
miscellaneous	: New Freelander is more of a sports utility vehicle than off-roader. Quality is on a higher level now, but so is the price.

FREELANDER 2.2 TD4

engine type	: diesel, inline-4
displacement	: 2179 cc
max. power	: 118 kW (160 bhp)
@	: 4000 rpm
max. torque	: 295 lb ft
@	: 2000 rpm
gears	: 6, optional 6-speed automatic
kerb weight	: 1770 kg
towing weight	: 2000 kg
consumption	: 37.7 mpg
acc. 0-60 mph	: 11.7 s
top speed	: 112 mph
miscellaneous	: Specifications apply to the diesel engine without the optional particle filter. The cleaner diesel version delivers 152 bhp.

LAND ROVER DEFENDER 90 / 110

engine type	: diesel, inline-4	kerb weight	: 1638 / 2055 kg
displacement	: 2402 cc	towing weight	: 3500 kg
max. power	: 90 kW (122 bhp)	boot space	: n.a.
@	: 3500 rpm	fuel capacity	: 93 l
max. torque	: 266 lb ft	consumption	: 28.3 / 25.7 mpg
@	: 2000 rpm	acc. 0-62 mph	: 15.8 s
gears	: 6	top speed	: 82 mph
AT	: -	EuroNCAP	: n.a.
drive	: 4WD	introduction	: January 1991
brakes f/r	: vent. discs / discs	last revised in	: January 2007
body type	: 3-dr. / 5-dr. SUV	warranty	: 3 years
l x w x h	: 3922 / 4599 x 1790 x 1980 mm	miscellaneous	: Old-school diesel-powered off-roader still going strong. Outdated in terms of safety equipment and build quality, but still very capable off-road.
wheelbase	: 2360 / 2794 mm		
turning circle	: 11.7 m		

LAND ROVER DISCOVERY TDV6 / V8

engine type	: diesel, V6 / petrol, V8	kerb weight	: 2394 / 2436 kg
displacement	: 2720 / 4394 cc	towing weight	: 3500 kg
max. power	: 140 kW (190 bhp) /	boot space	: 280 - 2558 l
	220 kW (300 bhp)	fuel capacity	: 82 / 86 l
@	: 4000 / 5500 rpm	consumption	: 30.1 / 18.8 mpg
max. torque	: 324 / 314 lb ft	acc. 0-62 mph	: 11.5 / 8.6 s
@	: 1900 / 4000 rpm	top speed	: 112 / 121 mph
gears	: 6	EuroNCAP	: n.a.
AT	: optional 6-speed / 6-speed	introduction	: May 2004
drive	: 4WD	last revised in	: -
brakes f/r	: vent. discs/ discs	warranty	: 3 years
body type	: 5-dr. SUV	miscellaneous	: Multi-talent. Unsurpassed offroad
l x w x h	: 4835 x 2190 x 1887 mm		performance, but onroad driving
wheelbase	: 2885 mm		characteristics fine too. Fresh,
turning circle	: 11.5 m		modern looks.

LAND ROVER RANGE ROVER SPORT V8 SUPERCHARGED

engine type	: petrol, V8	kerb weight	: 2572 kg
displacement	: 4197 cc	towing weight	: 3500 kg
max. power	: 287 kW (385 bhp)	boot space	: 960 l
@	: 5750 rpm	fuel capacity	: 84 l
max. torque	: 405 lb ft	consumption	: 17.8 mpg
@	: 3500 rpm	acc. 0-62 mph	: 7.2 s
gears	: -	top speed	: 140 mph
AT	: 6-speed	EuroNCAP	: -
drive	: 4WD	introduction	: March 2005
brakes f/r	: vent. discs	last revised in	: -
body type	: 5-dr. SUV	warranty	: 3 years
l x w x h	: 4788 x 1928 x 1817	miscellaneous	: The RR Sport is based on the
wheelbase	: 2745 mm		Discovery, not on the Range Rover.
turning circle	: 11.6 m		It can also be equipped with the
			4.4 V8 engine, as specified under
			the Discovery entry.

RANGE ROVER SPORT TDV6 / TDV8

engine type	: diesel, V6 / V8
displacement	: 2720 / 3630 cc
max. power	: 140 kW (188 bhp) /
	200 kW (268 bhp)
@	: 4000 rpm
max. torque	: 324 / 472 lb ft
@	: 1900 / 2000 rpm
gears	: 6-speed automatic
kerb weight	: 2455 / 2575 kg
towing weight	: 3500 kg
consumption	: 28.3 / 25.5 mpg
acc. 0-60 mph	: 12.7 / 9.2 s
top speed	: 120 / 130 mph
miscellaneous	: The new V8 diesel engine is now
	also available in the Range Rover
	Sport.

LAND ROVER RANGE ROVER V8 SUPERCHARGED

engine type	: petrol, V8	kerb weight	: 2450 / 2522 kg
displacement	: 4196 cc	towing weight	: 3500 kg
max. power	: 291 kW (396 bhp)	boot space	: 535 l
@	: 5750 rpm	fuel capacity	: 100 l
max. torque	: 413 lb ft	consumption	: 17.7 mpg
@	: 4000 rpm	acc. 0-62 mph	: 7.5 s
gears	: -	top speed	: 130 mph
AT	: 5-speed	EuroNCAP	: 4 stars
drive	: 4WD	introduction	: December 2002
brakes f/r	: vent. discs	last revised in	: December 2005
body type	: 5-dr. SUV	warranty	: 3 years
l x w x h	: 4950 x 1960 x 1820 mm	miscellaneous	: A majestic car as ever, but a suc-
wheelbase	: 2880 mm		cessor is at hand. It is likely that
turning circle	: 11.6 m		the new model will be consider-
			ably lighter.

RANGE ROVER TDV8

engine type	: diesel, V8
displacement	: 3630 cc
max. power	: 200 kW (271 bhp)
@	: 4000 rpm
max. torque	: 472 lb ft
@	: 2000 rpm
gears	: 5-speed automatic
kerb weight	: 2450 kg
towing weight	: 3500 kg
consumption	: 25.5 mpg
acc. 0-60 mph	: 9.2 s
top speed	: 124 mph
miscellaneous	: The Range Rover programme includes special variations such as an armour-plated version and the Autobiography model which can be tailored to your exacting demands.

LEXUS IS 250

engine type	: petrol, V6	kerb weight	: 1570 kg
displacement	: 2500 cc	towing weight	: 1500 kg
max. power	: 153 kW (208 bhp)	boot space	: 378 l
@	: 6400 rpm	fuel capacity	: 65 l
max. torque	: 186 lb ft	consumption	: 28.8 mpg
@	: 4800 rpm	acc. 0-62 mph	: 8.1 s
gears	: 6	top speed	: 144 mph
AT	: optional 6-speed	EuroNCAP	: n.a.
drive	: RWD	introduction	: December 2005
brakes f/r	: vent. discs/ discs	last revised in	: -
body type	: 4-dr. saloon	warranty	: 3 years
l x w x h	: 4575 x 1800 x 1440 mm	miscellaneous	: Lexus is obviously looking to
wheelbase	: 2730 mm		introduce a family look for its
turning circle	: 10.2 m		models, for car resembles new GS
			model. Smallest Lexus to compete
			with 3-series, A4 and C-class.
			More engines on their way.

IS 220D

engine type	: diesel, inline-4
displacement	: 2231 cc
max. power	: 130 kW (177 bhp)
@	: 3600 rpm
max. torque	: 295 lb ft
@	: 2000 rpm
gears	: 6
kerb weight	: 1585 kg
towing weight	: 1500 kg
consumption	: 44.8 mpg
acc. 0-60 mph	: 8.9 s
top speed	: 134 mph
miscellaneous	: Serious competition for established European contenders. Lovely diesel engine, ecological too.

LEXUS GS 300 / GS 400H

engine type	: petrol, V6	kerb weight	: 1695 / 1865 kg
displacement	: 2995 / 3456 cc	towing weight	: 2000 kg
max. power	: 183 kW (249 bhp) /	boot space	: 430 l
	218 kW (296 bhp)	fuel capacity	: 71 / 65 l
@	: 6200 / 6400 rpm	consumption	: 28.8 / 35.8 mpg
max. torque	: 228 / 272 lb ft	acc. 0-62 mph	: 7.2 / 5.9 s
@	: 3500 / 4800 rpm	top speed	: 148 / 155 mph
gears	: -	EuroNCAP	: 5 stars
AT	: 6-speed	introduction	: February 2005
drive	: RWD	last revised in	: -
brakes f/r	: vent. discs	warranty	: 3 years
body type	: 4-dr. saloon	miscellaneous	: GS 430 was replaced by hybrid
l x w x h	: 4820 x 1820 x 1425 mm		GS 450h. V8 power available by
wheelbase	: 2850 mm		special order.
turning circle	: 10.4 m		

LEXUS LS 460 / 600H

engine type	: petrol, V8		kerb weight	: 1945 / 2270 kg
displacement	: 4608 / 4969 cc		towing weight	: 2000 kg / -
max. power	: 280 kW (375 bhp) /		boot space	: 510 / 330 l
	290 kW (389 bhp)		fuel capacity	: 84 l
@	: 6400 rpm		consumption	: 25.4 / 30.4 mpg
max. torque	: 363 / 384 lb ft		acc. 0-62 mph	: 5.7 / 6.3 s
@	: 4100 / 4000 rpm		top speed	: 155 mph
gears	: -		EuroNCAP	: n.a.
AT	: 8-speed / CVT		introduction	: September 2006
drive	: RWD / 4WD		last revised in	: -
brakes f/r	: vent. discs		warranty	: 3 years
body type	: 4-dr. saloon		miscellaneous	: Extremely capable toplimo. Hybrid
l x w x h	: 5030 x 1875 x 1465 mm			LS 600h is unique in this high
wheelbase	: 2970 mm			segment of the car market. Model
turning circle	: 10.8 m			range includes a long-wheelbase
				version.

LEXUS SC 430

engine type	: petrol, V8	kerb weight	: 1740 kg
displacement	: 4293 cc	towing weight	: -
max. power	: 210 kW (286 bhp)	boot space	: 135 - 450 l
@	: 5600 rpm	fuel capacity	: 75 l
max. torque	: 309 lb ft	consumption	: 23.6 mpg
@	: 3500 rpm	acc. 0-62 mph	: 6.4 s
gears	: -	top speed	: 155 mph
AT	: 5-speed	EuroNCAP	: n.a.
drive	: RWD	introduction	: June 2001
brakes f/r	: vent. discs	last revised in	: November 2005
body type	: 2-dr. coupe, cabriolet	warranty	: 3 years
l x w x h	: 4515 x 1830 x 1370 mm	miscellaneous	: Fast, elegant car, particularly
wheelbase	: 2620 mm		successful in the United States.
turning circle	: 10.8 m		Build quality and hardtop beyond
			reproach.

LEXUS RX 350

engine type	: petrol, V6	**kerb weight**	: 1810 kg
displacement	: 3456 cc	**towing weight**	: 2000 kg
max. power	: 203 kW (276 bhp)	**boot space**	: 490 - 2130 l
@	: 6200 rpm	**fuel capacity**	: 75 l
max. torque	: 252 lb ft	**consumption**	: 25.2 mpg
@	: 4700 rpm	**acc. 0-62 mph**	: 7.8 s
gears	: -	**top speed**	: 124 mph
AT	: 5-speed	**EuroNCAP**	: n.a.
drive	: 4WD	**introduction**	: October 2000
brakes f/r	: vent. discs / discs	**last revised in**	: February 2003
body type	: 5-dr. SUV	**warranty**	: 3 years
l x w x h	: 4740 x 1845 x 1660 mm	**miscellaneous**	: With a more powerful and more economical new engine under the bonnet, the RX 350 is still only slightly cheaper than the more modern RX 400h.
wheelbase	: 2715 mm		
turning circle	: 12.2 m		

RX 400H

engine type	: petrol, V6 + two electrical engines
displacement	: 3311 cc
max. power	: 155 kW (211 bhp)
@	: 5600 rpm
max. torque	: 212 lb ft
@	: 4400 rpm
gears	: CVT
kerb weight	: 2000 kg
towing weight	: 2000 kg
consumption	: 34.9 mpg
acc. 0-60 mph	: 7.6 s
top speed	: 124 mph
miscellaneous	: Combined peak power of petrol engine and twin electric motors is 272 bhp. Not bad. Environmentally friendly model, with fuel consumption of an average middle-class car.

LOTUS ELISE S / R

engine type	: petrol, inline-4		kerb weight	: 860 kg
displacement	: 1796 cc		towing weight	: -
max. power	: 100 kW (136 bhp) /		boot space	: 112 l
	141 kW (192 bhp)		fuel capacity	: 38 l
@	: 6200 / 7800 rpm		consumption	: 34 / 32.1 mpg
max. torque	: 127 / 133 lb ft		acc. 0-62 mph	: 6.1 / 5.2 s
@	: 4200 / 6800 rpm		top speed	: 127 / 147 mph
gears	: 5		EuroNCAP	: n.a.
AT	: -		introduction	: October 1997
drive	: RWD		last revised in	: July 2004
brakes f/r	: vent. discs		warranty	: 2 years
body type	: 2-dr. convertible		miscellaneous	: S model is new entry level Lotus.
l x w x h	: 3785 x 1719 x 1143 mm			Just as quick as R model, but less
wheelbase	: 2301 mm			hot-blooded and less expensive.
turning circle	: 10.5 m			

LOTUS EXIGE / EXIGE S

engine type	: petrol, inline-4		**kerb weight**	: 875 / 935 kg
displacement	: 1796 cc		**towing weight**	: -
max. power	: 141 kW (192 bhp) /		**boot space**	: 112 l
	163 kW (221 bhp)		**fuel capacity**	: 40 l
@	: 7800 rpm		**consumption**	: 32.1 / 31 mpg
max. torque	:133 /158 lb ft		**acc. 0-62 mph**	: 5.2 / 4.3 s
@	: 6800 / 5500 rpm		**top speed**	: 147 / 148 mph
gears	: 6		**EuroNCAP**	: n.a.
AT	: -		**introduction**	: February 2005
drive	: RWD		**last revised in**	: -
brakes f/r	: vent. discs		**warranty**	: 2 years
body type	: 2-dr. coupe		**miscellaneous**	: Make no mistake: 'S' denotes
l x w x h	: 3797 x 1727 x 1163 mm			hottest Exige instead of entry
wheelbase	: 2301 mm			level version. A real street racer.
turning circle	: 10.5 m			

LOTUS EUROPA S

engine type	: petrol, inline-4	**kerb weight**	: 995 kg
displacement	: 1998 cc	**towing weight**	: -
max. power	: 147 kW (200 bhp)	**boot space**	: 154 l
@	: 5400 rpm	**fuel capacity**	: 43.5 l
max. torque	: 194 lb ft	**consumption**	: 30.4 mpg
@	: 5000 rpm	**acc. 0-62 mph**	: 5.8 s
gears	: 6	**top speed**	: 140 mph
AT	: -	**EuroNCAP**	: n.a.
drive	: RWD	**introduction**	: July 2006
brakes f/r	: vent. discs	**last revised in**	: -
body type	: 2-dr. coupe	**warranty**	: 2 years
l x w x h	: 3900 x 1714 x 1120 mm	**miscellaneous**	: Softer Lotus, aimed at drivers
wheelbase	: 2330 mm		who value comfort over
turning circle	: n.a.		performance.

MASERATI GRANTURISMO

engine type	: petrol, V8	kerb weight	: 1780 kg
displacement	: 4244 cc	towing weight	: -
max. power	: 298 kW (405 bhp)	boot space	: n.a.
@	: 7100 rpm	fuel capacity	: n.a.
max. torque	: 339 lb ft	consumption	: 19.7 mpg
@	: 4750 rpm	acc. 0-62 mph	: 5.2 s
gears	: -	top speed	: 177 mph
AT	: 6-speed automatic	EuroNCAP	: n.a.
drive	: RWD	introduction	: July 2007
brakes f/r	: vent. discs	last revised in	: -
body type	: 2-dr. coupe	warranty	: 3 years
l x w x h	: 4881 x 1847 x 1353 mm	miscellaneous	: A beautiful car, but not really
wheelbase	: 2942 mm		a direct successor to the Coupé.
turning circle	: n.a.		Newest 'Maser' intended for grand
			touring instead of racing.
			Hence the name.

MASERATI QUATTROPORTE

engine type	: petrol, V8	kerb weight	: 1930 kg
displacement	: 4244 cc	towing weight	: -
max. power	: 294 kW (400 bhp)	boot space	: 450 l
@	: 7000 rpm	fuel capacity	: 90 l
max. torque	: 333 lb ft	consumption	: 15 mpg
@	: 4500 rpm	acc. 0-62 mph	: 5.2 s
gears	: -	top speed	: 167 mph
AT	: seq. gearbox	EuroNCAP	: n.a.
drive	: RWD	introduction	: September 2003
brakes f/r	: vent. discs	last revised in	: -
body type	: 4-dr. saloon	warranty	: 3 years
l x w x h	: 5052 x 1895 x 1438 mm	miscellaneous	: Gorgeous looking car, and even
wheelbase	: 3064 mm		more fabulous to drive. Even
turning circle	: 12.3 m		though it has four doors, Italian
			flair doesn't come any better
			than this!

MAYBACH 57 / 57 S

engine type	: petrol, V12	**kerb weight**	: 2660 kg
displacement	: 5513 / 5980 cc	**towing weight**	: -
max. power	: 405 kW (550 bhp) /	**boot space**	: 605 l
	450 kW (612 bhp)	**fuel capacity**	: 110 l
@	: 5250 / 4800 rpm	**consumption**	: 17.8 / 17.2 mpg
max. torque	: 664 / 737 lb ft	**acc. 0-62 mph**	: 5.2 / 5.0 s
@	: 2300 / 2000 rpm	**top speed**	: 155 / 171 mph
gears	: -	**EuroNCAP**	: n.a.
AT	: 5-speed	**introduction**	: March 2002
drive	: RWD	**last revised in**	: -
brakes f/r	: vent. discs	**warranty**	: 4 years
body type	: 4-dr. saloon	**miscellaneous**	: Attempt by Mercedes to revive this
l x w x h	: 5728 x 1980 x 1572 mm		noble German brand. The already
wheelbase	: 3390 mm		huge limo is also available in 62
turning circle	: 13.4 m		and 62 S form with an even
			longer wheelbase of 3827 mm.

MAZDA 2 1.3 / 1.3 HP

engine type	: petrol, inline-4	**kerb weight**	: 955 kg
displacement	: 1348 cc	**towing weight**	: 900 kg
max. power	: 55 kW (75 bhp) / 63 kW (86 bhp)	**boot space**	: 250 l
@	: 6000 rpm	**fuel capacity**	: 43 l
max. torque	: 90 lb ft	**consumption**	: 52.3 mpg
@	: 3500 rpm	**acc. 0-62 mph**	: 14.0 / 12.9 s
gears	: 5	**top speed**	: 104 / 107 mph
AT	: -	**EuroNCAP**	: n.a.
drive	: FWD	**introduction**	: January 2008
brakes f/r	: vent. discs / discs	**last revised in**	: -
body type	: 5-dr. hatchback	**warranty**	: 3 years
l x w x h	: 3900 x 1695 x 1475 mm	**miscellaneous**	: Mazda opted for a conventional
wheelbase	: 2490 mm		small hatchback as a successor
turning circle	: 9.8 m		to the MPV-like Mazda2.

2 1.5

engine type	: petrol, inline-4
displacement	: 1498 cc
max. power	: 76 kW (103 bhp)
@	: 6000 rpm
max. torque	: 101 lb ft
@	: 4000 rpm
gears	: 5
kerb weight	: 960 kg
towing weight	: 900 kg
consumption	: 47.9 mpg
acc. 0-60 mph	: 10.4 s
top speed	: 117 mph
miscellaneous	: A Mazda2 with CiTD diesel
	power will enter the stage soon.

MAZDA 3 HATCHBACK 1.4 / 1.6

engine type	: petrol, inline-4
displacement	: 1349 / 1598 cc
max. power	: 62 kW (84 bhp) / 77 kW (105 bhp)
@	: 6000 rpm
max. torque	: 90 / 107 mph
@	: 4000 rpm
gears	: 5
AT	: - / optional 4-speed
drive	: FWD
brakes f/r	: vent. discs / discs
body type	: 5-dr. hatchback
l x w x h	: 4420 x 1755 x 1465 mm
wheelbase	: 2640 mm
turning circle	: 10.4 m

kerb weight	: 1165 kg
towing weight	: 900 / 1200 kg
boot space	: 346 l
fuel capacity	: 55 l
consumption	: 42.2 / 40.9 mpg
acc. 0-62 mph	: 14.9 / 11.0 s
top speed	: 106 / 114 mph
EuroNCAP	: n.a.
introduction	: September 2003
last revised in	: September 2006
warranty	: 3 years
miscellaneous	: Still one of the cleanest proposi-tions in this class. Refer to the saloon model for other engine types.

3 MPS

engine type	: petrol, inline-4
displacement	: 2261 cc
max. power	: 190 kW (265 bhp)
@	: 5500 rpm
max. torque	: 280 lb ft
@	: 3000 rpm
gears	: 6
kerb weight	: 1385 kg
towing weight	: -
consumption	: 29.1 mpg
acc. 0-60 mph	: 6.1 s
top speed	: 155 mph
miscellaneous	: Identical underneath to the Mazda6 MPS, but without the four-wheel drive. A limited-slip differential assists the front wheels in getting the power on the tarmac.

MAZDA 3 SALOON 2.0

engine type	: petrol, inline-4	kerb weight	: 1220 kg
displacement	: 1999 cc	towing weight	: 1300 kg
max. power	: 110 kW (150 bhp)	boot space	: 413 l
@	: 6500 rpm	fuel capacity	: 55 l
max. torque	: 138 lb ft	consumption	: 35.8 mpg
@	: 4000 rpm	acc. 0-62 mph	: 9.1 s
gears	: 5	top speed	: 130 mph
AT	: -	EuroNCAP	: n.a.
drive	: FWD	introduction	: September 2003
brakes f/r	: vent. discs / discs	last revised in	: September 2006
body type	: 4-dr. saloon	warranty	: 3 years
l x w x h	: 4490 x 1755 x 1465 mm	miscellaneous	: Not as popular as the Mazda3
wheelbase	: 2640 mm		Hatchback. Also available with the
turning circle	: 10.9 m		1.6 unit as described under that
			entry.

3 SALOON 1.6 CITD / 2.0 CITD

engine type	: diesel, inline-4
displacement	: 1560 / 1998 cc
max. power	: 80 kW (109 bhp) / 105 kW (143 bhp)
@	: 4000 / 3500 rpm
max. torque	: 177 / 266 lb ft
@	: 1750 / 2000 rpm
gears	: 5 / 6
kerb weight	: 1235 / 1370 kg
towing weight	: 1300 / 1500 kg
consumption	: 58.9 / 47.1 mpg
acc. 0-60 mph	: 11.5 / 9.9 s
top speed	: 115 / 126 mph
miscellaneous	: The 2.0 CiTD is new for the Mazda3.

MAZDA6 1.8 / 2.0

engine type	: petrol, inline-4
displacement	: 1798 / 1999 cc
max. power	: 88 kW (120 bhp) / 108 kW (147 bhp)
@	: 5500 / 6500 rpm
max. torque	: 122 / 136 lb ft
@	: 4300 / 4000 rpm
gears	: 5 / 6
AT	: - / optional 5-speed
drive	: FWD
brakes f/r	: vent. discs / discs
body type	: 4-dr. saloon
l x w x h	: 4735 x 1975 x 1440 mm
wheelbase	: 2725 mm
turning circle	: n.a.

kerb weight	: n.a.
towing weight	: n.a.
boot space	: n.a.
fuel capacity	: n.a.
consumption	: 41.5 / 40.4 mpg
acc. 0-62 mph	: n.a.
top speed	: 124 / 133 mph
EuroNCAP	: n.a.
introduction	: January 2008
last revised in	: -
warranty	: 3 years
miscellaneous	: Mazda kicks off with a totally new 6. The preliminary data refer to the four-door version, but the model range includes a hatchback and stationwagon (called SportBreak).

MAZDA6 2.5 / 2.0 CITD

engine type	: petrol / diesel, inline-4
displacement	: 2488 / 1998 cc
max. power	: 125 kW (170 bhp) / 103 kW (138 bhp)
@	: 6000 / 3500 rpm
max. torque	: 167 / 243 lb ft
@	: 4000 / 2000 rpm
gears	: 6
kerb weight	: n.a.
towing weight	: n.a.
consumption	: 34.9 / 50.4 mpg
acc. 0-60 mph	: n.a.
top speed	: 137 / 127 mph
miscellaneous	: The new 2.5 unit was developed from the 2.3 engine in the previous model. The faster MPS version will follow soon.

MAZDA 5 1.8 / 2.0

engine type	: petrol, inline-4	kerb weight	: 1370 / 1375 kg
displacement	: 1798 / 1999 cc	towing weight	: 1300 / 1400 kg
max. power	: 85 kW (115 bhp) /	boot space	: 112 l
	107 kW (145 bhp)	fuel capacity	: 60 l
@	: 5300 / 6000 rpm	consumption	: 35.8 / 34.5 mpg
max. torque	: 122 / 136 lb ft	acc. 0-62 mph	: 11.4 / 10.8 s
@	: 4000 / 4500 rpm	top speed	: 113 / 122 mph
gears	: 5	EuroNCAP	: 5 stars
AT	: -	introduction	: February 2005
drive	: FWD	last revised in	: -
brakes f/r	: vent. discs / discs	warranty	: 3 years
body type	: 5-dr. MPV	miscellaneous	: Sharp, mid-sized people carrier
l x w x h	: 4505 x 1755 x 1665 mm		with stowable seats in the third
wheelbase	: 2750		row.
turning circle	: 11.2 m		Reasonably quick with 2.0 engine.

5 2.0 CITD

engine type	: diesel, inline-4
displacement	: 1998 cc
max. power	: 81 kW (110 bhp) /
	105 kW (143 bhp)
@	: 3500 rpm
max. torque	: 228 / 266 lb ft
@	: 2000 rpm
gears	: 6
kerb weight	: 1510 kg
towing weight	: 1400 kg
consumption	: 44.9 / 44.9 mpg
acc. 0-60 mph	: 12.9 / 10.4 s
top speed	: 111 / 122 mph
miscellaneous	: Sales of Mazda 5 took off with
	introduction of diesel-powered
	version. Good match.

MAZDA MX-5 1.8 / 2.0

engine type	: petrol, inline-4
displacement	: 1798 / 1999 cc
max. power	: 93 kW (126 bhp) / 118 kW (160 bhp)
@	: 6500 rpm
max. torque	: 123 / 138 lb ft
@	: 4500 / 5000 rpm
gears	: 5
AT	: -
drive	: RWD
brakes f/r	: vent. discs / discs
body type	: 2-dr. convertible
l x w x h	: 3995 x 1720 x 1245 mm
wheelbase	: 2330 mm
turning circle	: 9.8 m

kerb weight	: 1055 / 1070 kg
towing weight	: -
boot space	: 150 l
fuel capacity	: 50 l
consumption	: 38.7 / 34.5 mpg
acc. 0-62 mph	: 9.4 / 7.9 s
top speed	: 122 / 131 mph
EuroNCAP	: n.a.
introduction	: March 2006
last revised in	: -
warranty	: 3 years
miscellaneous	: Third generation of very successful convertible. Still a real driver's car, now also available with a retractable hardtop roof. Manual 6-speed gearbox is an option in biggest version.

MAZDA RX-8 RENESIS / RENESIS HP

engine type	: petrol, birotary engine	kerb weight	: 1394 / 1390 kg
displacement	: 2 x 645 cc	towing weight	: 1200 kg
max. power	: 141 kW (192 bhp) /	boot space	: 250 l
	179 kW (231 bhp)	fuel capacity	: 61 l
@	: 7000 / 8200 rpm	consumption	: 26.7 / 25.2 mpg
max. torque	: 162 /155 lb ft	acc. 0-62 mph	: 7.2 / 6.4 s
@	: 5000 / 5500 rpm	top speed	: 139 /146 mph
gears	: 6	EuroNCAP	: n.a.
AT	: optional seq. gearbox,	introduction	: February 2003
	seq. gearbox	last revised in	: -
drive	: RWD	warranty	: 3 years
brakes f/r	: vent. discs	miscellaneous	: Unique model because of rotary
body type	: 4-dr. coupe		engine and rear 'suicide' doors.
l x w x h	: 4330 x 1770 x 1340 mm		Lovely, high-revving machine.
wheelbase	: 2700 mm		
turning circle	: 10.6 m		

MAZDA CX-7

engine type	: petrol, inline-4	kerb weight	: 1700 kg
displacement	: 2261 cc	towing weight	: -
max. power	: 191 kW (260 bhp)	boot space	: 845 l
@	: 5500 rpm	fuel capacity	: 69 l
max. torque	: 280 lb ft	consumption	: 27.7 mpg
@	: 3000 rpm	acc. 0-62 mph	: 7.9 s
gears	: 6	top speed	: 130 mph
AT	: -	EuroNCAP	: n.a.
drive	: 4WD	introduction	: August 2007
brakes f/r	: vent. discs / discs	last revised in	: -
body type	: 5-dr. SUV	warranty	: 3 years
l x w x h	: 4675 x 1872 x 1645 mm	miscellaneous	: Mazda's CX-7 truly lives up to
wheelbase	: 2750 mm		the 'sports' element in the 'SUV'
turning circle	: 11.4 m		abbreviation. A diesel version will
			be launched later in 2008.

MERCEDES-BENZ A 150 / A 170

engine type	: petrol, inline-4
displacement	: 1498 / 1699 cc
max. power	: 70 kW (95 bhp) / 85 kW (116 bhp)
@	: 5200 / 5500 rpm
max. torque	: 104 / 114 lb ft
@	: 3500 rpm
gears	: 5
AT	: optional, CVT
drive	: FWD
brakes f/r	: vent. discs / discs
body type	: 3- , 5-dr. hatchback
l x w x h	: 3838 x1764 x 1593 mm
wheelbase	: 2568 mm
turning circle	: 10.9 m

kerb weight	: 1095 / 1110 kg
towing weight	: 1000 / 1300 kg
boot space	: 435 -1370 l
fuel capacity	: 54 l
consumption	: 45.6 / 42.8 mpg
acc. 0-62 mph	: 12.6 / 10.9 s
top speed	: 109 / 117 mph
EuroNCAP	: 5 stars
introduction	: July 2004
last revised in	: -
warranty	: 2 years
miscellaneous	: Smallest Merc, but with ample interior space due to its clever platform. Original, modern looks, especially in 3-door form.

A 200 / A 200 TURBO

engine type	: petrol, inline-4
displacement	: 2034 cc
max. power	: 100 kW (136 bhp) / 142 kW (192 bhp)
@	: 5750 / 5000 rpm
max. torque	: 124 / 141 mph
@	: 3500 / 1800 rpm
gears	: 5 / 6
kerb weight	: 1140 / 1175 kg
towing weight	: 1500 kg
consumption	: 39.2 / 34.9 mpg
acc. 0-60 mph	: 9.8 / 7.5 s
top speed	: 124 / 141 mph
miscellaneous	: All petrol engines also available in B-class.

MERCEDES-BENZ B 180 CDI / B 200 CDI

engine type	: diesel, inline-4	kerb weight	: 1335 kg
displacement	: 1991 cc	towing weight	: 1500 kg
max. power	: 80 kW (109 bhp) /	boot space	: 544 - 2245 l
	103 kW (140 bhp)	fuel capacity	: 54 l
@	: 4200 rpm	consumption	: 50.4 / 50.4 mpg
max. torque	: 184 /221 lb ft	acc. 0-62 mph	: 11.3 / 9.6 s
@	: 1600 rpm	top speed	: 114 / 124 mph
gears	: 6	EuroNCAP	: -
AT	: optional, CVT	introduction	: March 2005
drive	: RWD	last revised in	: -
brakes f/r	: vent. discs / discs	warranty	: 2 years
body type	: 5-dr. hatchback	miscellaneous	: 82 bhp 160 CDI engine from
l x w x h	: 4270 x 1777 x 1603 mm		A-class not available in B-class,
wheelbase	: 2778 mm		but B 150, B 170, B 200 and B 200
turning circle	: 12.0 m		Turbo engines are.

MERCEDES-BENZ C 180 K SPORTCOUPÉ / C 200 K SPORTCOUPÉ

engine type	: petrol, inline-4
displacement	: 1796 cc
max. power	: 105 kW (143 bhp) /
	120 kW (163 bhp)
@	: 5200 / 5500 rpm
max. torque	: 162 / 177 lb ft
@	: 2500 / 3000 rpm
gears	: 6
AT	: optional, 5-speed
drive	: FWD
brakes f/r	: vent. discs / discs
body type	: 3-dr. hatchback
l x w x h	: 4343 x 1728 x 1406 mm
wheelbase	: 2715 mm
turning circle	: 10.7 m

kerb weight	: 1365 kg
towing weight	: 1500 kg
boot space	: 310 - 1100 l
fuel capacity	: 62 l
consumption	: 37.2 / 35.3 mpg
acc. 0-62 mph	: 9.7 / 9.1 s
top speed	: 139 / 145 mph
EuroNCAP	: 5 stars
introduction	: October 2000
last revised in	: February 2004
warranty	: 2 years
miscellaneous	: Smallest Benz with rear-wheel drive, competes with BMW 1-series and Audi A3. Twinpulse 1.8 also available as C 160 with 122 bhp.

C 230 / C 350 SPORTCOUPÉ

engine type	: petrol, V6
displacement	: 2496 / 3498 cc
max. power	: 150 kW (204 bhp) /
	200 kW (272 bhp)
@	: 6100 / 6000 rpm
max. torque	:180 / 258 lb ft
@	: 2900 / 2400 rpm
gears	: 6
kerb weight	: 1415 / 1440 kg
towing weight	: 1500 kg
consumption	: 30.4 / 29.1 mpg
acc. 0-60 mph	: 8.4 / 6.4 s
top speed	: 150 / 155 mph
miscellaneous	: Two brand-new V6 engines that perform well, particularly in combination with the 7-speed auto box.

C 200 CDI / C 220 CDI SPORTCOUPÉ

engine type	: diesel, inline-4
displacement	: 2148 cc
max. power	: 90 kW (122 bhp) /
	110 kW (150 bhp)
@	: 4200 rpm
max. torque	: 199 / 250 lb ft
@	: 1600 / 2000 rpm
gears	: 6
kerb weight	: 1390 / 1405 kg
towing weight	: 1500 / 1200 kg
consumption	: 43.5 / 42.8 mpg
acc. 0-60 mph	: 11.7 / 10.3 s
top speed	: 129 / 139 mph
miscellaneous	: 200 and 220 share the same engine, but they differ in horsepower. Their performance is more than adequate.

MERCEDES-BENZ C 180 K / C 200 K

engine type	: petrol, inline-4
displacement	: 1796 cc
max. power	: 115 kW (156 bhp) / 135 kW (184 bhp)
@	: 5200 / 5500 rpm
max. torque	: 170 / 184 lb ft
@	: 2500 / 2800 rpm
gears	: 6
AT	: optional 5-speed
drive	: RWD
brakes f/r	: vent. discs / discs
body type	: 4-dr. sedan
l x w x h	: 4581 x 1770 x 1447 mm
wheelbase	: 2760 mm
turning circle	: 10.8 m

kerb weight	: 1485 / 1490 kg
towing weight	: 1800 kg
boot space	: 475 l
fuel capacity	: 66 l
consumption	: 37.2 / 35.8 mpg
acc. 0-62 mph	: 9.6 / 8.6 s
top speed	: 138 / 146 mph
EuroNCAP	: n.a.
introduction	: March 2007
last revised in	: -
warranty	: 2 years
miscellaneous	: The Avantgarde is the sportier version and a popular alternative to a BMW 3-series. Refer to the Estate for diesel power.

MERCEDES-BENZ C 230 / C 280

engine type	: petrol, V6
displacement	: 2496 / 2996 cc
max. power	: 150 kW (204 bhp) / 170 kW (231 bhp)
@	: 6100 / 6000 rpm
max. torque	: 180 / 222 lb ft
@	: 2900 / 2500 rpm
gears	: 6 / 7-speed automatic
kerb weight	: 1540 / 1555 kg
towing weight	: 1800 kg
consumption	: 31.0 / 30.7 mpg
acc. 0-60 mph	: 8.5 / 7.5 s
top speed	: 149 / 152 mph
miscellaneous	: The third V6-powered model in the line-up is the C 350 with 272 bhp. The range also includes a 457 bhp strong C 63 AMG.

MERCEDES-BENZ C 200 CDI / C 220 CDI ESTATE

engine type	: diesel, inline-4	kerb weight	: 1485 / 1490 kg
displacement	: 2148 cc	towing weight	: 1800 kg
max. power	: 100 kW (136 bhp) /	boot space	: 485 l
	125 kW (170 bhp)	fuel capacity	: 66 l
@	: 3800 rpm	consumption	: 47.1 / 46.3 mpg
max. torque	: 199 / 295 lb ft	acc. 0-62 mph	: 10.8 / 8.9 s
@	: 1600 / 2000 rpm	top speed	: 129 / 139 mph
gears	: 6	EuroNCAP	: n.a.
AT	: optional 5-speed	introduction	: October 2007
drive	: RWD	last revised in	: -
brakes f/r	: vent. discs / discs	warranty	: 2 years
body type	: 5-dr. stationwagon	miscellaneous	: It stands to reason that a
l x w x h	: 4600 x 1770 x 1447 mm		stationwagon model is included
wheelbase	: 2760 mm		in the new C-class model range.
turning circle	: 10.8 m		

MERCEDES-BENZ C 320 CDI ESTATE

engine type	: diesel, V6
displacement	: 2987 cc
max. power	: 165 kW (224 bhp)
@	: 3800 rpm
max. torque	: 376 Nm
@	: 1600 rpm
gears	: 6, optional 7-speed automatic
kerb weight	: 1540 / 1555 kg
towing weight	: 1800 kg
consumption	: 39.8 mpg
acc. 0-60 mph	: 7.9 s
top speed	: 152 mph
miscellaneous	: Also available with the petrol
	engines listed for the saloon version.

MERCEDES-BENZ E 200 KOMPRESSOR

engine type	: benzine, inline-4
displacement	: 1796 cc
max. power	: 135 kW (184 bhp)
@	: 5500 rpm
max. torque	: 184 lb ft
@	: 3500 rpm
gears	: 6
AT	: optional 5-speed
drive	: RWD
brakes f/r	: vent. discs
body type	: 4-dr. saloon
l x w x h	: 4856 x 1822 x 1483 mm
wheelbase	: 2854 mm
turning circle	: 11.4 m

kerb weight	: 1480 / 1580 kg
towing weight	: 1700 / 1900 kg
boot space	: 540 l
fuel capacity	: 65 l
consumption	: 34.4 mpg
acc. 0-62 mph	: 9.1 s
top speed	: 147 mph
EuroNCAP	: 5 stars
introduction	: February 2002
last revised in	: April 2006
warranty	: 2 years
miscellaneous	: There is also a NGT version of the E 200 model, with an engine that runs on natural gas which is available for the estate model as well. Refer to the estate version for diesel power specifications.

E 280 / E 350

engine type	: petrol, V6
displacement	: 2996 / 3498 cc
max. power	: 170 kW (231 bhp) / 200 kW (272 bhp)
@	: 6000 rpm
max. torque	: 222 / 258 lb ft
@	: 2500 / 2400 rpm
gears	: 7-speed automatic
kerb weight	: 1560 / 1590 kg
towing weight	: 1900 kg
consumption	: 20.5 / 20.2 mpg
acc. 0-60 mph	: 7.3 / 6.9 s
top speed	: 155 mph
miscellaneous	: Specifications of the 500 and 63 AMG model are listed under the CLS entry. Another engine option is the E 420 CDI diesel unit, which can be found under the GL-class heading.

MERCEDES-BENZ E 220 CDI ESTATE

engine type	: diesel, inline-4	kerb weight	: 1785 / 1710 kg
displacement	: 2148 cc	towing weight	: 2100 kg
max. power	: 125 kW (170 pk)	boot space	: 690 l
@	: 3800 rpm	fuel capacity	: 70 l
max. torque	: 295 lb ft	consumption	: 39.8 mpg
@	: 1800 / 2000 rpm	acc. 0-62 mph	: 9.1 s
gears	: 6	top speed	: 135 mph
AT	: optional 5-speed	EuroNCAP	: 5 stars
drive	: RWD	introduction	: February 2002
brakes f/r	: vent. discs / discs	last revised in	: April 2006
body type	: 5-dr. stationwagon	warranty	: 2 years
l x w x h	: 4888 x 1822 x 1506 mm	miscellaneous	: All diesel engines on this page are
wheelbase	: 2854 mm		also available in the E-class
turning circle	: 11.4 m		saloon.

E 280 CDI ESTATE / E 320 CDI ESTATE

engine type	: diesel, V6
displacement	: 2987 cc
max. power	: 140 kW (190 bhp) /
	165 kW (224 bhp)
@	: 4000 / 3800 rpm
max. torque	: 324 / 398 lb ft
@	: 1400 / 1600 rpm
gears	: 7-speed automatic
kerb weight	: 1745 / 1785 kg
towing weight	: 1900 / 2100 kg
consumption	: 37.2 mpg
acc. 0-60 mph	: 8.2 / 7.3 s
top speed	: 143 / 149 mph
miscellaneous	: Not listed: the E 300 Bluetec. This
	version boasts a cleaner diesel
	engine of 210 bhp which complies
	with the EC stage V emission level.
	The engine is the same as the one in
	the E 280 and E 320 CDI.

MERCEDES-BENZ CLS 350 CGI / CLS 500

engine type	: petrol, V6 / V8
displacement	: 3498 / 5461 cc
max. power	: 215 kW (292 bhp) /
	285 kW (388 bhp)
@	: 6400 / 6000 rpm
max. torque	: 269 / 391 lb ft
@	: 3000 / 2800 rpm
gears	: -
AT	: 7-speed automatic
drive	: RWD
brakes f/r	: vent. discs
body type	: 4-dr. saloon
l x w x h	: 4913 x 1873 x 1390 / 1403 mm
wheelbase	: 2854 mm
turning circle	: 11.2 m

kerb weight	: 1635 / 1735 kg
towing weight	: -
boot space	: 505 l
fuel capacity	: 80 l
consumption	: 31.0 / 24.4 mpg
acc. 0-62 mph	: 6.7 / 5.4 s
top speed	: 155 mph
EuroNCAP	: n.a.
introduction	: July 2004
last revised in	: -
warranty	: 2 years
miscellaneous	: Elegant design on an E-class plat-form. There is also a CLS with a 3-litre diesel engine. For specifications, refer to the 320 CDI model of the Mercedes E-class.

CLS 63 AMG

engine type	: petrol, V8
displacement	: 6208 cc
max. power	: 378 kW (514 bhp)
@	: 6800 rpm
max. torque	: 464 lb ft
@	: 5200 rpm
gears	: 7-speed automatic
kerb weight	: 1805 kg
towing weight	: -
consumption	: 19.5 mpg
acc. 0-60 mph	: 4.5 s
top speed	: 155 mph
miscellaneous	: Big, normally aspirated powerhouse from AMG is available in nearly all Mercs, the CLS included.

MERCEDES-BENZ S 280 / 350

engine type	: petrol, V6	kerb weight	: 1780 / 1840 kg
displacement	: 2996 / 3498 cc	towing weight	: 2100 kg
max. power	: 170 kW (231 bhp) /	boot space	: 560 l
	200 kW (272 bhp)	fuel capacity	: 90 l
@	: 6000 rpm	consumption	: 28.5 / 28.0 mpg
max. torque	: 221 / 258 lb ft	acc. 0-62 mph	: 7.3 / 7.2 s
@	: 2500 / 2400 rpm	top speed	: 153 / 155 mph
gears	: -	EuroNCAP	: n.a.
AT	: 7-speed	introduction	: September 2005
drive	: RWD	last revised in	: -
brakes f/r	: vent. discs	warranty	: 2 years
body type	: 4-dr. saloon	miscellaneous	: The drive trains of all the other ver-
l x w x h	: 5076 x 1871 x 1473 mm		sions (S 500, S 600, S 63 AMG, S
wheelbase	: 3035 mm		65 AMG) are identical to those of
turning circle	: 11.8 m		the CL model and therefore listed
			under that heading.

S 320 CDI

engine type	: diesel, V6
displacement	: 2987 cc
max. power	: 173 kW (235 bhp)
@	: 3600 rpm
max. torque	: 398 lb ft
@	: 1600 rpm
gears	: 7-speed automatic
kerb weight	: 1855 / 1990 kg
towing weight	: 2100 kg
consumption	: 34.0 mpg
acc. 0-60 mph	: 7.5 s
top speed	: 155 mph
miscellaneous	: Upon special request, Das Haus will
	build a long-wheelbase version of
	the S-class model. It can also be
	equipped with four-wheel drive,
	should you so desire.

MERCEDES-BENZ R 350

engine type	: petrol, V6
displacement	: 3498 cc
max. power	: 200 kW (272 bhp)
@	: 6000 rpm
max. torque	: 258 lb ft
@	: 2400 rpm
gears	: -
AT	: 7-traps
drive	: RWD
brakes f/r	: vent. discs / discs
body type	: 5-dr. MPV
l x w x h	: 4780 x 1911 x 1779 mm
wheelbase	: 2915 mm
turning circle	: 11.7 m

kerb weight	: 2035 kg
towing weight	: 2100 kg
boot space	: 550 l
fuel capacity	: 80 l
consumption	: 24.8 mpg
acc. 0-62 mph	: 8.1 s
top speed	: 143 mph
EuroNCAP	: n.a.
introduction	: December 2005
last revised in	: June 2007
warranty	: 2 years
miscellaneous	: The R-class received a minor face-lift and was deprived of its 4Matic four-wheel drive system in order to abate its stiff price. Four-wheel drive remains an option however for the R 350 model, which is also available with a longer wheelbase.

R 280 CDI / R 320 CDI

engine type	: diesel, V6
displacement	: 2987 cc
max. power	: 140 kW (190 bhp) / 165 kW (224 bhp)
@	: 4000 / 3800 rpm
max. torque	: 324 / 376 lb fr
@	: 1400 / 1600 rpm
gears	: 7-speed automatic
kerb weight	: 2120 kg
towing weight	: 2100 kg
consumption	: 30.4 mpg
acc. 0-60 mph	: 9.9 / 8.7 s
top speed	: 130 / 134 mph
miscellaneous	: The R 63 AMG has been discontinued. For the specifications of the R 500 model, refer to the ML 500 which is identical from a technical point of view.

MERCEDES-BENZ CLK 200 KOMPRESSOR / CLK 280

engine type	: petrol, inline-4 / V6
displacement	: 1796 cc / 2.996 cc
max. power	: 120 kW (163 bhp) /
	170 kW (231 bhp)
@	: 5500 / 6000 rpm
max. torque	: 177 / 222 lb ft
@	: 3000 / 2500 rpm
gears	: 6
AT	: optional, 5-speed / 7-speed
drive	: RWD
brakes f/r	: vent. discs
body type	: 2-dr. coupe
l x w x h	: 4652 x 1740 x 1413 mm
wheelbase	: 2715 mm
turning circle	: 10.8 m

kerb weight	: 1440 / 1480 kg
towing weight	: 1500 kg
boot space	: 435 l
fuel capacity	: 62 l
consumption	: 33.6 / 30.7 mpg
acc. 0-62 mph	: 9.3 / 7.4 s
top speed	: 142 / 155 mph
EuroNCAP	: n.a.
introduction	: March 2002
last revised in	: June 2005
warranty	: 2 years
miscellaneous	: C-class based coupe offers
	some additional exclusivity…

CLK 220 CDI / CLK 320 CDI

engine type	: diesel, inline-4
displacement	: 2148 / 2987 cc
max. power	: 110 kW (150 bhp) /
	165 kW (224 bhp)
@	: 4200 / 3800 rpm
max. torque	: 251 / 376 lb ft
@	: 2000 / 1400 rpm
gears	: 6
kerb weight	: 1475 / 1560 kg
towing weight	: 1500 kg
consumption	: 44.1 / 38.2 mpg
acc. 0-60 mph	: 10.2 / 8.2 s
top speed	: 135 / 155 mph
miscellaneous	: … without sacrificing interior space.

MERCEDES-BENZ CLK 350 / CLK 500 CABRIOLET

engine type	: petrol, V6 / V8	**kerb weight**	: 1635 / 1700 kg
displacement	: 3498 / 5462 cc	**towing weight**	: 1500 kg
max. power	: 200 kW (272 bhp) / 285 kW (388 bhp)	**boot space**	: 390 l
@	: 6000 rpm	**fuel capacity**	: 62 l
max. torque	: 258 / 391 lb ft	**consumption**	: 28 / 24.4 mpg
@	: 2400 / 2800 rpm	**acc. 0-62 mph**	: 6.4 / 5.3 s
gears	: -	**top speed**	: 155 / 155 mph
AT	: 7-speed	**EuroNCAP**	: n.a.
drive	: RWD	**introduction**	: March 2003
brakes f/r	: vent. discs	**last revised in**	: June 2005
body type	: 2-dr. convertible	**warranty**	: 2 years
l x w x h	: 4652 x 1740 x 1413 mm	**miscellaneous**	: Why buy the AMG-version if you can have a CLK 500 with the new, powerful 5.5-litre V8 engine instead?
wheelbase	: 2715 mm		
turning circle	: 10.8 m		

CLK 63 AMG

engine type	: petrol, V8
displacement	: 6208 cc
max. power	: 354 kW (481 bhp)
@	: 6800 rpm
max. torque	: 464 lb ft
@	: 5000 rpm
gears	: 7-speed automatic
kerb weight	: 1775 kg
towing weight	: -
consumption	: 19.6 mpg
acc. 0-60 mph	: 4.7 s
top speed	: 155 mph
miscellaneous	: Coupe version is current safety car in Formula 1. Also available as a convertible.

MERCEDES-BENZ CL 500 / CL 600

engine type	: petrol, V8 / V12	kerb weight	: 1895 / 2085 kg
displacement	: 5462 / 5514 cc	towing weight	: -
max. power	: 285 kW (388 bhp) /	boot space	: 490 l
	380 kW (517 bhp)	fuel capacity	: 90 l
@	: 6000 / 5000 rpm	consumption	: 23.3 / 19.8 mpg
max. torque	: 391 / 612 lb ft	acc. 0-62 mph	: 5.5 / 4.6 s
@	: 2800 / 1900 rpm	top speed	: 155 mph
gears	: -	EuroNCAP	: n.a.
AT	: 7- / 5-speed	introduction	: September 2006
drive	: RWD	last revised in	: -
brakes f/r	: vent. discs	warranty	: 2 years
body type	: 2-dr. coupe	miscellaneous	: Giant coupé finds favour with a
l x w x h	: 5065 x 1871 x 1418 mm		small but loyal group of customers,
wheelbase	: 2955 mm		especially in Germany, the USA
turning circle	: 11.6 m		and the Middle East.

CL 63 AMG / CL 65 AMG

engine type	: petrol, V8 / V12
displacement	: 6209 / 5980 cc
max. power	: 386 kW (525 bhp) /
	450 kW (612 bhp)
@	: 6800 / 4800 rpm
max. torque	: 464 / 737 lb ft
@	: 5200 / 2000 rpm
gears	: 7- / 5-speed automatic
kerb weight	: 1985 / 2140 kg
towing weight	: -
consumption	: 19.0 / 19.1 mpg
acc. 0-60 mph	: 4.6 / 4.4 s
top speed	: 155 mph
miscellaneous	: Available engines do not differ much
	performance-wise, but they do in
	terms of character and price tag.

MERCEDES-BENZ SLR MCLAREN / 722 EDITION

engine type	: petrol, V8	**kerb weight**	: 1768 / 1724 kg
displacement	: 5439 cc	**towing weight**	: -
max. power	: 460 kW (626 bhp) /	**boot space**	: 272 l
	478 kW (650 bhp)	**fuel capacity**	: 97 l
@	: 6500 rpm	**consumption**	: 19.5 mpg
max. torque	: 575 / 605 lb ft	**acc. 0-62 mph**	: 3.8 / 3.6 s
@	: 3250 / 4000 rpm	**top speed**	: 208 / 210 mph
gears	: -	**EuroNCAP**	: n.a.
AT	: 5-speed	**introduction**	: September 2003
drive	: RWD	**last revised in**	: -
brakes f/r	: ceramic discs	**warranty**	: 2 years
body type	: 2-dr. coupe	**miscellaneous**	: The SLR McLaren can be ordered
l x w x h	: 4656 x 1908 x 1261 mm		with a softtop now. The 722
wheelbase	: 2700 mm		Edition pays tribute to the legend-
turning circle	: 12.2 m		ary 300 SLR with start number
			722 that won the Mille Miglia race
			of 1955.

MERCEDES-BENZ SLK 200 KOMPRESSOR / SLK 350

engine type	: petrol, inline-4 / V6	kerb weight	: 1290 / 1365 kg
displacement	: 1795 / 3498 cc	towing weight	: -
max. power	: 120 kW (163 bhp) /	boot space	: 210 - 300 l
	200 kW (272 bhp)	fuel capacity	: 70 l
@	: 5500 / 6000 rpm	consumption	: 32.5 / 29.1 mpg
max. torque	: 177 /258 lb ft	acc. 0-62 mph	: 7.9 / 5.6
@	: 3000 / 3500 rpm	top speed	: 143 / 155 mph
gears	: 6 u	EuroNCAP	: n.a.
AT	: optional, 5-speed	introduction	: January 2004
drive	: RWD	last revised in	: -
brakes f/r	: vent. discs / discs	warranty	: 2 years
body type	: 2-dr. convertible	miscellaneous	: SLK of second generation is a
l x w x h	: 4089 x 1777 x 1296 mm		proper sportscar now that
wheelbase	: 2430 mm		competes with the BMW Z4 and
turning circle	: 10.5 m		Porsche Boxster. Also available as
			SLK 280 with 231 bhp.

SLK 55 AMG

engine type	: petrol, V8
displacement	: 5439 cc
max. power	: 265 kW (360 bhp)
@	: 5750 rpm
max. torque	: 376 lb ft
@	: 4000 rpm
gears	: 7-speed automatic
kerb weight	: 1440 kg
towing weight	: n.a.
consumption	: 23.5 mpg
acc. 0-60 mph	: 4.9 s
top speed	: 155 mph
miscellaneous	: A big engine indeed for such a small convertible. Spectacular performance level, lovely V8 sound from quadruple end pipes.

MERCEDES-BENZ SL 500 / SL 55 AMG

engine type	: petrol, V8	kerb weight	: 1810 / 1860 kg
displacement	: 5461 / 5439 cc	towing weight	: -
max. power	: 285 kW (388 bhp) /	boot space	: 317 l
	380 kW (517 bhp)	fuel capacity	: 80 l
@	: 6000 / 6100 rpm	consumption	: 23.2 / 20.9 mpg
max. torque	: 391 / 531 lb ft	acc. 0-62 mph	: 5.4 / 4.5 s
@	: 2800 / 2600 rpm	top speed	: 155 / 155 mph
gears	: -	EuroNCAP	: n.a.
AT	: 7-speed / 5-speed	introduction	: August 2001
drive	: RWD	last revised in	: February 2006
brakes f/r	: vent. discs	warranty	: 2 years
body type	: 2-dr. convertible	miscellaneous	: SL was given a minor facelift.
l x w x h	: 4535 x 1827 x 1298 mm		V6-engined SL 350 also available.
wheelbase	: 2560 mm		
turning circle	: 11.0 m		

SL 600 / SL 65 AMG

engine type	: petrol, V12
displacement	: 5513 / 5980 cc
max. power	: 380 kW (517 bhp) /
	450 kW (612 bhp)
@	: 6100 / 5950 rpm
max. torque	: 612 / 737 lb ft
@	: 1900 / 2000 rpm
gears	: 5-speed automatic
kerb weight	: 1945 / 2020 kg
towing weight	: -
consumption	: 19.8 / 18.7 mpg
acc. 0-60 mph	: 4.5 / 4.2 s
top speed	: 155 / 155 mph
miscellaneous	: Although the difference in price
	between the two is considerable,
	the AMG is only marginally quicker
	off the line.

MERCEDES-BENZ ML 280 CDI / ML 320 CDI

engine type	: diesel, V6
displacement	: 2987 cc
max. power	: 140 kW (190 bhp) / 165 kW (224 bhp)
@	: 4000 / 3800 rpm
max. torque	: 324 / 376 lb ft
@	: 1400 / 1600 rpm
gears	: -
AT	: 7-speed
drive	: 4WD
brakes f/r	: vent. discs / discs
body type	: 5-dr. SUV
l x w x h	: 4780 x 1911 x 1815 mm
wheelbase	: 2915 mm
turning circle	: 11.6 m

kerb weight	: 2085 kg
towing weight	: 3500 kg
boot space	: 500 - 2050 l
fuel capacity	: 95 l
consumption	: 30.1 mpg
acc. 0-62 mph	: 9.8 / 8.6 s
top speed	: 127 / 134 m9h
EuroNCAP	: n.a.
introduction	: March 2005
last revised in	: -
warranty	: 2 years
miscellaneous	: The previous ML model sold well despite shortcomings in the quality department. The new ML however is a better car in every respect.

ML 350 / ML 500

engine type	: petrol, V6 / V8
displacement	: 3498 / 5461 cc
max. power	: 200 kW (272 bhp) / 285 kW (388 bhp)
@	: 6000 rpm
max. torque	: 258 / 339 lb ft
@	: 2400 / 2800 rpm
gears	: 7-speed automatic
kerb weight	: 2035 / 2085 kg
towing weight	: 3500 kg
consumption	: 24.6 / 21.1 mpg
acc. 0-60 mph	: 8.4 / 5.8 s
top speed	: 139 / 149 mph
miscellaneous	: Top-of-the-range model is the ML 63 AMG.

MERCEDES-BENZ G 320 CDI

engine type	: diesel, V6
displacement	: 2987 cc
max. power	: 165 kW (224 bhp)
@	: 3800 rpm
max. torque	: 398 lb ft
@	: 1600 rpm
gears	: -
AT	: 7-speed
drive	: 4WD
brakes f/r	: vent. discs / discs
body type	: 3-dr. SUV
l x w x h	: 4212 x 1760 x 1931 mm
wheelbase	: 2400 mm
turning circle	: 11.3 m

kerb weight	: 2175 kg
towing weight	: 3500 kg
boot space	: 250 l
fuel capacity	: 96 l
consumption	: 25.7 mpg
acc. 0-62 mph	: 8.8 s
top speed	: 110 mph
EuroNCAP	: n.a.
introduction	: 1979
last revised in	: March 2007
warranty	: 2 years
miscellaneous	: Military workhorse first shown in 1979 gradually evolved into a pleasure horse. Model variations are a convertible version and the five-door wagon with a wheelbase of 2850 mm.

G 500 / G 55 AMG

engine type	: petrol, V8
displacement	: 4966 / 5439 cc
max. power	: 218 kW (296 bhp) / 368 kW (500 bhp)
@	: 5500 / 6100 rpm
max. torque	: 336 / 516 lb ft
@	: 2800 / 2500 rpm
gears	: 7- / 5-speed automatic
kerb weight	: 2195 / 2550 kg
towing weight	: 3500 kg
consumption	: 17.9 / 17.3 mpg
acc. 0-60 mph	: 7.3 / 5.5 s
top speed	: 118 / 130 mph
miscellaneous	: The G-class models with V8-power under the bonnet are among the most expensive SUV's currently on the market.

MERCEDES-BENZ GL 450 / GL 500

engine type	: petrol, V8	kerb weight	: 2330 / 2345 kg
displacement	: 4663 / 5461 cc	towing weight	: 3500 kg
max. power	: 250 kW (340 bhp) /	boot space	: 620 l
	285 kW (388 bhp)	fuel capacity	: 100 l
@	: 6000 rpm	consumption	: 21 / 20.4 mpg
max. torque	: 339 /391 lb ft	acc. 0-62 mph	: 7.2 / 6.6 s
@	: 2700 / 2800 rpm	top speed	: 146 / 149 mph
gears	: -	EuroNCAP	: n.a.
AT	: 7-speed	introduction	: July 2006
drive	: 4WD	last revised in	: -
brakes f/r	: vent. discs	warranty	: 2 years
body type	: 5-dr. SUV	miscellaneous	: Not a successor to the G-class
l x w x h	: 5088 x 1920 x 1840 mm		models, but an enlarged version
wheelbase	: 3075 mm		of the ML.
turning circle	: 12.1 m		

GL 320 CDI / GL 420 CDI

engine type	: diesel, V6 / V8
displacement	: 2987 / 3996 cc
max. power	: 165 kW (224 bhp) /
	225 kW (306 bhp)
@	: 3800 / 3600 rpm
max. torque	: 376 / 516 lb ft
@	: 1600 / 2200 rpm
gears	: 7-speed automatic
kerb weight	: 2350 / 2450 kg
towing weight	: 3500 kg
consumption	: 28.9 / 24.6 mpg
acc. 0-60 mph	: 9.5 / 7.2 s
top speed	: 131 / 143 mph
miscellaneous	: V8 diesel engine also available
	in M-class.

MINI ONE / COOPER

engine type	: petrol, inline-4
displacement	: 1397 / 1598 cc
max. power	: 70 kW (95 bhp) / 88 kW (120 bhp)
@	: 6000 rpm
max. torque	: 103 / 118 lb ft
@	: 4000 / 4250 rpm
gears	: 6
AT	: optional 6-speed
drive	: FWD
brakes f/r	: vent. discs / discs
body type	: 3-dr. hatchback
l x w x h	: 3699 x 1683 x 1407 mm
wheelbase	: 2467 mm
turning circle	: 10.7 m

kerb weight	: 1035 / 1040 kg
towing weight	: 650 / 750 kg
boot space	: 160 l
fuel capacity	: 40 l
consumption	: 53.3 / 52.3 mpg
acc. 0-62 mph	: 10.9 / 9.1 s
top speed	: 115 / 126 mph
EuroNCAP	: 4 stars
introduction	: June 2001
last revised in	: December 2006
warranty	: 2 years
miscellaneous	: The revised New Mini is in great demand. Thanks to its fuel-efficient BMW-technology, the Mini is even more economical than before.

CLUBMAN COOPER S / COOPER D

engine type	: petrol / diesel, inline-4
displacement	: 1598 / 1560 cc
max. power	: 128 kW (175 bhp) / 80 kW (110 bhp)
@	: 5500 / 4000 rpm
max. torque	: 177 lb ft
@	: 1600 / 1750 rpm
gears	: 6
kerb weight	: 1105 / 1040 kg
towing weight	: 750 kg
consumption	: 45.6 / 72.4
acc. 0-60 mph	: 7.1 / 9.9 s
top speed	: 140 / 121 mph
miscellaneous	: The Clubman is a practical new addition to the model range. It was inspired by the old Mini Traveller. Both engines are also available in the standard Mini. There is no 'One' edition of the Clubman.

MINI ONE CONVERTIBLE

engine type	: petrol, inline-4	kerb weight	: 1140 kg
displacement	: 1598 cc	towing weight	: 650 kg
max. power	: 66 kW (90 bhp)	boot space	: 165 l
@	: 5500 rpm	fuel capacity	: 50 l
max. torque	: 103 lb ft	consumption	: 39.2 mpg
@	: 3000 rpm	acc. 0-62 mph	: 11.8 s
gears	: 5	top speed	: 109 mph
AT	: optional, CVT	EuroNCAP	: 4 stars
drive	: FWD	introduction	: April 2004
brakes f/r	: vent. discs / discs	last revised in	: -
body type	: 2-dr. convertible	warranty	: 2 years
l x w x h	: 3635 x 1688 x 1415 mm	miscellaneous	: Also available as Cooper and
wheelbase	: 2467 mm		Cooper S. New convertible not
turning circle	: 10.7 m		likely to make its appearance soon.

MITSUBISHI COLT 1.1 / 1.3

engine type	: petrol, inline-3 / inline-3
displacement	: 1124 / 1332 cc
max. power	: 55 kW (75 bhp) / 70 kW (95 bhp)
@	: 6000 rpm
max. torque	: 74 / 92 lb ft
@	: 3500 / 4000 rpm
gears	: 5
AT	: - / 6-speed seq.
drive	: FWD
brakes f/r	: vent. discs / discs
body type	: 5-dr. hatchback
l x w x h	: 3870 x 1695 x 1550 mm
wheelbase	: 2500 mm
turning circle	: 10.8 m

kerb weight	: 940 / 945 kg
towing weight	: 1000 kg
boot space	: 220 – 645 l
fuel capacity	: 47 l
consumption	: 51.4 / 47.1 mpg
acc. 0-62 mph	: 13.4 / 11.1 s
top speed	: 103 / 112 mph
EuroNCAP	: 4 stars
introduction	: April 2004
last revised in	: -
warranty	: 3 years
miscellaneous	: Pretty car that could help to make Mitsubishi profitable again. Also available with 1.5 engine.

COLT 1.5 DI-D

engine type	: diesel, inline-3
displacement	: 1493 cc
max. power	: 70 kW (95 bhp)
@	: 4000 rpm
max. torque	: 155 lb ft
@	: 1800 rpm
gears	: 5
kerb weight	: 1060 kg
towing weight	: 1000 kg
consumption	: 58.9 mpg
acc. 0-60 mph	: 9.9 s
top speed	: 112 mph
miscellaneous	: 68 bhp version of 3-cylinder diesel engine also available.

MITSUBISHI COLT CZ3 1.5 INSTYLE / CZT 1.5 TURBO

engine type	: petrol, inline-4	kerb weight	: 1045 / 935 kg
displacement	: 1499 cc	towing weight	: 1000 kg
max. power	: 80 kW (109 bhp) / 110 kW (150 bhp)	boot space	: 220 – 645 l
@	: 6000 rpm	fuel capacity	: 47 l
max. torque	: 107 / 155 lb ft	consumption	: 46.3 /41.5 mpg
@	: 4000 / 3500 rpm	acc. 0-62 mph	: 9.8 / 8 s
gears	: 5	top speed	: 118 / 131 mph
AT	: n.a.	EuroNCAP	: n.a.
drive	: FWD	introduction	: April 2004
brakes f/r	: vent. discs	last revised in	: -
body type	: 3-dr. hatchback	warranty	: 3 years
l x w x h	: 3810 x 1695 x 1520 mm	miscellaneous	: CZ3 also available with smaller
wheelbase	: 2500 mm		petrol engines. CZT is fastest of
turning circle	: 10.8 m		Colt range. Convertible is latest
			addition, with 1.5 and 1.5 turbo
			engines.

MITSUBISHI LANCER 1.5

engine type	: petrol, inline-4	kerb weight	: 1250 kg
displacement	: 1499 cc	towing weight	: 1100 kg
max. power	: 80 kW (109 bhp)	boot space	: n.a.
@	: 6000 rpm	fuel capacity	: 59 l
max. torque	: 105 lb ft	consumption	: 44.1 mpg
@	: 4000 rpm	acc. 0-62 mph	: 11.6 s
gears	: 5	top speed	: 119 mph
AT	: optional 4-speed	EuroNCAP	: n.a.
drive	: FWD	introduction	: December 2007
brakes f/r	: vent. discs / discs	last revised in	: -
body type	: 4-dr. saloon	warranty	: 3 years
l x w x h	: 4570 x 1760 x 1490 mm	miscellaneous	: Competitively priced company car, launched successfully in North-America earlier. A 1.8 version with 140 bhp, 2.0 version with 240 bhp and 300 bhp strong Evo X model will follow.
wheelbase	: 2635 mm		
turning circle	: 10.0 m		

LANCER 2.0 DI-D

engine type	: diesel, inline-4
displacement	: 1968 cc
max. power	: 103 kW (140 bhp)
@	: 4000 rpm
max. torque	: 229 lb ft
@	: 1750 rpm
gears	: 6
kerb weight	: 1425 kg
towing weight	: 1400 kg
consumption	: 48.9 mpg
acc. 0-60 mph	: 9.6 s
top speed	: 129 mph
miscellaneous	: Diesel engine from Volkswagen will be replaced by a unit from Mitsubishi.

MITSUBISHI LANCER WAGON 1.6 / 2.0

engine type	: petrol, inline-4	kerb weight	: 1250 / 1295 kg
displacement	: 1584 / 1997 cc	towing weight	: 1200 kg
max. power	: 72 kW (98 bhp) / 99 kW (135 bhp)	boot space	: 344 - 1079 l
@	: 5000 / 6000 rpm	fuel capacity	: 50 / 50 l
max. torque	: 111 / 130 lb ft	consumption	: 41.5 / 33.6 mpg
@	: 4000 / 4500 rpm	acc. 0-62 mph	: 12.6 / 10.0 s
gears	: 5	top speed	: 114 / 127 mph
AT	: -	EuroNCAP	: n.a.
drive	: FWD	introduction	: summer 2003
brakes f/r	: vent. discs / discs	last revised in	: autumn 2005
body type	: 5-dr. stationwagon	warranty	: 3 years
l x w x h	: 4485 x 1695 x 1480 mm	miscellaneous	: 'Plain' Lancer model now also
wheelbase	: 2600 mm		available as saloon. New Lancer
turning circle	: 10.0 m		on its way.

MITSUBISHI GRANDIS 2.4

engine type	: benzine, 4-cilinder lijn	kerb weight	: 1620 kg
displacement	: 2378 cm³	towing weight	: 1600 kg
max. power	: 121 kW (165 pk)	boot space	: 320 - 1545 l
@	: 6000 tpm	fuel capacity	: 65 l
max. torque	: 217 Nm	consumption	: 9,4 l/100 km
@	: 4000 tpm	acc. 0-62 mph	: 10,0 s
gears	: 5	top speed	: 200 km/u
AT	: n.b.	EuroNCAP	: n.b.
drive	: voorwielen	introduction	: april 2004
brakes f/r	: gev. schijven / schijven	last revised in	: zomer 2005
body type	: 5-drs. MPV	warranty	: 3 jaar
l x w x h	: 4765 x 1795 x 1655 mm	miscellaneous	: Mooie MPV met hoogwaardig
wheelbase	: 2830 mm		interieur en slimme gebruiks
turning circle	: 11,6 m		mogelijkheden.

GRANDIS 2.0 DI-D

engine type	: diesel, 4-cilinder lijn
displacement	: 1968 cm³
max. power	: 100 kW (136 pk)
@	: 4000 tpm
max. torque	: 310 Nm
@	: 1750 tpm
gears	: 6
kerb weight	: 1725 kg
towing weight	: 2000 kg
consumption	: 6,6 l/100 km
acc. 0-60 mph	: 10,8 s
top speed	: 195 km/u
miscellaneous	: Diesel is afkomstig van Volkswagen en dat is een goede keuze.

MITSUBISHI OUTLANDER SPORT 2.0 / 2.4

engine type	: petrol, inline-4
displacement	: 1997 / 2378 cc
max. power	: 100 kW (136 bhp) /
	118 kW (160 bhp)
@	: 6000 / 5750 rpm
max. torque	: 130 / 159 lb ft
@	: 4500 / 4000 rpm
gears	: 5
AT	: - / optional 4-speed
drive	: FWD / 4WD
brakes f/r	: vent. discs / discs
body type	: 5-dr. SUV
l x w x h	: 4545 x 1750 x 1670 mm
wheelbase	: 2625 mm
turning circle	: 11.4 m

kerb weight	: 1540 / 1555 kg
towing weight	: 1500 kg
boot space	: 402 - 1049 l
fuel capacity	: 60 l
consumption	: 29.9 / 28.9 mpg
acc. 0-62 mph	: 11.4 / 9.9 s
top speed	: 119 / 124 mph
EuroNCAP	: n.a.
introduction	: late 2003
last revised in	: 2005
warranty	: 3 years
miscellaneous	: 2-litre version has front-wheel drive, 2.4 has 4WD. Production of this robust and versatile model ends next year.

OUTLANDER SPORT 2.0 TURBO

engine type	: petrol, inline-4
displacement	: 1997 cc
max. power	: 148 kW (202 bhp)
@	: 5500 rpm
max. torque	: 224 lb ft
@	: 3500 rpm
gears	: 5
kerb weight	: 1505 kg
towing weight	: 1500 kg
consumption	: 28.1 mpg
acc. 0-60 mph	: 7.7 s
top speed	: 137 mph
miscellaneous	: Turbo-powered version is nice finale for popular crossover SUV.

MITSUBISHI OUTLANDER 2.0 DI-D / 2.2 DI-D

engine type	: diesel, inline-4
displacement	: 1968 / 2178 cc
max. power	: 103 kW (138 bhp) / 115 kW (156 bhp)
@	: 4000 rpm
max. torque	: 228 / 280 lb ft
@	: 1750 / 2000 rpm
gears	: 6
AT	: -
drive	: 4WD
brakes f/r	: vent. discs / discs
body type	: 5-dr. SUV
l x w x h	: 4646 x 1806 x 1680 mm
wheelbase	: 2670 mm
turning circle	: 10.6 m

kerb weight	: 1630 / 1747 kg
towing weight	: 2000 kg
boot space	: 771 l
fuel capacity	: 60 l
consumption	: 42.2 / 39.2 mpg
acc. 0-62 mph	: 10.8 / 9.9 s
top speed	: 116 / 124 mph
EuroNCAP	: 4 stars
introduction	: March 2007
last revised in	: -
warranty	: 3 years
miscellaneous	: Attractive SUV from Mitsubishi, usually ordered with diesel power under the bonnet. Two-litre version is supplied by Volkswagen, the larger 2.2 by Citroën/Peugeot.

OUTLANDER 2.4

engine type	: petrol, inline-4
displacement	: 2378 cc
max. power	: 125 kW (170 bhp)
@	: 6000 rpm
max. torque	: 171 lb ft
@	: 4100 rpm
gears	: 5, optional CVT
kerb weight	: n.a.
towing weight	: n.a.
consumption	: n.a.
acc. 0-60 mph	: n.a.
top speed	: n.a.
miscellaneous	: Mitsubishi uses a petrol engine of its own in the Outlander. Optional is the third row of seats which can accommodate two people.

MITSUBISHI SHOGUN SPORT 2.5 TD

engine type	: diesel, inline-4	kerb weight	: 1780 kg
displacement	: 2477 cc	towing weight	: 2800 kg
max. power	: 85 kW (115 bhp)	boot space	: 500 - 1720 l
@	: 4000 rpm	fuel capacity	: 74 l
max. torque	: 177 lb ft	consumption	: 27.2 mpg
@	: 2000 rpm	acc. 0-62 mph	: 18.5 s
gears	: 5	top speed	: 93 mph
AT	: -	EuroNCAP	: n.a.
drive	: 4WD	introduction	: September 2002
brakes f/r	: vent. discs	last revised in	: late 2005
body type	: 5-dr. SUV	warranty	: 3 years
l x w x h	: 4610 x 1695 x 1720 mm	miscellaneous	: Offroad vehicle based on pick-up
wheelbase	: 2725 mm		truck from Mitsubishi. Elegant, but
turning circle	: 11.8 m		no longer as refined as competi-
			tors.

PAJERO SPORT 3.0 V6 INTENSE AUTO

engine type	: petrol, V6
displacement	: 2972 cc
max. power	: 125 kW (170 bhp)
@	: 5000 rpm
max. torque	: 188 lb ft
@	: 4000 rpm
gears	: 4-speed automatic
kerb weight	: 1805 kg
towing weight	: 2800 kg
consumption	: 22.6 mpg
acc. 0-60 mph	: 13.2 s
top speed	: 109 mph
miscellaneous	: Rarely seen on our roads.

MITSUBISHI SHOGUN 3.2 DI-D / LONG BODY

engine type	: diesel, inline-4	kerb weight	: 2085 / 2265 kg
displacement	: 3200 cc	towing weight	: 2800 / 3300 kg
max. power	: 118 kW (158 bhp)	boot space	: 415 / 215 l
@	: 3800 rpm	fuel capacity	: 71 / 90 l
max. torque	: 281 lb ft	consumption	: 26.9 / 26.7 mpg
@	: 2000 rpm	acc. 0-62 mph	: 12.1 / 12.8 s
gears	: 5	top speed	: 110 mph
AT	: optional 5-speed	EuroNCAP	: n.a.
drive	: 4WD	introduction	: November 2006
brakes f/r	: vent. discs	last revised in	: -
body type	: 3-dr. / 5-dr. SUV	warranty	: 3 years
l x w x h	: 4385 / 4900 x 1850 / 1870 mm	miscellaneous	: Not a sports utility vehicle, but
wheelbase	: 2545 / 2780 mm		a well-appointed off-roader with
turning circle	: 10.6 / 11.4 m		good looks.

PAJERO 3.8 V6

engine type	: petrol, V6
displacement	: 3828 cc
max. power	: 184 kW (250 bhp)
@	: 6000 rpm
max. torque	: 243 lb ft
@	: 2750 rpm
gears	: 5-speed automatic
kerb weight	: 2215 kg
towing weight	: 3300 kg
consumption	: 20.9 mpg
acc. 0-60 mph	: 10.8 s
top speed	: 124 mph
miscellaneous	: Available with 'Long Body' bodywork only. Engine borrowed from American Mitsubishi's.

MORGAN 4/4 1.8 / MORGAN ROADSTER

engine type	: inline-4 / V6	kerb weight	: 868 / 940 kg
displacement	: 1798 / 2967 cc	towing weight	: n.a.
max. power	: 85 kW (115 bhp) / 166 kW (226 bhp)	boot space	: 102 l
	: 5500 / 6000 rpm	fuel capacity	: 50 l
@	: 118 / 206 lb ft	consumption	: 29.7 / 19.9 mpg
max. torque	: 4400 / 4900 rpm	acc. 0-62 mph	: 8.9 / 4.9 s
@	: 5	top speed	: 106 / 115 mph
gears	: -	EuroNCAP	: n.a.
AT	: RWD	introduction	: 1954
drive	: vent. discs / drum brakes	last revised in	: summer 2004
brakes f/r	: 2-dr. convertible	warranty	: 2 years
body type	: 3890 x 1500 x 1290 mm /	miscellaneous	: Not your average contemporary
l x w x h	: 4010 x 1720 x 1220 mm		model, but still on the shortlist
wheelbase	: 2440 / 2500 mm		of car buffs around the globe.
turning circle	: 10.0 m		Engines from Ford, including
			2.0 with 145 bhp. Plus 8 model
			replaced by Roadster.

MORGAN AERO 8

engine type	: petrol, V8	kerb weight	: 1145 kg
displacement	: 4398 cc	towing weight	: -
max. power	: 239 kW (325 bhp)	boot space	: n.a.
@	: 6100 rpm	fuel capacity	: 70 l
max. torque	: 331 lb ft	consumption	: 25.9 mpg
@	: 3600 rpm	acc. 0-62 mph	: 4.5 s
gears	: 6	top speed	: 170 mph
AT	: -	EuroNCAP	: n.a.
drive	: RWD	introduction	: late 2000
brakes f/r	: vent. discs	last revised in	: spring 2006
body type	: 2-dr. convertible	warranty	: 2 years
l x w x h	: 4120 x 1770 x 1200 mm	miscellaneous	: V8 from BMW and aluminium
wheelbase	: 2535 mm		chassis not in keeping with Morgan
turning circle	: 10.0 m		tradition, but ashwood bodyframe
			is. Fast, entertaining drive, but
			suspension is killing for your
			kidneys.

NISSAN MICRA 1.2

engine type	: petrol, inline-4
displacement	: 1240 cc
max. power	: 59 kW (80 bhp)
@	: 5200 rpm
max. torque	: 81 lb ft
@	: 3200 rpm
gears	: 5
AT	: optional 4-speed
drive	: FWD
brakes f/r	: vent. discs / drums
body type	: 3- / 5-dr. hatchback
l x w x h	: 3719 x 1660 x 1540 mm
wheelbase	: 2430 mm
turning circle	: 9.2 m

kerb weight	: 921 / 935 kg
towing weight	: 800 kg
boot space	: 251 l
fuel capacity	: 46 l
consumption	: 47.9 mpg
acc. 0-62 mph	: 13.5 s
top speed	: 104 mph
EuroNCAP	: 4 stars
introduction	: December 2002
last revised in	: July 2005
warranty	: 3 years
miscellaneous	: Car with an attractive design and favourable price. Also available with a 1.4 or 1.6 petrol engine, as described under the Micra C+C entry.

MICRA 1.5 DCI

engine type	: diesel, inline-4
displacement	: 1461 cc
max. power	: 63 kW (86 bhp)
@	: 4000 rpm
max. torque	: 147 lb ft
@	: 1900 rpm
gears	: 5
kerb weight	: 1018 kg
towing weight	: 900 kg
consumption	: 60.1 mpg
acc. 0-60 mph	: 11.9 s
top speed	: 106 mph
miscellaneous	: The diesel engine is an already familiar unit from the Renault Clio.

NISSAN MICRA C+C 1.4 / 1.6

engine type	: petrol, inline-4	kerb weight	: 1135 / 1150 kg
displacement	: 1386 / 1598 cc	towing weight	: 750 kg
max. power	: 65 kW (88 bhp) / 81 kW (110 bhp)	boot space	: 255 / 457 l
@	: 5200 / 6000 rpm	fuel capacity	: 46 l
max. torque	: 94 / 113 lb ft	consumption	: 42.8 /42.2 mpg
@	: 3200 / 4400 rpm	acc. 0-62 mph	: 12.8 / 10.6 s
gears	: 5	top speed	: 109 / 119 mph
AT	: -	EuroNCAP	: n.a.
drive	: FWD	introduction	: early 2006
brakes f/r	: discs / drum brakes	last revised in	: -
body type	: 2-dr. convertible	warranty	: 3 years
l x w x h	: 3806 x 1668 x 1441 mm	miscellaneous	: Small convertibles abound in
wheelbase	: 2432 mm		today's market, but Micra C+C
turning circle	: n.a.		stands out with panoramic glass
			roof and well-proportioned tail.

NISSAN QASHQAI 1.6 / 2.0

engine type	: petrol, inline-4	kerb weight	: 1297 / 1356 kg
displacement	: 1598 / 1997 cc	towing weight	: 1200 / 1400 kg
max. power	: 84 kW (115 bhp) / 104 kW (150 bhp)	boot space	: 410 l
@	: 6000 rpm	fuel capacity	: 65 l
max. torque	: 115 / 144 lb ft	consumption	: 42.2 / 34.4 mpg
@	: 4400 / 4800 rpm	acc. 0-62 mph	: 12.0 / 10.1 s
gears	: 5 / 6	top speed	: 109 / 119 mph
AT	: - / optional CVT	EuroNCAP	: 5 stars
drive	: FWD	introduction	: February 2007
brakes f/r	: vent. discs / discs	last revised in	: -
body type	: 5-dr. hatchback	warranty	: 3 years
l x w x h	: 4315 x 1780 x 1615 mm	miscellaneous	: The Qashqai is Nissan's new
wheelbase	: 2630 mm		trump card. 4WD is optional on
turning circle	: 10.6 m		the two-litre petrol and diesel
			models.

QASHQAI 1.5 DCI / 2.0 DCI

engine type	: diesel, inline-4
displacement	: 1461 / 1994 cc
max. power	: 78 kW (106 bhp) / 110 kW (150 bhp)
@	: 4000 rpm
max. torque	: 177 / 236 lb ft
@	: 2000 rpm
gears	: 6
kerb weight	: 1407 / 1520 kg
towing weight	: 1200 / 1400 kg
consumption	: 52.3 / 42.8 mpg
acc. 0-60 mph	: 12.2 / 10.5 s
top speed	: 108 / 119 mph
miscellaneous	: Familiar diesel units from
	partner Renault.

NISSAN NOTE 1.4 / 1.6

engine type	: petrol, inline-4
displacement	: 1386 / 1598 cc
max. power	: 65 kW (88 bhp) / 81 kW (110 bhp)
@	: 5200 / 6000 rpm
max. torque	: 94 / 113 lb ft
@	: 3200 / 4400 rpm
gears	: 5
AT	: -
drive	: FWD
brakes f/r	: discs / drum brakes
body type	: 5-dr. hatchback
l x w x h	: 4083 x 1690 x 1550 mm
wheelbase	: 2600 mm
turning circle	: 11.0 m

kerb weight	: 967 / 1082 kg
towing weight	: 945 / 1000 kg
boot space	: 437 l
fuel capacity	: 46 l
consumption	: 44.8 / 42.8 mpg
acc. 0-62 mph	: 13.1 / 10.7 s
top speed	: 103 / 114 mph
EuroNCAP	: 4 stars
introduction	: early 2006
last revised in	: -
warranty	: 3 years
miscellaneous	: New Note looks good and boasts a clever interior. Built in Britain.

NOTE 1.5 DCI LP / 1.5 DCI HP

engine type	: diesel, inline-4
displacement	: 1461 cc
max. power	: 50 kW (68 bhp) / 63 kW (86 bhp)
@	: 4000 / 3750 rpm
max. torque	: 118 / 148 lb ft
@	: 2000 rpm
gears	: 5
kerb weight	: 1140 kg
towing weight	: 790 / 900 kg
consumption	: 55.8 / 55.4 mpg
acc. 0-60 mph	: 16.5 / 13.0 s
top speed	: 96 / 101 mph
miscellaneous	: Diesel power promotes career of Note as small business car.

NISSAN 350Z

engine type	: petrol, V6		kerb weight	: 1534 kg
displacement	: 3498 cc		towing weight	: -
max. power	: 230 kW (313 bhp)		boot space	: 235 l
@	: 6400 rpm		fuel capacity	: 80 l
max. torque	: 264 lb ft		consumption	: 24.1 mpg
@	: 4800 rpm		acc. 0-62 mph	: 5.8 s
gears	: 6		top speed	: 155 mph
AT	: -		EuroNCAP	: n.a.
drive	: RWD		introduction	: March 2003
brakes f/r	: vent. discs		last revised in	: May 2007
body type	: 3-dr. coupe		warranty	: 3 years
l x w x h	: 4315 x 1815 x 1325 mm		miscellaneous	: Nissan keeps finetuning the 350Z,
wheelbase	: 2650 mm			which now features an upgraded
turning circle	: 11.3 m			V6 engine for more power. There is
				also a Roadster version.

NISSAN X-TRAIL 2.0 / 2.5

engine type	: petrol, inline-4
displacement	: 1997 / 2488 cc
max. power	: 104 kW (141 bhp) / 124 kW (169 bhp)
@	: 6000 rpm
max. torque	: 144 / 172 lb ft
@	: 4800 / 4400 rpm
gears	: 6
AT	: - / optional CVT
drive	: 4WD
brakes f/r	: vent. discs
body type	: 5-dr. SUV
l x w x h	: 4630 x 1785 x 1685 mm
wheelbase	: 2630 mm
turning circle	: 10.8 m

kerb weight	: 1482 / 1544 kg
towing weight	: 1500 / 2000 kg
boot space	: 603 l
fuel capacity	: 65 l
consumption	: 32.5 / 29.4 mpg
acc. 0-62 mph	: 11.1 / 9.8 s
top speed	: 114 / 120 mph
EuroNCAP	: n.a.
introduction	: July 2007
last revised in	: -
warranty	: 3 years
miscellaneous	: Bigger brother of Qashqai. New edition on Qashqai platform looks pretty much like before, but the changes are numerous.

X-TRAIL 2.0 DCI

engine type	: diesel, inline-4
displacement	: 1995 cc
max. power	: 110 kW (150 bhp) / 127 kW (173 bhp)
@	: 4000 / 3750 rpm
max. torque	: 236 / 266 lb ft
@	: 2000 rpm
gears	: 6, optional 6-speed automatic
kerb weight	: 1625 / 1651 kg
towing weight	: 2000 / 2200 kg
consumption	: 39.8 / 38.2 mpg
acc. 0-60 mph	: 11.2 / 10.0 s
top speed	: 117 / 124 mph
miscellaneous	: Previous diesel unit from Nissan has made way for a new generation of two-litre diesel engines.

NISSAN MURANO 3.5 V6 SE

engine type	: petrol, V6		kerb weight	: 1500 kg
displacement	: 3498 cc		towing weight	: 438 - 1965 l
max. power	: 172 kW (234 bhp)		boot space	: 82 l
@	: 6000 rpm		fuel capacity	: 23 mpg
max. torque	: 235 lb ft		consumption	: n.a.
@	: 3600 rpm		acc. 0-62 mph	: 8.9 s
gears	: -		top speed	: 124 mph
AT	: CVT		EuroNCAP	: n.a.
drive	: 4WD		introduction	: October 2004
brakes f/r	: vent. discs		last revised in	: -
body type	: 5-dr. SUV		warranty	: 3 years
l x w x h	: 4770 x 1880 x 1705 mm		miscellaneous	: No spare tyre on the rear door
wheelbase	: 2825 mm			of this modern SUV. Popular
turning circle	: 12.0 m			alternative to higher middle-class
				offerings. Available only with
				transversely mounted petrol engine
				and just one equipment level.

NISSAN PATROL 3.0 DI

engine type	: diesel, inline-4	kerb weight	: 2365 kg
displacement	: 2953 cc	towing weight	: 3500 kg
max. power	: 118 kW (160 bhp)	boot space	: 308 - 1652 l
@	: 3600 rpm	fuel capacity	: 95 l
max. torque	: 235 lb ft	consumption	: 26.2 mpg
@	: 2000 rpm	acc. 0-62 mph	: 14.8 s
gears	: 5	top speed	: 99 mph
AT	: optional, 4-speed	EuroNCAP	: n.a.
drive	: 4WD	introduction	: autumn 1997
brakes f/r	: vent. discs	last revised in	: autumn 2004
body type	: 5-dr. SUV	warranty	: 3 years
l x w x h	: 5045 x 1840 x 1855 mm	miscellaneous	: Classic offroader with externally
wheelbase	: 2970 mm		mounted spare tyre. Patrol often
turning circle	: 12.2 m		used professionally, more likely
			than not with a trailer on tow. Also
			available as 3-door with wheelbase
			of 2400 mm.

NISSAN PATHFINDER 2.5 DCI

engine type	: diesel, inline-4	**kerb weight**	: 2116 kg
displacement	: 2488 cc	**towing weight**	: 3000 kg
max. power	: 126 kW (172 bhp)	**boot space**	: 515 l
@	: 4000 rpm	**fuel capacity**	: 80 l
max. torque	: 297 lb ft	**consumption**	: 31.4 mpg
@	: 2000 rpm	**acc. 0-62 mph**	: 11.9 s
gears	: 6	**top speed**	: 112 mph
AT	: optional 5-speed	**EuroNCAP**	: 4 stars
drive	: 4WD	**introduction**	: March 2005
brakes f/r	: vent. discs	**last revised in**	: -
body type	: 5-dr. SUV	**warranty**	: 3 years
l x w x h	: 4740 x 1850 x 1760 mm	**miscellaneous**	: Americans like to call the
wheelbase	: 2850 mm		Pathfinder a 'midsize' SUV. An
turning circle	: 11.9 m		impressive car that is also very
			capable off-road.

NOBLE M15

engine type	: petrol, V6	**kerb weight**	: 1250 kg
displacement	: 2968 cc	**towing weight**	: -
max. power	: 339 kW (455 bhp)	**boot space**	: 185 l
@	: 6800 rpm	**fuel capacity**	: 70 l
max. torque	: 455 lb ft	**consumption**	: n.a.
@	: 4800 rpm	**acc. 0-62 mph**	: 3.5 s
gears	: 6	**top speed**	: 173 mph
AT	: -	**EuroNCAP**	: n.a.
drive	: RWD	**introduction**	: April 2006
brakes f/r	: vent. discs	**last revised in**	: -
body type	: 2-dr. coupe	**warranty**	: 2 years
l x w x h	: 4270 x 1905 x 1116 mm	**miscellaneous**	: M15 model intended to combat with the likes of Ferrari and Porsche. Can be used as a shopping car as well, according to its maker.
wheelbase	: 2438 mm		
turning circle	: n.a.		

OPEL (VAUXHALL) AGILA 1.0 12V / 1.2 16V

engine type	: petrol, inline-3	kerb weight	: n.a.
displacement	: 997 / 1242 cc	towing weight	: n.a.
max. power	: 48 kW (65 bhp) / 63 kW (86 bhp)	boot space	: 225 l
@	: 6000 rpm	fuel capacity	: n.a.
max. torque	: 66 / 84 lb ft	consumption	: 53.3 / 49.6 mpg
@	: 4000 rpm	acc. 0-62 mph	: 14.8 / 12.0 s
gears	: 5	top speed	: 100 / 108 mph
AT	: - / optional 4-speed	EuroNCAP	: n.a.
drive	: FWD	introduction	: November 2007
brakes f/r	: vent. discs / drums	last revised in	: -
body type	: 5-dr. hatchback	warranty	: 2 years
l x w x h	: 3740 x 1680 x 1590 mm	miscellaneous	: New model is an improvement
wheelbase	: 2350 mm		over the earlier boxy design.
turning circle	: 9.6 m		Identical to the Suzuki Splash from
			a technical point of view.

OPEL (VAUXHALL) CORSA 1.0 / 1.2

engine type	: petrol, inline-3 / -4
displacement	: 998 / 1229 cc
max. power	: 44 kW (60 bhp) / 59 kW (80 bhp)
@	: 5600 rpm
max. torque	: 65 / 81 lb ft
@	: 3800 / 4000 rpm
gears	: 5
AT	: - / optional 5-speed
drive	: FWD
brakes f/r	: vent. discs / drums
body type	: 5-dr. hatchback
l x w x h	: 3999 x 1713 x 1488 mm
wheelbase	: 2511 mm
turning circle	: 10.2 m

kerb weight	: 1045 / 1060 kg
towing weight	: 500 / 850 kg
boot space	: 285 l
fuel capacity	: 45 l
consumption	: 50.4 / 48.7 mpg
acc. 0-62 mph	: 18.2 / 13.9 s
top speed	: 93 / 104 mph
EuroNCAP	: 5 stars
introduction	: September 2006
last revised in	: n.v.t.
warranty	: 2 years
miscellaneous	: New Corsa is a big hit for Vauxhall. Specs refer to the five-door model, which is also available with the 1.4 and 1.7 CDTI engines described under the 3-door model.

CORSA 1.3 CDTI

engine type	: diesel, inline-4
displacement	: 1248 cc
max. power	: 55 kW (75 bhp) / 66 kW (90 bhp)
@	: 4000 rpm
max. torque	: 126 / 147 lb ft
@	: 1750 rpm
gears	: 5 / 6
kerb weight	: 1135 / 1165 kg
towing weight	: 1000 / 1200 kg
consumption	: 62.8 / 61.4 mpg
acc. 0-60 mph	: 14.5 / 12.7 s
top speed	: 101 / 107 mph
miscellaneous	: The Corsa is related to the Fiat Grande Punto from a technical point of view. What's more, both cars share the same diesel engines.

OPEL (VAUXHALL) CORSA 1.4 / VXR

engine type	: petrol, inline-4
displacement	: 1364 / 1598 cc
max. power	: 66 kW (90 bhp) / 141 kW (192 bhp)
@	: 5600 / 5850 rpm
max. torque	: 92 / 170 lb ft
@	: 4000 / 2000 rpm
gears	: 5 / 6
AT	: optional 4-speed / -
drive	: FWD
brakes f/r	: vent. discs, drums / discs
body type	: 3-dr. hatchback
l x w x h	: 3999 x 1713 x 1488 mm
wheelbase	: 2511 mm
turning circle	: 10.2 m

kerb weight	: 1040 / 1203 kg
towing weight	: 1000 kg / n.v.t.
boot space	: 285 l
fuel capacity	: 45 l
consumption	: 45.6 / 35.8 mpg
acc. 0-62 mph	: 12.4 / 7.2 s
top speed	: 107 / 140 mph
EuroNCAP	: 5 stars
introduction	: September 2006
last revised in	: -
warranty	: 2 years
miscellaneous	: Extravagant and extremely fast VXR reigns supreme over the Corsa model programme.

CORSA 1.7 CDTI

engine type	: diesel, inline-4
displacement	: 1686 cc
max. power	: 92 kW (125 bhp)
@	: 4000 rpm
max. torque	: 206 lb ft
@	: 2300 rpm
gears	: 6
kerb weight	: 1178 kg
towing weight	: 1300 kg
consumption	: 58.9 mpg
acc. 0-60 mph	: 10.1 s
top speed	: 121 mph
miscellaneous	: Vauxhall chose a powerplant of its own instead of the 1.9 unit from Fiat.

OPEL (VAUXHALL) TIGRA TWINTOP 1.4 / 1.8

engine type	: petrol, inline-4	**kerb weight**	: 1135 / 1165 kg
displacement	: 1364 / 1796 cc	**towing weight**	: -
max. power	: 66 kW (90 bhp) / 92 kW (125 bhp)	**boot space**	: 250 l
@	: 5600 / 6000 rpm	**fuel capacity**	: 45 l
max. torque	: 92 / 122 lb ft	**consumption**	: 46.3 / 36.7 mpg
@	: 4000 / 4600 rpm	**acc. 0-62 mph**	: 12.4 / 9.4 s
gears	: 5	**top speed**	: 112 / 127 mph
AT	: optional 5-speed / -	**EuroNCAP**	: n.a.
drive	: FWD	**introduction**	: late 2004
brakes f/r	: vent. discs / drum brakes	**last revised in**	: -
body type	: 2-dr. convertible	**warranty**	: 2 years
l x w x h	: 3921 x 1685 x 1364 mm	**miscellaneous**	: Charming convertible with foldable steel hardtop, built by Karmann. More rare than a Peugeot 206 CC.
wheelbase	: 2491 mm		
turning circle	: 10.6 m		

OPEL (VAUXHALL) TOUR 1.4

engine type	: petrol, inline-4		kerb weight	: 1135 kg
displacement	: 1364 cc		towing weight	: 1000 kg
max. power	: 66 kW (90 bhp)		boot space	: 510 -2695 l
@	: 5600 rpm		fuel capacity	: 52 l
max. torque	: 92 lb ft		consumption	: 44.8 mpg
@	: 4000 rpm		acc. 0-62 mph	: 14.0 s
gears	: 5		top speed	: 101 mph
AT	: -		EuroNCAP	: n.a.
drive	: FWD		introduction	: late 2002
brakes f/r	: vent. discs / drum brakes		last revised in	: autumn 2003
body type	: 5-dr. MPV		warranty	: 2 years
l x w x h	: 4332 x 1684 x 1801 mm		miscellaneous	: Corsa-based mini-MPV is not
wheelbase	: 2716 mm			nearly as successful as Meriva.
turning circle	: 10.8 m			

TOUR 1.3 CDTI / 1.7 CDTI

engine type	: diesel, inline-4
displacement	: 1248 / 1686 cc
max. power	: 55 kW (75 bhp) / 74 kW (100 bhp)
@	: 4000 / 4400 rpm
max. torque	: 125 / 148 lb ft
@	: 1750 / 2300 rpm
gears	: 5
kerb weight	: 1225 / 1265 kg
towing weight	: 1000 kg
consumption	: 55.4 / 54.3 mpg
acc. 0-60 mph	: 17.0 / 12.5 s
top speed	: 94 / 106 mph
miscellaneous	: No immediate successor planned on the basis of new Corsa.

OPEL (VAUXHALL) MERIVA 1.4 / 1.8

engine type	: petrol, inline-4
displacement	: 1364 / 1796 cc
max. power	: 66 kW (90 bhp) / 92 kW (125 bhp)
@	: 5600 / 6000 rpm
max. torque	: 92 / 122 lb ft
@	: 4000 / 4600 rpm
gears	: 5
AT	: optional 5-speed
drive	: FWD
brakes f/r	: vent. discs / discs
body type	: 5-dr. MPV
l x w x h	: 4052 x 1694 x 1624 mm
wheelbase	: 2630 mm
turning circle	: 10.5 m

kerb weight	: 1230 / 1280 kg
towing weight	: 1000 / 1200 kg
boot space	: 415 l
fuel capacity	: 53 l
consumption	: 44.1 / 35.8 mpg
acc. 0-62 mph	: 13.8 / 11.3 s
top speed	: 104 / 118 mph
EuroNCAP	: 4 stars
introduction	: spring 2003
last revised in	: January 2006
warranty	: 2 years
miscellaneous	: Successful, class-leading cross-over between Corsa and Astra boasts a spacious, flexible interior. Also available with 1.6 engine.

MERIVA 1.3 CDTI / 1.7 CDTI

engine type	: diesel, inline-4
displacement	: 1248 / 1686 cc
max. power	: 55 kW (75 bhp) / 74 kW (100 bhp)
@	: 4400 rpm
max. torque	: 170 / 240 lb ft
@	: 1750 / 2300 rpm
gears	: 5
kerb weight	: 1293 / 1355 kg
towing weight	: 1200 / 1000 kg
consumption	: 56.5 / 54.3 mpg
acc. 0-60 mph	: 17.8 / 13.4 s
top speed	: 98 / 111 mph
miscellaneous	: Frugal Merivas, thanks to reliable diesel engines.

OPEL (VAUXHALL) ASTRA 1.4 / 1.6

engine type	: petrol, inline-4	kerb weight	: 1130 / 1165 kg
displacement	: 1364 / 1598 cc	towing weight	: 1000 / 1200 kg
max. power	: 66 kW (90 bhp) / 85 kW (115 bhp)	boot space	: 380 l
@	: 5600 / 6000 rpm	fuel capacity	: 52 l
max. torque	: 92 / 114 lb ft	consumption	: 46.3 / 43.5 mpg
@	: 4000 rpm	acc. 0-62 mph	: 13.7 / 11.6 s
gears	: 5	top speed	: 112 / 119 mph
AT	: optional 5-speed	EuroNCAP	: 5 stars
drive	: FWD	introduction	: March 2004
brakes f/r	: vent. discs / drums	last revised in	: February 2007
body type	: 5-dr. hatchback	warranty	: 2 years
l x w x h	: 4249 x 1804 x 1460 mm	miscellaneous	: Facelift prolongs life of the Astra.
wheelbase	: 2614 mm		Bearing the name Saturn, it has
turning circle	: 10.8 m		now even started a new career in
			the States.

ASTRA 1.8

engine type	: petrol, inline-4
displacement	: 1796 cc
max. power	: 103 kW (140 bhp)
@	: 6300 rpm
max. torque	: 129 lb ft
@	: 3800 rpm
gears	: 5
kerb weight	: 1210 kg
towing weight	: 1300 kg
consumption	: 38.7 mpg
acc. 0-60 mph	: 10.2 s
top speed	: 129 mph
miscellaneous	: These petrol engines are also available for the Estate and Sport Hatch.

OPEL (VAUXHALL) ASTRA ESTATE 1.3 CDTI / 1.7 CDTI

O

engine type	: diesel, inline-4	kerb weight	: 1280 / 1293 kg
displacement	: 1248 / 1686 cc	towing weight	: 1400 kg
max. power	: 66 kW (90 bhp) / 74 kW (100 bhp)	boot space	: 500 l
@	: 4000 / 4400 rpm	fuel capacity	: 52 l
max. torque	: 147 / 177 lb ft	consumption	: 55.4 mpg
@	: 1750 / 2300 rpm	acc. 0-62 mph	: 14.1 / 12.5 s
gears	: 6 / 5	top speed	: 107 / 112 mph
AT	: -	EuroNCAP	: 5 stars
drive	: FWD	introduction	: July 2004
brakes f/r	: vent. discs / discs	last revised in	: February 2007
body type	: 5-dr. stationwagon	warranty	: 2 years
l x w x h	: 4515 x 1753 x 1500 mm	miscellaneous	: Spacious estate model. Turn to
wheelbase	: 2703 mm		the other Astra models for speci-
turning circle	: 11.1 m		fications of the available petrol
			engines.

OPEL (VAUXHALL) ASTRA SPORT HATCH 1.6T

engine type	: petrol, inline-4	kerb weight	: 1265 kg
displacement	: 1598 cc	towing weight	: 1500 kg
max. power	: 132 kW (180 bhp)	boot space	: 340 l
@	: 5500 tpm	fuel capacity	: 52 l
max. torque	: 169 lb ft	consumption	: 36.7 mpg
@	: 2000 rpm	acc. 0-62 mph	: 8.2 s
gears	: 6	top speed	: 139 mph
AT	: -	EuroNCAP	: 5 stars
drive	: FWD	introduction	: December 2005
brakes f/r	: vent. discs / discs	last revised in	: February 2007
body type	: 3-dr. hatchback	warranty	: 2 years
l x w x h	: 4288 x 1753 x 1413 mm	miscellaneous	: The 1.6 turbocharged engine is
wheelbase	: 2614 mm		new for the Astra and replaces
turning circle	: 10.8 m		the 2.0 T unit. With maximum
			power rated at 180 bhp, it is a very
			potent engine, yet also pleasantly
			economical.

OPEL (VAUXHALL) ASTRA TWINTOP 1.6 / 1.8

engine type	: petrol, inline-4	**kerb weight**	: 1415 / 1420 kg
displacement	: 1598 / 1796 cc	**towing weight**	: 1050 / 1200 kg
max. power	: 77 kW (105 bhp) /	**boot space**	: 205 - 440 l
	103 kW (140 bhp)	**fuel capacity**	: 52 l
@	: 6000 / 6300 rpm	**consumption**	: 40.4 / 36.7
max. torque	: 110 / 129 lb ft	**acc. 0-62 mph**	: 14.1 / 11.4 s
@	: 3900 / 3800 rpm	**top speed**	: 116 / 130 mph
gears	: 5	**EuroNCAP**	: n.a.
AT	: -	**introduction**	: April 2006
drive	: FWD	**last revised in**	: -
brakes f/r	: vent. discs / discs	**warranty**	: 2 years
body type	: 2-dr. convertible	**miscellaneous**	: Pretty 4-seater convertible with
l x w x h	: 4476 x 1831 x 1414 mm		clever roof top construction. Also
wheelbase	: 2614 mm		available as 2.0T with 170/200 bhp
turning circle	: 10.8 m		and 1.9 CDTi with 150 bhp.

OPEL (VAUXHALL) ZAFIRA 1.8 / 2.2

engine type	: petrol, inline-4
displacement	: 1796 / 2198 cc
max. power	: 103 kW (140 bhp) /
@	110 kW (150 bhp)
max. torque	: 6300 / 5600 rpm
@	: 129 / 159 lb ft
gears	: 3800 / 4000 rpm
AT	: 5 / 6
drive	: - / optional 4-speed
brakes f/r	: FWD
body type	: vent. discs / discs
l x w x h	: 5-dr. MPV
wheelbase	: 4467 x 1801 x 1635 mm
turning circle	: 2703 mm
	: 10.9 m

kerb weight	: 1403 / 1470 kg
towing weight	: 1200 kg
boot space	: 140 - 1820 l
fuel capacity	: 58 l
consumption	: 36.2 / 34.4 mpg
acc. 0-62 mph	: 11.5 / 10.6 s
top speed	: 122 / 124 mph
EuroNCAP	: 5 stars
introduction	: summer 2005
last revised in	: -
warranty	: 2 years
miscellaneous	: Second generation of pioneering model, positioned somewhat higher in the market now to make room for Meriva. FLEX-7 seating concept retained. Also available as 1.6, 2.0 T and VXR.

ZAFIRA 1.9 CDTI

engine type	: diesel, inline-4
displacement	: 1910 cc
max. power	: 88 kW (120 bhp) / 110 kW (150 bhp)
@	: 3500 / 4000 rpm
max. torque	: 206 / 236 lb ft
@	: 1700 / 2000 rpm
gears	: 6
kerb weight	: 1513 / 1528 kg
towing weight	: 1200 / 1500 kg
consumption	: 46.3 / 45.6 lb ft
acc. 0-60 mph	: 12.0 / 10.4 s
top speed	: 116 / 126 lb ft
miscellaneous	: Particle filter comes as standard.

OPEL (VAUXHALL) VECTRA 1.8 16V / 2.2 16V

engine type	: petrol, inline-4
displacement	: 1796 / 2198 cc
max. power	: 103 kW (140 bhp) /
	114 kW (155 bhp)
@	: 6300 / 5600 rpm
max. torque	: 129 / 162 lb ft
@	: 3800 rpm
gears	: 5 / 6
AT	: - / optional 5-speed
drive	: FWD
brakes f/r	: vent. discs / discs
body type	: 4-dr. saloon
l x w x h	: 4596 x 1798 x 1460 mm
wheelbase	: 2700 mm
turning circle	: 11.0 m

kerb weight	: 1295 / 1335 kg
towing weight	: 1400 / 1500 kg
boot space	: 500 - 1050 l
fuel capacity	: 60 l
consumption	: 39.2 / 37.7 mpg
acc. 0-62 mph	: 10.7 / 9.6 s
top speed	: 131 / 135 mph
EuroNCAP	: 4 stars
introduction	: autumn 2001
last revised in	: autumn 2005
warranty	: 2 years
miscellaneous	: Successful middle-class lease car. Available as saloon and hatchback. New headlights introduced with facelift.

VECTRA 2.0 T

engine type	: petrol, inline-4
displacement	: 1998 cc
max. power	: 129 kW (175 bhp)
@	: 5500 rpm
max. torque	: 195 lb ft
@	: 2500 rpm
gears	: 6
kerb weight	: 1465 kg
towing weight	: 1700 kg
consumption	: 32.8 mpg
acc. 0-60 mph	: 9.4 s
top speed	: 143 mph
miscellaneous	: Good performance, high equipment level.

OPEL (VAUXHALL) VECTRA ESTATE 1.9 CDTI

engine type	: petrol, inline-4
displacement	: 1910 cc
max. power	: 88 kW (120 bhp) / 110 kW (150 bhp)
@	: 3500 / 4000 rpm
max. torque	: 206 / 232 lb ft
@	: 2000 rpm
gears	: 6
AT	: - / optional 6-speed
drive	: FWD
brakes f/r	: vent. discs / discs
body type	: 5-dr. stationwagon
l x w x h	: 4822 x 1798 x 1500 mm
wheelbase	: 2830 mm
turning circle	: 10.9 m

kerb weight	: 1505 kg
towing weight	: 1500 kg
boot space	: 530 - 1850 l
fuel capacity	: 60 l
consumption	: 48.7 mpg
acc. 0-62 mph	: 12.0 / 10.5 s
top speed	: 121 / 130 mph
EuroNCAP	: 4 stars
introduction	: spring 2003
last revised in	: autumn 2005
warranty	: 2 years
miscellaneous	: One of the biggest stationwagons on the market, with a giant flat loading platform. Also available with both 4- and 6-cylinder petrol engines.

VECTRA ESTATE VXR

engine type	: petrol, inline-4
displacement	: 2792 cc
max. power	: 206 kW (280 bhp)
@	: 5500 rpm
max. torque	: 262 lb ft
@	: 1800 rpm
gears	: 6
kerb weight	: 1613 kg
towing weight	: 1800 kg
consumption	: 26.9 mpg
acc. 0-60 mph	: 6.5 s
top speed	: 155 mph
miscellaneous	: Recent power boost, but top speed limited to 155 mph. Previous VXR did 160 mph, enough to beat a BMW M5.

OPEL (VAUXHALL) SIGNUM 2.8 V6 TURBO / 3.0 V6 CDTI

O

engine type	: petrol, V6 / diesel, V6	kerb weight	: 1535 / 1610 kg
displacement	: 2792 / 2958 cc	towing weight	: 1700 kg
max. power	: 169 kW (230 bhp) /	boot space	: 365 - 1410 l
	130 kW (184 bhp)	fuel capacity	: 60 l
@	: 5500 / 4000 rpm	consumption	: 26.6 / 40.4 mpg
max. torque	: 243 / 295 lb ft	acc. 0-62 mph	: 7.6 / 9.6 s
@	: 1800 / 1900 rpm	top speed	: 151 / 139 mph
gears	: 6	EuroNCAP	: 4 stars
AT	: optional 6-speed	introduction	: March 2003
drive	: FWD	last revised in	: September 2005
brakes f/r	: vent. discs	warranty	: 2 years
body type	: 5-dr. hatchback	miscellaneous	: Spacious hatchback on Vectra
l x w x h	: 4636 x 1798 x 1466 mm		Estate platform, with two separate
wheelbase	: 2830 mm		seats in the back.
turning circle	: 11.4 m		

OPEL (VAUXHALL) GT

engine type	: petrol, inline-4	kerb weight	: 1306kg
displacement	: 1998 cc	towing weight	: -
max. power	: 194 kW (260 bhp)	boot space	: 157 l
@	: 5300 rpm	fuel capacity	: 52 l
max. torque	: 258 lb ft	consumption	: 30.7 mpg
@	: 2500 rpm	acc. 0-62 mph	: 5.7 s
gears	: 5	top speed	: 142 mph
AT	: -	EuroNCAP	: n.a.
drive	: RWD	introduction	: April 2007
brakes f/r	: vent. discs	last revised in	: -
body type	: 2-dr. convertible	warranty	: 2 years
l x w x h	: 4091 x 1813 x 1274 mm	miscellaneous	: The GT nomenclature is back on a
wheelbase	: 2614 mm		roadster model based on the
turning circle	: 10.4 m		American Saturn Sky. Fast car at
			an honest price.

OPEL (VAUXHALL) ANTARA 2.4

engine type	: petrol, inline-4		kerb weight	: 1805 / 1865 kg
displacement	: 2405 cc		towing weight	: 1500 / 2000 kg
max. power	: 103 kW (140 bhp)		boot space	: 405 l
@	: 5200 rpm		fuel capacity	: 65 l
max. torque	: 162 lb ft		consumption	: 29.4 mpg
@	: 2400 rpm		acc. 0-62 mph	: 11.9 s
gears	: 5		top speed	: 109 mph
AT	: -		EuroNCAP	: n.a.
drive	: FWD		introduction	: September 2006
brakes f/r	: vent. discs / discs		last revised in	: -
body type	: 5-dr. SUV		warranty	: 2 years
l x w x h	: 4575 x 1850 x 1704 mm		miscellaneous	: Based on the Chevrolet Captiva, but without the third row of seats. Antara faster and more economical than American.
wheelbase	: 2707 mm			
turning circle	: 12.4 m			

ANTARA 2.0 CDTI

engine type	: diesel, inline-4
displacement	: 1991 cc
max. power	: 110 kW (150 bhp)
@	: 4000 rpm
max. torque	: 236 lb ft
@	: 2000 rpm
gears	: 5, optional 5-speed automatic
kerb weight	: n.a.
towing weight	: 2000 kg
consumption	: 37.7 mpg
acc. 0-60 mph	: 10.3 s
top speed	: 112 mph
miscellaneous	: Diesel-powered version likely to be bestseller of Antara range.

PEUGEOT 107 1.0

engine type	: petrol, inline-3	kerb weight	: 865 kg
displacement	: 998 cc	towing weight	: -
max. power	: 50 kW (68 bhp)	boot space	: 139 - 751 l
@	: 6000 rpm	fuel capacity	: 35 l
max. torque	: 70 lb ft	consumption	: 61.4 mpg
@	: 3600 rpm	acc. 0-62 mph	: 13.7 s
gears	: 5	top speed	: 100 mph
AT	: optional 5-speed	EuroNCAP	: 4 stars
drive	: FWD	introduction	: December 2005
brakes f/r	: vent. discs / discs	last revised in	: -
body type	: 3- / 5-dr. hatchback	warranty	: 2 years
l x w x h	: 3430 x 1630 x 1470 mm	miscellaneous	: Front has typical Peugeot family
wheelbase	: 2340 mm		look. More versions of this budget
turning circle	: 9.5 m		car not planned.

PEUGEOT 1007 1.4 / 1.6 16V

engine type	: petrol, inline-4
displacement	: 1360 / 1587 cc
max. power	: 55 kW (75 bhp) / 80 kW (110 bhp)
@	: 5400 / 5800 rpm
max. torque	: 88 / 110 lb ft
@	: 3300 / 4000 rpm
gears	: 5
AT	: optional, 2Tronic
drive	: FWD
brakes f/r	: vent. discs, drum brakes / discs
body type	: 3-dr. hatchback
l x w x h	: 3731 x 1686 x 1620 mm
wheelbase	: 2315 mm
turning circle	: 10.1 m

kerb weight	: 1115 / 1178 kg
towing weight	: 987 / 1090 kg
boot space	: 326 - 977 l
fuel capacity	: 40 l
consumption	: 43.5 / 40.9 mpg
acc. 0-62 mph	: 15.6 / 11.1 s
top speed	: 103 / 118 mph
EuroNCAP	: 5 stars
introduction	: Summer 2005
last revised in	: -
warranty	: 2 years
miscellaneous	: Trendy city car with sliding doors for ease of entry in confined parking spaces. More expensive than comparable cars. Also 90 bhp 1.4 engine available.

1007 1.4 HDI

engine type	: diesel, inline-4
displacement	: 1398 cc
max. power	: 50 kW (70 bhp)
@	: 4000 rpm
max. torque	: 120 lb ft
@	: 2000 rpm
gears	: 5
kerb weight	: 1143 kg
towing weight	: 1137 kg
consumption	: 60.1 mpg
acc. 0-60 mph	: 16.7 s
top speed	: 99 mph
miscellaneous	: Diesel power makes small 1007 thrifty.

PEUGEOT PARTNER 1.4 / 1.6

engine type	: petrol, inline-4	kerb weight	: 1163 / 1226 kg
displacement	: 1360 / 1587 cc	towing weight	: 900 / 1100 kg
max. power	: 55 kW (75 bhp) / 80 kW (110 bhp)	boot space	: 624 - 2800 l
@	: 5500 / 5750 rpm	fuel capacity	: 55 l
max. torque	: 90 / 110 lb ft	consumption	: 39.8 / 37.5 mpg
@	: 3400 / 4000 rpm	acc. 0-62 mph	: 14.5 / 11.2 s
gears	: 5	top speed	: 93 / 107 mph
AT	: -	EuroNCAP	: n.a.
drive	: FWD	introduction	: 1996
brakes f/r	: vent. discs / drum brakes	last revised in	: September 2002
body type	: 4-dr. MPV	warranty	: 2 years
l x w x h	: 4137 x 1724 x 1801 mm	miscellaneous	: Already in its tenth year of
wheelbase	: 2693 mm		production. Good alternative to
turning circle	: 11.3 m		marginally higher positioned car
			when spaciousness is more
			important than chassis or looks.

PARTNER 1.6 HDI 90

engine type	: diesel, inline-4
displacement	: 1560 cc
max. power	: 66 kW (90 bhp)
@	: 4000 rpm
max. torque	: 161 lb ft
@	: 1900 rpm
gears	: 5
kerb weight	: 1244 / 1215 kg
towing weight	: 1100 kg
consumption	: 52.3 mpg
acc. 0-60 mph	: 12.9 s
top speed	: 99 mph
miscellaneous	: Diesel versions account for majority of commercial Partner sales. Version of 1.4 that runs on natural gas also available, for added tax benefits.

PEUGEOT 206 1.4

engine type	: petrol, inline-4		**kerb weight**	: 925 kg
displacement	: 1360 cc		**towing weight**	: 1100 kg
max. power	: 55 kW (75 bhp)		**boot space**	: 245 l
@	: 5500 rpm		**fuel capacity**	: 50 l
max. torque	: 90 lb ft		**consumption**	: 44.1 mpg
@	: 2800 rpm		**acc. 0-62 mph**	: 12.2 s
gears	: 5		**top speed**	: 106 mph
AT	: -		**EuroNCAP**	: 4 stars
drive	: FWD		**introduction**	: July 1998
brakes f/r	: discs / drums		**last revised in**	: September 2002
body type	: 3-dr. hatchback		**warranty**	: 2 years
l x w x h	: 3835 x 1652 x 1428 mm		**miscellaneous**	: Peugeot decided to prolong
wheelbase	: 2442 mm			production of the 206 as a cheap
turning circle	: 9.8 m			base level model, something which
				Renault did with the Clio and Fiat
				with the Punto.

206 1.4 HDI

engine type	: diesel, inline-4
displacement	: 1398 cc
max. power	: 50 kW (68 bhp)
@	: 4000 rpm
max. torque	: 120 lb ft
@	: 1750 rpm
gears	: 5
kerb weight	: 949 kg
towing weight	: 1100 kg
consumption	: 64.2 mpg
acc. 0-60 mph	: 13.1 s
top speed	: 104 mph
miscellaneous	: Buyers can choose between a three-door and five-door hatchback.

PEUGEOT 207 1.4 / 1.4 VTI

engine type	: petrol, inline-4
displacement	: 1360 cc
max. power	: 55 kW (75 bhp) / 70 kW (95 bhp)
@	: 5400 / 6000 rpm
max. torque	: 90 / 100 lb ft
@	: 3250 / 1400 rpm
gears	: 5
AT	: -
drive	: FWD
brakes f/r	: vent. discs / discs
body type	: 3- / 5-dr. hatchback
l x w x h	: 4030 x 1748 x 1470 mm
wheelbase	: 2540 mm
turning circle	: 10,4 m

kerb weight	: 1113 / 1140 kg
towing weight	: 900 / 1150 kg
boot space	: 270 l
fuel capacity	: 60 l
consumption	: 44.8 / 44.1 mpg
acc. 0-62 mph	: 14.5 / 11.5 s
top speed	: 106 / 112 mph
EuroNCAP	: 5 stars
introduction	: March 2006
last revised in	: -
warranty	: 2 years
miscellaneous	: The new 1.4 VTi engine is the same unit as in the Mini One. Refer to the 207 SW and 207 CC models for specifications of the other available engines.

207 RC

engine type	: petrol, inline-4
displacement	: 1598 cc
max. power	: 128 kW (175 bhp)
@	: 6000 rpm
max. torque	: 195 lb ft
@	: 1600 rpm
gears	: 6
kerb weight	: 1225 kg
towing weight	: 1150 kg
consumption	: 39.2 mpg
acc. 0-60 mph	: 7.1 s
top speed	: 137 mph
miscellaneous	: Peugeot said goodbye to the GTI tag, fastest versions are now called RC.

207 1.4 HDI

engine type	: diesel, inline-4
displacement	: 1398 cc
max. power	: 50 kW (68 bhp)
@	: 4000 rpm
max. torque	: 120 lb ft
@	: 1750 rpm
gears	: 5
kerb weight	: 1151 kg
towing weight	: 1150 kg
consumption	: 62.7 mpg
acc. 0-60 mph	: 15.5 s
top speed	: 104 mph
miscellaneous	: An economical rather than quick car and therefore also clean: emission of CO2 is only 120 grammes per kilometre.

PEUGEOT 207 SW 1.6 HDI / HDIF

P

engine type	: diesel, inline-4
displacement	: 1560 cc
max. power	: 66 kW (90 bhp) / 80 kW (110 bhp)
@	: 4000 rpm
max. torque	: 161 / 180 lb ft
@	: 1750 rpm
gears	: 5
AT	: -
drive	: FWD
brakes f/r	: vent. discs / discs
body type	: 5-dr. stationwagon
l x w x h	: 4149 x 1748 x 1510 mm
wheelbase	: 2442 mm
turning circle	: 10.4 m

kerb weight	: 1264 / 1275kg
towing weight	: 1150 kg
boot space	: 428 l
fuel capacity	: 66 l
consumption	: 61.4 / 56.4 mpg
acc. 0-62 mph	: 11.8 / 10.3 s
top speed	: 123 / 131 mph
EuroNCAP	: 5 stars
introduction	: July 2007
last revised in	: -
warranty	: 2 years
miscellaneous	: There is also an estate version of the new 207. It is one of the few stationwagons in this segment, together with the Skoda Fabia Estate.

PEUGEOT 207 CC 1.6 VTI / 1.6 THP

engine type	: petrol, inline-4	kerb weight	: 1327 / 1393 kg
displacement	: 1598 cc	towing weight	: -
max. power	: 88 kW (120 bhp) / 110 kW (150 bhp)	boot space	: 370 l
@	: 6000 / 5800 rpm	fuel capacity	: 50 l
max. torque	: 120 / 180 lb ft	consumption	: 43.5 / 39.2 mpg
@	: 4250 / 1400 rpm	acc. 0-62 mph	: 10.7 / 8.6 s
gears	: 5	top speed	: 124 / 129 mph
AT	: optional 4-speed	EuroNCAP	: 5 stars
drive	: FWD	introduction	: March 2007
brakes f/r	: vent. discs / discs	last revised in	: -
body type	: 2-dr. convertible	warranty	: 2 years
l x w x h	: 4037 x 1750 x 1397 mm	miscellaneous	: Because of its success, the 206
wheelbase	: 2540 mm		CC deserved a worthy successor.
turning circle	: 10.6 m		Officially a four-seater, the 207 CC
			in reality only seats two.

PEUGEOT 308 1.6 VTI / 1.6 THP

engine type	: petrol, inline-4
displacement	: 1598 cc
max. power	: 88 kW (120 bhp) / 110 kW (150 bhp)
@	: 6000 / 5800 rpm
max. torque	: 120 / 180 lb ft
@	: 4250 / 1400 rpm
gears	: 5
AT	: optional 4-speed
drive	: FWD
brakes f/r	: vent. discs / discs
body type	: 3- / 5-dr. hatchback
l x w x h	: 4276 x 1815 x 1498 mm
wheelbase	: 2608 mm
turning circle	: n.a.

kerb weight	: 1277 / 1314 kg
towing weight	: n.a.
boot space	: n.a.
fuel capacity	: 60 l
consumption	: 42.2 / 39.8 mpg
acc. 0-62 mph	: 10.8 / 8.8 s
top speed	: 122 / 133 mph
EuroNCAP	: n.a.
introduction	: September 2007
last revised in	: -
warranty	: 2 years
miscellaneous	: New medium-sized model shares technology with old 307 and new 207. A convertible and station-wagon will follow.

308 1.6 HDIF / 2.0 HDIF

engine type	: diesel, inline-4
displacement	: 1560 / 1997 cc
max. power	: 80 kW (110 bhp) / 100 kW (136 bhp)
@	: 4000 tpm
max. torque	: 180 / 240 lb ft
@	: 1750 / 2000 rpm
gears	: 6
kerb weight	: 1312 / 1408 kg
towing weight	: n.a.
consumption	: 60.1 / 51.4 mpg
acc. 0-60 mph	: 11.3 / 10.1 s
top speed	: 119 / 129 mph
miscellaneous	: Both diesel engines are equipped with a particle filter.

PEUGEOT 307 SW 1.6 HDI / 2.0 HDIF

engine type	: diesel, inline-4	kerb weight	: 1369 / 1475 kg
displacement	: 1560 / 1997 cc	towing weight	: 1300 / 1500 kg
max. power	: 66 kW (90 bhp) / 100 kW (136 bhp)	boot space	: 598 - 2082 l
@	: 4000 rpm	fuel capacity	: 60 / 60 l
max. torque	: 180 / 240 lb ft	consumption	: 55.3 / 50.4 mpg
@	: 1750 / 2000 rpm	acc. 0-62 mph	: 13.3 / 10.8 s
gears	: 5 / 6	top speed	: 114 / 122 mph
AT	: -	EuroNCAP	: n.a.
drive	: FWD	introduction	: April 2002
brakes f/r	: vent. discs / discs	last revised in	: September 2005
body type	: 5-dr. stationwagon	warranty	: 2 years
l x w x h	: 4432 x 1757 x 1544 mm	miscellaneous	: SW has glass roof section, Estate
wheelbase	: 2708 mm		has more sober equipment.
turning circle	: 11.0 m		Spacious and popular models.

PEUGEOT 307 CC 1.6 16V / CC 2.0 16V

engine type	: petrol, inline-4
displacement	: 1587 / 1997 cc
max. power	: 80 kW (110 bhp) / 103 kW (143 bhp)
@	: 5800 / 6000 rpm
max. torque	: 110 / 150 lb ft
@	: 4000 / 4000 rpm
gears	: 5
AT	: - / optional 4-speed
drive	: FWD
brakes f/r	: vent. discs / discs
body type	: 2-dr. convertible
l x w x h	: 4360 x 1759 x 1424 mm
wheelbase	: 2608 mm
turning circle	: 11.0 m

kerb weight	: 1428 / 1443 kg
towing weight	: 1200 / 1320 kg
boot space	: 232 l
fuel capacity	: 50 l
consumption	: 37.2 / 34.9 mpg
acc. 0-62 mph	: 12.7 / 10.1 s
top speed	: 119 / 129 mph
EuroNCAP	: 4 stars
introduction	: April 2003
last revised in	: September 2005
warranty	: 2 years
miscellaneous	: Former concept car now a big hit in convertible market. Also available with 2.0 diesel unit with particle filter and 136 bhp.

PEUGEOT 407 1.8 16V

engine type	: petrol, inline-4	kerb weight	: 1375 kg
displacement	: 1749 cc	towing weight	: 1600 kg
max. power	: 92 kW (125 bhp)	boot space	: 407 l
@	: 6000 rpm	fuel capacity	: 66 l
max. torque	: 127 lb ft	consumption	: 36.6 mpg
@	: 3750 rpm	acc. 0-62 mph	: 10.3 s
gears	: 5	top speed	: 126 mph
AT	: -	EuroNCAP	: 5 stars
drive	: FWD	introduction	: April 2004
brakes f/r	: vent. discs / discs	last revised in	: -
body type	: 4-dr. saloon	warranty	: 2 years
l x w x h	: 4676 x 1811 x 1445 mm	miscellaneous	: Spacious, modern saloon with fine
wheelbase	: 2725 mm		driving characteristics and bold
turning circle	: 11.2 m		design. Also available with four
			different diesel engines, refer to
			407 SW for specifications.

407 2.0 16V / 2.2 16V

engine type : petrol, inline-4
displacement : 1997 / 2230 cc
max. power : 103 kW (140 bhp) /
120 kW (163 bhp)
@ : 6000 / 5875 rpm
max. torque : 150 / 165 lb ft
@ : 4000 / 4150 rpm
gears : 5 / 6
kerb weight : 1390 / 1491 kg
towing weight : 1800 / 1800 kg
consumption : 34.8 / 31.2 mpg
acc. 0-60 mph : 9.1 / 9.0 s
top speed : 132 / 137 mph
miscellaneous : Strong petrol engines, but 3.0 V6
is best of them all. Refer to 407
Coupe for specifications of V6.

PEUGEOT 407 SW 1.6 HDIF 16V

engine type	: diesel, inline-4	kerb weight	: 1467 kg
displacement	: 1560 cc	towing weight	: 1000 kg
max. power	: 80 kW (110 bhp)	boot space	: 448 - 1365 l
@	: 4000 rpm	fuel capacity	: 66 l
max. torque	: 180 lb ft	consumption	: 50.4 mpg
@	: 1750 rpm	acc. 0-62 mph	: 12.1 s
gears	: 5	top speed	: 117 mph
AT	: -	EuroNCAP	: 5 stars
drive	: FWD	introduction	: September 2004
brakes f/r	: vent. discs / discs	last revised in	: -
body type	: 5-dr. stationwagon	warranty	: 2 years
l x w x h	: 4763 x 1811 x 1486 mm	miscellaneous	: Looks were more important than interior space, which is not unusual with more expensive middle-class stationwagons of this type.
wheelbase	: 2725 mm		
turning circle	: 11.2 m		

407 SW 2.0 HDIF 16V / 2.2 HDIF 16V

engine type	: diesel, inline-4
displacement	: 1997 / 2179 cc
max. power	: 100 kW (136 bhp) / 125 kW (170 bhp)
@	: 4000 rpm
max. torque	: 240 / 277 lb ft
@	: 2000 / 1500 rpm
gears	: 6
kerb weight	: 1523 / 1650 kg
towing weight	: 1600 / 1900 kg
consumption	: 47.1 / 45.5 mpg
acc. 0-60 mph	: 10.1 / 9.4 s
top speed	: 126 / 137 mph
miscellaneous	: Diesel engines in SW topped by 2.7 HDiF (refer to 407 Coupe), but 2.7 hardly faster than 2.2 and a lot more expensive.

PEUGEOT 407 COUPÉ 2.2 / 3.0 V6

engine type	: petrol, inline-4 / V6
displacement	: 2230 / 2946 cc
max. power	: 120 kW (163 bhp) /
	155 kW (211 bhp)
@	: 5875 / 6000 rpm
max. torque	: 165 / 218 lb ft
@	: 4150 / 3750 rpm
gears	: 6
AT	: - / optional 6-speed
drive	: FWD
brakes f/r	: vent. discs
body type	: 2-dr. coupe
l x w x h	: 4815 x 1868 x 1400 mm
wheelbase	: 2720 mm
turning circle	: 11.5 m

kerb weight	: 1525 / 1612 kg
towing weight	: n.a.
boot space	: 400 l
fuel capacity	: 66 l
consumption	: 30.7 / 27.6 mpg
acc. 0-62 mph	: 9.2 / 8.4 s
top speed	: 138 / 151 mph
EuroNCAP	: 5 stars
introduction	: January 2006
last revised in	: -
warranty	: 2 years
miscellaneous	: Stretched profile masks long front overhang. Designed in-house, whereas predecessors were styled by Pininfarina.

407 COUPÉ 2.7 HDIF

engine type	: diesel, V6
displacement	: 2720 cc
max. power	: 150 kW (205 bhp)
@	: 4000 rpm
max. torque	: 330 lb ft
@	: 1900 rpm
gears	: 6-speed automatic
kerb weight	: 1724 kg
towing weight	: n.a.
consumption	: 33.2 mpg
acc. 0-60 mph	: 8.5 s
top speed	: 143 mph
miscellaneous	: Top-of-the-range has diesel power under the bonnet, combined with a 6-speed automatic transmission.

PEUGEOT 607 2.2 16V / 3.0 V6 24V

engine type	: petrol, inline-4 / V6
displacement	: 2230 / 2946 cc
max. power	: 120 kW (163 bhp) / 155 kW (211 bhp)
@	: 5875 / 6000 rpm
max. torque	: 162 / 218 lb ft
@	: 4150 / 3750 rpm
gears	: 6 / -
AT	: - / 6-speed
drive	: FWD
brakes f/r	: vent. discs / discs
body type	: 4-dr. saloon
l x w x h	: 4902 x 1800 x 1442 mm
wheelbase	: 2800 mm
turning circle	: 11.4 m

kerb weight	: 1510 / 1619 kg
towing weight	: 1850 / 1800 kg
boot space	: 577 l
fuel capacity	: 80 l
consumption	: 30.7 / 27.7 mpg
acc. 0-62 mph	: 9.9 / 9.2 s
top speed	: 137 / 145 mph
EuroNCAP	: 4 stars
introduction	: September 1999
last revised in	: November 2005
warranty	: 2 years
miscellaneous	: It is traditionally difficult for outsiders to sell big cars in a segment that is dominated by expensive models from Germany. 607 is really a fine alternative but remains a rare car.

607 2.0 HDIF 16V / 2.2 HDIF 16V

engine type	: diesel, inline-4
displacement	: 1997 / 2179 cc
max. power	: 100 kW (136 bhp) / 125 kW (170 bhp)
@	: 4000 rpm
max. torque	: 240 / 277 lb ft
@	: 2000 / 1500 rpm
gears	: 6
kerb weight	: 1565 / 1595 kg
towing weight	: 1760 / 1800 kg
consumption	: 46.3 / 44.1 mpg
acc. 0-60 mph	: 10.8 / 9.3 s
top speed	: 128 / 139 mph
miscellaneous	: More horsepower now for 2.0 and 2.2 diesel engines.

607 2.7 HDIF V6

engine type	: diesel, V6
displacement	: 2720 cc
max. power	: 150 kW (204 bhp)
@	: 4000 rpm
max. torque	: 325 lb ft
@	: 1900 rpm
gears	: 6-speed automatic
kerb weight	: 1698 kg
towing weight	: 1700 kg
consumption	: 33.6 mpg
acc. 0-60 mph	: 8.7 s
top speed	: 143 mph
miscellaneous	: V6 engine developed by PSA and Ford but also used by Jaguar and Land Rover.

PEUGEOT 807 2.0 16V / 2.0 HDIF 16V

engine type	: petrol / diesel, inline-4	kerb weight	: 1606 / 1718 kg
displacement	: 1997 cc	towing weight	: 1700 / 1850 kg
max. power	: 103 kW (140 bhp) /	boot space	: 480 - 2948 l
	100 kW (136 bhp)	fuel capacity	: 80 l
@	: 6000 / 4000 rpm	consumption	: 31.4 / 39.8 mpg
max. torque	: 150 / 236 lb ft	acc. 0-62 mph	: 11.6 / 12.5 s
@	: 4000 / 2000 rpm	top speed	: 115 / 118 mph
gears	: 5 / 6	EuroNCAP	: 5 stars
AT	: optional 4-speed / -	introduction	: July 2002
drive	: FWD	last revised in	: -
brakes f/r	: vent. discs / discs	warranty	: 2 years
body type	: 5-dr. MPV	miscellaneous	: 807 model range much smaller
l x w x h	: 4727 x 1854 x 1752 mm		now, but 110 bhp HDiF version
wheelbase	: 2825 mm		with
turning circle	: 10.8 m		automatic transmission also
			available.

PEUGEOT 4007 2.2 HDI

engine type	: diesel, inline-4
displacement	: 2178 cc
max. power	: 115 kW (156 bhp)
@	: 4000 rpm
max. torque	: 285 lb ft
@	: 2000 rpm
gears	: 6
AT	: -
drive	: 4WD
brakes f/r	: vent. discs / discs
body type	: 5-dr. SUV
l x w x h	: 4635 x 1805 x 1713 mm
wheelbase	: 2670 mm
turning circle	: 10.6 m

kerb weight	: 1717 kg
towing weight	: 2000 kg
boot space	: 184 l
fuel capacity	: 60 l
consumption	: 39.2 mpg
acc. 0-62 mph	: 9.9 s
top speed	: 124 mph
EuroNCAP	: n.a.
introduction	: July 2007
last revised in	: -
warranty	: 2 years
miscellaneous	: Very first SUV from Peugeot is in fact a Mitsubishi Outlander in disguise. Its diesel engine however is a Peugeot unit, which in turn is used by Mitsubishi as well.

P

PORSCHE BOXSTER / BOXSTE R S

engine type	: petrol, flat-6	kerb weight	: 1350 / 1395 kg
displacement	: 2687 / 3387 cc	towing weight	: n.a.
max. power	: 180 kW (245 bhp) /	boot space	: 280 l
	217 kW (295 bhp)	fuel capacity	: 64 l
@	: 6400 / 6250 rpm	consumption	: 30.4 / 26.6 mpg
max. torque	: 202 / 251 lb ft	acc. 0-62 mph	: 6.1 / 5.4 s
@	: 4600 / 4400 rpm	top speed	: 160 / 169 mph
gears	: 5 / 6	EuroNCAP	: n.a.
AT	: optional 5-speed	introduction	: July 2004
drive	: RWD	last revised in	: -
brakes f/r	: vent. discs	warranty	: 2 years
body type	: 2-dr. convertible	miscellaneous	: Boxster engine line-up now
l x w x h	: 4329 x 1801 x 1295 mm		identical to that of fixed-roof
wheelbase	: 2415 mm		Cayman.
turning circle	: 10.9 m		

PORSCHE CAYMAN S

engine type	: petrol, flat-6
displacement	: 3387 cc
max. power	: 217 kW (295 bhp)
@	: 6250 rpm
max. torque	: 251 lb ft
@	: 4400 rpm
gears	: 6
AT	: optional 5-speed
drive	: RWD
brakes f/r	: vent. discs
body type	: 2-dr. coupe
l x w x h	: 4329 x 1801 x 1305 mm
wheelbase	: 2415 mm
turning circle	: 10.9 m

kerb weight	: 1415 kg
towing weight	: -
boot space	: 410 l
fuel capacity	: 64 l
consumption	: 26.6 mpg
acc. 0-62 mph	: 5.4 s
top speed	: 171 mph
EuroNCAP	: n.a.
introduction	: September 2005
last revised in	: -
warranty	: 2 years
miscellaneous	: Coupe based on Boxster. Also available with 2.7 boxer engine with 245 bhp.

PORSCHE 911 CARRERA / CARRERA S

engine type	: petrol, flat-6	kerb weight	: 1470 / 1495 kg
displacement	: 3596 / 3824 cc	towing weight	: n.a.
max. power	: 239 kW (325 bhp) /	boot space	: 135 l
	261 kW (355 bhp)	fuel capacity	: 64 / 64 l
@	: 6800 / 6600 rpm	consumption	: 25.7 / 24.6 mpg
max. torque	: 273 / 295 lb ft	acc. 0-62 mph	: 5.0 / 4.8 s
@	: 4250 / 4600 rpm	top speed	: 177 / 182 mph
gears	: 6	EuroNCAP	: n.a.
AT	: optional 5-speed	introduction	: July 2004
drive	: RWD	last revised in	: -
brakes f/r	: vent. discs	warranty	: 2 years
body type	: 2-dr. coupe	miscellaneous	: 997 model also available as
l x w x h	: 4427 x 1808 x 1310 mm		Carrera 4 and 4S with 4WD and
wheelbase	: 2350 mm		likewise with convertible body.
turning circle	: 12.1 m		All-round sportscar: spacious,
			very fast and great build quality.
			Expensive however.

PORSCHE 911 TURBO / GT2

engine type	: petrol, flat-6	kerb weight	: 1585 / 1515 kg
displacement	: 3600 cc	towing weight	: -
max. power	: 353 kW (480 bhp) /	boot space	: 105 l
	390 kW (530 bhp)	fuel capacity	: 67 l
@	: 6000 / 6500 rpm	consumption	: 22.1 / 22.6 mpg
max. torque	: 457 / 501 lb ft	acc. 0-62 mph	: 3.9 / 3.7 s
@	: 1950 / 2200 rpm	top speed	: 193 / 204 mph
gears	: 6	EuroNCAP	: n.a.
AT	: optional 5-speed / -	introduction	: July 2006
drive	: 4WD / RWD	last revised in	: -
brakes f/r	: vent. discs	warranty	: 2 years
body type	: 2-dr. coupe	miscellaneous	: 'Turbo' and 'Porsche' are inextrica-
l x w x h	: 4450 x 1852 x 1300 mm		bly linked notions. The blown 911
wheelbase	: 2350 mm		is now also available as a convert-
turning circle	: n.a.		ible. The GT2 is the ultimate 'Elfer'.

911 GT3

engine type	: petrol, flat-6
displacement	: 3600 cc
max. power	: 305 kW (415 bhp)
@	: 7600 rpm
max. torque	: 298 lb ft
@	: 5500 rpm
gears	: 6
kerb weight	: 1395 kg
towing weight	: -
consumption	: 22.1 mpg
acc. 0-60 mph	: 4.3 s
top speed	: 192 mph
miscellaneous	: There is also a GT3 RS version, which weighs 20 kg less and is marginally quicker than the GT3. Only for purists.

PORSCHE CAYENNE / CAYENNE S

engine type	: petrol, V6 / V8	kerb weight	: 2160 / 2225 kg
displacement	: 3598 / 4806 cc	towing weight	: 3500 kg
max. power	: 213 kW (290 bhp) /	boot space	: 540 l
	283 kW (385 bhp)	fuel capacity	: 100 l
@	: 6200 rpm	consumption	: 21.9 / 19.0 mpg
max. torque	: 284 / 386 lb ft	acc. 0-62 mph	: 8.1 / 6.6 s
@	: 3000 / 3500 rpm	top speed	: 141 / 157 mph
gears	: 6	EuroNCAP	: n.a.
AT	: optional Tiptronic	introduction	: April 2002
drive	: 4WD	last revised in	: April 2007
brakes f/r	: vent. discs	warranty	: 2 years
body type	: 5-dr. SUV	miscellaneous	: New Cayenne is now equipped
l x w x h	: 4798 x 1928 x 1699 mm		with a new entry level engine that
wheelbase	: 2855 mm		is more suited to a car this big.
turning circle	: 11.4 m		The facelift included a nose job
			as well.

CAYENNE TURBO

engine type	: petrol, V8
displacement	: 4806 cc
max. power	: 368 kW (500 bhp)
@	: 6000 rpm
max. torque	: 516 lb ft
@	: 4500 rpm
gears	: 6-speed Tiptronic
kerb weight	: 2355 kg
towing weight	: 3500 kg
consumption	: 19.0 mpg
acc. 0-60 mph	: 5.1 s
top speed	: 171 mph
miscellaneous	: There are no plans yet for a return of
	the more potent Turbo S model.

RENAULT TWINGO 1.2 16V

engine type	: petrol, inline-4	**kerb weight**	: 925 / 950 kg
displacement	: 1149 cc	**towing weight**	: -
max. power	: 55 kW (75 bhp)	**boot space**	: 230 l
@	: 5500 rpm	**fuel capacity**	: 40 l
max. torque	: 79 lb ft	**consumption**	: 49.5 mpg
@	: 4250 rpm	**acc. 0-62 mph**	: 12.0 s
gears	: 5	**top speed**	: 106 mph
AT	: optional 5-speed	**EuroNCAP**	: 4 stars
drive	: FWD	**introduction**	: September 2007
brakes f/r	: vent. discs / drums	**last revised in**	: -
body type	: 3-dr. hatchback	**warranty**	: 2 years
l x w x h	: 3600 x 1654 x 1470 mm	**miscellaneous**	: More business-like than its
wheelbase	: 2367 mm		predecessor, but also very
turning circle	: 10.3 m		practical and very cheap.

P
R

TWINGO GT

engine type	: petrol, inline-4
displacement	: 1149 cc
max. power	: 74 kW (100 bhp)
@	: 5500 rpm
max. torque	: 107 lb ft
@	: 3000 rpm
gears	: 5
kerb weight	: 980 kg
towing weight	: -
consumption	: 47.8 mpg
acc. 0-60 mph	: 9.8 s
top speed	: 117 mph
miscellaneous	: The fastest Twingo ever. The GT can be distinguished by its set of bumpers and wheels.

RENAULT KANGOO 1.6 / 1.6 16V

engine type	: petrol, inline-4	**kerb weight**	: n.a.
displacement	: 1598 cc	**towing weight**	: n.a.
max. power	: 66 kW (90 bhp) / 77 kW (105 bhp)	**boot space**	: 660 l
@	: 5500 / 5750 rpm	**fuel capacity**	: n.a.
max. torque	: 94 / 109 lb ft	**consumption**	: 35.8 / 36.7 mpg
@	: 3000 / 3750 rpm	**acc. 0-62 mph**	: n.a.
gears	: 5	**top speed**	: n.a.
AT	: - / optional 4-speed	**EuroNCAP**	: n.a.
drive	: FWD	**introduction**	: January 2008
brakes f/r	: vent. discs / discs	**last revised in**	: -
body type	: 5-dr. MPV	**warranty**	: 2 years
l x w x h	: 4213 x 1829 x n.b. mm	**miscellaneous**	: The new Kangoo is much bigger than the previous model. Renault therefore plans to build a version with a shorter wheelbase. Unaltered drive train.
wheelbase	: 2697 mm		
turning circle	: n.a.		

KANGOO 1.5 DCI

engine type	: diesel, inline-4
displacement	: 1461 cc
max. power	: 50 kW (68 bhp) / 68 kW (84 bhp)
@	: 4000 / 3750 rpm
max. torque	: 118 / 148 lb ft
@	: 1500 / 1750 rpm
gears	: 5
kerb weight	: n.a.
towing weight	: n.a.
consumption	: 54.3 / 53.3 mpg
acc. 0-60 mph	: n.a.
top speed	: n.a.
miscellaneous	: Also available with the 105 bhp strong 1.5 dCi engine, the only diesel unit fitted with a particle filter.

RENAULT CLIO CAMPUS 1.2 8V / 1.2 16V

engine type	: petrol, inline-4	**kerb weight**	: 890 / 920 kg
displacement	: 1149 cc	**towing weight**	: 1100 / 1150 kg
max. power	: 43 kW (60 bhp) / 55 kW (75 bhp)	**boot space**	: 255 – 1035 l
@	: 5250 / 5500 rpm	**fuel capacity**	: 50 l
max. torque	: 68 / 78 lb ft	**consumption**	: 47.1 / 47.9 mpg
@	: 2500 / 4250 rpm	**acc. 0-62 mph**	: 15.0 / 13.0 s
gears	: 5	**top speed**	: 98 / 106 mph
AT	: -	**EuroNCAP**	: 4 stars
drive	: FWD	**introduction**	: April 1998
brakes f/r	: vent. discs / drums	**last revised in**	: July 2006
body type	: 3- / 5-dr. hatchback	**warranty**	: 2 years
l x w x h	: 3812 x 1639 x 1417 mm	**miscellaneous**	: The old Clio model is still available
wheelbase	: 2472 mm		for the moment, but only in entry
turning circle	: 10.3 m		level form. It can also be ordered
			with the 1.5 dCi diesel unit.

R

RENAULT CLIO 1.2 16V / 1.4 16V

engine type	: petrol, inline-4
displacement	: 1149 / 1598 cc
max. power	: 74 kW (100 bhp) / 82 kW (111 bhp)
@	: 5500 / 6000 rpm
max. torque	: 107 / 112 lb ft
@	: 3000 / 4250 rpm
gears	: 5 / -
AT	: - / 4-speed
drive	: FWD
brakes f/r	: vent. discs / discs
body type	: 3- / 5–dr. hatchback
l x w x h	: 3986 x 1707 x 1493 mm
wheelbase	: 2575 mm
turning circle	: 10.7 m
kerb weight	: 1090 / 1150 kg
towing weight	: 1200 kg
boot space	: 288 l
fuel capacity	: 55 l
consumption	: 47.9 / 37.7 mpg
acc. 0-62 mph	: 11.1 / 12.2 s
top speed	: 114 / 116 mph
EuroNCAP	: 5 stars
introduction	: September 2005
last revised in	: -
warranty	: 2 years
miscellaneous	: Small and economical turbocharged engine is new in the Clio range. There is also a 1.2 unit with either 65 or 75 bhp.

CLIO 1.6 16V / RS

engine type	: petrol, inline-4
displacement	: 1998 cc
max. power	: 102 kW (140 bhp) / 145 kW (197 bhp)
@	: 6000 / 7250 rpm
max. torque	: 143 / 158 lb ft
@	: 3750 / 5550 rpm
gears	: 6
kerb weight	: 1180 / 1235 kg
towing weight	: 1200 kg / -
consumption	: 38.7 / 31.7 mpg
acc. 0-60 mph	: 8.5 / 6.9 s
top speed	: 127 / 134 mph
miscellaneous	: The RS ranks at the top of the range, but the rather inconspicuous 2.0 model is very quick too.

RENAULT MODUS 1.5 DCI 70 / 85

engine type	: diesel, inline-4
displacement	: 1461 cc
max. power	: 50 kW (68 bhp) / 63 kW (86 bhp)
@	: 4000 rpm
max. torque	: 118 / 148 lb ft
@	: 1700 / 1900 rpm
gears	: 5
AT	: - / optional Quickshift
drive	: FWD
brakes f/r	: vent. discs / drum brakes
body type	: 5-dr. MPV
l x w x h	: 3792 x 1695 x 1589 mm
wheelbase	: 2482 mm
turning circle	: 9.9 m

kerb weight	: 1155 / 1160 kg
towing weight	: 900 kg
boot space	: 274 - 1283 l
fuel capacity	: 49 l
consumption	: 60.1 / 62.8 mpg
acc. 0-62 mph	: 15.3 / 13.0 s
top speed	: 97 / 106 mph
EuroNCAP	: 5 stars
introduction	: August 2004
last revised in	: -
warranty	: 2 years
miscellaneous	: Drivetrain shared with Clio. Refer to Clio for specifications of petrol engines.

MODUS 1.5 DCI 105

engine type	: diesel, inline-4
displacement	: 1461 cc
max. power	: 78 kW (105 bhp)
@	: 4000 rpm
max. torque	: 177 lb ft
@	: 2000 rpm
gears	: 6
kerb weight	: 1175 kg
towing weight	: 900 kg
consumption	: 60.1 mpg
acc. 0-60 mph	: 11.2 s
top speed	: 116 mph
miscellaneous	: Excellent diesel engine, also fitted in Clio.

RENAULT MÉGANE 1.4 16V / 1.6 16V

engine type	: petrol, inline-4	kerb weight	: 1140 / 1150 kg
displacement	: 1390 / 1598 cc	towing weight	: 1300 kg
max. power	: 72 kW (100 bhp) / 82 kW (110 bhp)	boot space	: 330 - 1190 l
@	: 6000 rpm	fuel capacity	: 60 l
max. torque	: 94 / 112 lb ft	consumption	: 40.9 mpg
@	: 3750 / 4250 rpm	acc. 0-62 mph	: 12.5 / 10.9 s
gears	: 5	top speed	: 114 / 119 mph
AT	: - / optional 4-speed	EuroNCAP	: 5 stars
drive	: FWD	introduction	: October 2002
brakes f/r	: vent. discs / discs	last revised in	: January 2006
body type	: 3- / 5-dr. hatchback	warranty	: 2 years
l x w x h	: 4209 x 1777 x 1457 mm	miscellaneous	: Already striking design
wheelbase	: 2625 mm		received minor facelift.
turning circle	: 10.5 m		

MÉGANE 2.0 TURBO

engine type	: petrol, inline-4
displacement	: 1998 cc
max. power	: 165 kW (225 bhp)
@	: 5500 rpm
max. torque	: 221 lb ft
@	: 3000 rpm
gears	: 6
kerb weight	: 1330 kg
towing weight	: 1000 kg
consumption	: 32.1 mpg
acc. 0-60 mph	: 6.5 s
top speed	: 147 mph
miscellaneous	: Biggest engine available in Megane, but only in hatchback version with either 3 or 5 doors. Fast 'hot hatch' is built by Renault Sport in Dieppe.

RENAULT MÉGANE SPORTS TOURER 1.5 DCI 85 / 105

engine type	: diesel, inline-4	kerb weight	: 1210 / 1235 kg
displacement	: 1461 cc	towing weight	: 1300 / 1250 kg
max. power	: 63 kW (85 bhp) / 78 kW (105 bhp)	boot space	: 520 - 1600 l
@	: 3750 / 4000 rpm	fuel capacity	: 60 l
max. torque	: 148 / 177 lb ft	consumption	: 60.1 mpg
@	: 1900 / 2000 rpm	acc. 0-62 mph	: 13.1 / 11.4 s
gears	: 5 / 6	top speed	: 108 / 115 mph
AT	: -	EuroNCAP	: 5 stars
drive	: FWD	introduction	: October 2002
brakes f/r	: vent. discs / discs	last revised in	: January 2006
body type	: 5-dr. stationwagon	warranty	: 2 years
l x w x h	: 4500 x 1777 x 1467 mm	miscellaneous	: Sports Tourer and Saloon share
wheelbase	: 2686 mm		same wheelbase, longer than
turning circle	: 10.7 m		hatchback. Engine range identical.

R

MÉGANE SPORTS TOURER 1.9 DCI

engine type	: diesel, inline-4
displacement	: 1870 cc
max. power	: 96 kW (130 bhp)
@	: 4000 rpm
max. torque	: 222 lb ft
@	: 2000 rpm
gears	: 6
kerb weight	: 1285 kg
towing weight	: 1300 kg
consumption	: 51.4 mpg
acc. 0-60 mph	: 9.3 s
top speed	: 124 mph
miscellaneous	: 'FAP' addition to model name
	indicates standard fitment of
	particle filter.

RENAULT MÉGANE COUPÉ-CABRIOLET 2.0 / 2.0 T

engine type	: petrol, inline-4
displacement	: 1998 cc
max. power	: 99 kW (135 bhp) / 120 kW (165 bhp)
@	: 5500 / 5000 rpm
max. torque	: 141 / 199 lb ft
@	: 3750 / 3250 rpm
gears	: 6
AT	: optional 4-speed
drive	: FWD
brakes f/r	: vent. discs / discs
body type	: 2-dr. convertible
l x w x h	: 4355 x 1777 x 1404 mm
wheelbase	: 2522 mm
turning circle	: 10.1 m

kerb weight	: 1365 / 1390 kg
towing weight	: 1200 kg
boot space	: 490 l
fuel capacity	: 60 l
consumption	: 34.4 / 35.3 mpg
acc. 0-62 mph	: 9.9 / 8.7 s
top speed	: 127 / 137 mph
EuroNCAP	: 5 stars
introduction	: September 2003
last revised in	: January 2006
warranty	: 2 years
miscellaneous	: Comfortable 4-seater convertible which doubles as a coupe. Entry level model is 1.6 with 115 bhp. 165 bhp 2.0-litre turbo engine is faster and also available in hatchback.

MÉGANE COUPÉ-CABRIOLET 2.0 DCI

engine type	: diesel, inline-4
displacement	: 1995 cc
max. power	: 110 kW (150 bhp)
@	: 4000 rpm
max. torque	: 250 lb ft
@	: 2000 rpm
gears	: 6
kerb weight	: 1470 kg
towing weight	: 1200 kg
consumption	: 49.6 mpg
acc. 0-60 mph	: 9.6 s
top speed	: 132 mph
miscellaneous	: The number of diesel-powered convertibles continues to grow. Laid-back nature of diesel engine matches well with open-top motoring.

RENAULT SCÉNIC 1.4 16V / 1.6 16V

engine type	: petrol, inline-4	kerb weight	: 1290 / 1295 kg
displacement	: 1390 / 1598 cc	towing weight	: 1300 kg
max. power	: 72 kW (100 bhp) / 82 kW (110 bhp)	boot space	: 406 - 1840 l
@	: 6000 rpm	fuel capacity	: 60 l
max. torque	: 94 / 114 lb ft	consumption	: 39.2 mpg
@	: 3750 / 4250 rpm	acc. 0-62 mph	: 14.3 / 11.8 s
gears	: 5 / 6	top speed	: 108 / 115 mph
AT	: - / optional 4-speed	EuroNCAP	: 5 stars
drive	: FWD	introduction	: July 2003
brakes f/r	: vent. discs / discs	last revised in	: September 2006
body type	: 5-dr. MPV	warranty	: 2 years
l x w x h	: 4259 x 1805 x 1620 mm	miscellaneous	: Received minor facelift like
wheelbase	: 2685 mm		Megane sister. Refer to Grand
turning circle	: 10.7 m		Scenic with longer wheelbase for
			specifications of 2.0 and 2.0 T
			engines.

SCÉNIC 1.5 DCI 85 / 105

engine type	: diesel, inline-4
displacement	: 1461 cc
max. power	: 63 kW (85 bhp) / 78 kW (105 bhp)
@	: 4000 rpm
max. torque	: 148 / 177 lb ft
@	: 2000 rpm
gears	: 5 / 6
kerb weight	: 1315 / 1340 kg
towing weight	: 1300 kg
consumption	: 55.4 / 54.3 mpg
acc. 0-60 mph	: 14.6 / 12.4 s
top speed	: 104 / 111 mph
miscellaneous	: Two additional diesel engines available, more powerful still. Refer to Grand Scenic for specifications.

RENAULT GRAND SCÉNIC 2.0 16V / 2.0 T

engine type	: petrol, inline-4	**kerb weight**	: 1455 / 1480 kg
displacement	: 1998 cc	**towing weight**	: 1300 kg
max. power	: 99 kW (135 bhp) /	**boot space**	: 200 - 1920 l
	120 kW (165 bhp)	**fuel capacity**	: 60 l
@	: 6000 / 5500 rpm	**consumption**	: 34.4 / 34.9 mpg
max. torque	: 141 / 199 lb ft	**acc. 0-62 mph**	: 10.9 / 9.6 s
@	: 3750 / 3250 rpm	**top speed**	: 121 / 128 mph
gears	: 6	**EuroNCAP**	: 5 stars
AT	: optional, 4-speed / -	**introduction**	: January 2004
drive	: FWD	**last revised in**	: September 2006
brakes f/r	: vent. discs / discs	**warranty**	: 2 years
body type	: 5-dr. MPV	**miscellaneous**	: Grand Scenic can accommodate
l x w x h	: 4493 x 1810 x 1636 mm		seven people, due to longer
wheelbase	: 2736 mm		wheelbase and three rows of
turning circle	: 10.8 m		seats. Extra luggage possible as
			well of course.

GRAND SCÉNIC 1.9 DCI / 2.0 DCI

engine type	: diesel, inline-4
displacement	: 1870 / 1995 cc
max. power	: 96 kW (130 bhp) /
	110 kW (150 bhp)
@	: 4000 rpm
max. torque	: 222 / 251 lb ft
@	: 2000 rpm
gears	: 6
kerb weight	: 1475 / 1505 kg
towing weight	: 1300 kg
consumption	: 47.1 / 48.7 mpg
acc. 0-60 mph	: 9.6 / 9.8 s
top speed	: 118 / 127 mph
miscellaneous	: Grand Scenic is now also available
	in 5-seater configuration.

RENAULT LAGUNA 2.0 16V

engine type	: benzine, inline-4	kerb weight	: 1369 kg
displacement	: 1997 cc	towing weight	: 1300 kg
max. power	: 103 kW (140 bhp)	boot space	: 450 l
@	: 6000 rpm	fuel capacity	: 66 l
max. torque	: 144 lb ft	consumption	: 35.7 mpg
@	: 3750 rpm	acc. 0-62 mph	: 9.1 s
gears	: 6	top speed	: 130 mph
AT	: -	EuroNCAP	: n.a.
drive	: FWD	introduction	: October 2007
brakes f/r	: vent. discs / discs	last revised in	: -
body type	: 5-dr. hatchback	warranty	: 3 years
l x w x h	: 4695 x 1811 x 1445 mm	miscellaneous	: Renault claims that the new
wheelbase	: 2756 mm		Laguna can match its class-top-
turning circle	: 11.1 m		ping opponents in terms of reliabil-
			ity. Same choice of petrol engines
			for the estate version.

R

LAGUNA 2.0 TURBO

engine type	: petrol, inline-4
displacement	: 1998 cc
max. power	: 125 kW (170 bhp)
@	: 5000 rpm
max. torque	: 199 lb ft
@	: 3250 rpm
gears	: 6-speed automatic
kerb weight	: 1467 kg
towing weight	: 1300 kg
consumption	: 31.7 mpg
acc. 0-60 mph	: 9.2 s
top speed	: 137 mph
miscellaneous	: Biggest Laguna engine for the time being. The French manufacturer keeps an even more powerful unit up his sleeve for the imminent Laguna Coupé.

RENAULT LAGUNA SPORT TOURER 1.5 DCI

engine type	: diesel, inline-4	kerb weight	: 1483 kg
displacement	: 1461 cc	towing weight	: 1500 kg
max. power	: 81 kW (110 bhp)	boot space	: 508 l
@	: 4000 rpm	fuel capacity	: 66 l
max. torque	: 177 lb ft	consumption	: 56.5 mpg
@	: 2000 rpm	acc. 0-62 mph	: 12.3 s
gears	: 6	top speed	: 116 mph
AT	: -	EuroNCAP	: n.a.
drive	: FWD	introduction	: December 2007
brakes f/r	: vent. discs / discs	last revised in	: -
body type	: 5-drs. stationwagon	warranty	: 2 years
l x w x h	: 4803 x 1811 x 1445 mm	miscellaneous	: Most Laguna buyers will probably
wheelbase	: 2756 mm		opt for the stationwagon version.
turning circle	: 11.1 m		The same range of diesel engines
			is also available for the saloon
			model.

LAGUNA SPORT TOURER 2.0 DCI

engine type	: diesel, inline-4
displacement	: 1995 cc
max. power	: 96 kW (130 bhp) / 110 kW (150 bhp)
@	: 4000 rpm
max. torque	: 222 / 251 lb ft
@	: 2000 rpm
gears	: 6
kerb weight	: 1501 / 1513 kg
towing weight	: 1500 kg
consumption	: 46.3 mpg
acc. 0-60 mph	: 10.8 / 9.7 s
top speed	: 124 / 131 mph
miscellaneous	: The Laguna 1.5 dCi is the only diesel-powered model without a particle filter. This filter is a standard fitment on all other diesel engines.

RENAULT VEL SATIS 2.0 T / 3.5 V6 24V

engine type	: petrol, inline-4 / V6	kerb weight	: 1615 / 1695 kg
displacement	: 1998 / 3498 cc	towing weight	: 1600 kg
max. power	: 125 kW (170 bhp) /	boot space	: 460 - 1468 l
	177 kW (245 bhp)	fuel capacity	: 80 l
@	: 5000 / 6000 tpm	consumption	: 30.1 / 24.6 mpg
max. torque	: 199 / 243 lb ft	acc. 0-62 mph	: 9.6 / 8.3 s
@	: 3250 / 3600 rpm	top speed	: 130 / 146 mph
gears	: 6 / -	EuroNCAP	: 5 stars
AT	: optional / 5-speed	introduction	: April 2002
drive	: FWD	last revised in	: March 2005
brakes f/r	: vent. discs / discs	warranty	: 2 years
body type	: 5-dr. hatchback	miscellaneous	: Renault's unorthodox proposition
l x w x h	: 4860 x 1860 x 1577 mm		for this segment of the market
wheelbase	: 2840 mm		proved unsuccessful.
turning circle	: 11.3 m		

R

VEL SATIS 2.0 DCI / 3.0 DCI

engine type	: diesel, inline-4 / V6
displacement	: 1997 / 2958 cc
max. power	: 110 kW (150 bhp) /
	133 kW (182 bhp)
@	: 4000 / 4400 rpm
max. torque	: 251 / 295 lb ft
@	: 2000 / 1800 rpm
gears	: 6 / 5-speed automatic
kerb weight	: 1565 / 1710 kg
towing weight	: 1600 / 1650 kg
consumption	: 39.8 / 32.5 mpg
acc. 0-60 mph	: 9.5 / 10.4 s
top speed	: 131 / 132 mph
miscellaneous	: The new 2.0 dCi replaces the old
	2.2 dCi, but this 2.2 is still avail-
	able in combination with an
	automatic transmission.

RENAULT ESPACE 2.0 16V / 2.0 T 16V

engine type	: petrol, inline-4	kerb weight	: 1640 / 1660 kg
displacement	: 1998 cc	towing weight	: 1800 / 2000 kg
max. power	: 100 kW (140 bhp) /	boot space	: 291 l
	125 kW (170 bhp)	fuel capacity	: 83 l
@	: 5500 / 5000 rpm	consumption	: 30.1 / 29.7 mpg
max. torque	: 141 / 199 lb ft	acc. 0-62 mph	: 12.5 / 9.7 s
@	: 3750 / 3250 rpm	top speed	: 115 / 128 mph
gears	: 6	EuroNCAP	: 5 stars
AT	: - / optional 5-speed	introduction	: August 2002
drive	: FWD	last revised in	: February 2006
brakes f/r	: vent. discs / discs	warranty	: 2 years
body type	: 5-dr. MPV	miscellaneous	: The best of the large MPV's.
l x w x h	: 4656 x 1860 x 1728 mm		Spacious, practical, original and
wheelbase	: 2803 mm		safe. Beats an aeroplane as means
turning circle	: 11.0 m		of transport on holidays.

ESPACE 3.5 V6 24V

engine type	: petrol, V6
displacement	: 3498 cc
max. power	: 177 kW (245 bhp)
@	: 6000 rpm
max. torque	: 243 lb ft
@	: 3600 rpm
gears	: 5-speed automatic
kerb weight	: 1745 kg
towing weight	: 2000 kg
consumption	: 23.2 mpg
acc. 0-60 mph	: 8.1 s
top speed	: 140 mph
miscellaneous	: Also available in the Grand Espace.

RENAULT GRAND ESPACE 2.0 DCI

engine type	: diesel, inline-4		**kerb weight**	: 1850 kg
displacement	: 1998 cc		**towing weight**	: 2000 kg
max. power	: 110 kW (150 bhp) /		**boot space**	: 456 - 3050 l
	127 kW (175 bhp)		**fuel capacity**	: 83 l
@	: 4000 / 3750 rpm		**consumption**	: 38.2 / 37.2 mpg
max. torque	: 236 / 266 lb ft		**acc. 0-62 mph**	: 10.6 / 9.8 s
@	: 2000 / 1750 rpm		**top speed**	: 117 / 127 mph
gears	: 6		**EuroNCAP**	: 5 stars
AT	: optional 6-speed		**introduction**	: August 2002
drive	: FWD		**last revised in**	: February 2006
brakes f/r	: vent. discs / discs		**warranty**	: 2 years
body type	: 5-dr. MPV		**miscellaneous**	: The same choice of engines exists
l x w x h	: 4856 x 1860 x 1746 mm			for the Grand Espace as for the
wheelbase	: 2868 mm			shorter Espace model, with the
turning circle	: 11.4 m			exception of the 2.0 16V unit. The
				larger Espace is also available with
				a 130 bhp strong 2.0 dCi diesel
				engine.

GRAND ESPACE 3.0 DCI V6 24V

engine type	: diesel, V6
displacement	: 2958 cc
max. power	: 133 kW (180 bhp)
@	: 4000 rpm
max. torque	: 295 lb ft
@	: 1800 rpm
gears	: 6-speed automatic
kerb weight	: 1910 kg
towing weight	: 2000 kg
consumption	: 30.1 mpg
acc. 0-60 mph	: 10.9 s
top speed	: 130 mph
miscellaneous	: More expensive but less economical than the modern 2.0 dCi unit and yet not faster.

ROLLS-ROYCE PHANTOM

engine type	: petrol, V12	kerb weight	: 2495 kg
displacement	: 6749 cc	towing weight	: -
max. power	: 338 kW (453 bhp)	boot space	: 460 l
@	: 5350 rpm	fuel capacity	: 100 l
max. torque	: 531 lb ft	consumption	: 17.8 mpg
@	: 3500 rpm	acc. 0-62 mph	: 5.9 s
gears	: -	top speed	: 149 mph
AT	: 6-speed	EuroNCAP	: n.a.
drive	: RWD	introduction	: January 2003
brakes f/r	: vent. discs	last revised in	: -
body type	: 4-dr. saloon	warranty	: 3 years
l x w x h	: 5834 x 1990 x 1632	miscellaneous	: The long-wheelbase version of the
wheelbase	: 3570 mm		Phantom offers 250 mm of extra
turning circle	: 13.8 m		rear leg room. Recently, a beautiful
			convertible version of the Phantom
			was introduced, called Drophead
			Coupé.

SAAB 9-3 SPORT SALOON 1.8I / 1.8T

engine type	: petrol, inline-4	kerb weight	: 1340 / 1395 kg
displacement	: 1796 / 1998 cc	towing weight	: 1400 / 1600 kg
max. power	: 90 kW (122 bhp) / 110 kW (150 bhp)	boot space	: 425 l
@	: 6000 / 5500 rpm	fuel capacity	: 58 l
max. torque	: 123 / 177 lb ft	consumption	: 36.7 / 37.7 mpg
@	: 3800 / 2000 rpm	acc. 0-62 mph	: 11.5 / 9.5 s
gears	: 5	top speed	: 124 / 131 mph
AT	: - / optional 5-speed	EuroNCAP	: n.a.
drive	: FWD	introduction	: September 2002
brakes f/r	: vent. discs / discs	last revised in	: September 2007
body type	: 4-dr. saloon	warranty	: 2 years
l x w x h	: 4647 x 1802 x 1450 mm	miscellaneous	: Nose of Aero X conceptcar looks good on 9-3 model. Car benefits from improved detailing.
wheelbase	: 2675 mm		
turning circle	: 10.8 m		

9-3 SPORT SALOON 2.0T / 2.0T

engine type	: petrol, inline-4
displacement	: 1998 cc
max. power	: 129 kW (175 bhp) / 155 kW (210 bhp)
@	: 5500 / 5300 rpm
max. torque	: 195 / 221 lb ft
@	: 2500 rpm
gears	: 6, optional 5-speed automatic
kerb weight	: 1395 / 1435 kg
towing weight	: 1600 kg
consumption	: 35.8 / 34.9 mpg
acc. 0-60 mph	: 8.5 / 7.7 s
top speed	: 137 / 146 mph
miscellaneous	: Both the 1.8t and 2.0t models are available in a BioPower version which runs on bioethanol (E85). Refer to the Convertible for specs.

9-3 SPORT SALOON TURBO X

engine type	: petrol, V6
displacement	: 2792 cc
max. power	: 206 kW (280 bhp)
@	: 5500 rpm
max. torque	: 295 lb ft
@	: 2100 rpm
gears	: 6
kerb weight	: n.a.
towing weight	: n.a.
consumption	: 25.9 mpg
acc. 0-60 mph	: 5.7 s
top speed	: 155 mph
miscellaneous	: Flagship model is Saab's first car with four-wheel drive. The 'old' 2.8 V6 is still available and is now 255 bhp strong.

SAAB 9-3 SPORTWAGON 1.9 TID 8V / 16V

engine type	: diesel, inline-4	kerb weight	: 1495 / 1510 kg
displacement	: 1910 cc	towing weight	: 1500 kg
max. power	: 88 kW (120 bhp) / 110 kW (150 bhp)	boot space	: 425 l
@	: 3500 / 4000 rpm	fuel capacity	: 58 l
max. torque	: 206 / 236 lb ft	consumption	: 51.4 / 47.9 mpg
@	: 2000 rpm	acc. 0-62 mph	: 12.0 / 10.2 s
gears	: 6	top speed	: 121 / 124 mph
AT	: - / optional 6-speed	EuroNCAP	: n.a.
drive	: FWD	introduction	: September 2002
brakes f/r	: vent. discs / discs	last revised in	: September 2007
body type	: 5-dr. stationwagon	warranty	: 2 years
l x w x h	: 4670 x 1802 x 1498 mm	miscellaneous	: Diesel engines are available in
wheelbase	: 2675 mm		saloon model too. The Convertible
turning circle	: 10.8 m		(see next page) is not available
			with the 120 bhp unit.

9-3 SPORTWAGON 1.9 TTID 16V

engine type	: diesel, inline-4
displacement	: 1910 cc
max. power	: 132 kW (180 bhp)
@	: 4000 rpm
max. torque	: 295 lb ft
@	: 1850 rpm
gears	: 6
kerb weight	: 1695 kg
towing weight	: 1600 kg
consumption	: 47.1 mpg
acc. 0-60 mph	: 8.7 s
top speed	: 137 mph
miscellaneous	: Saab uses diesel engines from Fiat and benefits from this range-topping unit which will be mounted in Alfa Romeo models as well.

SAAB 9-3 CONVERTIBLE 1.8T / 2.0T BIOPOWER

engine type	: petrol/ethanol, inline-4	kerb weight	: 1550 kg
displacement	: 1998 cc	towing weight	: 1600 kg
max. power	: 129 kW (175 bhp) /	boot space	: 352 l
	147 kW (200 bhp)	fuel capacity	: 58 l
@	: 5500 rpm	consumption	: n.a.
max. torque	: 195 / 221 lb ft	acc. 0-62 mph	: 8.9 / 8.2 s
@	: 2500 rpm	top speed	: 131 / 140 mph
gears	: 5 / 6	EuroNCAP	: n.a.
AT	: optional 5-speed	introduction	: September 2002
drive	: FWD	last revised in	: September 2007
brakes f/r	: vent. discs / discs	warranty	: 2 years
body type	: 2-dr. convertible	miscellaneous	: Bioethanol power (E85) is a suc-
l x w x h	: 4647 x 1780 x 1437 mm		cess in Sweden, thanks to govern-
wheelbase	: 2675 mm		ment support. E85 service stations
turning circle	: 10.8 m		are merging in Great Britain as
			well.

S

SAAB 9-5 2.0T / 2.3T

engine type	: petrol, inline-4	kerb weight	: 1470 kg
displacement	: 1985 / 2290 cc	towing weight	: 1800 kg
max. power	: 110 kW (150 bhp) /	boot space	: 500 l
	136 kW (185 bhp)	fuel capacity	: 75 l
@	: 5500 rpm	consumption	: 32.8 / 31.7 mpg
max. torque	: 177 / 206 lb ft	acc. 0-62 mph	: 9.8 / 8.3 s
@	: 1800 / 1800 rpm	top speed	: 134 / 143 mph
gears	: 5	EuroNCAP	: 5 stars
AT	: optional 5-speed	introduction	: July 1997
drive	: FWD	last revised in	: September 2005
brakes f/r	: vent. discs	warranty	: 2 years
body type	: 4-dr. saloon	miscellaneous	: 9-5 also available as
l x w x h	: 4827 x 1792 x 1449		environmentally friendly BioPower
wheelbase	: 2703 mm		version that runs on E85 (ethanol).
turning circle	: 10.8 m		2.3T with 220 bhp available too.

9-5 AERO

engine type	: petrol, inline-4
displacement	: 2290 cc
max. power	: 191 kW (260 bhp)
@	: 5300 rpm
max. torque	: 258 lb ft
@	: 5400 rpm
gears	: 5
kerb weight	: 1495 kg
towing weight	: 1800 kg
consumption	: 30.7 mpg
acc. 0-60 mph	: 6.9 s
top speed	: 155 mph
miscellaneous	: Fastest version, with 4-cylinder turbo engine in the best Saab tradition. V6 from Vauxhall no longer available.

SAAB 9-5 SPORT ESTATE 1.9 TID

engine type	: diesel, inline-4	**kerb weight**	: 1555 kg
displacement	: 1910 cc	**towing weight**	: 1800 kg
max. power	: 110 kW (150 bhp)	**boot space**	: 416 – 1490 l
@	: 4000 rpm	**fuel capacity**	: 75 l
max. torque	: 236 lb ft	**consumption**	: 41.5 mpg
@	: 2000 rpm	**acc. 0-62 mph**	: 10.7 s
gears	: 5	**top speed**	: 127 mph
AT	: optional 5-speed	**EuroNCAP**	: 5 stars
drive	: FWD	**introduction**	: September 1998
brakes f/r	: vent. discs	**last revised in**	: September 2005
body type	: 5-dr. stationwagon	**warranty**	: 2 years
l x w x h	: 4828 x 1792 x 1459 mm	**miscellaneous**	: The only diesel unit available in
wheelbase	: 2703 mm		the 9-5, but a popular choice in
turning circle	: 10.8 m		business circles.

S

SEAT IBIZA 1.2 12V / 1.4 16V

engine type	: petrol, inline-3 / -4	kerb weight	: 995 / 1034 kg
displacement	: 1198 / 1390 cc	towing weight	: 800 kg
max. power	: 51 kW (70 bhp) / 63 kW (85 bhp)	boot space	: 267 - 960 l
@	: 5400 / 5000 rpm	fuel capacity	: 45 l
max. torque	: 83 / 96 lb ft	consumption	: 47.9 / 43.5 mpg
@	: 3000 / 3600 rpm	acc. 0-62 mph	: 14.2 / 11.9 s
gears	: 5	top speed	: 106 / 112 mph
AT	: -	EuroNCAP	: 4 stars
drive	: FWD	introduction	: April 2002
brakes f/r	: vent. discs / drum brakes	last revised in	: March 2006
body type	: 3-dr. hatchback	warranty	: 2 years
l x w x h	: 3953 x 1698 x 1441 mm	miscellaneous	: Dynamic, sporting alternative to
wheelbase	: 2460 mm		Volkswagen Polo and Skoda Fabia.
turning circle	: 10.6 m		1.4 16V also available with 100 bhp.

IBIZA 1.4 TDI / 1.9 TDI

engine type	: diesel, inline-3 / -4
displacement	: 1422/ 1896 cc
max. power	: 51 kW (70 bhp) / 74 kW (100 bhp)
@	: 4000 rpm
max. torque	: 114 / 177 lb ft
@	: 2200 / 1900 rpm
gears	: 5
kerb weight	: 1106 / 1165 kg
towing weight	: 1000 / 1200 kg
consumption	: 60.1 / 57.6 mpg
acc. 0-60 mph	: 14.8 / 10.8 s
top speed	: 103 / 118 mph
miscellaneous	: Engines also available in Cordoba.

SEAT IBIZA FR / CUPRA

engine type	: petrol, inline-4
displacement	: 1781 cc
max. power	: 110 kW (150 bhp) / 132 kW (180 bhp)
@	: 5800 / 5500 rpm
max. torque	: 162 / 180 lb ft
@	: 1950 / 2000 rpm
gears	: 5
AT	: -
drive	: FWD
brakes f/r	: vent. discs / discs
body type	: 3-dr. hatchback
l x w x h	: 3953 x 1698 x 1441 mm
wheelbase	: 2460 mm
turning circle	: 10.6 m

kerb weight	: 1154 / 1177 kg
towing weight	: 1200 kg / -
boot space	: 267 - 960 l
fuel capacity	: 45 l
consumption	: 35.8 / 35.3 mpg
acc. 0-62 mph	: 8.4 / 7.3 s
top speed	: 134 / 143 mph
EuroNCAP	: 4 stars
introduction	: April 2002
last revised in	: March 2006
warranty	: 2 years
miscellaneous	: Compact, affordable and fiery models, but not that often found on buyers' shortlists.

S

IBIZA FR TDI / CUPRA TDI

engine type	: diesel, inline-4
displacement	: 1896 cc
max. power	: 96 kW (130 bhp) / 118 kW (160 bhp)
@	: 4000 / 3750 rpm
max. torque	: 228 / 243 lb ft
@	: 1900 rpm
gears	: 6
kerb weight	: 1192 / 1215 kg
towing weight	: 1200 kg / -
consumption	: 53.3 / 51.4 mpg
acc. 0-60 mph	: 9.4 / 7.6 s
top speed	: 129 / 137 mph
miscellaneous	: 'FR' stands for Formula Racing. Engines also used in other cars of Volkswagen Group.

SEAT CORDOBA 1.4 16V / 1.6 16V

engine type	: petrol, inline-4	kerb weight	: 1082 / 1065 kg
displacement	: 1390 / 1598 cc	towing weight	: 800 / 1000 kg
max. power	: 55 kW (75 bhp) / 77 kW (105 bhp)	boot space	: 485 l
@	: 5000 / 5600 rpm	fuel capacity	: 45 l
max. torque	: 93 / 113 lb ft	consumption	: 37.7 / 40.9 mpg
@	: 3800 rpm	acc. 0-62 mph	: 15.9 / 10.6 s
gears	: - / 5	top speed	: 107 / 120 mph
AT	: 4-speed / -	EuroNCAP	: 4 stars
drive	: FWD	introduction	: April 2002
brakes f/r	: vent. discs / drums	last revised in	: March 2006
body type	: 4-dr. saloon	warranty	: 2 years
l x w x h	: 4280 x 1698 x 1441 mm	miscellaneous	: The current Cordoba model is not
wheelbase	: 2460 mm		nearly as popular as the first edi-
turning circle	: 10.6 m		tion. Same range of engines as in
			the Ibiza.

SEAT LEON FR / CUPRA

engine type	: petrol, inline-4	kerb weight	: 1334 / 1350 kg
displacement	: 1984 cc	towing weight	: 1400 kg
max. power	: 147 kW (200 bhp) /	boot space	: 341 l
	177 kW (240 bhp)	fuel capacity	: 55 l
@	: 5100 / 5700 rpm	consumption	: 35.8 / 34.0 mpg
max. torque	: 206 / 221 lb ft	acc. 0-62 mph	: 7.3 / 6.8 s
@	: 1800 / 2200 rpm	top speed	: 142 / 153 mph
gears	: 6	EuroNCAP	: 5 stars
AT	: optional 6-speed / -	introduction	: September 2005
drive	: FWD	last revised in	: n.v.t.
brakes f/r	: vent. discs / discs	warranty	: 2 jaar
body type	: 5-dr. hatchback	miscellaneous	: Sporty looking car with clev-
l x w x h	: 4323 x 1768 x 1458 mm		erly disguised rear door handles.
wheelbase	: 2578 mm		Also available with less tweaked
turning circle	: 10.9 m		engines which can be found under
			the Altea and Toledo entries.

S

SEAT ALTEA 1.9 TDI

engine type	: diesel, inline-4	kerb weight	: 1380 kg
displacement	: 1896 cc	towing weight	: 1400 kg
max. power	: 77 kW (105 bhp)	boot space	: 409 l
@	: 4000 rpm	fuel capacity	: 55 l
max. torque	: 184 lb ft	consumption	: 51.4 mpg
@	: 1900 rpm	acc. 0-62 mph	: 12.3 s
gears	: 5	top speed	: 114 mph
AT	: -	EuroNCAP	: 5 stars
drive	: FWD	introduction	: November 2004
brakes f/r	: vent. discs / discs	last revised in	: -
body type	: 5-dr. hatchback	warranty	: 2 years
l x w x h	: 4280 x 1768 x 1568 mm	miscellaneous	: Engine range includes 102 bhp
wheelbase	: 2578 mm		strong 1.6 petrol engine and 2.0
turning circle	: 10.9 m		TFSI with 200 bhp.

ALTEA 2.0 TDI / 2.0 TDI FR

engine type	: diesel, inline-4
displacement	: 1968 cc
max. power	: 103 kW (140 bhp) / 125 kW (170 bhp)
@	
max. torque	: 4000 / 4200 rpm
@	: 236 / 258 lb ft
gears	: 1750 / 1800 rpm
kerb weight	: 6
towing weight	: 1405 / 1421 kg
consumption	: 1400 kg
acc. 0-60 mph	: 47.9 / 45.6 mpg
top speed	: 9.9 / 8.6 s
miscellaneous	: 125 / 130 mph
	: Also available with Volkswagen's DSG automatic transmission with double clutch, a fine alternative to a manual gearbox.

SEAT ALTEA FREETRACK 2.0 TSI

engine type	: petrol, inline-4		**kerb weight**	: 1546 kg
displacement	: 1984 cc		**towing weight**	: 1400 kg
max. power	: 147 kW (200 bhp)		**boot space**	: 490 l
@	: 5100 rpm		**fuel capacity**	: 55 l
max. torque	: 206 lb ft		**consumption**	: 30.1 mpg
@	: 1800 rpm		**acc. 0-62 mph**	: 7.5 s
gears	: 6		**top speed**	: 133 mph
AT	: -		**EuroNCAP**	: 5 stars
drive	: 4WD		**introduction**	: July 2007
brakes f/r	: vent. discs / discs		**last revised in**	: -
body type	: 5-dr. SUV		**warranty**	: 2 years
l x w x h	: 4493 x 1788 x 1622 mm		**miscellaneous**	: Seat's first SUV is built
wheelbase	: 2576 mm			on the platform of the Altea XL.
turning circle	: 10.9 m			

ALTEA FREETRACK 2.0 TDI

engine type	: diesel, inline-4
displacement	: 1968 cc
max. power	: 125 kW (170 bhp)
@	: 4200 rpm
max. torque	: 258 lb ft
@	: 1800 rpm
gears	: 6
kerb weight	: 1543 kg
towing weight	: 1400 kg
consumption	: 41.5 mpg
acc. 0-60 mph	: 8.7 s
top speed	: 127 mph
miscellaneous	: In other European markets Seat also campaigns a 2.0 TDI version with front-wheel drive and 140 instead of 170 bhp.

SEAT TOLEDO 1.6 / 2.0 FSI

engine type	: petrol, inline-4	kerb weight	: 1319 / 1434 kg
displacement	: 1595 / 1798 cc	towing weight	: 1200 / 1400 kg
max. power	: 75 kW (102 bhp) /	boot space	: 500 l
	118 kW (160 bhp)	fuel capacity	: 55 l
@	: 5600 / 5000 rpm	consumption	: 36.7 / 36.2 mpg
max. torque	: 109 / 184 lb ft	acc. 0-62 mph	: 12.9 / 8.5 s
@	: 3800 / 1500 rpm	top speed	: 112 / 126 mph
gears	: 5 / 6	EuroNCAP	: 5 stars
AT	: -	introduction	: November 2004
drive	: FWD	last revised in	: -
brakes f/r	: vent. discs / discs	warranty	: 2 years
body type	: 5-dr. hatchback	miscellaneous	: The 'Altea saloon' is not a very
l x w x h	: 4457 x 1768 x 1568 mm		popular derivation. It is also avail-
wheelbase	: 2578 mm		able with the 1.9 TDI and 2.0 TDI
turning circle	: 10.9 m		diesel units, and so are the Seat
			Leon and Seat Altea.

SEAT ALHAMBRA 2.0 / 1.8 T

engine type	: petrol, inline-4
displacement	: 1984 / 1781 cc
max. power	: 85 kW (115 bhp) / 110 kW (150 bhp)
@	: 5200 / 5800 rpm
max. torque	: 125 / 162 lb ft
@	: 2600 / 1800 rpm
gears	: 6 / 6
AT	: - / optional 5-speed
drive	: FWD
brakes f/r	: vent. discs / discs
body type	: 5-dr. MPV
l x w x h	: 4634 x 1810 x 1759 mm
wheelbase	: 2841 mm
turning circle	: 11.9 m

kerb weight	: 1553 / 1574 kg
towing weight	: 1800 / 1900 kg
boot space	: 852 - 2610 l
fuel capacity	: 70 l
consumption	: 30.1 mpg
acc. 0-62 mph	: 15.2 / 10.9 s
top speed	: 110 / 124 mph
EuroNCAP	: 3 stars
introduction	: December 1997
last revised in	: April 2000
warranty	: 2 years
miscellaneous	: Conventional MPV from Seat is a relative of VW's Sharan. Spacious interior.

S

ALHAMBRA 2.8 V6 AUTO

engine type	: petrol, V6
displacement	: 2792 cc
max. power	: 150 kW (204 bhp)
@	: 6200 rpm
max. torque	: 195 lb ft
@	: 3400 rpm
gears	: 5
kerb weight	: 1627 kg
towing weight	: 2000 kg
consumption	: 24.8 mpg
acc. 0-60 mph	: 10.4 s
top speed	: 132 mph
miscellaneous	: Powerful, refined V6 engine offers excellent performance.

ALHAMBRA 1.9 TDI / 2.0 TDI

engine type	: diesel, inline-4
displacement	: 1896 / 1968 cc
max. power	: 85 kW (115 bhp) / 103 kW (140 bhp)
@	: 4000 rpm
max. torque	: 229 lb ft
@	: 1900 rpm
gears	: 6
kerb weight	: 1624 / 1640 kg
towing weight	: 2000 kg
consumption	: 43.3 / 42.2 mpg
acc. 0-60 mph	: 13.7 / 12.2 s
top speed	: 112 / 119 mph
miscellaneous	: Oldest model in Seat programme is still going strong.

SKODA FABIA 1.2 / 1.4

engine type	: petrol, inline-3 / -4	kerb weight	: 1050 / 1060 kg
displacement	: 1198 / 1390 cc	towing weight	: 900 / 1200 kg
max. power	: 51 kW (70 bhp) / 63 kW (85 bhp)	boot space	: 300 l
@	: 5400 / 5000 rpm	fuel capacity	: 45 l
max. torque	: 82 / 98 lb ft	consumption	: 47.9 / 43.5 mpg
@	: 3000 / 3800 rpm	acc. 0-62 mph	: 14.9 / 12.3 s
gears	: 5	top speed	: 101 / 108 mph
AT	: -	EuroNCAP	: n.a.
drive	: FWD	introduction	: March 2007
brakes f/r	: vent. discs / drums	last revised in	: -
body type	: 5-dr. hatchback	warranty	: 2 years
l x w x h	: 3992 x 1642 x 1498 mm	miscellaneous	: New Fabia is among the most
wheelbase	: 2462 mm		spacious cars in its class. The
turning circle	: 10.0 m		entry level model is equipped with
			a 1.2 engine with maximum power
			of 60 bhp.

FABIA 1.6

engine type	: petrol, inline-4
displacement	: 1598 cc
max. power	: 77 kW (105 bhp)
@	: 5600 rpm
max. torque	: 113 lb ft
@	: 3800 rpm
gears	: 5, optional 6-speed automatic
kerb weight	: 1070 kg
towing weight	: 1200 kg
consumption	: 40.9 mpg
acc. 0-60 mph	: 10.1 s
top speed	: 118 mph
miscellaneous	: The fastest Fabia yet. Whether
	there will be an even faster RS
	version, remains to be seen.

SKODA FABIA COMBI 1.4 TDI

engine type	: diesel, inline-4	kerb weight	: n.a.
displacement	: 1422 cc	towing weight	: n.a.
max. power	: 59 kW (80 bhp)	boot space	: 480 l
@	: 4000 rpm	fuel capacity	: 45 l
max. torque	: 144 lb ft	consumption	: 58.9 mpg
@	: 2200 rpm	acc. 0-62 mph	: 13.4 s
gears	: 5	top speed	: 106 mph
AT	: -	EuroNCAP	: n.a.
drive	: FWD	introduction	: October 2007
brakes f/r	: vent. discs / drums	last revised in	: -
body type	: 5-dr. stationwagon	warranty	: 2 years
l x w x h	: 4239 x 1642 x 1498 mm	miscellaneous	: The previous Fabia Combi proved
wheelbase	: 2462 mm		so popular that it called for a suc-
turning circle	: 10.2 m		cessor, which will be based on the
			new Fabia.

S

FABIA COMBI 1.9 TDI

engine type	: diesel, inline-4
displacement	: 1896 cc
max. power	: 77 kW (105 bhp)
@	: 4000 rpm
max. torque	: 177 lb ft
@	: 1800 rpm
gears	: 5
kerb weight	: n.a.
towing weight	: n.a.
consumption	: 55.4 mpg
acc. 0-60 mph	: 11.0 s
top speed	: 117 mph
miscellaneous	: All petrol engines of the saloon model are also available for the stationwagon version, with the exception of the 60 bhp strong 1.2 engine. A particle filter is standard on this diesel engine but optional on the 1.4 TDI unit.

SKODA ROOMSTER 1.4 / 1.6

engine type	: petrol, inline-4	kerb weight	: 1155 / 1175 kg
displacement	: 1390 / 1598 cc	towing weight	: 900 / 1000 kg
max. power	: 63 kW (86 bhp) / 77 kW (105 bhp)	boot space	: 450 – 1780 l
@	: 5000 / 5600 rpm	fuel capacity	: 55 l
max. torque	: 97 / 113 lb ft	consumption	: 41.5 / 40.4 mpg
@	: 3800 rpm	acc. 0-62 mph	: 13.0 / 10.9 s
gears	: 5	top speed	: 106 / 114 mph
AT	: -	EuroNCAP	: n.a.
drive	: FWD	introduction	: September 2006
brakes f/r	: vent. discs / discs	last revised in	: -
body type	: 5-drs. MPV	warranty	: 2 years
l x w x h	: 4210 x 1684 x 1607 mm	miscellaneous	: Refreshing mini-MPV with
wheelbase	: 2620 mm		adjustable rear bench. Steep price
turning circle	: 10.5 m		not in the best Skoda tradition.
			Also available with 1.2 12V petrol
			engine and diesel power (refer to
			Fabia Estate for specifications).

SKODA OCTAVIA 1.4

engine type	: petrol, inline-4	**kerb weight**	: 1205 kg
displacement	: 1390 cc	**towing weight**	: 900 kg
max. power	: 59 kW (80 bhp)	**boot space**	: 560 l
@	: 5000 rpm	**fuel capacity**	: 55 l
max. torque	: 98 lb ft	**consumption**	: 40.4 mpg
@	: 3800 rpm	**acc. 0-62 mph**	: 14.2 s
gears	: 5	**top speed**	: 107 mph
AT	: -	**EuroNCAP**	: 4 stars
drive	: FWD	**introduction**	: June 2004
brakes f/r	: vent. discs / discs	**last revised in**	: -
body type	: 5-dr. hatchback	**warranty**	: 2 years
l x w x h	: 4572 x 1769 x 1462 mm	**miscellaneous**	: Although it resembles a saloon, this car is in fact a hatchback. It is also a strong seller.
wheelbase	: 2578 mm		
turning circle	: 10.9 m		

S

OCTAVIA 1.6 FSI / 1.8 TSI

engine type	: petrol, inline-4
displacement	: 1598 / 1798 cc
max. power	: 85 kW (115 bhp) / 118 kW (160 bhp)
@	: 6000 / 5000 rpm
max. torque	: 114 / 184 lb ft
@	: 4000 / 1500 rpm
gears	: 5 / 6
kerb weight	: 1240 / 1300 kg
towing weight	: 1200 / 1300 kg
consumption	: 42.8 / 38.2 mpg
acc. 0-60 mph	: 11.4 / 8.1 s
top speed	: 123 / 139 mph
miscellaneous	: The 1.8 TFSI engine (here TSI) has found its way under the bonnet of the Octavia too.

SKODA OCTAVIA COMBI 1.9 TDI / 2.0 TDI

engine type	: diesel, inline-4	kerb weight	: 1300 / 1325 kg
displacement	: 1896 / 1968 cc	towing weight	: 1400 kg
max. power	: 77 kW (105 bhp) /	boot space	: 580 - 1620 l
	103 kW (140 bhp)	fuel capacity	: 55 l
@	: 4000 rpm	consumption	: 55.4 / 51.4 mpg
max. torque	: 184 / 236 lb ft	acc. 0-62 mph	: 11.9 / 9.7 s
@	: 1900 / 1750 rpm	top speed	: 119 / 129 mph
gears	: 5 / 6	EuroNCAP	: 4 stars
AT	: optional 6-speed	introduction	: June 2004
drive	: FWD	last revised in	: n.v.t.
brakes f/r	: vent. discs / discs	warranty	: 2 years
body type	: 5-dr. stationwagon	miscellaneous	: The Scout is a four-wheel drive
l x w x h	: 4572 x 1769 x 1468 mm		model based on the Octavia
wheelbase	: 2578 mm		Combi. It is available with either a
turning circle	: 10.2 m		2.0 TDI or a 2.0 FSI petrol engine
			which delivers 150 bhp.

OCTAVIA VRS COMBI 2.0 TFSI / 2.0 TDI

engine type	: petrol / diesel, inline-4
displacement	: 1984 / 1968 cc
max. power	: 147 kW (200 bhp) /
	125 kW (170 bhp)
@	: 5100 / 4200 rpm
max. torque	: 206 / 258 lb ft
@	: 1800 rpm
gears	: 6
kerb weight	: 1390 / 1420 kg
towing weight	: 1400 kg
consumption	: 35.8 / 49.6 mpg
acc. 0-60 mph	: 7.5 / 8.6 s
top speed	: 149 / 140 mph
miscellaneous	: Diesel power is now available
	for the vRS model as well.

SKODA SUPERB 2.0 / 1.8T

engine type	: petrol, inline-4	**kerb weight**	: 1387 / 1413 kg
displacement	: 1984 / 1781 cm3	**towing weight**	: 1400 / 1300 kg
max. power	: 85 kW (115 bhp) /	**boot space**	: 462 l
	110 kW (150 bhp)	**fuel capacity**	: 62 l
@	: 5400 / 5700 rpm	**consumption**	: 33.2 / 34.0 mpg
max. torque	: 127 / 155 lb ft	**acc. 0-62 mph**	: 11.6 / 9.5 s
@	: 3500 / 1750 rpm	**top speed**	: 122 / 134 mph
gears	: 5	**EuroNCAP**	: 4 stars
AT	: - / optional 5-speed	**introduction**	: July 2002
drive	: FWD	**last revised in**	: July 2006
brakes f/r	: vent. discs / discs	**warranty**	: 2 years
body type	: 4-dr. saloon	**miscellaneous**	: The Superb is based on the
l x w x h	: 4803 x 1765 x 1469 mm		previous VW Passat model, with
wheelbase	: 2803 mm		engines from that period too. The
turning circle	: 11.8 m		car is popular among taxi drivers
			because of its generous leg room
			in the rear.

SUPERB 2.8 V6 / 2.5 TDI

engine type	: petrol / diesel, V6
displacement	: 2771 / 2496 cc
max. power	: 142 kW (193 bhp) /
	120 kW (160 bhp)
@	: 6000 / 4000 rpm
max. torque	: 206 / 258 lb ft
@	: 3200 / 1250 rpm
gears	: 5 / 5-speed automatic
kerb weight	: 1476 / 1545 kg
towing weight	: 1600 kg
consumption	: 29.4 / 36.2 mpg
acc. 0-60 mph	: 8.0 / 10.3 s
top speed	: 147 / 135 mph
miscellaneous	: Specifications of the 1.9 TDI and
	2.0 TDI are listed under the Octavia
	Combi entry on the previous page.

SMART FORTWO

engine type	: petrol, inline-3	kerb weight	: 750 / 770 kg
displacement	: 999 cc	towing weight	: -
max. power	: 52 kW (71 bhp) / 62 kW (84 bhp)	boot space	: 220 l
@	: 5800 / 5250 rpm	fuel capacity	: 33 l
max. torque	: 68 / 88 lb ft	consumption	: 60.1 / 57.6 mpg
@	: 4500 / 3250 rpm	acc. 0-62 mph	: 13.3 / 10.9 s
gears	: -	top speed	: 90 mph
AT	: 5-speed sequential	EuroNCAP	: n.a.
drive	: RWD	introduction	: February 2007
brakes f/r	: vent. discs / discs	last revised in	: -
body type	: 3-dr. hatchback	warranty	: 2 years
l x w x h	: 2700 x 1560 x 1540 mm	miscellaneous	: Somewhat bigger but much better
wheelbase	: 1870 mm		than before. Its competitors how-
turning circle	: 8.8 m		ever offer four seats for the same
			kind of money. Also available with
			45 kW unit.

FORTWO BRABUS

engine type	: petrol, inline-3
displacement	: 999 cc
max. power	: 72 kW (98 kW)
@	: 3800 rpm
max. torque	: 104 lb ft
@	: 2000 rpm
gears	: 5-speed sequentieel
kerb weight	: 770 kg
towing weight	: -
consumption	: 54.3 mpg
acc. 0-60 mph	: 9.9 s
top speed	: 95 mph
miscellaneous	: Tuner Brabus is responsible for
	the exterior styling of this Smart.

SPYKER C8

engine type	: petrol, V8	**kerb weight**	: approx. 1250 kg
displacement	: 4172 cc	**towing weight**	: -
max. power	: 298 kW (400 bhp)	**boot space**	: n.a.
@	: 7000 rpm	**fuel capacity**	: 75 l
max. torque	: 354 lb ft	**consumption**	: n.a.
@	: 3400 rpm	**acc. 0-62 mph**	: 4.5 s
gears	: 6	**top speed**	: 186 mph
AT	: -	**EuroNCAP**	: n.a.
drive	: RWD	**introduction**	: 2004
brakes f/r	: vent. discs	**last revised in**	: -
body type	: 2-dr. convertible	**warranty**	: 2 years
l x w x h	: 4185 x 1880 x 1080 mm	**miscellaneous**	: Small Dutch car manufacturer
wheelbase	: 2570 mm		builds on the foundations of
turning circle	: n.a.		forgotten pre-war luxury marque.
			Latest addition is C12 La Turbie
			model with 500 bhp Audi W12-
			engine.

S

SPYKER D12 PEKING-TO-PARIS

engine type	: petrol, W12	kerb weight	: 1850 kg
displacement	: 5998 cc	towing weight	: -
max. power	: 368 kW (500 bhp)	boot space	: n.a.
@	: n.a.	fuel capacity	: 100 l
max. torque	: 450 lb ft	consumption	: n.a.
@	: n.a.	acc. 0-62 mph	: 5.0 s
gears	: 6	top speed	: 186 mph
AT	: -	EuroNCAP	: n.a.
drive	: 4WD	introduction	: 2006
brakes f/r	: vent. discs	last revised in	: -
body type	: 4-dr. SUV	warranty	: 2 years
l x w x h	: 4950 x 2000 x 1680 mm	miscellaneous	: New SSUV, Spyker speak for
wheelbase	: 2855 mm		Super
turning circle	: n.a.		Sports Utility Vehicle. Majority of
			customers to be found in
			Middle-East.

SSANGYONG ACTYON 230 / 200 XDI

engine type	: petrol / diesel, inline-4	**kerb weight**	: 1748 kg
displacement	: 2295 / 1998 cc	**towing weight**	: 2100 kg
max. power	: 110 kW (150 bhp) / 104 kW (141 bhp)	**boot space**	: 661 l
		fuel capacity	: 75 l
@	: 5500 / 4000 rpm	**consumption**	: 24.6 / 36.2 mpg
max. torque	: 158 / 229 lb ft	**acc. 0-62 mph**	: 12.2 / 14.4 s
@	: 3500 / 1800 rpm	**top speed**	: 102 / 101 mph
gears	: 5	**EuroNCAP**	: n.a.
AT	: optional 4-speed	**introduction**	: September 2006
drive	: RWD	**last revised in**	: -
brakes f/r	: vent. discs / discs	**warranty**	: 3 years
body type	: 5-dr. SUV	**miscellaneous**	: Car with a bold design but a rather conventional drive train.
l x w x h	: 4450 x 1880 x 1740 mm		
wheelbase	: 2740 mm		
turning circle	: 11.2 m		

S

SSANGYONG KYRON 200 XDI

engine type	: diesel, inline-4	kerb weight	: 1796 kg
displacement	: 1998 cc	towing weight	: 2100 kg
max. power	: 104 kW (141 bhp)	boot space	: 625 l
@	: 4000 rpm	fuel capacity	: 75 l
max. torque	: 229 lb ft	consumption	: 36.7 mpg
@	: 1800 rpm	acc. 0-62 mph	: 16.2 s
gears	: 5	top speed	: 104 mph
AT	: optional 4-speed	EuroNCAP	: n.a.
drive	: 2WD	introduction	: autumn 2005
brakes f/r	: vent. discs / discs	last revised in	: -
body type	: 3-dr. SUV	warranty	: 3 years
l x w x h	: 4660 x 1880 x 1755 mm	miscellaneous	: New model replaces Musso. Just
wheelbase	: 2740 mm		one engine available, but choice of
turning circle	: n.a.		2WD and 4WD. Better-looking than
			predecessor.

SSANGYONG REXTON 270 XDI / XVT

engine type	: diesel, inline-5	**kerb weight**	: 1961 / 1970 kg
displacement	: 2696 cc	**towing weight**	: 3500 kg
max. power	: 121 kW (165 bhp) /	**boot space**	: 935 l
	137 kW (186 bhp)	**fuel capacity**	: 80 l
@	: 4000 rpm	**consumption**	: 32.9 / 30.7 mpg
max. torque	: 251 / 296 lb ft	**acc. 0-62 mph**	: 13.2 / 11.2 s
@	: 2400 / 1600 rpm	**top speed**	: 110 / 113 mph
gears	: 5 / -	**EuroNCAP**	: n.a.
AT	: optional / 5-speed	**introduction**	: December 2002
drive	: 4WD	**last revised in**	: July 2006
brakes f/r	: vent. discs / discs	**warranty**	: 3 years
body type	: 5-dr. SUV	**miscellaneous**	: Ageing but reliable Mercedes-Benz
l x w x h	: 4720 x 1870 x 1830 mm		diesel engine soldiers on in the
wheelbase	: 2820 mm		Rexton. And in the well-equipped
turning circle	: 11.2 m		XVT model it delivers even more
			power

S

SSANGYONG RODIUS 270

engine type	: diesel, inline-5	kerb weight	: 1982 kg
displacement	: 2696 cc	towing weight	: 2500 kg
max. power	: 121 kW (163 bhp)	boot space	: 893 - 3322 l
@	: 4000 rpm	fuel capacity	: 80 l
max. torque	: 165 lb ft	consumption	: 32.9 mpg
@	: 3000 rpm	acc. 0-62 mph	: 13.5 s
gears	: 5	top speed	: 105 mph
AT	: optional 5-speed	EuroNCAP	: n.a.
drive	: RWD	introduction	: July 2005
brakes f/r	: vent. discs	last revised in	: -
body type	: 5-dr. MPV	warranty	: 3 years
l x w x h	: 5125 x 1915 x 1845 mm	miscellaneous	: Very big car with lots of space and
wheelbase	: 3000 mm		8 seats. Old but capable diesel
turning circle	: 11.6 m		engine. Also available as SV 270X.

SUBARU JUSTY

engine type	: petrol, inline-3	**kerb weight**	: 890 kg
displacement	: 998 cc	**towing weight**	: 750 kg
max. power	: 51 kW (68 bhp)	**boot space**	: 225 l
@	: 6000 rpm	**fuel capacity**	: 40 l
max. torque	: 69 lb ft	**consumption**	: 56.5 mpg
@	: 3600 rpm	**acc. 0-62 mph**	: 13.9 s
gears	: 5	**top speed**	: 100 mph
AT	: -	**EuroNCAP**	: n.a.
drive	: FWD	**introduction**	: September 2007
brakes f/r	: discs / drums	**last revised in**	: -
body type	: 5-dr. hatchback	**warranty**	: 3 years
l x w x h	: 3600 x 1665 x 1550	**miscellaneous**	: The Justy is not a derivative
wheelbase	: 2430 mm		of a Suzuki model this time.
turning circle	: 8.6 m		It is based on the Daihatsu Sirion.

S

SUBARU IMPREZA 1.5R / 2.0R

engine type	: petrol, flat-4
displacement	: 1498 / 1994 cc
max. power	: 79 kW (107 bhp) / 110 kW (150 bhp)
@	: 6000 / 6400 rpm
max. torque	: 105 / 145 lb ft
@	: 3200 rpm
gears	: 5
AT	: optional 4-speed
drive	: 4WD
brakes f/r	: vent. discs / discs
body type	: 5-dr. hatchback
l x w x h	: 4415 x 1740 x 1475 mm
wheelbase	: 2620 mm
turning circle	: 10.6 m

kerb weight	: 1310 / 1345 kg
towing weight	: 1500 / 1600 kg
boot space	: 538 l
fuel capacity	: 60 l
consumption	: 37.7 / 33.6 mpg
acc. 0-62 mph	: 13.9 / 9.4 s
top speed	: 109 mph / n.a.
EuroNCAP	: n.a.
introduction	: September 2007
last revised in	: -
warranty	: 3 years
miscellaneous	: No longer a saloon, but a respect- able hatchback. In due course Subaru's own diesel engine will be fitted in the Impreza too.

IMPREZA 2.5 WRX

engine type	: petrol, flat-4
displacement	: 2457 cc
max. power	: 169 kW (230 bhp)
@	: 5200 rpm
max. torque	: 236 lb ft
@	: 2800 rpm
gears	: 5
kerb weight	: 1395 kg
towing weight	: 1200 kg
consumption	: 27.2 mpg
acc. 0-60 mph	: 5.6 s
top speed	: n.a.
miscellaneous	: It is only logical that the Impreza line-up includes a fast WRX version. Subaru has confirmed the return of a 280 bhp strong WRX STi.

SUBARU LEGACY 2.0R

engine type	: petrol, flat-4		**kerb weight**	: 1305 kg
displacement	: 1994 cc		**towing weight**	: 1300 kg
max. power	: 121 kW (165 bhp)		**boot space**	: 433 l
@	: 6800 rpm		**fuel capacity**	: 64 l
max. torque	: 138 lb ft		**consumption**	: 32.5 mpg
@	: 3200 rpm		**acc. 0-62 mph**	: 11.2 s
gears	: 5		**top speed**	: 133 mph
AT	: optional 4-speed		**EuroNCAP**	: n.a.
drive	: 4WD		**introduction**	: October 2003
brakes f/r	: vent. discs / discs		**last revised in**	: September 2006
body type	: 4-dr. saloon		**warranty**	: 3 years
l x w x h	: 4665 x 1730 x 1425 mm		**miscellaneous**	: Exclusively equipped Japanese
wheelbase	: 2670 mm			alternative for fast rivals from
turning circle	: 10.8 m			Germany. New 2.0 petrol engine
				replaces previous 2.0 as well as
				2.5. Wagon version also available.

S

SUBARU OUTBACK 3.0R

engine type	: petrol, flat-6	kerb weight	: 1495 kg
displacement	: 3000 cc	towing weight	: 1800 kg
max. power	: 180 kW (245 bhp)	boot space	: 459 - 1649 l
@	: 6600 rpm	fuel capacity	: 64 l
max. torque	: 219 lb ft	consumption	: 28.5 mpg
@	: 4200 rpm	acc. 0-62 mph	: 8.5 s
gears	: -	top speed	: 139 mph
AT	: 5-speed	EuroNCAP	: 4 stars
drive	: 4WD	introduction	: October 2003
brakes f/r	: vent. discs / discs	last revised in	: September 2006
body type	: 5-dr. stationwagon	warranty	: 3 years
l x w x h	: 4730 x 1770 x 1545 mm	miscellaneous	: Outback is wilder version of
wheelbase	: 2670 mm		Subaru Legacy Wagon. 6-cylinder
turning circle	: 10.8 m		boxer engine refined and full of
			character.

SUBARU FORESTER 2.0 X / 2.5

engine type	: petrol, flat-4		kerb weight	: 1465 / 1560 kg
displacement	:1994 / 2457 cc		towing weight	: 1500 / 2000 kg
max. power	: 116 kW (158 bhp) /		boot space	: 387 – 1629 l
	169 kW (230 bhp)		fuel capacity	: 60 l
@	: 6400 / 5600 rpm		consumption	: 30.4 / 26.4 mpg
max. torque	: 137 / 236 lb ft		acc. 0-62 mph	: 9.7 / 6.0 s
@	: 3200 / 3600 rpm		top speed	: 122 / 134 mph
gears	: 5		EuroNCAP	: n.a.
AT	: optional 4-speed		introduction	: September1998
drive	: 4WD		last revised in	: September 2005
brakes f/r	: vent. discs / discs		warranty	: 3 years
body type	: 5-dr. stationwagon		miscellaneous	: Practical and spacious
l x w x h	: 4485 x 1735 x 1590 mm			Impreza-based stationwagon is
wheelbase	: 2525 mm			great tow car.
turning circle	: 10.6 m			

SUBARU TRIBECA

engine type	: petrol, flat-6	kerb weight	: 1880 kg
displacement	: 3630 cc	towing weight	: 2000 kg
max. power	: 191 kW (260 bhp)	boot space	: 525 l
@	: 6000 rpm	fuel capacity	: 64 l
max. torque	: 247 lb ft	consumption	: n.a.
@	: 4400 rpm	acc. 0-62 mph	: n.a.
gears	: -	top speed	: n.a.
AT	: 5-speed	EuroNCAP	: n.a.
drive	: 4WD	introduction	: July 2006
brakes f/r	: vent. discs	last revised in	: March 2007
body type	: 5-dr. SUV	warranty	: 3 years
l x w x h	: 4864 x 1877 x 1687 mm	miscellaneous	: The Tribeca made it to Europe
wheelbase	: 2750 mm		only recently, but has now been
turning circle	: 11.4 m		subjected to a facelift already.
			Engine bigger and more potent.

SUZUKI WAGON R+ 1.0 / 1.2

engine type	: petrol, inline-3 / inline-4	kerb weight	: 940 / 955 kg
displacement	: 998 / 1229 cc	towing weight	: 650 kg
max. power	: 44 kW (60 bhp) / 59 kW (80 bhp)	boot space	: 248 l
@	: 5600 rpm	fuel capacity	: 41 l
max. torque	: 65 / 81 lb ft	consumption	: 48.7 / 47.1 mpg
@	: 3800 / 4000 rpm	acc. 0-62 mph	: 17.7 / 13.2 s
gears	: 5	top speed	: 90 / 100 mph
AT	: -	EuroNCAP	: n.a.
drive	: FWD	introduction	: May 2000
brakes f/r	: vent. discs / drum brakes	last revised in	: -
body type	: 5-dr. MPV	warranty	: 3 years
l x w x h	: 3540 x 1600 x 1660 mm	miscellaneous	: Roomy and practical car with low running costs. 94 bhp 1.3 also available, with either 5-speed manual or 4-speed automatic.
wheelbase	: 2360 mm		
turning circle	: 9.8 m		

S

SUZUKI SPLASH 1.0 12V / 1.2 16V

engine type	: petrol, inline-3	kerb weight	: n.a.
displacement	: 997 / 1242 cc	towing weight	: n.a.
max. power	: 48 kW (65 bhp) / 63 kW (86 bhp)	boot space	: 225 l
@	: 6000 rpm	fuel capacity	: n.a.
max. torque	: 66 / 84 lb ft	consumption	: 53.3 / 49.6 mpg
@	: 4000 rpm	acc. 0-62 mph	: 14.8 / 12.0 s
gears	: 5	top speed	: 100 / 108 mph
AT	: - / optional 4-speed	EuroNCAP	: n.a.
drive	: FWD	introduction	: Spring 2008
brakes f/r	: vent. discs / drums	last revised in	: -
body type	: 5-dr. hatchback	warranty	: 3 years
l x w x h	: 3740 x 1680 x 1590 mm	miscellaneous	: According to Suzuki, this car does
wheelbase	: 2350 mm		not replace the Wagon R+,
turning circle	: 9.6 m		although the Splash is similar in
			size. It is the twin sister of the
			Vauxhall Agila.

SUZUKI SWIFT 1.3 / 1.5

engine type	: petrol, inline-4
displacement	: 1328 / 1490 cc
max. power	: 68 kW (92 bhp) / 75 kW (102 bhp)
@	: 5800 / 5900 rpm
max. torque	: 85 / 98 lb ft
@	: 4200 / 4100 tpm
gears	: 5
AT	: - / optional 4-speed
drive	: FWD
brakes f/r	: vent. discs / drums
body type	: 3- / 5-dr. hatchback
l x w x h	: 3695 x 1690 x 1500 mm
wheelbase	: 2380 mm
turning circle	: 9.4 m

kerb weight	: 945 / 955 kg
towing weight	: 1000 kg
boot space	: 213 l
fuel capacity	: 45 l
consumption	: 46.3 / 43.5 mpg
acc. 0-62 mph	: 11.0 / 10.0 s
top speed	: 109 / 115 mph
EuroNCAP	: 4 stars
introduction	: March 2005
last revised in	: n.v.t.
warranty	: 3 years
miscellaneous	: The Swift is one of the better cars in its class. Modern looks, fine driving behaviour. Also available with a 1.3 diesel engine.

S

SWIFT SPORT

engine type	: petrol, inline-4
displacement	: 1586 cc
max. power	: 92 kW (125 bhp)
@	: 6800 rpm
max. torque	: 110 lb ft
@	: 4800 rpm
gears	: 5
kerb weight	: 1005 kg
towing weight	: 1000 kg
consumption	: 39.2 mpg
acc. 0-60 mph	: 8.9 s
top speed	: 124 mph
miscellaneous	: Little 'hot hatches' do not need lots of horsepower in order to be great fun to drive. Evidence the Swift Sport.

SUZUKI SX4 1.5 / 1.6 16V

engine type	: petrol, inline-4
displacement	: 1490 / 1586 cc
max. power	: 73 kW (99 bhp) / 79 kW (107 bhp)
@	: 5600 rpm
max. torque	: 98 / 107 lb ft
@	: 4100 / 4000 rpm
gears	: 5
AT	: - / optional 4-speed
drive	: FWD
brakes f/r	: vent. discs / drum brakes
body type	: 5-dr. hatchback
l x w x h	: 4100 x 1730 x 1555 mm
wheelbase	: 2500 mm
turning circle	: 10.6 m

kerb weight	: 1105 kg
towing weight	: 1200 kg
boot space	: 270 - 670 l
fuel capacity	: 50 l
consumption	: 41.5 / 39.8 mpg
acc. 0-62 mph	: 11.0 / 10.7 s
top speed	: 109 / 112 mph
EuroNCAP	: 4 stars
introduction	: April 2006
last revised in	: -
warranty	: 3 years
miscellaneous	: Identical to Fiat Sedici, but cheaper since Italian sister car is offered with 4WD only. Wild SX4 4Grip model however also boasts 4 driven wheels.

SX4 1.9 DDIS

engine type	: diesel, inline-4
displacement	: 1910 cc
max. power	: 88 kW (120 bhp)
@	: 4000 rpm
max. torque	: 206 lb ft
@	: 2000 rpm
gears	: 6
kerb weight	: 1240 kg
towing weight	: 1200 kg
consumption	: 44.8 mpg
acc. 0-60 mph	: 10.5 s
top speed	: 118 mph
miscellaneous	: Diesel version intended to promote SX4 as company car.

SUZUKI JIMNY

engine type	: petrol, inline-4	kerb weight	: 1135 / 1220 kg
displacement	: 1328 cc	towing weight	: 1300 kg
max. power	: 63 kW (85 bhp)	boot space	: 113-816 l
@	: 6000 rpm	fuel capacity	: 40 l
max. torque	: 81 lb ft	consumption	: 38.7 mpg
@	: 4100 rpm	acc. 0-62 mph	: 14.1 s
gears	: 5	top speed	: 87 mph
AT	: -	EuroNCAP	: n.a.
drive	: 4WD	introduction	: September 1998
brakes f/r	: discs / drum brakes	last revised in	: December 2005
body type	: 2-dr. SUV	warranty	: 3 years
l x w x h	: 3625 x 1600 x 1670 mm	miscellaneous	: Suzuki built itself a reputation with
wheelbase	: 2250 mm		small offroad vehicles. Cute looks
turning circle	: 9.8 m		and determined behaviour. Also
			available as convertible.

S

SUZUKI GRAND VITARA 1.6 / 2.0

engine type	: petrol, inline-4
displacement	: 1586 / 1995 cc
max. power	: 78 kW (106 bhp) / 103 kW (140 bhp)
@	: 5900 / 6000 rpm
max. torque	: 107 / 135 lb ft
@	: 4100 / 4000 rpm
gears	: 5
AT	: - / optional 4-speed
drive	: 4WD
brakes f/r	: vent. discs / drum brakes
body type	: 3-dr. / 5-dr. SUV
l x w x h	: 4005 / 4470 (5-d) x 1810 x 1695 mm
wheelbase	: 2440 / 2640 (5-d) mm
turning circle	: 10.2 / 11.0 m

kerb weight	: 1370 / 1505 kg
towing weight	: 1600 / 1850 kg
boot space	: 184 − 964 / 398 − 1386 l
fuel capacity	: 55 / 66 l
consumption	: 32.5 / 31.0 mpg
acc. 0-62 mph	: 14.4 / 12.5 s
top speed	: 99 / 109 mph
EuroNCAP	: n.a.
introduction	: September 2005
last revised in	: -
warranty	: 3 years
miscellaneous	: Completely new model. 1.6 version only available with 3 doors, 2.0 only with 5 doors. Fine companion with adequate performance level.

GRAND VITARA 1.9 DDIS

engine type	: diesel, inline-4
displacement	: 1870 cc
max. power	: 95 kW (129 bhp)
@	: 3750 rpm
max. torque	: 221 lb ft
@	: 2000 rpm
gears	: 5
kerb weight	: 1495 kg
towing weight	: 1600 kg
consumption	: 36.7 mpg
acc. 0-60 mph	: 12.8 s
top speed	: 106 mph
miscellaneous	: Available with 3-door and 5-door bodywork.

TOYOTA AYGO 1.0

engine type	: petrol, inline-3
displacement	: 998 cc
max. power	: 50 kW (68 bhp)
@	: 6000 rpm
max. torque	: 68 lb ft
@	: 3600 rpm
gears	: 5
AT	: optional 5-speed
drive	: FWD
brakes f/r	: vent. discs / drum brakes
body type	: 3- / 5-dr. hatchback
l x w x h	: 3410 x 1615 x 1465 mm
wheelbase	: 2340 mm
turning circle	: n.a.

kerb weight	: 765 kg
towing weight	: n.a.
boot space	: 130 - 782 l
fuel capacity	: 35 l
consumption	: 61.4 mpg
acc. 0-62 mph	: 14.2 s
top speed	: 98 mph
EuroNCAP	: 4 stars
introduction	: May 2005
last revised in	: -
warranty	: 3 years
miscellaneous	: Cute and original design, aimed at young clientele. Technically identical to Citroën C1 and Peugeot 107.

S
T

AYGO 1.4 DIESEL

engine type	: diesel, inline-4
displacement	: 1398 cc
max. power	: 40 kW (54 bhp)
@	: 4000 rpm
max. torque	: 96 lb ft
@	: 1750 rpm
gears	: 5
kerb weight	: 880 kg
towing weight	: n.a.
consumption	: 68.9 mpg
acc. 0-60 mph	: 16.8 s
top speed	: 96 mph
miscellaneous	: There are not that many cars around anymore of comparable size and weight.

TOYOTA YARIS 1.3 / SR

engine type	: petrol, inline-4	kerb weight	: 985 / 1090 kg
displacement	: 1298 / 1798 cc	towing weight	: 900 / 1050 kg
max. power	: 64 kW (87 bhp) / 98 kW (131 bhp)	boot space	: 363 l
@	: 6000 rpm	fuel capacity	: 42 l
max. torque	: 90 / 128 lb ft	consumption	: 47.1 / 39.2 mpg
@	: 4200 / 4400 rpm	acc. 0-62 mph	: 11.5 / 9,3 s
gears	: 5	top speed	: 106 / 121 mph
AT	: optional 5-speed / -	EuroNCAP	: 5 stars
drive	: FWD	introduction	: January 2006
brakes f/r	: vent. discs, drums / discs	last revised in	: -
body type	: 3- / 5-dr. hatchback	warranty	: 3 years
l x w x h	: 3750 x 1695 x 1530 mm	miscellaneous	: Popular small car, built in France.
wheelbase	: 2460 mm		Refer to the Toyota Aygo for
turning circle	: 9.4 m		specifications of the 1.0 engine.

YARIS 1.4 D-4D

engine type	: diesel, inline-4
displacement	: 1364 cc
max. power	: 66 kW (90 bhp)
@	: 3800 rpm
max. torque	: 140 lb ft
@	: 1800 rpm
gears	: 5
kerb weight	: 1030 kg
towing weight	: 1050 kg
consumption	: 62.8 mpg
acc. 0-60 mph	: 10.7 s
top speed	: 109 mph
miscellaneous	: Lively diesel engine.

TOYOTA AURIS 1.4 / 1.6

engine type	: petrol, inline-4
displacement	: 1398 / 1598 cc
max. power	: 71 kW (96 bhp) / 91 kW (122 bhp)
@	: 6000 rpm
max. torque	: 96 / 116 lb ft
@	: 4600 / 5200 rpm
gears	: 5
AT	: - / optional MMT
drive	: FWD
brakes f/r	: vent. discs / discs
body type	: 5-dr. hatchback
l x w x h	: 4220 x 1760 x 1515 mm
wheelbase	: 2600 mm
turning circle	: 10.4 m

kerb weight	: 1195 / 1205 kg
towing weight	: 1000 / 1300 kg
boot space	: 354 l
fuel capacity	: 55 l
consumption	: 40.9 / 39.8 mpg
acc. 0-62 mph	: 13.0 / 10.4 s
top speed	: 106 / 118 mph
EuroNCAP	: 5 stars
introduction	: February 2007
last revised in	: -
warranty	: 3 years
miscellaneous	: The Auris replaces the Corolla, but is identical in concept. It can also be ordered with two doors less.

AURIS 1.4 D-4D / 2.0 D-4D

engine type	: diesel, inline-4
displacement	: 1364 / 1998 cc
max. power	: 66 kW (89 bhp) / 93 kW (124 bhp)
@	: 3800 / 3600 rpm
max. torque	: 140 / 221 lb ft
@	: 1800 rpm
gears	: 5 / 6
kerb weight	: 1235 / 1360 kg
towing weight	: 1000 / 1500 kg
consumption	: 56.5 / 52.3 mpg
acc. 0-60 mph	: 12.0 / 10.3 s
top speed	: 109 / 121 mph
miscellaneous	: Third diesel option is the 177 bhp strong 2.2 D-4D. Refer to the Avensis for details.

TOYOTA COROLLA 1.6 16V

engine type	: petrol, inline-4	kerb weight	: 1240 kg
displacement	: 1598 cc	towing weight	: 1300 kg
max. power	: 91 kW (122 bhp)	boot space	: 450 l
@	: 6000 rpm	fuel capacity	: 55 l
max. torque	: 116 lb ft	consumption	: 40.9 mpg
@	: 5200 rpm	acc. 0-62 mph	: 10.4 s
gears	: 5	top speed	: 121 mph
AT	: optional 5-speed MMT	EuroNCAP	: 5 stars
drive	: FWD	introduction	: September 2007
brakes f/r	: vent. discs / discs	last revised in	: n.v.t.
body type	: 4-dr. saloon	warranty	: 3 jaar
l x w x h	: 4540 x 1760 x 1470 mm	miscellaneous	: The trusted Corolla nomenclature
wheelbase	: 2600 mm		is still in use for a down-to-earth
turning circle	: 10.4 m		saloon.

COROLLA 2.0 D-4D

engine type	: diesel, inline-4
displacement	: 1998 cc
max. power	: 93 kW (124 bhp)
@	: 3600 rpm
max. torque	: 221 lb ft
@	: 1800 rpm
gears	: 6
kerb weight	: 1305 kg
towing weight	: 1300 kg
consumption	: 49.6 mpg
acc. 0-60 mph	: 10.3 s
top speed	: 124 mph
miscellaneous	: The limited range of available engines consists of the above petrol engine and this diesel unit which, by the way, is excellent.

TOYOTA VERSO 1.6 16V / 1.8 16V

engine type	: petrol, inline-4	kerb weight	: 1320 / 1340 kg
displacement	: 1598 / 1794 cc	towing weight	: 1200 / 1300 kg
max. power	: 81 kW (110 bhp) / 95 kW (129 bhp)	boot space	: 397 - 779 l
@	: 6000 rpm	fuel capacity	: 60 l
max. torque	: 111 / 126 lb ft	consumption	: 37.7 / 36.7 mpg
@	: 3800 / 4200 rpm	acc. 0-62 mph	: 12.7 / 10.8 s
gears	: 5	top speed	: 109 / 121 mph
AT	: - / optional 5-speed	EuroNCAP	: 5 stars
drive	: FWD	introduction	: February 2004
brakes f/r	: vent. discs / discs	last revised in	: July 2007
body type	: 5-dr. MPV	warranty	: 3 years
l x w x h	: 4360 x 1770 x 1620 mm	miscellaneous	: Minor facelift for a fine family car. The Verso is available with five or even seven seats, in which case the third row of seats can be folded flat.
wheelbase	: 2750 mm		
turning circle	: 11.6 m		

VERSO 2.2 D-4D / T180

engine type	: diesel, inline-4
displacement	: 2231 cc
max. power	: 100 kW (136 bhp) / 130 kW (177 bhp)
@	: 3600 rpm
max. torque	: 228 / 295 lb ft
@	: 2000 rpm
gears	: 5
kerb weight	: 1450 kg
towing weight	: 1300 kg
consumption	: 44.8 / 41.5
acc. 0-60 mph	: 9.4 / 8.8 s
top speed	: 122 / 128 mph
miscellaneous	: A particle filter is now also standard on the smaller diesel unit.

TOYOTA AVENSIS 1.6 16V / 1.8 16V

engine type	: petrol, inline-4
displacement	: 1598 / 1794 cc
max. power	: 81 kW (110 bhp) / 95 kW (129 bhp)
@	: 6000 rpm
max. torque	: 111 / 125 lb ft
@	: 3800 / 4200 rpm
gears	: 5
AT	: - / optional 4-speed
drive	: FWD
brakes f/r	: vent. discs / discs
body type	: 4-dr. saloon
l x w x h	: 4645 x 1760 x 1480 mm
wheelbase	: 2700 mm
turning circle	: 10.8 m

kerb weight	: 1255 kg
towing weight	: 1300 kg
boot space	: 520 l
fuel capacity	: 60 l
consumption	: 39.2 mpg
acc. 0-62 mph	: 12.0 / 10.3 s
top speed	: 121 / 124 mph
EuroNCAP	: 5 stars
introduction	: February 2003
last revised in	: April 2006
warranty	: 3 years
miscellaneous	: Very successful car. Representative looks, excellent build quality, fine engines, high safety level.

AVENSIS 2.0 D4 / 2.4 D4

engine type	: petrol, inline-4
displacement	: 1998 / 2362 cc
max. power	: 108 kW (147 bhp) / 120 kW (163 bhp)
@	: 5700 / 5800 rpm
max. torque	: 114 / 170 lb ft
@	: 4000 / 3800 rpm
gears	: 5 / 5-speed automatic
kerb weight	: 1305 kg
towing weight	: 1400 kg
consumption	: 34.9 / 29.7 mpg
acc. 0-60 mph	: 9.4 / 9.1 s
top speed	: 130 / 137 mph
miscellaneous	: D4 stands for direct fuel injection. Fine petrol engines.

TOYOTA AVENSIS TOURER T180

engine type	: diesel, inline-4	kerb weight	: 1460 kg
displacement	: 2231 cc	towing weight	: 1300 kg
max. power	: 130 kW (177 bhp)	boot space	: 520 - 1500 l
@	: 3600 rpm	fuel capacity	: 60 l
max. torque	: 295 lb ft	consumption	: 45.6 mpg
@	: 2000 rpm	acc. 0-62 mph	: 8.6 s
gears	: 6	top speed	: 137 mph
AT	: -	EuroNCAP	: 5 stars
drive	: FWD	introduction	: February 2003
brakes f/r	: vent. discs / discs	last revised in	: -
body type	: 5-dr. stationwagon	warranty	: 3 years
l x w x h	: 4700 x 1760 x 1525 mm	miscellaneous	: Catalytic convertor of diesel
wheelbase	: 2700 mm		engine
turning circle	: 11.2 m		very efficient against soot particles
			and nitrogen oxide. Toyota has a
			lead on rest of industry.

T

AVENSIS WAGON 2.0 D-4D / 2.2 D-4D

engine type	: diesel, inline-4
displacement	: 1995 / 2231 cc
max. power	: 93 kW (126 bhp) / 110 kW (150 bhp)
@	: 3600 rpm
max. torque	: 222 / 228 lb ft
@	: 2800 / 2000 rpm
gears	: 6
kerb weight	: 1440 / 1455 kg
towing weight	: 1300 kg
consumption	: 49.6 / 47.1 mpg
acc. 0-60 mph	: 10.6 / 9.3 s
top speed	: 124 / 130 mph
miscellaneous	: 2.0 D4-D engine upgraded
	together with facelift.

TOYOTA PRIUS HSD

engine type	: petrol, inline-4 + electrical engine	**kerb weight**	: 1104 kg
displacement	: 1497 cc	**towing weight**	: -
max. power	: 57 kW (77 bhp)	**boot space**	: 408 – 1210 l
@	: 5000 rpm	**fuel capacity**	: 50 l
max. torque	: 85 lb ft	**consumption**	: 65.7 mpg
@	: 4000 rpm	**acc. 0-62 mph**	: 10.9 s
gears	: -	**top speed**	: 106 mph
AT	: CVT	**EuroNCAP**	: 5 stars
drive	: FWD	**introduction**	: November 2003
brakes f/r	: vent. discs / discs	**last revised in**	: October 2005
body type	: 5-dr. hatchback	**warranty**	: 5 years
l x w x h	: 4450 x 1725 x 1490 mm	**miscellaneous**	: Complex hybrid drivetrain results
wheelbase	: 2700 mm		in low consumption and emission
turning circle	: 10.2 m		figures. Sales enhanced by unique
			looks and favourable tax condi-
			tions.

TOYOTA RAV4 2.0 16V

engine type	: petrol, inline-4	**kerb weight**	: 1440 kg
displacement	: 1998 cc	**towing weight**	: 2000 kg
max. power	: 112 kW (152 bhp)	**boot space**	: 513 l
@	: 6000 rpm	**fuel capacity**	: 60 l
max. torque	: 143 lb ft	**consumption**	: 32.8 mpg
@	: 4000 rpm	**acc. 0-62 mph**	: 10.6 s
gears	: 5	**top speed**	: 115 mph
AT	: optional 4-speed	**EuroNCAP**	: 4 stars
drive	: 4WD	**introduction**	: December 2005
brakes f/r	: vent. discs / discs	**last revised in**	: -
body type	: 5-dr. SUV	**warranty**	: 3 years
l x w x h	: 4395 x 1815 x 1720 mm	**miscellaneous**	: Third generation of successful SUV much bigger than predecessors. Front-wheel drive and 3-door bodywork no longer available.
wheelbase	: 2560 mm		
turning circle	: 10.2 m		

T

RAV4 2.2 D-4D

engine type	: diesel, inline-4
displacement	: 2231 cc
max. power	: 100 kW (136 bhp) / 130 kW (177 bhp)
@	: 3600 rpm
max. torque	: 228 / 295 lb ft
@	: 2000 rpm
gears	: 6
kerb weight	: 1560 / 1570 kg
towing weight	: 2000 kg
consumption	: 42.8 / 40.4 mpg
acc. 0-60 mph	: 10.5 / 9.3 s
top speed	: 112 / 124 mph
miscellaneous	: Diesel-powered RAV4 shines with low consumption and emission figures. Not your average thirsty and polluting SUV therefore.

TOYOTA LAND CRUISER 3.0 D-4D / 4.0 V6

engine type	: diesel, inline-4 / petrol, V6	kerb weight	: 1835 / 1845 kg
displacement	: 2982 / 3956 cc	towing weight	: 2800 kg
max. power	: 127 kW (164 bhp) /	boot space	: 620 l
	183 kW (245 bhp)	fuel capacity	: 87 l
@	: 3400 / 5200 rpm	consumption	: 31.4 / 22.2 mpg
max. torque	: 302 / 281 lb ft	acc. 0-62 mph	: 11.5 / 9.1 s
@	: 1600 / 3800 rpm	top speed	: 109 / 112 mph
gears	: 6 / -	EuroNCAP	: n.a.
AT	: optional 5-speed / 5-speed	introduction	: December 2002
drive	: 4WD	last revised in	: -
brakes f/r	: vent. discs	warranty	: 3 years
body type	: 5-dr. SUV	miscellaneous	: Although updated occasionally,
l x w x h	: 4810 x 1790 x 1890 mm		looks of Land Cruiser remain
wheelbase	: 2790 mm		unaltered. Robust offroader,
turning circle	: 11.4 m		comfortable too. 3.0 D4 version
			also available with 3-door body on
			shorter wheelbase.

TOYOTA LAND CRUISER 100 4.2 D-4D

engine type	: diesel, inline-6	**kerb weight**	: 2420 kg
displacement	: 4164 cc	**towing weight**	: 3500 kg
max. power	: 150 kW (201 bhp)	**boot space**	: 1318 - 2212 l
@	: 3400 rpm	**fuel capacity**	: 96 l
max. torque	: 317 lb ft	**consumption**	: 25.4 mpg
@	: 1200 rpm	**acc. 0-62 mph**	: 13.6 s
gears	: 5	**top speed**	: 106 mph
AT	: optional 5-speed	**EuroNCAP**	: n.a.
drive	: 4WD	**introduction**	: 1998
brakes f/r	: vent. discs	**last revised in**	: December 2005
body type	: 5-dr. SUV	**warranty**	: 3 years
l x w x h	: 4890 x 1940 x 1890 mm	**miscellaneous**	: Bigger Land Cruiser Amazon also
wheelbase	: 2850 mm		available with V8 petrol engine.
turning circle	: 11.8 m		

TVR TUSCAN 2

engine type	: petrol, inline-6	kerb weight	: 1207 kg
displacement	: 3996 cc	towing weight	: -
max. power	: 287 kW (390 bhp)	boot space	: 275 l
@	: 7000 rpm	fuel capacity	: 57 l
max. torque	: 310 lb ft	consumption	: n.a.
@	: 5250 rpm	acc. 0-62 mph	: 3.8 s
gears	: 5	top speed	: 195 mph
AT	: -	EuroNCAP	: n.a.
drive	: RWD	introduction	: 2000
brakes f/r	: vent. discs	last revised in	: 2005
body type	: 2-dr. targa / convertible	warranty	: 2 years
l x w x h	: 4235 x 1810 x 1200 mm	miscellaneous	: The expression 'a hairy car' could
wheelbase	: 2361 mm		have been cued for TVRs in
turning circle	: n.a.		particular. Tuscan convertible
			available soon.

TVR SAGARIS

engine type	: petrol, inline-6	**kerb weight**	: 1078 kg
displacement	: 3996 cc	**towing weight**	: -
max. power	: 294 kW (400 bhp)	**boot space**	: n.a.
@	: 7000 rpm	**fuel capacity**	: 57 l
max. torque	: 350 lb ft	**consumption**	: n.a.
@	: 6000 rpm	**acc. 0-62 mph**	: 3.9 s
gears	: 5	**top speed**	: > 160 mph
AT	: -	**EuroNCAP**	: n.a.
drive	: RWD	**introduction**	: December 2005
brakes f/r	: vent. discs	**last revised in**	: -
body type	: 2-dr. coupe	**warranty**	: 2 years
l x w x h	: 4057 x 1850 x 1175 mm	**miscellaneous**	: Astonishing car with wild looks and wild engine. Phenomenal performance..
wheelbase	: 2361 mm		
turning circle	: n.a.		

T

VOLKSWAGEN FOX 1.2 / 1.4

engine type	: petrol, inline-3 / inline-4
displacement	: 1198 / 1390 cc
max. power	: 40 kW (55 bhp) / 55 kW (75 bhp)
@	: 4750 / 5000 rpm
max. torque	: 80 / 92 lb ft
@	: 3000 / 2750 rpm
gears	: 5
AT	: -
drive	: FWD
brakes f/r	: vent. discs / drum brakes
body type	: 3-dr. hatchback
l x w x h	: 3828 x 1660 x 1544 mm
wheelbase	: 2465 mm
turning circle	: 11.0 m

kerb weight	: 973 / 987 kg
towing weight	: -
boot space	: 260-1016 l
fuel capacity	: 45 l
consumption	: 46.3 / 41.5 mpg
acc. 0-62 mph	: 17.5 / 13.0 s
top speed	: 92 / 104 mph
EuroNCAP	: 4 stars
introduction	: September 2005
last revised in	: -
warranty	: 2 years
miscellaneous	: Cheapest VW in ages. Good alternative to Toyota Aygo and similar models. Spacious interior with adequate front and rear legroom.

VOLKSWAGEN FOX 1.4 TDI

engine type	: diesel, inline-3
displacement	: 1422 cc
max. power	: 51 kW (70 bhp)
@	: 4000 rpm
max. torque	: 114 lb ft
@	: 1600 rpm
gears	: 5
kerb weight	: 1060 kg
towing weight	: -
consumption	: 57.6 mpg
acc. 0-60 mph	: 14.7 s
top speed	: 100 mph
miscellaneous	: Smallest VW is built in Brazil. Only available in 3-door version, in order to make life easier for VW Polo.

VOLKSWAGEN POLO 1.2

engine type	: petrol, inline-3	**kerb weight**	: 989 / 991 kg
displacement	: 1198 cc	**towing weight**	: 700 / 800 kg
max. power	: 40 kW (55 bhp) / 47 kW (64 bhp)	**boot space**	: 270 -1030 l
@	: 4750 / 5400 rpm	**fuel capacity**	: 45 l
max. torque	: 80 / 83 lb ft	**consumption**	: 47.1 mpg
@	: 3000 rpm	**acc. 0-62 mph**	: 17.5 / 14.9 s
gears	: 5	**top speed**	: 95 / 101 mph
AT	: -	**EuroNCAP**	: 4 stars
drive	: FWD	**introduction**	: September 2001
brakes f/r	: vent. discs / drum brakes	**last revised in**	: September 2005
body type	: 3- / 5-dr. hatchback	**warranty**	: 2 years
l x w x h	: 3916 x 1650 x 1467 mm	**miscellaneous**	: Bestseller in B-segment. Also
wheelbase	: 2465 mm		available with 1.4 (75 or 80 bhp),
turning circle	: 10.6 m		1.6 (105 bhp) and four different TDi
			engines.

V

POLO GTI

engine type	: petrol, inline-4
displacement	: 1781 cc
max. power	: 110 kW (150 bhp)
@	: 5800 rpm
max. torque	: 162 lb ft
@	: 1950 rpm
gears	: 5
kerb weight	: 1139 kg
towing weight	: 800 kg
consumption	: 35.8 mpg
acc. 0-60 mph	: 8.2 s
top speed	: 134 mph
miscellaneous	: Engine from VW Golf IV GTI transforms Polo into a nice and quick 'hot hatch'.

VOLKSWAGEN CROSSPOLO 1.4 16V / 1.6 16V

engine type	: petrol, inline-4	kerb weight	: 1062 / 1065 kg
displacement	: 1390 / 1598 cc	towing weight	: 800 / 1200 kg
max. power	: 59 kW (80 bhp) / 77 kW (105 bhp)	boot space	: 288 l
@	: 5000 / 5600 rpm	fuel capacity	: 45 l
max. torque	: 97 / 113 lb ft	consumption	: 42.2 / 40.9 mpg
@	: 3800 rpm	acc. 0-62 mph	: 13.5 / 12.1 s
gears	: 5	top speed	: 106 / 119 mph
AT	: optional 4-speed / optional 6-speed	EuroNCAP	: 4 stars
drive	: FWD	introduction	: March 2006
brakes f/r	: vent. discs / discs	last revised in	: -
body type	: 5-dr. hatchback	warranty	: 2 years
l x w x h	: 3908 x 1675 x 1527 mm	miscellaneous	: New Polo Dune is the first in a series of wild looking VWs.
wheelbase	: 2462 mm		
turning circle	: 10.6 m		

CROSSPOLO 1.4 TDI / 1.9 TDI

engine type	: diesel, inline-3 / inline-4
displacement	: 1422 / 1896 cc
max. power	: 51 kW (70 bhp) / 74 kW (100 bhp)
@	: 4000 rpm
max. torque	: 114 / 177 lb ft
@	: 1600 / 1800 rpm
gears	: 5
kerb weight	: 1130 / 1165 kg
towing weight	: 900 / 1200 kg
consumption	: 56.5 / 55.4 mpg
acc. 0-60 mph	: 15.9 / 11.5 s
top speed	: 100 / 113 mph
miscellaneous	: Same 1.4 TDI engine also mounted in frugal Polo BlueMotion.

VOLKSWAGEN GOLF 1.4 16V / 1.4 TSI

engine type	: petrol, inline-4	kerb weight	: 1129 / 1205 kg
displacement	: 1390 cc	towing weight	: 1000 kg / -
max. power	: 59 kW (80 bhp) / 90 kW (122 bhp)	boot space	: 350 l
@	: 5000 / 5500 rpm	fuel capacity	: 55 l
max. torque	: 97 / 147 lb ft	consumption	: 40.9 / 44.8 mpg
@	: 3800 / 1500 rpm	acc. 0-62 mph	: 13.9 / 9.4 s
gears	: 5 / 6	top speed	: 104 / 122 mph
AT	: -	EuroNCAP	: 5 stars
drive	: FWD	introduction	: September 2003
brakes f/r	: vent. discs / discs	last revised in	: -
body type	: 3- / 5-dr. hatchback	warranty	: 2 years
l x w x h	: 4204 x 1759 x 1485 mm	miscellaneous	: Still a bestseller. Available with
wheelbase	: 2578 mm		many other engine alternatives, as
turning circle	: 10.9 m		described under the other entries
			(Golf Plus, Touran, Jetta).

GOLF 2.0 SDI

engine type	: diesel, inline-4
displacement	: 1968 cc
max. power	: 55 kW (75 bhp)
@	: 4200 rpm
max. torque	: 103 lb ft
@	: 2200 rpm
gears	: 5
kerb weight	: 1227 kg
towing weight	: 1000 kg
consumption	: 52.3 mpg
acc. 0-60 mph	: 16.7 s
top speed	: 101 mph
miscellaneous	: Not very quick, but good. This 2.0 SDI model is the spiritual successor to the successful Golf II 1.6 D. Also available with 1.9 TDI unit of either 90 or 105 bhp and 2.0 TDI with 140 or 170 bhp.

VOLKSWAGEN GOLF GTI / R32

engine type	: petrol, inline-4 / V6	kerb weight	: 1303 / 1594 kg
displacement	: 1984 / 3189 cc	towing weight	: 1400 kg / n.a.
max. power	: 147 kW (200 bhp) /	boot space	: 350 – 1305 / 275 -1230 l
	184 kW (250 bhp)	fuel capacity	: 55 / 60 l
@	: 5100 / 6300 rpm	consumption	: 34.9 / 26.2 mpg
max. torque	: 207 / 236 lb ft	acc. 0-62 mph	: 7.2 / 6.5 s
@	: 1800 / 2500 rpm	top speed	: 146 / 155 mph
gears	: 6	EuroNCAP	: 5 stars
AT	: optional 6-speed DSG	introduction	: September 2004 /
drive	: FWD / 4WD	last revised in	September 2005
brakes f/r	: vent. discs, discs /	warranty	: -
	vent. discs	miscellaneous	: 2 years
body type	: 3- / 5-dr. hatchback		: Golf range features two top
l x w x h	: 4204 x 1759 x 1485 mm		models. Legendary GTI makes a
wheelbase	: 2578 mm		comeback, 6-cylinder R32 is even
turning circle	: 10.9 m		faster.

VOLKSWAGEN GOLF PLUS 1.6 FSI

engine type	: petrol, inline-4	kerb weight	: 1283 kg
displacement	: 1598 cc	towing weight	: 1200 kg
max. power	: 85 kW (115 bhp)	boot space	: 395 l
@	: 6000 rpm	fuel capacity	: 55 l
max. torque	: 114 lb ft	consumption	: 39.8 mpg
@	: 4000 rpm	acc. 0-62 mph	: 12.0 s
gears	: 6	top speed	: 117 mph
AT	: optional 6-speed	EuroNCAP	: n.a.
drive	: FWD	introduction	: February 2005
brakes f/r	: vent. discs / discs	last revised in	: -
body type	: 5-dr. hatchback	warranty	: 2 years
l x w x h	: 4206 x 1759 x 1580 mm	miscellaneous	: Its dimensions put it in between
wheelbase	: 2578 mm		the Golf and Touran models.
turning circle	: 10.8 m		

V

CROSSGOLF 1.9 TDI / 2.0 TDI

engine type	: diesel, inline-4
displacement	: 1896 / 1968 cc
max. power	: 77 kW (105 bhp) / 103 kW (140 bhp)
@	: 4000 rpm
max. torque	: 155 / 236 lb ft
@	: 1900 / 1750 rpm
gears	: 5 / 6
kerb weight	: 1395 / 1426 kg
towing weight	: 1400 kg
consumption	: 52.3 / 48.7 mpg
acc. 0-60 mph	: 12.1 / 9.9 s
top speed	: 114 / 125 mph
miscellaneous	: The CrossGolf is not a proper off-road vehicle but rather an 'SUV light' for fans of the off-road look.

VOLKSWAGEN CADDY KOMBI 1.4 16V / 1.6

engine type	: petrol, inline-4	kerb weight	: 1317 / 1336 kg
displacement	: 1390 / 1598 cc	towing weight	: 1200 / 1300 kg
max. power	: 55 kW (75 bhp) / 75 kW (102 bhp)	boot space	: 626 – 2300 l
@	: 5000 / 5600 rpm	fuel capacity	: 60 l
max. torque	: 94 / 109 lb ft	consumption	: 34.5 / 34.9 mpg
@	: 3300 / 3800 rpm	acc. 0-62 mph	: 17.9 / 13.7 s
gears	: 5	top speed	: 92 / 102 mph
AT	: -	EuroNCAP	: n.a.
drive	: FWD	introduction	: April 2004
brakes f/r	: vent. discs	last revised in	: -
body type	: 5-dr. MPV	warranty	: 2 years
l x w x h	: 4405 x 1802 x 1833 mm	miscellaneous	: Sliding doors, sturdy grey-coloured
wheelbase	: 2682 mm		bumpers and simple rear axle
turning circle	: n.a.		distinguish Caddy from equally
			spacious but more expensive
			Touran.

CADDY KOMBI 1.9 TDI

engine type	: diesel, inline-4
displacement	: 1895 / 1896 cc
max. power	: 55 kW (75 bhp) / 77 kW (105 bhp)
@	: 4000 rpm
max. torque	: 155 / 177 lb ft
@	: 1900 rpm
gears	: 5
kerb weight	: 1401 kg
towing weight	: 1400 / 1500 kg
consumption	: 45.6 / 47.1 mpg
acc. 0-60 mph	: 17.7 / 13.3 s
top speed	: 93 / 103 mph
miscellaneous	: 2.0 TDI engine reserved for
	other models.

VOLKSWAGEN TOURAN 1.4 TSI

engine type	: petrol, inline-4	kerb weight	: 1478 / 1522 kg
displacement	: 1390 cc	towing weight	: 1500 / 1500 kg
max. power	: 103 kW (140 bhp) /	boot space	: 695 l
	125 kW (170 bhp)	fuel capacity	: 60 l
@	: 5600 / 6000 rpm	consumption	: 38.2 / 37.2 mpg
max. torque	: 162 / 177 lb ft	acc. 0-62 mph	: 9.8 / 8.5 s
@	: 1500 rpm	top speed	: 124 / 132 mph
gears	: 6 / -	EuroNCAP	: 5 stars
AT	: - / 6-speed DSG	introduction	: February 2004
drive	: FWD	last revised in	: November 2006
brakes f/r	: vent. discs / discs	warranty	: 2 years
body type	: 5-dr. MPV	miscellaneous	: Revised Touran benefits from
l x w x h	: 4407 x 1794 x 1635 mm		potent yet frugal TSI engine.
wheelbase	: 2678 mm		
turning circle	: 11.2 m		

V

CROSSTOURAN 2.0 TDI

engine type	: diesel, inline-4
displacement	: 1968 cc
max. power	: 125 kW (170 bhp)
@	: 4200 rpm
max. torque	: 258 lb ft
@	: 1750 rpm
gears	: 6, optional 6-speed DSG
kerb weight	: 1596 kg
towing weight	: 1600 kg
consumption	: 42.8 mpg
acc. 0-60 mph	: 9.2 s
top speed	: 132 mph
miscellaneous	: CrossTouran follows the path of the CrossPolo and CrossGolf. The car looks much better than the conservatively styled model it is based on.

VOLKSWAGEN GOLF ESTATE 1.6

engine type	: petrol, inline-4	kerb weight	: 1278 kg
displacement	: 1595 cc	towing weight	: 1200 kg
max. power	: 75 kW (102 bhp)	boot space	: 505 l
@	: 5600 rpm	fuel capacity	: 55 l
max. torque	: 109 lb ft	consumption	: 38.2 mpg
@	: 3800 rpm	acc. 0-62 mph	: 12.3 s
gears	: 5	top speed	: 114 mph
AT	: -	EuroNCAP	: 5 stars
drive	: FWD	introduction	: July 2007
brakes f/r	: vent. discs / discs	last revised in	: -
body type	: 5-dr. stationwagon	warranty	: 2 years
l x w x h	: 4556 x 1781 x 1504 mm	miscellaneous	: Estate version of the Golf arrives
wheelbase	: 2578 mm		late on the scene. Very roomy
turning circle	: 11.0 m		model with a large choice of
			engines. Refer to the Golf, Golf
			Plus and Touran for specifications.

JETTA 1.9 TDI

engine type	: diesel, inline-4
displacement	: 1896 cc
max. power	: 77 kW (105 bhp)
@	: 4000 rpm
max. torque	: 184 lb ft
@	: 1900 rpm
gears	: 5
kerb weight	: 1320 kg
towing weight	: 1400 kg
consumption	: 54.3 mpg
acc. 0-60 mph	: 11.9 s
top speed	: 117 mph
miscellaneous	: Car is built in Mexico together with Golf Estate, with which it shares its drive train.

VOLKSWAGEN NEW BEETLE 1.4 16V / 1.6

engine type	: petrol, inline-4	kerb weight	: 1157 / 1177 kg
displacement	: 1390 / 1596 cc	towing weight	: 1000 kg
max. power	: 55 kW (75 bhp) / 75 kW (102 bhp)	boot space	: 214 -769 l
@	: 5000 / 5600 rpm	fuel capacity	: 55 l
max. torque	: 93 / 109 lb ft	consumption	: 39.8 / 36.7 mpg
@	: 3300 / 3800 rpm	acc. 0-62 mph	: 14.6 / 11.6 s
gears	: 5	top speed	: 100 / 111 mph
AT	: -	EuroNCAP	: 4 stars
drive	: FWD	introduction	: November 1998
brakes f/r	: vent. discs / discs	last revised in	: September 2005
body type	: 3-dr. hatchback	warranty	: 2 years
l x w x h	: 4081 x 1724 x 1498 mm	miscellaneous	: Long-term model received a minor
wheelbase	: 2508 mm		facelift, in order to enhance sales.
turning circle	: 10.9 m		However, those who liked it, will
			already have bought one by now.

V

NEW BEETLE 1.9 TDI

engine type	: diesel, inline-4
displacement	: 1896 cc
max. power	: 77 kW (105 bhp)
@	: 4000 rpm
max. torque	: 177 lb ft
@	: 1800 rpm
gears	: 5
kerb weight	: 1266 kg
towing weight	: 1000 kg
consumption	: 51.4 mpg
acc. 0-60 mph	: 11.5 s
top speed	: 112 mph
miscellaneous	: Same engines used in
	hatchback and convertible.

VOLKSWAGEN NEW BEETLE CABRIOLET 2.0 / 1.8T

engine type	: petrol, inline-4	kerb weight	: 1304 / 1363 kg
displacement	: 1984 / 1781 cc	towing weight	: 1000 kg
max. power	: 85 kW (115 bhp) /	boot space	: 201 l
	110 kW (150 bhp)	fuel capacity	: 55 l
@	: 5200 / 5800 rpm	consumption	: 32.1 / 34.0 mpg
max. torque	: 127 / 162 lb ft	acc. 0-62 mph	: 11.7 / 9.3 s
@	: 3200 / 2000 rpm	top speed	: 114 / 125 mph
gears	: 5	EuroNCAP	: 4 stars
AT	: optional 4-speed / -	introduction	: April 2003
drive	: FWD	last revised in	: September 2005
brakes f/r	: vent. discs / discs	warranty	: 2 years
body type	: 2-dr. convertible	miscellaneous	: Romantic model in down-to-earth
l x w x h	: 4081 x 1724 x 1502 mm		Volkswagen programme.
wheelbase	: 2509 mm		
turning circle	: 10.9 m		

VOLKSWAGEN EOS 3.2 V6

engine type	: petrol, V6		**kerb weight**	: 1627 kg
displacement	: 3189 cc		**towing weight**	: 1500 kg
max. power	: 184 kW (250 bhp)		**boot space**	: 358 l
@	: 6300 rpm		**fuel capacity**	: 55 l
max. torque	: 244 lb ft		**consumption**	: 30.7 mpg
@	: 2500 rpm		**acc. 0-62 mph**	: 7.3 s
gears	: -		**top speed**	: 153 lb ft
AT	: 6-speed DSG		**EuroNCAP**	: n.a.
drive	: FWD		**introduction**	: April 2006
brakes f/r	: vent. discs / discs		**last revised in**	: -
body type	: 2-dr. convertible		**warranty**	: 2 years
l x w x h	: 4407 x 1791 x 1437 mm		**miscellaneous**	: Good-looking coupé-convertible.
wheelbase	: 2578 mm			Also available with 1.6 FSI (115
turning circle	: 10.9 m			bhp), 2.0 FSI (150 bhp), 2.0 TFSI
				(200 bhp) or 2.0 TDI (140 bhp).

V

VOLKSWAGEN TIGUAN 1.4 TSI

engine type	: petrol, inline-4		**kerb weight**	: 1546 kg
displacement	: 1390 cc		**towing weight**	: 2000 kg
max. power	: 110 kW (150 bhp)		**boot space**	: 505 l
@	: 5800 rpm		**fuel capacity**	: 64 l
max. torque	: 177 lb ft		**consumption**	: 33.6 mpg
@	: 1750 rpm		**acc. 0-62 mph**	: 9.6 s
gears	: 6		**top speed**	: 119 mph
AT	: -		**EuroNCAP**	: n.a.
drive	: 4WD		**introduction**	: November 2007
brakes f/r	: vent. discs / discs		**last revised in**	: -
body type	: 5-dr. SUV		**warranty**	: 2 years
l x w x h	: 4427 x 1809 x 1683 mm		**miscellaneous**	: Choice of engines for the Tiguan
wheelbase	: 2604 mm			is limited to these two engines.
turning circle	: 12.0 m			The car is available in a regular
				and off-road version.

TIGUAN 2.0 TDI

engine type	: diesel, inline-4
displacement	: 1968 cc
max. power	: 103 kW (140 bhp)
@	: 4200 rpm
max. torque	: 236 lb ft
@	: 1750 rpm
gears	: 6, optional 6-speed automatic
kerb weight	: 1590 kg
towing weight	: 2200 kg
consumption	: 39.2 mpg
acc. 0-60 mph	: 10.5 s
top speed	: 116 mph
miscellaneous	: The Tiguan is the first Volkswagen with a common-rail diesel engine. A unit with 170 bhp will follow.

VOLKSWAGEN PASSAT 1.6 / 1.6 16V FSI

engine type	: petrol, inline-4
displacement	: 1595 / 1598 cc
max. power	: 75 kW (102 bhp) / 85 kW (115 bhp)
@	: 5600 / 6000 rpm
max. torque	: 109 / 114 lb ft
@	: 3800 / 4000 rpm
gears	: 5 / 6
AT	: - / optional 6-speed
drive	: FWD
brakes f/r	: vent. discs / discs
body type	: 4-dr. saloon
l x w x h	: 4765 x 1820 x 1472 mm
wheelbase	: 2709 mm
turning circle	: 11.4 m

kerb weight	: 1318 / 1323 kg
towing weight	: 1300 kg
boot space	: 565 l
fuel capacity	: 70 l
consumption	: 36.7 / 36.2 mpg
acc. 0-62 mph	: 12.4 / 11.4 s
top speed	: 118 / 122 mph
EuroNCAP	: 5 stars
introduction	: November 2004
last revised in	: -
warranty	: 2 years
miscellaneous	: New Passat has striking front. Familiar, excellent build quality.

V

PASSAT 2.0 16V FSI / 2.0 TFSI

engine type	: petrol, inline-4
displacement	: 1984 cc
max. power	: 110 kW (150 bhp) / 147 kW (200 bhp)
@	: 6000 / 5100 rpm
max. torque	: 148 / 207 lb ft
@	: 3500 / 1800 rpm
gears	: 6
kerb weight	: 1364 / 1420 kg
towing weight	: 1500 / 1600 kg
consumption	: 33.2 / 34.4 mpg
acc. 0-60 mph	: 9.4 / 7.6 s
top speed	: 130 / 144 mph
miscellaneous	: FSI stands for Fuel Stratified Injection, Volkswagen speak for direct fuel injection. Lower consumption figures due to combustion of leaner mixture at constant engine speed.

PASSAT 3.2 V6 FSI

engine type	: petrol, V6
displacement	: 3189 cc
max. power	: 184 kW (250 bhp)
@	: 6400 rpm
max. torque	: 236 lb ft
@	: 3200 rpm
gears	: 6-speed DSG
kerb weight	: 1635 kg
towing weight	: 2200 kg
consumption	: 28.0 mpg
acc. 0-60 mph	: 7.2 s
top speed	: 151 mph
miscellaneous	: Previous Passat was related to Audi A4/A6, with longitudinal engines. New Passat has transverse engines, meaning V6 is in fact VR6. Now with fuel injection.

VOLKSWAGEN PASSAT ESTATE 2.0 TDI

engine type	: diesel, inline-4	kerb weight	: 1485 / 1432 kg
displacement	: 1968 / 1968 cc	towing weight	: 1800 kg
max. power	: 103 kW (140 bhp) /	boot space	: 603 l
	125 kW (170 bhp)	fuel capacity	: 62 l
@	: 4000 / 4200 rpm	consumption	: 47.9 / 44.1 mpg
max. torque	: 236 / 258 lb ft	acc. 0-62 mph	: 10.1 / 8.6 s
@	: 1750 / 1800 rpm	top speed	: 128 / 137 mph
gears	: 6	EuroNCAP	: 5 stars
AT	: optional 6-speed DSG	introduction	: July 2005
drive	: FWD	last revised in	: -
brakes f/r	: vent. discs / discs	warranty	: 2 years
body type	: 5-dr. stationwagon	miscellaneous	: Elegantly sloping roof hides large
l x w x h	: 4774 x 1820 x 1517 mm		storage compartment. Available
wheelbase	: 2709 mm		with same engines as saloon
turning circle	: 11.4 m		model, with the exception of the
			smallest 1.6 unit.

PASSAT ESTATE BLUEMOTION

engine type	: diesel, inline-4
displacement	: 1896 cc
max. power	: 77 kW (105 bhp)
@	: 4000 rpm
max. torque	: 184 lb ft
@	: 1900 rpm
gears	: 5
kerb weight	: 1477 kg
towing weight	: 1500 kg
consumption	: 54.3 mpg
acc. 0-60 mph	: 12.4 s
top speed	: 118 mph
miscellaneous	: Thanks to minor technical changes, this model is more economical than the regular 1.9 TDI.

VOLKSWAGEN PHAETON 3.2 V6 / 4.2 V8

engine type	: petrol, V6 / V8	**kerb weight**	: 2176 / 2232 kg
displacement	: 3189 / 4172 cc	**towing weight**	: 2300 / 2400 kg
max. power	: 177 kW (241 bhp) /	**boot space**	: 500 l
	246 kW (335 bhp)	**fuel capacity**	: 90 l
@	: 6200 / 6500 rpm	**consumption**	: 23.2 / 21.6 mpg
max. torque	: 232 / 317 lb ft	**acc. 0-62 mph**	: 9.4 / 6.9 s
@	: 2400 / 3500 rpm	**top speed**	: 148 / 155 mph
gears	: -	**EuroNCAP**	: n.a.
AT	: 6-speed	**introduction**	: April 2002
drive	: 4WD	**last revised in**	: -
brakes f/r	: vent. discs	**warranty**	: 2 years
body type	: 4-dr. saloon	**miscellaneous**	: Not to everyone's taste. Also
l x w x h	: 5055 x 1903 x 1450 mm		available with longer wheelbase
wheelbase	: 2881 mm		and with a choice of 2 separate
turning circle	: 12.0 m		seats or 3-seat bench in the rear.

V

PHAETON 6.0 W12

engine type	: petrol, W12
displacement	: 5998 cc
max. power	: 331 kW (450 bhp)
@	: 6050 rpm
max. torque	: 413 lb ft
@	: 2750 rpm
gears	: 5
kerb weight	: 2294 kg
towing weight	: 2400 kg
consumption	: 19.5 mpg
acc. 0-60 mph	: 6.1 s
top speed	: 155 mph
miscellaneous	: Compact 12-cylinder engine offers fabulous performance.

PHAETON 3.0 V6 TDI

engine type	: diesel, V6
displacement	: 2967 cc
max. power	: 165 kW (225 bhp)
@	: 4000 rpm
max. torque	: 332 lb ft
@	: 1400 rpm
gears	: 6
kerb weight	: 2227 kg
towing weight	: 2500 kg
consumption	: 29.4 mpg
acc. 0-60 mph	: 9.1 s
top speed	: 145 mph
miscellaneous	: Introduction of V6 diesel option has done wonders for popularity of big Phaeton.

VOLKSWAGEN TOUAREG 2.5 TDI / 3.0 V6 TDI

engine type	: diesel, inline-5 / V6
displacement	: 2460 / 2967 cc
max. power	: 128 kW (174 bhp) / 165 kW (225 bhp)
@	: 3500 / 4000 rpm
max. torque	: 295 / 369 lb ft
@	: 2000 / 1750 rpm
gears	: 6 / -
AT	: optional / 6-speed
drive	: 4WD
brakes f/r	: vent. discs
body type	: 5-dr. SUV
l x w x h	: 4754 x 1928 x 1726 mm
wheelbase	: 2855 mm
turning circle	: 11.6 m

kerb weight	: 2179 / 2287 kg
towing weight	: 3500 kg
boot space	: 555 – 1570 l
fuel capacity	: 100 l
consumption	: 28.8 / 25.9 mpg
acc. 0-62 mph	: 12.4 / 9.9 s
top speed	: 114 / 125 mph
EuroNCAP	: n.a.
introduction	: September 2002
last revised in	: -
warranty	: 2 years
miscellaneous	: Diesel power best choice for this model. Successful VW SUV shares technology with Porsche Cayenne.

TOUAREG 3.6 V6 / 4.2 FSI V8

engine type	: petrol, V6 / V8
displacement	: 3597 / 4172 cc
max. power	: 206 kW (280 bhp) / 228 kW (310 bhp)
@	: 6200 rpm
max. torque	: 266 / 302 lb ft
@	: 3000 rpm
gears	: 6
kerb weight	: 2204 / 2217 kg
towing weight	: 3500 kg
consumption	: 20.5 / 19.1 mpg
acc. 0-60 mph	: 8.7 / 8.1 s
top speed	: 134 / 135 mph
miscellaneous	: Strongest version is 450 bhp 6.0 W12, available upon special request.

TOUAREG 5.0 V10 TDI

engine type	: diesel, V10
displacement	: 4921 cc
max. power	: 230 kW (313 bhp)
@	: 3750 rpm
max. torque	: 553 lb ft
@	: 2000 rpm
gears	: 6
kerb weight	: 2424 kg
towing weight	: 3500 kg
consumption	: 23.0 mpg
acc. 0-60 mph	: 7.8 s
top speed	: 140 mph
miscellaneous	: Fairly economical beast. Output of big diesel engine however already beaten by three other manufacturers from Germany.

VOLKSWAGEN SHARAN 2.0 / 1.8T

engine type	: petrol, inline-4		kerb weight	: 1553 / 1574 kg
displacement	: 1984 / 1781 cc		towing weight	: 1800 / 1900 kg
max. power	: 85 kW (115 bhp) /		boot space	: 255 - 2610 l
	110 kW (150 bhp)		fuel capacity	: 70 l
@	: 5200 / 5800 rpm		consumption	: 29.1 mpg
max. torque	: 125 / 162 lb ft		acc. 0-62 mph	: 15.2 / 10.9 s
@	: 2600 / 1800 rpm		top speed	: 110 / 124 mph
gears	: 6		EuroNCAP	: 3 stars
AT	: optional 4- / 5-speed		introduction	: July 2000
drive	: FWD		last revised in	: -
brakes f/r	: vent. discs / discs		warranty	: 2 years
body type	: 5-dr. MPV		miscellaneous	: Sharan model is past its prime.
l x w x h	: 4634 x 1810 x 1759 mm			Also two diesel engines available,
wheelbase	: 2841 mm			1.9 TDI and 2.0 TDI. Refer to
turning circle	: 11.0 m			identical Seat Alhambra for
				specifications.

V

SHARAN 2.8 V6

engine type	: petrol, V6
displacement	: 2792 cc
max. power	: 150 kW (204 bhp)
@	: 6200 rpm
max. torque	: 195 lb ft
@	: 3400 rpm
gears	: 6, optional 5-speed automatic
kerb weight	: 1594 kg
towing weight	: 2000 kg
consumption	: 26.6 mpg
acc. 0-60 mph	: 9.9 s
top speed	: 135 mph
miscellaneous	: If you have money to spare, opt for the 2.8 V6 with 4Motion four-wheel drive. Ideally suited for winter sports holidays!

VOLVO C30 1.6

engine type	: petrol, inline-4	kerb weight	: 1175 kg
displacement	: 1596 cc	towing weight	: 1200 kg
max. power	: 74 kW (100 bhp)	boot space	: 251 l
@	: 6000 rpm	fuel capacity	: 55 l
max. torque	: 110 lb ft	consumption	: 40.4 mpg
@	: 4000 rpm	acc. 0-62 mph	: 11.8 s
gears	: 5	top speed	: 115 mph
AT	: -	EuroNCAP	: n.a.
drive	: FWD	introduction	: January 2007
brakes f/r	: vent. discs / discs	last revised in	: -
body type	: 3-dr. hatchback	warranty	: 2 years
l x w x h	: 4248 x 1780 x 1452 mm	miscellaneous	: Popular, trendy hatchback based on S40 and V50. Refer to these models for the other available engines in the C30.
wheelbase	: 2640 mm		
turning circle	: 10.6 m		

VOLVO S40 1.8 / 2.0

engine type	: petrol, inline-4
displacement	: 1798 / 1999 cc
max. power	: 92 kW (125 bhp) / 107 kW (145 bhp)
@	: 6000 rpm
max. torque	: 122 / 136 lb ft
@	: 4000 rpm
gears	: 5
AT	: -
drive	: FWD
brakes f/r	: vent. discs / discs
body type	: 4-dr. saloon
l x w x h	: 4476 x 1770 x 1454 mm
wheelbase	: 2640 mm
turning circle	: 10.6 m

kerb weight	: 1266 / 1271 kg
towing weight	: 1300 / 1350 kg
boot space	: 404 l
fuel capacity	: 55 l
consumption	: 38.7 / 38.2 mpg
acc. 0-62 mph	: 10.9 / 9.5 s
top speed	: 124 / 130 mph
EuroNCAP	: 5 stars
introduction	: September 2003
last revised in	: July 2007
warranty	: 2 years
miscellaneous	: Smaller saloon model bears a bigger resemblance to the S80 now. Also available with 100 bhp strong 1.6 (see C30 model) and 170 bhp strong 2.4 unit. There is also a FlexiFuel version of the 1.8 engine which runs on bioethanol (E85).

V

S40 T5

engine type	: petrol, inline-5
displacement	: 2521 cc
max. power	: 169 kW (230 bhp)
@	: 5000 rpm
max. torque	: 236 lb ft
@	: 1500 rpm
gears	: 6
kerb weight	: 1368 kg
towing weight	: 1500 kg
consumption	: 32.5 mpg
acc. 0-60 mph	: 6.8 s
top speed	: 149 mph
miscellaneous	: Rapid T5 model gets even more power. The AWD version features 4WD.

VOLVO V50 1.6D / 2.0D

engine type	: diesel, inline-4	kerb weight	: 1311 / 1472 kg
displacement	: 1560 / 1997 cc	towing weight	: 1300 / 1500 kg
max. power	: 80 kW (109 bhp) / 100 kW (136 bhp)	boot space	: 417 l
@	: 4000 rpm	fuel capacity	: 52 l
max. torque	: 177 / 236 lb ft	consumption	: 56.5 / 48.7 mpg
@	: 1750 / 2000 rpm	acc. 0-62 mph	: 12.1 / 9.6 s
gears	: 5 / 6	top speed	: 118 / 127 mph
AT	: -	EuroNCAP	: 5 stars
drive	: FWD	introduction	: December 2004
brakes f/r	: vent. discs / discs	last revised in	: July 2007
body type	: 5-dr. stationwagon	warranty	: 2 years
l x w x h	: 4522 x 1770 x 1457 mm	miscellaneous	: Facelift ensures that the V50 is
wheelbase	: 2640 mm		moredistinguishable from the S40
turning circle	: 10.6 m		at the front. Specifications of petrol
			engines are listed under the C30
			and S40 entries.

V50 D5

engine type	: diesel, inline-5
displacement	: 2401 cc
max. power	: 132 kW (180 bhp)
@	: 4000 rpm
max. torque	: 258 lb ft
@	: 1750 rpm
gears	: 5-speed automatic
kerb weight	: 1435 kg
towing weight	: 1500 kg
consumption	: 40.4 mpg
acc. 0-60 mph	: 8.5 s
top speed	: 137 mph
miscellaneous	: Biggest diesel engine is available only in combination with an automatic transmission.

VOLVO S60 2.4 / 2.0T

engine type	: petrol, inline-5		kerb weight	: 1466 / 1388 kg
displacement	: 2435 / 1984 cc		towing weight	: 1600 kg
max. power	: 103 kW (140 bhp) /		boot space	: 424 – 1034 l
	132 kW (180 bhp)		fuel capacity	: 70 l
@	: 4500 / 5300 rpm		consumption	: 31.7 mpg
max. torque	: 148 / 177 lb ft		acc. 0-62 mph	: 10.2 / 8.8 s
@	: 3750 / 2200 rpm		top speed	: 130 / 140 mph
gears	: 5		EuroNCAP	: 4 stars
AT	: optional 6-speed		introduction	: July 2000
drive	: FWD		last revised in	: July 2004
brakes f/r	: vent. discs		warranty	: 2 years
body type	: 4-dr. saloon		miscellaneous	: S60 available with choice of ten
l x w x h	: 4603 x 1813 x 1428 mm			different 5-cylinder engines,
wheelbase	: 2715 mm			including three diesels. 2.4 also
turning circle	: 10.8 m			available with 170 bhp and in
				Bi-fuel version that runs both on
				petrol and natural gas.

V

S60 T5

engine type	: petrol, inline-5
displacement	: 2401 cc
max. power	: 191 kW (260 bhp)
@	: 5500 rpm
max. torque	: 258 lb ft
@	: 2100 rpm
gears	: 6
kerb weight	: 1477 kg
towing weight	: 1600 kg
consumption	: 30.4 mpg
acc. 0-60 mph	: 6.5 s
top speed	: 155 mph
miscellaneous	: Not the most spacious Volvo on
	offer, but often chosen for its
	sporty aura.

VOLVO V70 D / 2.4 D

engine type	: diesel, inline-5	kerb weight	: 1604 kg
displacement	: 2400 cc	towing weight	: 1800 kg
max. power	: 120 kW (163 bhp)	boot space	: 575 l
@	: 4000 rpm	fuel capacity	: 70 l
max. torque	: 251 lb ft	consumption	: 43.5 mpg
@	: 1750 rpm	acc. 0-62 mph	: 9.9 s
gears	: 6	top speed	: 130 mph
AT	: optional 6-speed	EuroNCAP	: n.a.
drive	: FWD	introduction	: September 2007
brakes f/r	: vent. discs / discs	last revised in	: -
body type	: 5-dr. stationwagon	warranty	: 2 years
l x w x h	: 4823 x 1861 x 1578 mm	miscellaneous	: The cornerstone of Volvo's model programme. Turn to the XC70 model for details of the 3.2 and D5 engines.
wheelbase	: 2816 mm		
turning circle	: 11.7 m		

V70 2.5T / T6

engine type	: petrol, inline-5 / -6
displacement	: 2521 / 2953 cc
max. power	: 147 kW (200 bhp) / 210 kW (285 bhp)
@	: 4800 / 5000 rpm
max. torque	: 222 / 295 lb ft
@	: 1500 rpm
gears	: 6 / 6-speed automatic
kerb weight	: 1573 / 1715 kg
towing weight	: 1800 / 2000 kg
consumption	: 30.4 / 25.0 mpg
acc. 0-60 mph	: 8.1 / 7.2 s
top speed	: 130 / 152 mph
miscellaneous	: Less powerful four-cylinders are on their way in order to abate the price.

VOLVO XC70 D5

engine type	: diesel, inline-5	kerb weight	: 1721 kg
displacement	: 2400 cc	towing weight	: 2100 kg
max. power	: 136 kW (185 bhp)	boot space	: 575 l
@	: 4000 rpm	fuel capacity	: 70 l
max. torque	: 295 lb ft	consumption	: 34.0 mpg
@	: 2000 rpm	acc. 0-62 mph	: 8.9 s
gears	: 6	top speed	: 130 mph
AT	: optional 6-speed	EuroNCAP	: n.a.
drive	: 4WD	introduction	: September 2007
brakes f/r	: vent. discs / discs	last revised in	: -
body type	: 5-dr. stationwagon	warranty	: 2 years
l x w x h	: 4838 x 1861 x 1604 mm	miscellaneous	: A tough-looking version of the V70 is again included in the revised model range. Off-road the car performs respectably too.
wheelbase	: 2815 mm		
turning circle	: 11.5 m		

V

XC70 3.2

engine type	: petrol, inline-4
displacement	: 3192 cc
max. power	: 175 kW (238 bhp)
@	: 6200 rpm
max. torque	: 236 lb ft
@	: 3200 rpm
gears	: 6-speed automatic
kerb weight	: 1744 kg
towing weight	: 1800 kg
consumption	: 24.8 mpg
acc. 0-60 mph	: 8.4 s
top speed	: 134 mph
miscellaneous	: The in-line 'six' is an already familiar unit from the S80 and Land Rover Freelander.

VOLVO C70 2.4 / T5

engine type	: petrol, inline-5	kerb weight	: 1692 kg
displacement	: 2435 / 2521 cc	towing weight	: 1500 kg
max. power	: 103 kW (138 bhp) /	boot space	: 200 - 404 l
	162 kW (218 bhp)	fuel capacity	: 62 l
@	: 5000 rpm	consumption	: 31.7 / 31.0 mpg
max. torque	: 162 / 236 lb ft	acc. 0-62 mph	: 11.0 / 7.6 s
@	: 4000 / 1500 rpm	top speed	: 127 / 150 mph
gears	: 5 / 6	EuroNCAP	: n.a.
AT	: optional 5-speed	introduction	: November 2006
drive	: FWD	last revised in	: -
brakes f/r	: vent. discs	warranty	: 2 years
body type	: 2-dr. convertible	miscellaneous	: New model is the prettiest of Volvo
l x w x h	: 4580 x 1820 x 1400 mm		family. Beautiful convertible with
wheelbase	: 2640 mm		typical Volvo styling cues. Safer
turning circle	: 12.7 m		than many fixed-roof cars. Also
			available with 168 bhp 2.4i and D5
			diesel engine.

VOLVO S80 2.5T / 3.2

engine type	: petrol, inline-5 / inline-6
displacement	: 2521 / 3192 cc
max. power	: 147 kW (200 bhp) /
	175 kW (238 bhp)
@	: 4800 / 6200 rpm
max. torque	: 222 / 236 lb ft
@	: 1500 / 3200 rpm
gears	: 6 / -
AT	: optional, 6-speed / 6-speed
drive	: FWD
brakes f/r	: vent. discs
body type	: 4-dr. saloon
l x w x h	: 4851 x 1861 x 1492 mm
wheelbase	: 2835 mm
turning circle	: n.a.

kerb weight	: 1415 / 1556 kg
towing weight	: 1800 /kg
boot space	: 480 l
fuel capacity	: 70 l
consumption	: 30.7 / 28.5 mpg
acc. 0-62 mph	: 7.7 / 7.9 s
top speed	: 146 / 149 mph
EuroNCAP	: n.a.
introduction	: April 2006
last revised in	: -
warranty	: 2 years
miscellaneous	: New S80 widens the gap with S60 and V70 models more so than predecessor. Amiable car. Also available with V8 from XC90.

V

S80 2.4D / D5

engine type	: diesel, inline-5
displacement	: 2401 cc
max. power	: 120 kW (163 bhp) /
	136 kW (185 bhp)
@	: 4000 rpm
max. torque	: 251 / 295 lb ft
@	: 1750 / 2000 rpm
gears	: 6
kerb weight	: 1541 / 1545 kg
towing weight	: 1800 kg
consumption	: 44.8 / 44.1 mpg
acc. 0-60 mph	: 9.5 / 8.5 s
top speed	: 130 / 143 mph
miscellaneous	: D5 diesel option logical addition to engine range of flagship model.

VOLVO XC90 2.5T / 3.2

engine type	: petrol, inline-5 / inline-6
displacement	: 2521 / 3192 cc
max. power	: 154 kW (210 bhp) / 175 kW (231 bhp)
@	: 5000 / 6200 rpm
max. torque	: 236 lb ft
@	: 1500 / 3200 rpm
gears	: 6 / -
AT	: optional 5-speed / 6-speed
drive	: 4WD
brakes f/r	: vent. discs / discs
body type	: 5-dr. SUV
l x w x h	: 4807 x 1898 x 1784 mm
wheelbase	: 2857 mm
turning circle	: 12.5 m

kerb weight	: 1967 / 2025 kg
towing weight	: 2250 / 2250 kg
boot space	: 613 – 1837 l
fuel capacity	: 80 l
consumption	: 25.2 / 23.9 mpg
acc. 0-62 mph	: 9.5 s
top speed	: 130 mph
EuroNCAP	: 5 stars
introduction	: September 2002
last revised in	: April 2006
warranty	: 2 years
miscellaneous	: Big hit everywhere, in car parks of tennis clubs, shopping malls, you name it. Safe and fairly economical SUV with option of seven seats.

XC90 V8

engine type	: petrol, V8
displacement	: 4414 cc
max. power	: 232 kW (315 bhp)
@	: 5850 rpm
max. torque	: 324 lb ft
@	: 3900 rpm
gears	: 6-speed automatic
kerb weight	: 2077 kg
towing weight	: 2250 kg
consumption	: 20.9 mpg
acc. 0-60 mph	: 7.3 s
top speed	: 130 mph
miscellaneous	: V8 engine developed by Yamaha and aimed at American market.

XC90 D5

engine type	: diesel, inline-5
displacement	: 2401 cc
max. power	: 136 kW (185 bhp)
@	: 4000 rpm
max. torque	: 295 lb ft
@	: 2000 rpm
gears	: 6
kerb weight	: 2029 kg
towing weight	: 2250 kg
consumption	: 34.0 mpg
acc. 0-60 mph	: 10.9 s
top speed	: 121 mph
miscellaneous	: Perfect towing car for boat trailers and horse trailers.

Contacts

Marque	Postal address	Brochures	Web address
Alfa Romeo	240 Bath Road, Slough, Berkshire	0800 718 000	alfaromeo.co.uk
Alpina	Alpina GB, Sytner of Nottingham, Lenton Lane, Nottingham	0115 934 1414	sytner.co.uk
Ascari		01295 254 800	ascari.net
Aston Martin	Banbury Road, Gaydon, Warwick	01908 610 620	astonmartin.co.uk
Audi	Yeomans Drive, Blakelands, Milton Keynes MK14 5AN	0845 699 777	audi.co.uk
Bentley	Pyms Lane, Crewe, Cheshire CW1 3PL	01270 535 032	bentleymotors.com
BMW	Ellesfield Avenue, Bracknell, Berks RG12 8TA	0800 325 600	bmw.co.uk
Brooke		01404 548 885	brookecars.co.uk
Cadillac	Trinity Court, Wokingham Road, Bracknell, Berks RG42 1PL	0845 330 776	cadillaceurope.com
Caterham	Station Avenue, Caterham, Surrey, CR3 6LB	01883 333 700	caterham.co.uk
Chevrolet	Wyvern House, Kimpton Road, Luton LU2 0DW	0800 666 222	chevrolet.co.uk
Chrysler	Tongwell, Milton Keynes, Bucks MK15 8BA	0800 616 159	chryslerjeep.co.uk
Citroen	221 Bath Road, Slough, Berks SL1 4BA	0800 262 262	citroen.co.uk
Corvette	Wyvern House, Kimpton Road, Luton LU2 0DW		stratstonecorvette.co.uk
Daihatsu	Ryder Street, West Bromwich, West Midlands B70 0EJ	0800 618 618	daihatsu.co.uk
Dodge	Tongwell, Milton Keynes, Bucks MK15 8BA	0800 616 159	dodge.co.uk
Ferrari	272 Leigh Road, Slough, Berks SL1 4HF		ferrari.co.uk
Fiat	240 Bath Road, Slough, Berkshire	0800 717 000	fiat.co.uk
Ford	Eagle Way, Warley, Brentwood, Essex CM13 8BW	08457 111 888	ford.co.uk
Honda	470 London Road, Slough, Berks SL3 8QY	0845 200 8000	honda.co.uk
Hummer	325 Deansgate, Manchester, M3 4LQ	0161 831 7447	hummer.co.uk
Hyundai	St John's Court, Easton Street, High Wycombe, Bucks HP11 1JX	0800 981 981	hyundai.co.uk
Invicta	9-12 Westpoint Business Park, Bumpers Farm, Chippenham, Wilts SN14 8RB	01249 651 000	invictacar.com
Isuzu	Ryder Street, West Bromwich, West Midlands B70 0RR		isuzu.co.uk
Jaguar	Browns Lane, Allesley, Coventry, West Midlands CV5 9DR	0800 708 060	jaguar.com
Jeep	Tongwell, Milton Keynes, Bucks MK15 8BA	0800 616 159	chryslerjeep.co.uk
Kia	2 The Heights, Brooklands, Weybridge, Surrey KT13 0NY	0800 775 777	kia.co.uk
Lamborghini	Melton Court, 25 Old Brompton Road, South Kensington, London SW7 3TD	020 7589 1472	lamborghini.co.uk
Land Rover	Banbury Road, Gaydon, Warks CV35 0RR	0800 110 110	landrover.co.uk
Lexus	Great Burgh, Burgh Heath, Epsom, Surrey KT18 5UX	0845 278 8888	lexus.co.uk
Lotus	Potash Lane, Hethel, Norfolk NR18 8EXZ	0870 9000 565	lotuscars.co.uk
Marcos		01373 301 376	marcos-eng.com
Maserati	272 Leigh Road, Slough, Berks SL1 4HF	0800 064 6468	maserati.co.uk
Mazda	Riverbridge House, Anchor Boulevard, Dartford, Kent DA2 6QH	08457 484 848	mazda.co.uk
Mercedes-Benz	Tongwell, Milton Keynes, Bucks MK15 8BA	0800 181 361	mercedes.co.uk
Mini	Ellesfield Avenue, Bracknell, Berks RG12 8TA	08000 836 464	mini.co.uk
Mitsubishi	Watermoor, Cirencester, Glos GL7 4LF	0845 070 2000	mitsubishi-cars.co.uk
Morgan	Pickersleigh Road, Malvern Link, Worcs WR14 2LL	01684 573 104	morgan-motor.co.uk
Nissan	The Rivers Office Park, Denham Way, Maple Cross, Rickmansworth, Herts WD3 9YS	08457 669 966	nissan.co.uk
Noble	16 Moat Way Industrial Estate, Barwell, Leics LE9 8EY	01455 844 052	noblecars.com
Pagani		01753 663 012	paganiautomobili.it
Perodua	Craigmore House, Remenham Hill, Henley-on-Thames, Oxon RG9 3EP	01491 415 230	perodua-uk.com
Peugeot	Aldermoor House, PO Box 227, Aldermoor Lane, Coventry CV3 1LT	08457 565 556	peugeot.co.uk
Porsche	Bath Road, Calcot, Reading, Berks RG31 7SE	08457 911 911	porsche.co.uk
Proton	Walton House, 56-58 Richmond Hill, Bournemouth BH2 6EX	08000 521 521	proton.co.uk
Renault	The Rivers Office Park, Denham Way, Maple Cross, Rickmansworth, Herts WD3 9YS	0800 525 150	renault.co.uk
Rolls-Royce	The Drive, Westhampnett, Chichester, West Sussex PO18 0SH	01243 384 000	rolls-royce.co.uk
Saab	150 Bath Road, Maidenhead, Berks FL6 4LB	0800 626 556	saab.co.uk
Seat	Yeomans Drive, Blakelands, Milton Keynes MK14 5AN	0800 222 222	seat.co.uk
Skoda	Yeomans Drive, Blakelands, Milton Keynes MK14 5AN	0845 774 745	skoda.co.uk
Smart	Tongwell, Milton Keynes, Bucks MK15 8BA	08000 379 966	thesmart.co.uk
Spyker	Station Road, Pangbourne, Berkshire RG8 7AN	0118 976 6366	spyker-cars.co.uk
SsangYong	1 St Andrew's Court, Wellington Street, Thame, Oxford OX9 3WT	01252 775 428	syukcars.co.uk
Subaru	Ryder Street, West Bromwich, West Midlands B70 0EJ	08708 502 503	subaru.co.uk
Suzuki	46-62 Gatwick Road, Crawley, West Sussex RH10 2XF	01892 707 007	suzuki.co.uk
Toyota	Great Burgh, Burgh Heath, Epsom, Surrey KT18 5UX	0845 275 5555	toyota.co.uk
TVR	Bristol Avenue, Blackpool, Lancs FY2 0JF	01253 509 055	tvr.co.uk
Vauxhall	Griffin House, Osborne Road, Luton, Beds LU1 3YT	08457 400 800	vauxhall.co.uk
Volkswagen	Yeomans Drive, Blakelands, Milton Keynes MK14 5AN	0800 333 666	volkswagen.co.uk
Volvo	Globe Park, Marlow, Bucks SL7 1YQ	0800 400 430	volvocars.com
Westfield	Gibbons Industrial Park, Dudley Road, Kingswinford DY6 8XF	01384 400 077	westfield-sportscars.co.uk

New car prices in the UK

On the following pages are prices for every new car on sale in the United Kingdom, which were correct as of mid-October 2007. They're all on-the-road prices, which means all delivery and first registration charges have been taken into account. However, because they're list prices, they're not necessarily what you'll actually be charged if you come to buy a new car; some manuacturers are keener to haggle than others!

The list of models covered in the following pages is not exactly the same as the ones detailed already in this book. As this book went to press, we had technical details of some of the latest models, but not the costs. Examples of this include the Jaguar XF, Fiat 500 and Peugeot 308 – as well as replacement models such as the Mercedes C-Class estate and Audi A4. However, even where we have been able to include list prices, they're all subject to change, while fresh derivatives often join model ranges, and others get dropped. That's why you need to do some online research if you want to research your new car purchase in minute detail – the new car market moves very quickly!

Model	Derivative	BHP	UK price
ALFA ROMEO			
147	1.6 TS Turismo 3dr	120	14,950
147	1.6 TS Turismo 5dr	120	15,450
147	1.6 TS Lusso 3dr	120	16,150
147	1.6 TS Lusso 5dr	120	16,650
147	1.6 TS Sport 3dr	120	13,450
147	1.6 TS Sport 5dr	120	13,950
147	2.0 TS Lusso 3dr	120	17,350
147	2.0 TS Lusso 5dr	120	17,850
147	1.9 JTDm Turismo 8v 3dr	115	16,150
147	1.9 JTDm Turismo 8v 5dr	115	16,650
147	1.9 JTDm Lusso 8v 3dr	115	17,350
147	1.9 JTDm Lusso 8v 5dr	115	17,850
147	1.9 JTDm Sport 8v 3dr	115	14,950
147	1.9 JTDm Sport 8v 5dr	115	15,450
147	1.9 JTDm Turismo 16v 3dr	150	17,350
147	1.9 JTDm Turismo 16v 5dr	150	17,850
147	1.9 JTDm Lusso 16v 3dr	150	18,550
147	1.9 JTDm Lusso 16v 5dr	150	19,050
147	1.9 JTDm Q2 16v 3dr	150	18,850
147	1.9 JTDm Q2 16v 5dr	150	19,350
147	1.9 JTDm Sport Q2 16v 3dr	150	16,950
147	1.9 JTDm Sport Q2 16v 5dr	150	17,450
159	1.9 JTS Turismo	160	20,250
159	2.2 JTS Turismo	185	21,250
159	2.2 JTS Lusso	185	22,650
159	2.2 JTS TI	185	23,400
159	3.2 JTS Q4 Turismo	256	27,050
159	3.2 JTS Q4 Lusso	256	28,450
159	3.2 JTS Q4 TI	256	29,200
159	1.9 JTDm Turismo	150	20,750
159	1.9 JTDm Lusso	150	22,150
159	2.4 JTDm Turismo	200	23,250
159	2.4 JTDm Lusso	200	24,650
159	2.4 JTDm TI	200	25,400
159	2.4 JTDm Q4 TI	200	27,400
159	Sportwagon 1.9 JTS Turismo	160	21,350
159	Sportwagon 2.2 JTS Turismo	185	22,350
159	Sportwagon 2.2 JTS Lusso	185	23,750
159	Sportwagon 2.2 JTS TI	185	23,750
159	Sportwagon 3.2 JTS V6 Q4	256	29,550
159	Sportwagon 3.2 JTS V6 Q4	256	29,550
159	Sportwagon 1.9 JTDm Turismo	150	21,850
159	Sportwagon 1.9 JTDm Lusso	150	23,250
159	Sportwagon 2.4 JTDm Lusso	200	25,750
159	Sportwagon 2.4 JTDm TI	200	25,750
159	Sportwagon 2.4 JTDm Q4 TI	200	25,750
GT	2.0 JTS Turismo	165	20,400
GT	2.0 JTS Lusso	165	22,200
GT	3.2 V6 Lusso	240	26,400
GT	1.9 JTDm Turismo	150	21,600
GT	1.9 JTDm Lusso	150	23,400
GT	1.9 JTDm Q2	150	24,100
Brera	2.2 JTS SV	185	23,995
Brera	3.2 JTS Q4 SV	256	29,250
Brera	2.4 JTDm SV	200	26,995
Spider	2.2 JTS SV	185	25,995
Spider	3.2 JTS Q4 SV	256	31,250
Spider	2.4 JTDm SV	200	28,995
ALPINA			
B3S	3.4	300	40,850
B3S	3.4 cabrio	300	43,850
D3	2.0d	197	26,995
B5	4.4 V8	500	63,850
B7	4.4 V8	500	79,850
Roadster S	3.4 S	300	37,850
Roadster S	3.4 S Lux	300	39,850
B6	Coupé	493	83,950
B6	Convertible	493	79,950
ASCARI			
KZ-1		500	235,000
ASTON MARTIN			
V8 Vantage	Coupé	380	82,800
V8 Vantage	Roadster	380	91,000
DB9	Coupé	450	109,750
DB9	Volante manual	450	118,750
Vanquish	S	520	177,100
AUDI			
A3	1.4T FSi 3dr	123	16,365

Model	Derivative	BHP	UK price
A3	1.6 3dr	100	15,540
A3	1.6 SE 3dr	100	17,540
A3	1.6 Sport 3dr	100	17,540
A3	1.6 FSI 3dr	113	16,180
A3	1.6 FSI SE 3dr	113	18,180
A3	1.6 FSI S Line 3dr	113	19,730
A3	1.6 FSI Sport 3dr	113	18,180
A3	1.8T FSI 3dr	158	18,085
A3	1.8T FSI SE 3dr	158	20,085
A3	1.8T FSI Sport 3dr	158	20,085
A3	1.8T FSI S-Line 3dr	158	21,885
A3	2.0 FSI 3dr	148	17,805
A3	2.0 FSI SE 3dr	148	19,805
A3	2.0 FSI Sport 3dr	148	19,805
A3	2.0 FSI S Line 3dr	148	21,355
A3	2.0 T 3dr	197	19,355
A3	2.0 T FSI Sport 3dr	197	21,355
A3	2.0 T FSI Sport DSG 3dr	197	21,095
A3	2.0 T FSI SE 3dr	197	21,355
A3	2.0 T FSI S Line 3dr	197	23,135
A3	2.0 T FSI S Line SE DSG 3dr	197	24,005
A3	2.0 T FSI quattro Sport 3dr	197	22,755
A3	2.0 T FSI quattro S Line 3dr	197	24,555
A3	3.2 quattro Sport 3dr	247	25,020
A3	3.2 quattro S Line 3dr	247	26,820
A3	3.2 quattro S Line 3dr	247	26,820
S3	3dr	261	27,000
A3	1.9 TDI 3dr	103	16,725
A3	1.9 TDI SE 3dr	103	18,725
A3	1.9 TDI Sport 3dr	103	18,725
A3	2.0 TDI 3dr	138	18,355
A3	2.0 TDI SE 3dr	138	20,355
A3	2.0 TDI Sport 3dr	138	20,355
A3	2.0 TDI S Line 3dr	138	22,155
A3	2.0 TDI 170 3dr	168	19,180
A3	2.0 TDI 170 SE 3dr	168	21,180
A3	2.0 TDI 170 Sport 3dr	168	21,180
A3	2.0 TDI 170 S Line 3dr	168	22,980
A3	2.0 TDI 170 quattro Sport 3dr	168	22,605
A3	2.0 TDI 170 quattro S Line 3dr	168	24,405
A3	1.6 Sportback	100	16,040
A3	1.6 SE Sportback	100	18,040
A3	1.6 Sport Sportback	100	18,040
A3	1.6 FSI Sportback	113	16,680
A3	1.6 FSI SE Sportback	113	18,680
A3	1.6 FSI Sport Sportback	113	18,680
A3	1.6 FSI S Line Sportback	113	20,505
A3	1.8T FSI Sportback	158	18,585
A3	1.8T FSI SE Sportback	158	20,585
A3	1.8T FSI Sport Sportback	158	20,585
A3	1.8T FSI S Line Sportback	158	22,385
A3	2.0 T FSI Sportback	197	19,855
A3	2.0 T FSI SE Sportback	197	21,855
A3	2.0 T FSI Sport Sportback	197	21,855
A3	2.0 T FSI S Line Sportback	197	23,655
A3	2.0 T FSI quattro Sport Sportback	197	23,255
A3	2.0 T FSI quattro S Line Sportback	197	25,055
A3	3.2 quattro Sport Sportback	247	25,520
A3	3.2 quattro S Line Sportback	247	27,320
A3	1.9 TDI Sportback	103	17,225
A3	1.9 TDI SE Sportback	103	19,225
A3	1.9 TDI Sport Sportback	103	19,225
A3	2.0 TDI Sportback	138	18,855
A3	2.0 TDI SE Sportback	138	20,855
A3	2.0 TDI Sport Sportback	138	20,855
A3	2.0 TDI S Line Sportback	138	22,655
A3	2.0 TDI 170 Sportback	168	19,680
A3	2.0 TDI 170 SE Sportback	168	21,680
A3	2.0 TDI 170 Sport Sportback	168	21,680
A3	2.0 TDI 170 S Line Sportback	168	23,480
A3	2.0 TDI 170 quattro Sport Sportback	168	23,105
A3	2.0 TDI 170 quattro S Line Sportback	168	24,905
A4	1.8 T	161	21,810
A4	1.8 T SE	161	21,810
A4	1.8 T S Line	161	22,560
A4	1.8 T quattro	161	23,210
A4	1.8 T quattro SE	161	23,210
A4	1.8 T quattro S Line	161	23,960
A4	2.0	129	19,925
A4	2.0 SE	129	19,925
A4	2.0 S Line	129	20,675
A4	2.0 T FSI	197	23,170
A4	2.0 T FSI SE	197	23,170

Model	Derivative	BHP	UK price
A4	2.0 T FSI S Line	197	23,920
A4	2.0 T FSI quattro	197	24,610
A4	2.0 T FSI quattro SE	197	24,610
A4	2.0 T FSI quattro S Line	197	25,360
A4	3.2 FSI	252	28,115
A4	3.2 FSI SE	252	28,115
A4	3.2 FSI S Line	252	28,865
A4	3.2 FSI quattro	252	28,065
A4	3.2 FSI quattro SE	252	28,065
A4	3.2 FSI quattro S Line	252	28,815
S4	Saloon	339	37,515
RS4	Saloon	414	51,030
A4	1.9 TDI	114	21,445
A4	1.9 TDI	114	21,445
A4	1.9 TDI S Line	114	22,195
A4	2.0 TDI	138	22,740
A4	2.0 TDI SE	138	22,740
A4	2.0 TDI S Line	138	23,490
A4	2.0 TDI	170	23,675
A4	2.0 TDI	170	23,675
A4	2.0 TDI SE	170	24,425
A4	2.0 TDI S Line SE	170	24,425
A4	2.0 TDI quattro	170	25,100
A4	2.0 TDI quattro SE	170	25,100
A4	2.0 TDI quattro S Line	170	25,850
A4	2.7 TDI	180	25,780
A4	2.7 TDI SE	180	25,780
A4	2.7 TDI S Line	180	26,530
A4	3.0 TDI quattro	201	28,175
A4	3.0 TDI quattro SE	201	28,175
A4	3.0 TDI quattro S Line	201	28,925
A4	Avant 2.0	129	21,075
A4	Avant 2.0 SE	129	21,075
A4	Avant 2.0 S Line	129	21,825
A4	Avant 1.8 T	161	22,960
A4	Avant 1.8 T SE	161	22,960
A4	Avant 1.8 T S Line	161	23,710
A4	Avant 1.8 T quattro	161	24,360
A4	Avant 1.8 T quattro SE	161	24,360
A4	Avant 1.8 T quattro S Line	161	25,110
A4	Avant 2.0 T FSI	197	24,360
A4	Avant 2.0 T FSI SE	197	24,360
A4	Avant 2.0 T FSI S Line	197	25,110
A4	Avant 2.0 T FSI quattro	197	25,760
A4	Avant 2.0 T FSI quattro SE	197	25,760
A4	Avant 2.0 T FSI quattro S Line	197	26,510
A4	Avant 3.2 FSI	252	29,625
A4	Avant 3.2 FSI SE	252	29,625
A4	Avant 3.2 FSI S Line	252	30,015
A4	Avant 3.2 FSI quattro	252	29,215
A4	Avant 3.2 FSI quattro SE	252	29,215
S4	Avant quattro	339	38,665
RS4	Avant quattro	414	52,180
A4	Avant 1.9 TDI	114	22,595
A4	Avant 1.9 TDI SE	114	22,595
A4	Avant 1.9 TDI S Line	114	23,345
A4	Avant 2.0 TDI	140	23,890
A4	Avant 2.0 TDI	140	23,890
A4	Avant 2.0 TDI SE	140	24,640
A4	Avant 2.0 TDI	170	24,825
A4	Avant 2.0 TDI	170	24,825
A4	Avant 2.0 TDI SE	170	25,575
A4	Avant 2.0 TDI S Line	170	25,575
A4	Avant 2.0 TDI quattro	170	26,250
A4	Avant 2.0 TDI quattro SE	170	26,250
A4	Avant 2.0 TDI quattro S Line	170	27,000
A4	Avant 2.7 TDI	180	26,930
A4	Avant 2.7 TDI SE	180	26,930
A4	Avant 2.7 TDI S Line	180	27,680
A4	Avant 3.0 TDI quattro	201	29,325
A4	Avant 3.0 TDI quattro SE	201	29,325
A4	Avant 3.0 TDI quattro S Line	201	30,075
A4	cabrio 1.8 T	161	26,210
A4	cabrio 1.8 T Sport	161	26,960
A4	cabrio 1.8 T S Line	161	28,610
A4	cabrio 2.0 T FSI	197	27,860
A4	cabrio 2.0 T FSI Sport	197	28,610
A4	cabrio 2.0 T FSI S Line	197	30,260
A4	cabrio 3.2	252	32,675
A4	cabrio 3.2 Sport	252	33,425
A4	cabrio 3.2 S Line	252	35,075
A4	cabrio 3.2 quattro	252	32,625
A4	cabrio 3.2 quattro Sport	252	33,375
A4	cabrio 3.2 quattro S Line	252	35,025
S4	cabrio quattro	342	43,125
RS4	cabrio quattro	414	59,900
A4	cabrio 2.0 TDI	138	27,020
A4	cabrio 2.0 TDI	138	27,770
A4	cabrio 2.0 TDI S Line	138	29,420
A4	cabrio 3.0 TDI quattro	230	33,210
A4	cabrio 3.0 TDI quattro Sport	230	33,960
A4	cabrio 3.0 TDI quattro S Line	230	35,610
A5	3.2 V6 FSI	261	33,230
A5	3.2 V6 FSI quattro	261	33,375
A5	3.2 V6 FSI Sport	261	34,180
S5	Coupe	349	39,825
A5	2.7 TDi	187	31,640
A5	2.7 TDi Sport	187	32,590
A5	3.0 TDi quattro	237	33,430
A5	3.0 TDi quattro Sport	237	34,380
A6	2.0 T FSI SE	165	25,390
A6	2.0 T FSI S Line	165	28,430
A6	2.4 SE	177	25,525
A6	2.4 S Line	177	28,495
A6	2.4 quattro SE	177	27,125
A6	2.4 quattro S Line	177	30,015
A6	2.8 FSI SE	207	27,580
A6	3.2 FSI SE	252	31,625
A6	3.2 FSI S Line	252	34,595
A6	3.2 FSI quattro SE	252	33,225
A6	3.2 FSI quattro S Line	252	36,195
A6	4.2 quattro SE	335	44,575
A6	4.2 quattro S Line	335	46,355
S6	Saloon	429	55,475
A6	2.0 TDI SE	138	25,510
A6	2.0 TDI S Line	138	28,550
A6	2.7 TDI S Line	178	27,495
A6	2.7 TDI quattro SE	178	30,535
A6	2.7 TDI quattro S Line	178	33,425
A6	3.0 TDI quattro SE	225	32,050
A6	3.0 TDI quattro S Line	225	34,940
A6	Avant 2.0 T FSI SE	165	26,960
A6	Avant 2.0 T FSI S Line	165	30,000
A6	Avant 2.4 SE	177	27,095
A6	Avant 2.4 S Line	177	29,985
A6	Avant 2.4 quattro SE	177	28,395
A6	Avant 2.4 quattro S Line	177	31,285
A6	Avant 2.8 FSI SE	207	29,150
A6	Avant 2.8 FSI S Line	207	32,040
A6	Avant 3.2 FSI SE	252	33,195
A6	Avant 3.2 FSI S Line	252	36,085
A6	Avant 3.2 FSI quattro SE	252	34,495
A6	Avant 3.2 FSI quattro S Line	252	37,385
A6	Avant 4.2 quattro SE	335	45,845
A6	Avant 4.2 quattro S Line	335	47,625
S6	Avant quattro	429	57,645
A6	Avant 2.0 TDI SE	138	27,060
A6	Avant 2.0 TDI S Line	138	30,120
A6	Avant 2.7 TDI SE	178	29,105
A6	Avant 2.7 TDI S Line	178	31,995
A6	Avant 2.7 TDI quattro SE	178	31,805
A6	Avant 2.7 TDI quattro S Line	178	34,695
A6	Avant 3.0 TDI quattro SE	225	33,320
A6	Avant 3.0 TDI quattro S Line	225	36,210
A6	Allroad quattro 3.2 FSi	252	36,515
A6	Allroad quattro 4.2 FSi	345	47,865
A6	Allroad quattro 2.7 TDi	178	33,530
A6	Allroad quattro 3.0 TDi	201	34,980
A8	3.2 SE	256	50,325
A8	3.2 LWB	256	53,695
A8	3.2 Sport	256	52,825
A8	3.2 Sport LWB	256	56,195
A8	3.2 FSI quattro SE	256	52,225
A8	3.2 FSI quattro SE Sport	256	54,725
A8	4.2 FSI quattro SE	325	59,915
A8	4.2 FSI quattro SE LWB	325	63,285
A8	4.2 FSI quattro Sport	325	62,415
A8	4.2 FSI quattro Sport LWB	325	65,785
A8	6.0 quattro LWB	444	79,755
S8	V10	444	70,925
A8	3.0 TDI quattro SE	230	49,680
A8	3.0 TDI quattro SE LWB	230	53,125
A8	3.0 TDI quattro Sport	230	52,180
A8	3.0 TDI quattro Sport LWB	230	55,625
A8	4.2 TDI quattro SE	321	60,595
A8	4.2 TDI quattro SE LWB	321	63,965
A8	4.2 TDI quattro Sport	321	63,095
A8	4.2 TDI quattro Sport LWB	321	66,465
Q7	3.6 V6	276	38,325
Q7	3.6 V6 SE	276	40,825
Q7	3.6 V6 S Line	276	41,725
Q7	4.2 FSI quattro SE	345	48,475
Q7	4.2 FSI quattro S Line	345	49,375
Q7	3.0 TDI quattro	230	38,075
Q7	3.0 TDI quattro SE	230	40,575
Q7	3.0 TDI quattro S Line	230	41,475
Q7	4.2 TDI quattro SE	345	49,995
TT	Coupé 2.0 T FSI	197	24,625
TT	Coupé 2.0 T FSI S-Tronic	197	26,025
TT	Coupé 3.2 quattro	247	29,285
TT	Coupé 3.2 quattro S-Tronic	247	30,685
TT	Roadster 2.0 T FSI	197	26,915
TT	Roadster 3.2 quattro	247	31,535
R8	4.2 FSi	414	76,825

Model	Derivative	BHP	UK price
BENTLEY			
Continental	GT	552	120,500
Continental	GTC	552	132,500
Continental	Flying Spur	552	117,500
Arnage	R	400	166,000
Arnage	RL	400	193,000
Arnage	T	450	175,500
Azure		450	222,500

Model	Derivative	BHP	UK price
BMW			
116i		115	16,390
116i	ES	115	17,215
116i	SE	115	18,340
116i	M Sport	115	20,000
118i	3dr	141	17,815
118i	5dr	141	18,345
118i	ES 3dr	141	18,640
118i	ES 5dr	141	19,170
118i	SE 3dr	141	19,765
118i	SE 5dr	141	20,295
118i	M Sport 3dr	141	21,460
118i	M Sport 5dr	141	21,955
120i	3dr	168	18,845
120i	5dr	168	19,375
120i	ES 3dr	168	19,670
120i	ES 5dr	168	20,200
120i	SE 3dr	168	20,795
120i	SE 5dr	168	21,325
120i	M Sport 3dr	168	22,420
120i	M Sport 5dr	168	22,915
130i	M Sport 3dr	261	26,385
130i	M Sport 5dr	261	26,915
118d	3dr	141	18,225

Model	Derivative	BHP	UK price
118d	5dr	141	18,755
118d	ES 3dr	141	19,050
118d	ES 5dr	141	19,580
118d	SE 3dr	141	20,175
118d	SE 5dr	141	20,705
118d	M Sport 3dr	141	21,870
118d	M Sport 5dr	141	22,365
120d	3dr	175	19,650
120d	5dr	175	20,180
120d	ES 3dr	175	20,475
120d	ES 5dr	175	21,005
120d	SE 3dr	175	21,600
120d	SE 5dr	175	22,130
120d	M Sport 3dr	175	23,225
120d	M Sport 5dr	175	23,720
318i	ES saloon	127	20,735
318i	SE saloon	127	21,765
318i	M Sport saloon	127	24055
320i	ES saloon	150	22,385
320i	SE saloon	150	23,415
320i	M Sport saloon	150	25,705
325i	SE saloon	215	16,165
325i	M Sport saloon	215	28,805
330i	SE saloon	254	29,530
330i	M Sport saloon	254	32,340
335i	SE saloon	302	31,390
335i	M Sport saloon	302	34,200
318d	ES saloon	122	23,090
318d	SE saloon	122	24,120
318d	M Sport saloon	122	26,410
320d	ES saloon	163	24,255
320d	SE saloon	163	25,285
320d	M Sport saloon	163	27,575
325d	SE saloon	194	27,675
325d	M Sport saloon	194	30,315
330d	SE saloon	227	30,075
330d	M Sport saloon	227	32,885
335d	SE saloon	282	33,385
335d	M Sport saloon	282	36,125
318i	ES Touring	141	21,915
318i	SE Touring	141	22,945
318i	M Sport Touring	141	25,235
320i	ES Touring	150	23,565
320i	SE Touring	150	24,595
320i	M Sport Touring	150	26,885
325i	SE Touring	215	27,345
325i	M Sport Touring	215	29,985
330i	SE Touring	254	30,710
330i	M Sport Touring	254	33,520
335i	SE Touring	302	32,570
335i	M Sport Touring	302	35,380
318d	ES Touring	121	24,295
318d	SE Touring	121	25,325
318d	M Sport Touring	121	27,615
320d	ES Touring	163	25,435
320d	SE Touring	163	26,465
320d	M Sport Touring	163	28,755
325d	SE Touring	194	28,855
325d	M Sport Touring	194	31,495
330d	SE Touring	231	31,255
330d	M Sport Touring	231	34,065
335d	SE Touring	282	34,562
335d	M Sport Touring	282	37,305
320Ci	SE coupé	168	25,735
320Ci	M Sport coupé	168	28,360
325Ci	SE coupé	215	28,445
325Ci	M Sport coupé	215	31,070
330Ci	SE coupé	268	31,675
330Ci	M Sport coupé	268	34,230
335Ci	SE coupé	306	33,900
335Ci	M Sport coupé	306	35,775
M3	Coupé	414	50,625
320Cd	SE coupé	174	27,890
320Cd	M Sport coupé	174	30,515
325Cd	SE coupé	194	29,920
325Cd	M Sport coupé	194	32,545
330Cd	SE coupé	228	32,220
330Cd	M Sport coupé	228	34,775
335Cd	SE coupé	282	35,895
335Cd	M Sport coupé	282	37,770
320Ci	SE cabrio	168	30,660
320Ci	M Sport cabrio	168	33,285
325Ci	SE cabrio	215	33,095
325Ci	M Sport cabrio	215	35,720
330Ci	SE cabrio	268	36,425
330Ci	M Sport cabrio	268	38,980
335Ci	SE cabrio	306	38,035
335Ci	M Sport cabrio	306	40,355
330Cd	SE cabrio	228	36,790
330Cd	M Sport cabrio	228	39,345
523i	SE saloon	187	28,655
523i	M Sport saloon	187	31,775
525i	SE saloon	215	30,300
525i	M Sport saloon	215	33,420
530i	SE saloon	268	34,295
530i	M Sport saloon	268	37,415
540i	SE saloon	302	38,700
540i	M Sport saloon	302	41,820
550i	SE saloon	362	45,310
550i	M Sport saloon	362	47,870
M5	Saloon	507	64,600
520d	SE saloon	161	27,000
520d	M Sport saloon	161	30,120
525d	SE saloon	174	30,755
525d	M Sport saloon	174	33,875
530d	SE saloon	232	34,655
530d	M Sport saloon	232	37,775
535d	SE saloon	268	39,065

Model	Derivative	BHP	UK price
535d	M Sport saloon	268	42,185
523i	SE Touring	187	30,690
523i	M Sport Touring	187	33,810
525i	SE Touring	215	32,335
525i	M Sport Touring	215	35,455
530i	SE Touring	268	36,375
530i	M Sport Touring	268	39,495
550i	SE Touring	362	47,350
550i	M Sport Touring	362	49,910
M5	Touring	507	67,180
520d	SE Touring	161	29,010
520d	M Sport Touring	161	32,130
525d	SE Touring	194	32,865
525d	M Sport Touring	194	35,985
530d	SE Touring	232	36,710
530d	M Sport Touring	232	39,830
535d	SE Touring	282	41,135
535d	M Sport Touring	282	44,255
630i		254	47,975
630i	Sport	254	50,175
650i		361	54,075
650i	Sport	361	55,925
M6		500	82,710
635d		290	53,910
635d	Sport	290	56,110
630i	cabrio	254	53,685
630i	Sport cabrio	254	55,885
650i	cabrio	367	59,515
650i	Sport cabrio	367	61,365
M6	cabrio	500	87,365
635d	cabrio	290	59,600
635d	Sport cabrio	290	61,800
730i	SE	254	52,925
730i	Sport	254	56,550
730	Li SE	254	55,545
740i		301	57,290
740i	Sport	301	60,920
740	Li	301	60,070
750i		361	61,785
750i	Sport	361	65,415
750	Li	361	64,535
760i		445	82,545
760	Li	445	84,695
730d	SE	227	51,435
730	Ld SE	227	54,060
730d	Sport	227	55,060
X3	2.5si SE	218	30,915
X3	2.5si M Sport	218	33,000
X3	3.0i SE	272	34,440
X3	3.0i M Sport	272	36,525
X3	2.0d SE	175	28,900
X3	2.0d M Sport	175	31,060
X3	3.0d SE	218	32,925
X3	3.0d M Sport	218	35,010
X3	3.0sd SE	282	36,905
X3	3.0sd M Sport	282	38,665
X5	3.0i SE	268	39,645
X5	4.8i SE	350	50,085
X5	4.8i M Sport	350	53,440
X5	3.0d SE	232	42,630
X5	3.0sd SE	282	39,110
Z4	Roadster 2.0i SE	150	24,005
Z4	Roadster 2.0i Sport	150	26,590
Z4	Roadster 2.5i SE	174	26,040
Z4	Roadster 2.5i Sport	174	28,625
Z4	Roadster 2.5si SE	218	28,780
Z4	Roadster 2.5si Sport	218	34,140
Z4	Roadster 3.0si SE	261	33,200
Z4	Roadster 3.0si Sport	261	34,630
Z4	M Roadster	338	43,405
Z4	Coupé 3.0si SE	265	31,820
Z4	Coupé 3.0si Sport	265	33,345
Z4	M Coupé	343	41,880

BROOKE

Double R	2.0 200	200	27,995
Double R	2.3 260	260	31,995
Double R	2.0 300	300	36,995

CADILLAC

BLS	2.0 T SE	173	19,950
BLS	2.0 T Luxury	173	23,500
BLS	2.0 T Luxury	207	24,900
BLS	2.8 V6 Elegance	252	25,350
BLS	2.8 V6 Sport Luxury	252	30,200
BLS	1.9D SE	148	20,750
BLS	1.9D Luxury	148	24,350
CTS	2.8 V6 Elegance	215	24,000
CTS	2.8 V6 Sport Luxury	215	26,500
CTS	3.6 V6 Sport Luxury	257	29,000
Escalade	6.2 V8 Elegance	405	46,000
Escalade	6.2 V8 Sport Luxury	405	49,000
SRX	3.6 V6 Elegance	258	29,000
SRX	3.6 V6 Sport Luxury	258	33,700
SRX	4.6 V8 Sport Luxury	316	39,100

CATERHAM

Seven	Classic	105	15,495
Seven	Roadsport	120	19,195
Seven	SV Roadsport	125	20,695
Seven	Superlight	150	23,895
Seven	Superlight SV	150	25,395
Seven	Superlight R400	210	29,495
Seven	Superlight R400 SV	210	30,995
CSR	200 Roadster	200	32,295
CSR	260 Superlight	260	40,495
Sigma	1.6 Roadsport	125	16,695
Sigma	1.6 Roadsport	150	18,195

Model	Derivative	BHP	UK price
Sigma	1.6 Superlight	150	21,395
CHEVROLET			
Matiz	0.8 S	50	6,245
Matiz	0.8 SE auto	50	7,315
Matiz	1.0 SE	64	6,865
Matiz	1.0 SE+	64	8,277
Kalos	1.2 S 3dr	71	7,295
Kalos	1.2 S 5dr	71	7,815
Kalos	1.2 SE	71	8,365
Kalos	1.4 SX 5dr	93	9,365
Lacetti	1.4 SE 5dr	93	9,995
Lacetti	1.6 SX 5dr	108	11,115
Lacetti	1.8 CDX saloon	120	12,715
Lacetti	1.6 SX estate	108	11,615
Tacuma	1.6 SX	103	11,495
Tacuma	2.0 CDX	119	13,695
Captiva	2.4 LS	140	16,995
Captiva	2.0 VCDi LT 5st	148	19,995
Captiva	2.0 VCDi LT 7st	148	21,140
Captiva	2.0 VCDi LTX 5st	148	23,740
CHRYSLER			
Sebring	2.0 Limited	154	17,995
Sebring	2.4 Limited	167	18,995
Sebring	2.0 CRD Limited	138	18,995
PT Cruiser	2.4 Classic	141	12,995
PT Cruiser	2.4 Touring	141	14,580
PT Cruiser	2.4 Limited	141	16,080
PT Cruiser	2.2 CRD Classic	148	14,245
PT Cruiser	2.2 CRD Touring	148	15,745
PT Cruiser	2.2 CRD Limited	148	17,245
PT Cruiser	cabrio 2.4 Touring	148	16,680
PT Cruiser	cabrio 2.4 Limited	141	18,180
300 C	3.5i V6	249	26,315
300 C	SRT-8	425	39,870
300 C	3.0 CRD	218	26,315
300 C	SRT-8	425	41,110
300 C	Touring 3.0 CRD	218	27,815
Crossfire	3.2i V6 coupé	215	24,995
Crossfire	3.2i V6 roadster	215	25,995
Voyager	2.4 SE	145	18,855
Voyager	2.4 Executive	145	22,080
Voyager	2.5 CRD SE	141	19,995
Voyager	2.8 CRD Executive	150	23,970
Grand Voyager	2.8 CRD LX	150	25,995
Grand Voyager	2.8 CRD Executive	150	28,320
Grand Voyager	2.8 CRD Executive XS	150	32,010
CITROEN			
C1	1.0 Vibe 3dr	67	6,995
C1	1.0 Vibe 5dr	67	7,355
C1	1.0 Cool 3dr	67	7,495
C1	1.0 Cool 5dr	67	7,855
C1	1.0 Rhythm 3dr	55	7,485
C1	1.0 Rhythm 5dr	55	7,835
C1	1.0 Airplay+ 3dr	55	7,595
C1	1.0 Airplay+ 5dr	55	7,945
C1	1.4 HDi Rhythm 5dr	55	8,825
C2	1.1 L	61	8,395
C2	1.1 Airplay+	61	7,995
C2	1.1 SX	61	9,595
C2	1.4 Furio	61	9,395
C2	1.4 SX	75	10,095
C2	1.4 Stop & Start	90	10,895
C2	1.4 Furio	75	9,895
C2	1.6 VTR Sensodrive	110	11,600
C2	1.6 VTS	123	12,400
C2	1.6 Code	123	10,545
C2	1.4 HDi L	70	9,535
C2	1.4 HDi SX	70	10,735
C2	1.4 HDi Furio	70	10,535
C3	1.1 L	60	9,395
C3	1.1 Airplay+	60	7,995
C3	1.1 Cool	60	10,195
C3	1.4 Cool	74	10,695
C3	1.4 SX	74	11,145
C3	1.4 Stop & Start	88	11,745
C3	1.6 SX auto	110	12,525
C3	1.6 VTR	110	12,850
C3	1.6 Exclusive Sensodrive	110	13,045
C3	1.4 HDi L	69	10,635
C3	1.4 HDi Cool	69	11,385
C3	1.6 HDi SX	91	12,435
C3	1.6 HDi Exclusive	91	13,135
C3	1.6 HDi VTR	110	13,435
C3	Pluriel 1.4 Cote d-Azur	75	12,950
C3	Pluriel 1.4 Latte	75	14,460
C3	Pluriel 1.4 Kiwi	75	14,690
C3	Pluriel 1.6 Exclusive Sensodrive	75	16,050
C3	Pluriel 1.4 HDi Exclusive	110	14,885
C4	1.4 VT coupé	90	12,050
C4	1.4 VTR coupé	90	13,250
C4	1.6 VTR coupé	110	13,850
C4	1.6 Cool coupé	110	13,750
C4	1.6 VTR+ coupé	110	14,750
C4	2.0 VTS 180 coupé	178	18,150
C4	1.6 HDi VTR coupé	91	14,635
C4	1.6 HDi Cool coupé	108	14,535
C4	1.6 HDi VTR+ coupé	108	16,485
C4	1.6 HDi VTR+ DPFS coupé	108	17,015
C4	2.0 HDi VTS coupé	136	18,435
C4	1.4 LX 5dr	90	12,050
C4	1.4 SX 5dr	90	13,250
C4	1.4 Cool 5dr	90	13,150
C4	1.6 SX 5dr	110	13,850
C4	1.6 Cool 5dr	110	13,750
C4	1.6 VTR+ 5dr	110	14,750
C4	2.0 VTR Plus 5dr	141	15,850
C4	2.0 Exclusive auto 5dr	141	17,775
C4	1.6 HDi LX	91	13,435
C4	1.6 HDi SX	91	14,635
C4	1.6 HDi Cool	91	14,535
C4	1.6 HDi SX	108	15,585
C4	1.6 HDi VTR+	108	16,485
C4	1.6 HDi VTR+ DPFS	108	17,015
C4	2.0 HDi VTR Plus	136	17,335
C4	2.0 HDi Exclusive	136	18,435
C4	Picasso 1.8 LX	127	14,550
C4	Picasso 1.8 SX	127	15,550
C4	Picasso 1.8 VTR+	127	16,250
C4	Picasso 2.0 SX	143	16,800
C4	Picasso 2.0 VTR+	143	17,500
C4	Picasso 2.0 Exclusive	143	19,400
C4	Picasso 1.6 HDi LX	108	16,040
C4	Picasso 1.6 HDi SX	108	17,740
C4	Picasso 1.6 HDi Exclusive	108	20,140
C4	Picasso 2.0 HDi VTR+	138	19,340
C4	Picasso 2.0 HDi Exclusive	138	21,240
C4	Grand Picasso 1.8 LX	127	15,225
C4	Grand Picasso 1.8 SX	127	16,225
C4	Grand Picasso 1.8 VTR+	127	16,925
C4	Grand Picasso 2.0 SX	143	17,260
C4	Grand Picasso 2.0 VTR+	143	17,960
C4	Grand Picasso 2.0 Exclusive	143	19,860
C4	Grand Picasso 1.6 HDi LX	108	16,715
C4	Grand Picasso 1.6 HDi SX	108	17,715
C4	Grand Picasso 1.6 HDi VTR+	108	18,415
C4	Grand Picasso 1.6 HDi Exclusive	108	20,600
C4	Grand Picasso 2.0 HDi VTR+	138	19,800
C4	Grand Picasso 2.0 HDi Exclusive	138	21,700
C5	1.8 LX	115	15,850
C5	1.8 Design	115	16,450
C5	1.8 VTR	115	17,050
C5	2.0 VTR	141	17,375
C5	2.0 Exclusive auto	141	20,675
C5	3.0 V6 Exclusive	207	22,370
C5	1.6 HDi VTX	108	14,335
C5	1.6 HDi VTX+	108	15,335
C5	1.6 HDi LX	108	16,335
C5	1.6 HDi Design	108	16,935
C5	1.6 HDi VTR	108	17,535
C5	2.0 HDi VTR	136	18,740
C5	2.0 HDi Exclusive	136	21,040
C5	2.2 HDi VTX+	173	18,034
C5	2.2 HDi Exclusive	173	22,540
C5	2.0 VTR estate	141	18,475
C5	1.6 HDi LX estate	108	17,435
C5	1.6 HDi Design estate	108	18,035
C5	1.6 HDi VTX estate	108	18,635
C5	1.6 HDi VTR estate	108	15,435
C5	1.6 HDi VTX+ estate	108	16,435
C5	2.0 HDi VTR estate	136	19,840
C5	2.0 HDi Exclusive estate	136	22,140
C5	2.2 HDi VTX+ estate	173	19,135
C5	2.2 HDi Exclusive estate	173	23,640
C6	3.0 V6	212	29,900
C6	3.0 V6 Lignage	212	33,000
C6	3.0 V6 Exclusive	212	36,200
C6	2.2 HDi V6	173	28,315
C6	2.2 HDi V6 Lignage	173	31,415
C6	2.2 HDi V6 Exclusive	173	34,615
C6	2.7 HDi V6	205	31,895
C6	2.7 HDi V6 Lignage	205	34,995
C6	2.7 HDi V6 Exclusive	205	38,195
Berlingo	1.4 Forte	75	10,610
Berlingo	1.6 Forte	75	11,110
Berlingo	1.6 Desire	110	11,620
Berlingo	1.6 HDi Forte	75	11,395
Berlingo	1.6 HDi Desire	75	11,905
Berlingo	1.6 HDi Forte	92	11,945
Berlingo	1.6 HDi Desire	92	12,455
Xsara Picasso	1.6 Desire	110	14,950
Xsara Picasso	1.6 VTX	110	11,505
Xsara Picasso	1.6 HDi Desire	92	15,985
Xsara Picasso	1.6 HDi VTX	92	11,895
Xsara Picasso	1.6 HDi Desire	108	17,035
C8	2.0 LX	141	19,690
C8	2.0 SX	141	20,850
C8	2.0 Exclusive auto	141	24,370
C8	2.0 HDi LX	120	21,145
C8	2.0 HDi SX	120	22,305
C8	2.0 HDi SX	134	23,175
C8	2.0 HDi Exclusive	134	25,570
C-Crosser	2.2 HDi VTR+	156	22,790
C-Crosser	2.2 HDi Exclusive	156	25,490
CORVETTE			
Corvette	C6	400	47,495
Corvette	C6 Convertible	400	53,495
Corvette	Z06	505	62,695
DAIHATSU			
Charade	1.0 EL 3dr	58	6,460
Charade	1.0 EL 5dr	58	6,960
Sirion	1.0 S	68	7,460
Sirion	1.0 SE	68	7,960
Sirion	1.3 S	86	8,105
Sirion	1.3 SE	86	8,705
Sirion	1.3 SX	86	9,305
Materia	1.5 S	86	10,995
Terios	1.5 S	103	12,995
Terios	1.5 SX	103	14,295
Terios	1.5 SE	103	14,995
Copen	1.3	67	10,995

Model	Derivative	BHP	UK price
DODGE			
Caliber	1.8 S	148	11,695
Caliber	1.8 SE	148	12,225
Caliber	1.8 SXT	148	14,025
Caliber	2.0 SXT	154	14,025
Caliber	2.0 SXT Sport	154	14,195
Caliber	2.0 CRD SE	138	14,295
Caliber	2.0 CRD SXT	138	15,615
Caliber	2.0 CRD SXT Sport	138	15,785
Avenger	2.0 SE	154	14,995
Avenger	2.0 SXT	154	16,995
Avenger	2.4 SXT auto	168	17,995
Avenger	2.0 CRD SE	138	15,995
Avenger	2.0 CRD SXT	138	17,995
Nitro	3.7 V6 SXT	211	23,590
Nitro	2.8 CRD SE	180	18,995
Nitro	2.8 CRD SXT	180	22,590
Viper	SRT-10 cabrio	500	70,985
FERRARI			
F430		483	129,009
F430	F1	483	134,002
F430	Spider	483	137,852
F430	F1 Spider	483	142,852
599	GTB Fiorano	611	179,902
612	Scaglietti	532	182,952
612	Scaglietti F1	532	187,952
FIAT			
Panda	1.1 Active	54	6,995
Panda	1.2 Dynamic	60	7,455
Panda	1.2 Dynamic air-con	60	8,005
Panda	1.2 Dynamic SkyDome	60	8,005
Panda	1.2 Eleganza	60	8,655
Panda	1.2 4x4	60	9,660
Panda	1.4 100HP	99	10,160
Grande Punto	1.3 Multijet Dynamic	70	8,295
Grande Punto	1.2 Active 3dr	65	8,450
Grande Punto	1.2 Active 5dr	65	9,050
Grande Punto	1.2 Active Air-Con 3dr	65	8,950
Grande Punto	1.2 Active Air-Con 5dr	65	9,550
Grande Punto	1.2 Dynamic 3dr	65	9,550
Grande Punto	1.2 Dynamic 5dr	65	10,150
Grande Punto	1.4 Active Sport 3dr	77	9,350
Grande Punto	1.4 Active Sport 5dr	77	9,950
Grande Punto	1.4 Dynamic 3dr	77	10,150
Grande Punto	1.4 Dynamic 5dr	77	10,650
Grande Punto	1.4 Eleganza 3dr	77	10,250
Grande Punto	1.4 Eleganza 5dr	77	10,850
Grande Punto	1.4 16v Active Sport 3dr	95	10,050
Grande Punto	1.4 16v Active Sport 5dr	95	10,650
Grande Punto	1.4 16v Dynamic Sport 3dr	95	10,750
Grande Punto	1.4 16v Dynamic Sport 5dr	95	11,350
Grande Punto	1.4 16v Sporting 3dr	95	11,350
Grande Punto	1.4 T-Jet Sporting 3dr	120	11,995
Grande Punto	1.4 T-Jet Sporting 5dr	120	12,595
Grande Punto	1.3 Multijet Active 3dr	75	9,620
Grande Punto	1.3 Multijet Active 5dr	75	10,220
Grande Punto	1.3 Multijet Air-Con Active 3dr	75	10,120
Grande Punto	1.3 Multijet Air-Con Active 5dr	75	10,720
Grande Punto	1.3 Multijet Dynamic 3dr	75	10,720
Grande Punto	1.3 Multijet Dynamic 3dr	75	11,320
Grande Punto	1.9 Multijet Sporting	130	12,740
Bravo	1.4 5dr	89	10,995
Bravo	1.4 Active	89	11,795
Bravo	1.4 Active Sport	89	12,495
Bravo	1.4 Dynamic	89	12,895
Bravo	1.4 T-Jet 150 Active	148	12,895
Bravo	1.4 T-Jet 150 Dynamic	148	13,995
Bravo	1.4 T-Jet 150 Sport	148	14,295
Bravo	1.9 Multijet Active	120	13,295
Bravo	1.9 Multijet Active Sport	120	13,995
Bravo	1.9 Multijet Dynamic	150	15,195
Bravo	1.9 Multijet Sport	150	15,495
Doblò	1.4 Active	77	10,010
Doblò	1.4 Dynamic	77	10,910
Doblò	1.3 Multijet Active	85	10,995
Doblò	1.3 Multijet Family	85	11,795
Doblò	1.9 Multijet Active	105	11,300
Doblò	1.9 Multijet Dynamic	105	12,200
Doblò	1.9 Multijet Active	120	11,700
Doblò	1.9 Multijet Family	120	12,500
Doblò	1.9 Multijet Dynamic	120	12,600
Sedici	1.6 Dynamic	107	12,710
Sedici	1.6 Eleganza	107	13,710
Sedici	1.9 Multijet Dynamic	120	14,700
Sedici	1.9 Multijet Eleganza	120	15,700
Multipla	1.6 Dynamic Family	103	13,785
Multipla	1.9 JTD Dynamic Family	120	15,050
Multipla	1.9 JTD Dynamic Plus	120	16,650
Multipla	1.9 JTD Eleganza	120	17,650
FORD			
Ka	1.3 Style	69	7,410
Ka	1.3 Style Climate	69	7,985
Ka	1.3 Zetec	69	8,010
Ka	1.3 Zetec Climate	69	8,610
Ka	1.3 Luxury	69	9,210
Sportka	1.6 SE	94	10,010
Fiesta	1.25 Freedom 3dr	75	9,817
Fiesta	1.25 Freedom 5dr	75	10,417
Fiesta	1.25 Studio 3dr	75	8,422
Fiesta	1.25 Studio 5dr	75	9,022
Fiesta	1.25 Style 3dr	75	9,022
Fiesta	1.25 Style 5dr	75	9,622
Fiesta	1.25 Style Climate 3dr	75	9,622
Fiesta	1.25 Style Climate 5dr	75	10,222
Fiesta	1.25 Zetec Climate 3dr	75	10,222

Model	Derivative	BHP	UK price
Fiesta	1.25 Zetec Climate 5dr	75	10,822
Fiesta	1.4 Freedom 3dr	79	10,117
Fiesta	1.4 Freedom 5dr	79	10,717
Fiesta	1.4 Style 3dr	79	9,322
Fiesta	1.4 Style 5dr	79	9,922
Fiesta	1.4 Style Climate 3dr	79	9,922
Fiesta	1.4 Style Climate 5dr	79	10,522
Fiesta	1.4 Zetec Climate 3dr	79	10,522
Fiesta	1.4 Zetec Climate 5dr	79	11,122
Fiesta	1.4 Ghia 3dr	79	11,422
Fiesta	1.4 Ghia 5dr	79	12,022
Fiesta	1.6 Style 3dr	98	10,922
Fiesta	1.6 Style 5dr	98	11,522
Fiesta	1.6 Style Climate 3dr	98	11,522
Fiesta	1.6 Style Climate 5dr	98	12,122
Fiesta	1.6 Ghia 5dr	98	12,622
Fiesta	1.6 Zetec-S 3dr	98	11,622
Fiesta	ST	148	13,622
Fiesta	1.4 TDCi Studio 3dr	67	9,292
Fiesta	1.4 TDCi Style 3dr	67	9,892
Fiesta	1.4 TDCi Style 5dr	67	10,492
Fiesta	1.4 TDCi Style Climate 3dr	67	10,492
Fiesta	1.4 TDCi Style Climate 5dr	67	11,092
Fiesta	1.4 TDCi Zetec Climate 3dr	67	11,092
Fiesta	1.4 TDCi Zetec Climate 5dr	67	11,692
Fiesta	1.4 TDCi Ghia 5dr	67	12,592
Fiesta	1.6 TDCi Zetec Climate 3dr	89	11,592
Fiesta	1.6 TDCi Zetec Climate 5dr	89	12,292
Fiesta	1.6 TDCi Ghia 5dr	89	13,192
Fiesta	1.6 TDCi Zetec-S 3dr	89	12,492
Fusion	1.4 Style	78	10,745
Fusion	1.4 Style Climate	78	11,945
Fusion	1.4 Zetec	78	11,245
Fusion	1.4 Zetec Climate	78	11,845
Fusion	1.4 +	78	12,545
Fusion	1.4 Pursuit	78	11,022
Fusion	1.4 Pursuit Climate	78	11,622
Fusion	1.6 Zetec Climate	99	12,472
Fusion	1.6 +	99	13,145
Fusion	1.4 TDCi Style	67	11,445
Fusion	1.4 TDCi Style Climate	67	12,045
Fusion	1.4 TDCi Zetec Climate	67	12,645
Fusion	1.4 TDCi +	67	13,245
Fusion	1.4 TDCi Pursuit	67	11,612
Fusion	1.4 TDCi Pursuit Climate	67	12,212
Fusion	1.6 TDCi Zetec Climate	89	13,245
Fusion	1.6 TDCi +	89	13,642
Focus	1.4 Studio 3dr	79	11,522
Focus	1.4 Studio 5dr	79	12,122
Focus	1.4 Style 3dr	79	13,022
Focus	1.4 Style 5dr	79	13,622
Focus	1.6 Style 3dr	99	13,522
Focus	1.6 Style 5dr	99	14,122
Focus	1.6 Zetec Climate 3dr	99	14,272
Focus	1.6 Zetec Climate 5dr	99	14,872
Focus	1.6 Ghia 5dr	99	15,622
Focus	1.6 Ti-VCT Style 5dr	113	14,372
Focus	1.6 Ti-VCT Zetec Climate 3dr	113	14,522
Focus	1.6 Ti-VCT Zetec Climate 5dr	113	15,122
Focus	1.6 Ti-VCT Ghia 5dr	113	15,872
Focus	1.6 Ti-VCT Titanium 5dr	113	15,872
Focus	1.8 Style 5dr	123	14,622
Focus	1.8 Zetec Climate 3dr	123	14,772
Focus	1.8 Zetec Climate 5dr	123	15,372
Focus	1.8 Ghia 5dr	123	16,122
Focus	1.8 Titanium 5dr	123	16,122
Focus	2.0 Zetec Climate 3dr	143	15,272
Focus	2.0 Zetec Climate 5dr	143	15,872
Focus	2.0 Ghia 5dr	143	16,622
Focus	2.0 Titanium 5dr	143	16,622
Focus	ST 3dr	222	18,010
Focus	ST 5dr	222	18,610
Focus	ST 2 3dr	222	19,010
Focus	ST 2 5dr	222	19,610
Focus	ST 3 3dr	222	20,010
Focus	ST 3 5dr	222	20,610
Focus	1.6 TDCi Studio 5dr	89	13,612
Focus	1.6 TDCi Style 5dr	89	15,112
Focus	1.6 TDCi Style 5dr	108	15,612
Focus	1.6 TDCi Zetec Climate 3dr	108	15,762
Focus	1.6 TDCi Zetec Climate 5dr	108	16,362
Focus	1.6 TDCi Ghia 5dr	108	17,112
Focus	1.6 TDCi Titanium 5dr	108	17,112
Focus	1.8 TDCi Style 5dr	113	15,612
Focus	1.8 TDCi Zetec Climate 3dr	113	15,762
Focus	1.8 TDCi Zetec Climate 5dr	113	16,362
Focus	1.8 TDCi Ghia 5dr	113	17,112
Focus	1.8 TDCi Titanium 5dr	113	17,112
Focus	2.0 TDCi Zetec Climate 3dr	134	16,812
Focus	2.0 TDCi Zetec Climate 5dr	134	17,412
Focus	2.0 TDCi Ghia 5dr	134	18,162
Focus	2.0 TDCi Titanium 5dr	134	18,162
Focus	1.6 Ghia saloon	99	15,622
Focus	1.6 Ti-VCT Ghia saloon	113	15,872
Focus	1.6 Ti-VCT Titanium saloon	113	15,872
Focus	2.0 Ghia saloon	143	16,622
Focus	2.0 Titanium saloon	143	16,622
Focus	1.6 TDCi Ghia saloon	108	17,112
Focus	1.6 TDCi Titanium saloon	108	17,112
Focus	1.8 TDCi Ghia saloon	113	17,112
Focus	1.8 TDCi Titanium saloon	113	17,112
Focus	2.0 TDCi Ghia saloon	134	18,162
Focus	2.0 TDCi Titanium saloon	134	18,162
Focus	1.6 Style estate	99	14,972
Focus	1.6 Zetec Climate estate	99	15,722
Focus	1.6 Ghia estate	99	16,472
Focus	1.6 Ti-VCT Style estate	113	15,222
Focus	1.6 Ti-VCT Zetec Climate estate	113	15,972

Model	Derivative	BHP	UK price
Focus	1.6 Ti-VCT Ghia estate	113	16,722
Focus	1.6 Ti-VCT Titanium estate	113	16,722
Focus	1.8 Style estate	123	15,472
Focus	1.8 Zetec Climate estate	123	16,222
Focus	1.8 Ghia estate	123	16,972
Focus	1.8 Titanium estate	123	16,972
Focus	2.0 Zetec Climate estate	143	16,722
Focus	2.0 Ghia estate	143	17,472
Focus	2.0 Titanium estate	143	17,472
Focus	1.6 TDCi Studio estate	89	14,462
Focus	1.6 TDCi Style estate	89	15,962
Focus	1.6 TDCi Style estate	108	16,462
Focus	1.6 TDCi Zetec Climate estate	108	17,212
Focus	1.6 TDCi Ghia estate	108	17,962
Focus	1.6 TDCi Titanium estate	108	17,962
Focus	1.8 TDCi Style estate	113	16,462
Focus	1.8 TDCi Zetec Climate estate	113	17,212
Focus	1.8 TDCi Ghia estate	113	17,962
Focus	1.8 TDCi Titanium estate	113	17,962
Focus	2.0 TDCi Zetec Climate estate	134	18,262
Focus	2.0 TDCi Ghia estate	134	19,012
Focus	2.0 TDCi Titanium estate	134	19,012
Focus	1.6 coupé-cabrio CC-1	99	16,810
Focus	2.0 16v coupé-cabrio CC-2	143	17,822
Focus	2.0 16v coupé-cabrio CC-3	143	18,822
Focus	2.0 TDCi coupé-cabrio CC-2	134	19,287
Focus	2.0 TDCi coupé-cabrio CC-3	134	20,287
C-MAX	1.6 Studio 5dr	99	13,022
C-MAX	1.6 Style 5dr	99	14,022
C-MAX	1.6 Zetec 5dr	99	15,022
C-MAX	1.8 Style	123	14,522
C-MAX	1.8 Zetec	123	15,522
C-MAX	1.8 Titanium	123	16,522
C-MAX	1.8 FFV Style	123	14,512
C-MAX	1.8 FFV Zetec	123	15,512
C-MAX	1.8 FFV Titanium	123	16,512
C-MAX	2.0 Zetec	143	16,022
C-MAX	2.0 Titanium	143	17,022
C-MAX	1.6 TDCi Style	89	15,012
C-MAX	1.6 TDCi Zetec	89	16,012
C-MAX	1.6 TDCi Style	107	16,012
C-MAX	1.6 TDCi Zetec	107	17,012
C-MAX	1.6 TDCi Titanium	107	18,012
C-MAX	1.8 TDCi Style	113	16,012
C-MAX	1.8 TDCi Zetec	113	17,012
C-MAX	1.8 TDCi Titanium	113	18,012
C-MAX	2.0 TDCi Zetec	134	17,762
C-MAX	2.0 TDCi Titanium	134	19,045
C-MAX	2.0 TDCi DPF Zetec	134	18,062
C-MAX	2.0 TDCi DPF Titanium	134	19,062
Mondeo	1.6 Edge 5dr	108	14,995
Mondeo	1.6 Edge 5dr	123	15,695
Mondeo	1.6 Zetec 5dr	123	16,695
Mondeo	2.0 Edge 5dr	145	16,195
Mondeo	2.0 Zetec 5dr	145	17,195
Mondeo	2.0 Ghia 5dr	145	18,445
Mondeo	2.0 Titanium 5dr	145	18,445
Mondeo	2.0 Titanium X 5dr	145	20,445
Mondeo	2.3 Edge 5dr	159	17,695
Mondeo	2.3 Zetec 5dr	159	18,695
Mondeo	2.3 Ghia 5dr	159	19,945
Mondeo	2.3 Titanium 5dr	159	19,445
Mondeo	2.3 Titanium X 5dr	159	21,945
Mondeo	2.5T Ghia 5dr	217	20,945
Mondeo	2.5T Titanium 5dr	217	20,945
Mondeo	2.5T Titanium X 5dr	217	22,945
Mondeo	1.8 TDCi Edge 5dr	99	16,495
Mondeo	1.8 TDCi Edge 5dr	123	16,795
Mondeo	1.8 TDCi Edge 6-speed 5dr	123	16,995
Mondeo	1.8 TDCi Zetec 5dr	123	17,995
Mondeo	1.8 TDCi Ghia 5dr	123	19,245
Mondeo	1.8 TDCi Titanium 5dr	123	19,245
Mondeo	1.8 TDCi Titanium X 5dr	123	21,245
Mondeo	2.0 TDCi Edge auto 5dr	128	18,495
Mondeo	2.0 TDCi Zetec auto 5dr	128	19,495
Mondeo	2.0 TDCi Ghia auto 5dr	128	20,745
Mondeo	2.0 TDCi Titanium auto 5dr	128	20,745
Mondeo	2.0 TDCi Titanium X auto 5dr	128	22,745
Mondeo	2.0 TDCi Edge 5dr	138	17,395
Mondeo	2.0 TDCi Zetec 5dr	138	18,395
Mondeo	2.0 TDCi Ghia 5dr	138	19,645
Mondeo	2.0 TDCi Titanium 5dr	138	19,645
Mondeo	2.0 TDCi Titanium X 5dr	138	21,645
Mondeo	1.6 Edge saloon	123	15,695
Mondeo	1.6 Zetec saloon	123	16,695
Mondeo	2.0 Edge saloon	145	16,195
Mondeo	2.0 Zetec saloon	145	17,195
Mondeo	2.0 Ghia saloon	145	18,445
Mondeo	2.0 Titanium saloon	145	18,445
Mondeo	2.3 Edge auto saloon	159	17,695
Mondeo	2.3 Zetec auto saloon	159	18,695
Mondeo	2.3 Ghia auto saloon	159	19,445
Mondeo	2.3 Titanium X auto saloon	159	21,945
Mondeo	2.5T Ghia saloon	217	20,945
Mondeo	2.5T Titanium saloon	217	20,945
Mondeo	2.5T Titanium X saloon	217	22,945
Mondeo	1.8 TDCi Edge saloon	123	16,795
Mondeo	1.8 TDCi Edge 6-speed saloon	123	16,995
Mondeo	1.8 TDCi Zetec saloon	123	17,995
Mondeo	1.8 TDCi Ghia saloon	123	19,245
Mondeo	1.8 TDCi Titanium saloon	123	19,245
Mondeo	1.8 TDCi Titanium X saloon	123	21,245
Mondeo	2.0 TDCi Edge saloon	128	18,495
Mondeo	2.0 TDCi Zetec auto saloon	128	19,495
Mondeo	2.0 TDCi Ghia auto saloon	128	20,745
Mondeo	2.0 TDCi Titanium auto saloon	128	20,745
Mondeo	2.0 TDCi Titanium X auto saloon	128	22,745

Model	Derivative	BHP	UK price
Mondeo	2.0 TDCi Edge saloon	138	17,395
Mondeo	2.0 TDCi Zetec saloon	138	18,395
Mondeo	2.0 TDCi Ghia saloon	138	19,645
Mondeo	2.0 TDCi Titanium saloon	138	19,645
Mondeo	2.0 TDCi Titanium X saloon	138	21,645
Mondeo	1.6 Edge estate	108	16,245
Mondeo	1.6 Edge estate	123	16,945
Mondeo	1.6 Zetec estate	123	17,945
Mondeo	2.0 Edge estate	145	17,445
Mondeo	2.0 Zetec estate	145	18,445
Mondeo	2.0 Ghia estate	145	19,695
Mondeo	2.0 Titanium estate	145	19,695
Mondeo	2.0 Titanium X estate	145	21,695
Mondeo	2.3 Edge estate	159	18,945
Mondeo	2.3 Zetec estate	159	19,945
Mondeo	2.3 Ghia estate	159	21,195
Mondeo	2.3 Titanium estate	159	21,195
Mondeo	2.3 Titanium X estate	159	23,195
Mondeo	2.5T Ghia estate	217	22,195
Mondeo	2.5T Titanium estate	217	22,195
Mondeo	2.5T Titanium X estate	217	24,195
Mondeo	1.8 TDCi Edge estate	99	17,745
Mondeo	1.8 TDCi Edge estate	123	18,045
Mondeo	1.8 TDCi Edge 6-speed estate	123	18,245
Mondeo	1.8 TDCi Zetec estate	123	19,245
Mondeo	1.8 TDCi Ghia estate	123	20,495
Mondeo	1.8 TDCi Titanium estate	123	20,495
Mondeo	1.8 TDCi Titanium X estate	123	22,495
Mondeo	2.0 TDCi Edge auto estate	128	19,745
Mondeo	2.0 TDCi Zetec auto estate	128	20,745
Mondeo	2.0 TDCi Ghia auto estate	128	21,995
Mondeo	2.0 TDCi Titanium auto estate	128	21,995
Mondeo	2.0 TDCi Titanium X auto estate	128	23,995
Mondeo	2.0 TDCi Edge estate	138	18,645
Mondeo	2.0 TDCi Zetec estate	138	19,645
Mondeo	2.0 TDCi Ghia estate	138	20,895
Mondeo	2.0 TDCi Titanium estate	138	20,895
Mondeo	2.0 TDCi Titanium X estate	138	22,895
Galaxy	2.0 LX	143	19,495
Galaxy	2.0 Zetec	143	21,495
Galaxy	2.0 Ghia	143	22,495
Galaxy	1.8 TDCi LX	99	19,495
Galaxy	1.8 TDCi LX 5-speed	123	20,295
Galaxy	1.8 TDCi LX 6-speed	123	20,495
Galaxy	1.8 TDCi Zetec 5-speed	123	22,295
Galaxy	1.8 TDCi Zetec 6-speed	123	22,495
Galaxy	1.8 TDCi Zetec	123	22,295
Galaxy	1.8 TDCi Ghia	123	23,495
Galaxy	2.0 TDCi LX	128	21,995
Galaxy	2.0 TDCi Zetec	128	23,995
Galaxy	2.0 TDCi auto Zetec	128	23,995
Galaxy	2.0 TDCi auto Ghia	128	24,995
Galaxy	2.0 TDCi auto LX	138	20,995
Galaxy	2.0 TDCi Zetec	138	22,995
Galaxy	2.0 TDCi Ghia	138	23,995
S-MAX	2.0 LX	143	17,495
S-MAX	2.0 Zetec	143	18,995
S-MAX	2.0 Titanium	143	20,495
S-MAX	2.5 Zetec	217	20,995
S-MAX	2.5 Titanium	217	22,495
S-MAX	1.8 TDCi LX 5-speed	123	18,295
S-MAX	1.8 TDCi Zetec 5-speed	123	19,795
S-MAX	1.8 TDCi Titanium 5-speed	123	21,295
S-MAX	1.8 TDCi LX 6-speed	123	18,495
S-MAX	1.8 TDCi Zetec 6-speed	123	19,995
S-MAX	1.8 TDCi Titanium 6-speed	123	21,495
S-MAX	2.0 TDCi auto LX	128	19,995
S-MAX	2.0 TDCi auto Zetec	128	21,495
S-MAX	2.0 TDCi auto Titanium	128	22,995
S-MAX	2.0 TDCi LX	138	18,995
S-MAX	2.0 TDCi Zetec	138	20,495
S-MAX	2.0 TDCi Titanium	138	21,995

Model	Derivative	BHP	UK price
HONDA			
Jazz	1.2	76	9,067
Jazz	1.4 SE	82	10,967
Jazz	1.4 Sport	82	11,697
Civic	1.4 S	82	13,207
Civic	1.4 SE	82	14,927
Civic	1.8 ES	138	16,127
Civic	1.8 EX	138	17,227
Civic	1.8 S	138	15,285
Civic	1.8 SE	138	14,927
Civic	1.8 Sport	138	15,727
Civic	1.8 Type S	138	15,277
Civic	1.8 Type S GT	138	16,277
Civic	2.0 Type R	138	17,627
Civic	2.0 Type R GT	138	18,627
Civic	2.2 i-CTDi ES	138	17,367
Civic	2.2 i-CTDi EX	138	18,467
Civic	2.2 i-CTDi S	138	15,505
Civic	2.2 i-CTDi SE	138	16,167
Civic	2.2 i-CTDi Sport	138	16,967
Civic	2.2 i-CTDi Type S	138	16,567
Civic	2.2 i-CTDi Type S GT	138	17,567
Civic	1.4 VTEC hybrid	113	16,600
Civic	1.4 VTEC EX hybrid	113	19,300
Accord	2.0 SE	153	17,177
Accord	2.0 Type-S	153	19,127
Accord	2.0 EX	153	20,227
Accord	2.4 Type-S	187	20,027
Accord	2.4 EX	187	21,127
Accord	2.2 i-CTDi SE	138	18,600
Accord	2.2 i-CTDi Sport	138	19,367
Accord	2.2 i-CTDi Sport GT	138	20,767
Accord	2.2 i-CTDi EX	138	21,167
Accord	Tourer 2.0i SE	153	18,377
Accord	Tourer 2.0i EX	153	21,427
Accord	Tourer 2.4i Type-S	187	21,302

389

Model	Derivative	BHP	UK price
Accord	Tourer 2.4i EX	187	22,402
Accord	Tourer 2.2 i-CTDi Sport	138	20,567
Accord	Tourer 2.2 i-CTDi EX	138	22,367
Legend	3.5 EX	291	36,340
Legend	3.5 EX 18in alloys	291	37,350
Legend	3.5 EX (ADAS & CMBS)	291	39,090
Legend	3.5 EX (ADAS & 18in alloys)	291	40,190
S2000		237	27,402
S2000	GT	237	27,952
FR-V	1.8 SE	138	16,127
FR-V	1.8 ES	138	17,227
FR-V	1.8 EX	138	18,347
FR-V	2.2 i-CDTi SE	138	17,617
FR-V	2.2 i-CDTi ES	138	18,717
FR-V	2.2 i-CDTi EX	138	19,837
CR-V	2.0i SE	148	18,827
CR-V	2.0i ES	148	20,227
CR-V	2.0i ES sat-nav	148	21,627
CR-V	2.0i EX	148	23,527
CR-V	2.0i EX advanced safety	148	25,527
CR-V	2.2 i-CDTi SE	138	20,017
CR-V	2.2 i-CDTi ES	138	21,417
CR-V	2.2 i-CDTi ES sat-nav	138	22,817
CR-V	2.2 i-CDTi EX	138	24,717
CR-V	2.2 i-CDTi EX advanced safety	138	26,717

HYUNDAI

Model	Derivative	BHP	UK price
Amica	1.1 GSi 5dr	62	6,017
Amica	1.1 CDX 5dr	62	6,617
Getz	1.1 GSi 3dr	66	6,495
Getz	1.1 GSi 5dr	66	6,995
Getz	1.1 CDX 5dr	66	8,617
Getz	1.4 GSi 3dr	95	8,117
Getz	1.4 GSi 5dr	95	8,617
Getz	1.4 CDX 5dr	95	9,367
Getz	1.5 CRTD GSi 5dr	87	9,207
Getz	1.5 CRTD CDX+ 3dr	87	10,057
Accent	1.4 Atlantic	96	9,022
i30	1.4 Comfort	108	10,995
i30	1.4 Style	108	12,545
i30	1.6 Comfort	120	12,295
i30	1.6 Style	120	13,295
i30	1.6 Premium	120	14,895
i30	1.6 CRDi Comfort	113	12,995
i30	1.6 CRDi Style	113	13,995
i30	1.6 CRDi Premium	113	15,595
i30	2.0 CRDi Style	138	14,995
i30	2.0 CRDi Premium	138	16,595
Matrix	1.6 GSi	102	11,022
Matrix	1.8 CDX	121	12,235
Matrix	1.5 CRTD GSi	81	11,707
Coupé	1.6 S	103	15,772
Coupé	2.0 SE	141	18,022
Coupé	2.7 V6	165	19,597
Sonata	2.0 CDX	143	17,022
Sonata	3.3 V6 CDX	232	20,097
Sonata	2.0 CRTD CDX	138	18,012
Tucson	2.0 GSi 2WD	140	14,847
Tucson	2.0 GSi 4WD	140	15,847
Tucson	2.0 CDX	140	17,197
Tucson	2.7 CDX	173	19,692
Tucson	2.0 CRTD 2WD GSi	111	16,842
Tucson	2.0 CRTD 2WD CDX	111	18,192
Tucson	2.0 CRTD 4WD GSi	138	16,842
Tucson	2.0 CRTD 4WD CDX	138	18,192
Tucson	2.0 CRTD 4WD Zenith	138	20,670
Santa Fe	2.7 CDX 5str	186	24,157
Santa Fe	2.7 CDX 7str	186	25,257
Santa Fe	2.7 CDX+ 5str	186	25,357
Santa Fe	2.7 CDX+ 7str	186	26,457
Santa Fe	2.2 CRTD GSi 5str	148	21,877
Santa Fe	2.2 CRTD GSi 7str	148	22,977
Santa Fe	2.2 CRTD CDX 5str	148	23,677
Santa Fe	2.2 CRTD CDX 7str	148	24,777
Santa Fe	2.2 CRTD CDX+ 5str	148	24,877
Santa Fe	2.2 CRTD CDX+ 7str	148	25,977
Terracan	2.9 CRTD	160	19,370

INVICTA

Model	Derivative	BHP	UK price
S1		320	106,000
S1		420	120,000
S1		600	150,000

JAGUAR

Model	Derivative	BHP	UK price
X-type	2.5 S	191	23,500
X-type	2.5 SE	191	27,500
X-type	2.5 Sport Premium	191	28,500
X-type	2.5 Sovereign	191	30,000
X-type	2.0d S	128	21,500
X-type	2.0d SE	128	25,500
X-type	2.0d Sport Premium	128	26,500
X-type	2.0d Sovereign	128	28,000
X-type	2.2d S	152	22,500
X-type	2.2d SE	152	26,500
X-type	2.2d Sport Premium	152	27,500
X-type	2.2d Sovereign	152	29,000
X-type	2.5 S estate	191	24,900
X-type	2.5 SE estate	191	28,900
X-type	2.5 Sport Premium estate	191	29,900
X-type	2.5 Sovereign estate	191	31,400
X-type	3.0 Sport Premium estate	228	30,300
X-type	3.0 Sovereign estate	228	31,800
X-type	2.0d S estate	126	22,900
X-type	2.0d SE estate	126	26,900
X-type	2.0d Sport Premium estate	126	27,900
X-type	2.0d Sovereign estate	126	29,400
X-type	2.2d S estate	152	22,500
X-type	2.2d SE estate	152	27,900

Model	Derivative	BHP	UK price
X-type	2.2d Sport Premium estate	152	28,900
X-type	2.2d Sovereign estate	152	30,400
S-type	3.0 Spirit	240	29,085
S-type	3.0 XS	240	32,085
S-type	3.0 SE	240	33,585
S-type	R	400	45,090
S-type	2.7d Spirit	206	30,005
S-type	2.7d XS	206	33,005
S-type	2.7d SE	206	34,505
XJ6	3.0 Executive	240	43,642
XJ6	3.0 Sovereign	240	49,642
XJ8	4.2 Sovereign	300	58,142
XJ8	4.2 Sovereign LWB	300	59,892
XJR		400	60,252
XJ6	2.7D Executive	206	45,542
XJ6	2.7D Executive LWB	206	47,292
XJ6	2.7D Sport Premium	206	51,542
XJ6	2.7D Sovereign	206	51,542
XJ6	2.7D Sovereign LWB	206	53,292
XK	4.2	300	60,097
XK	4.2 Convertible	300	66,097
XKR	4.2	420	70,097
XKR	4.2 Convertible	420	76,097

JEEP

Model	Derivative	BHP	UK price
Patriot	2.4 Sport	168	15,995
Patriot	2.4 Limited	168	17,795
Patriot	2.0 CRD Sport	138	16,995
Patriot	2.0 CRD Limited	138	18,795
Wrangler	3.8 Rubicon	196	22,595
Wrangler	2.8 CRD Sport	161	17,995
Wrangler	2.8 CRD Sahara auto	161	21,090
Wrangler	2.8 CRD Sport Unlimited	161	19,995
Wrangler	2.8 CRD Sahara Unlimited	161	22,090
Compass	2.4 Limited	168	17,995
Compass	2.0 CRD Limited	138	19,010
Cherokee	2.8 CRD Sport	161	20,095
Cherokee	2.8 CRD Limited	161	22,635
Grand Cherokee	SRT-8	425	41,295
Grand Cherokee	3.0 CRD Predator	215	26,590
Grand Cherokee	3.0 CRD Overland	215	34,090
Grand Cherokee	3.0 CRD Limited	215	30,590
Commander	3.0 CRD Predator	215	27,590
Commander	3.0 CRD Limited	215	31,590

KIA

Model	Derivative	BHP	UK price
Picanto	1.0 GS	64	5,995
Picanto	1.1 LS	64	6,645
Rio	1.4 S	96	7,495
Rio	1.4 GS	96	8,045
Rio	1.4 LS	96	9,045
Rio	1.5 CRDi GS	109	9,045
Rio	1.5 CRDi LX	109	10,045
Cee'd	1.4 S	103	10,995
Cee'd	1.4 GS	103	11,795
Cee'd	1.6 S	120	11,545
Cee'd	1.6 GS	120	12,295
Cee'd	1.6 LS	120	13,295
Cee'd	1.6 D S	89	12,295
Cee'd	1.6 D LS	89	13,045
Cee'd	1.6 D L S	113	14,295
Cee'd SW	1.6 GS	120	12,995
Cee'd SW	1.6 LS	120	13,995
Cee'd SW	1.6 D GS	89	13,745
Cee'd SW	1.6 D L S	113	14,995
Magentis	2.0 GS	142	14,545
Magentis	2.0 LS	142	16,045
Magentis	2.7 LS	185	17,545
Magentis	2.0 CRDi GS	138	15,545
Magentis	2.0 CRDi GLS	138	17,045
Carens	2.0 S	142	11,995
Carens	2.0 GS	142	13,045
Carens	2.0 CRDi GS 5str	138	14,045
Carens	2.0 CRDi GS 7str	138	14,545
Carens	2.0 CRDi LS 7str	138	16,045
Sedona	2.7 V6 GS	186	15,995
Sedona	2.9 CRDi GS	182	17,545
Sedona	2.9 CRDi LS	182	19,545
Sedona	2.9 CRDi TS	182	21,545
Sportage	2.0 XE	140	15,345
Sportage	2.0 XS	140	17,045
Sportage	2.7 XS	173	19,435
Sportage	2.0 CRDi XE	111	16,545
Sportage	2.0 CRDi XS	111	18,245
Sorento	3.3 XT	192	26,085
Sorento	2.5 CRDi XE	168	19,995
Sorento	2.5 CRDi XS	168	23,045
Sorento	2.5 CRDi XT	168	25,045

LAMBORGHINI

Model	Derivative	BHP	UK price
Gallardo	5.0	512	125,000
Gallardo	5.0 Spyder	520	135,000
Murciélago	LP640	631	192,000
Murciélago	LP640 Roadster	631	211,000

LAND ROVER

Model	Derivative	BHP	UK price
Defender	90 TD5 hard top 3dr	122	19,455
Defender	90 TD5 station wagon 3dr	122	21,280
Defender	90 TD5 County hard top 3dr	122	20,895
Defender	90 TD5 County 3dr	122	22,530
Defender	90 TD5 XS 3dr	122	26,135
Defender	110 TD5 hard top 5dr	122	21,055
Defender	110 TD5 station wagon 5dr	122	23,495
Defender	110 TD5 County hard top 5dr	122	22,355
Defender	110 TD5 County 5dr	122	24,795
Defender	110 TD5 XS 5dr	122	28,395
Freelander	3.2 GS	230	26,595
Freelander	3.2 XS	230	28,645

Model	Derivative	BHP	UK price
Freelander	3.2 SE	230	31,645
Freelander	3.2 HSE	230	34,095
Freelander	TD4 S	160	20,960
Freelander	TD4 GS	160	23,460
Freelander	TD4 XS	160	25,510
Freelander	TD4 SE	160	28,510
Freelander	TD4 HSE	160	30,960
Discovery	4.4 V8 S	295	38,040
Discovery	4.4 V8 SE	295	43,040
Discovery	4.4 V8 HSE	295	48,540
Discovery	TDV6 5str	193	27,315
Discovery	TDV6 GS	193	29,815
Discovery	TDV6 XS	193	32,815
Discovery	TDV6 SE	193	37,595
Discovery	TDV6 HSE	193	44,535
Range Rover	Sport V8 Supercharged HSE	385	57,750
Range Rover	Sport TDV6 S	188	35,750
Range Rover	Sport TDV6 SE	188	42,450
Range Rover	Sport TDV6 HSE	188	47,700
Range Rover	Sport TDV8 HSE	268	53,550
Range Rover	V8 Supercharged Vogue SE	400	74,900
Range Rover	TDV8 HSE	272	55,100
Range Rover	TDV8 Vogue	272	62,600
Range Rover	TDV8 Vogue SE	272	70,600

LEXUS

Model	Derivative	BHP	UK price
IS 250		204	23,972
IS 250	SE	204	26,610
IS 250	SE-L	204	28,722
IS 250	Sport	204	27,722
IS 220d		175	23,132
IS 220d	SE	175	25,782
IS 220d	SE-L	175	27,882
IS 220d	Sport	175	27,387
GS 300		245	31,650
GS 300	SE	245	37,650
GS 300	SE-L	245	39,250
GS 430		279	48,005
GS 450h		292	38,080
GS 450h	SE	292	43,985
GS 450h	SE-L	292	46,830
RX 350		272	32,035
RX 350	SE	272	36,185
RX 350	SE-L	272	42,650
RX 400h		269	36,415
RX 400h	SR	269	37,500
RX 400h	SR (ICE)	269	39,700
RX 400h	SR (multimedia)	269	40,745
RX 400h	SR (ICE & multimedia)	269	42,945
RX 400h	SE	269	40,310
RX 400h	SE-L	269	45,280
SC 430		282	54,880
LS460		375	57,102
LS460	SE	375	65,102
LS460	SE-L	375	71,102
LS60		439	81,400
LS600	L	439	83,645
LS600	L (rear relaxation pack)	439	88,000

LOTUS

Model	Derivative	BHP	UK price
Elise	S	134	24,500
Elise	S Sport	134	25,490
Elise	S Touring	134	25,990
Elise	S Super Touring	134	27,985
Elise	R	189	29,945
Elise	R Sport	189	30,490
Elise	R Super Touring	189	30,990
Exige		189	30,945
Exige	Sport	189	32,440
Exige	Super Sport	189	34,935
Exige	Touring	189	32,940
Exige	S	218	34,895
Exige	S Sport	218	36,390
Exige	S Touring	218	36,890
Europa	S	197	33,895
Europa	S Luxury Touring	197	33,895

MARCOS

Model	Derivative	BHP	UK price
TSO	GT2	475	49,950

MASERATI

Model	Derivative	BHP	UK price
Coupé	GT	390	56,650
Coupé	Gransport	395	66,965
Spyder	Gransport	390	69,040
Granturismo	Coupé	399	78,500
Quattroporte	4.2	400	77,102
Quattroporte	4.2 Sport GT	400	83,302
Quattroporte	4.2 Executive GT	400	86,002

MAYBACH

Model	Derivative	BHP	UK price
Maybach	57	543	263,137
Maybach	57 S	612	297,837
Maybach	62	543	303,072
Maybach	62 S	612	345,687

MAZDA

Model	Derivative	BHP	UK price
2	1.3 TS	74	8,499
2	1.3 TS2	85	9,999
2	1.5 Sport	102	11799
3	1.4 S 5dr	83	11,430
3	1.4 TS 5dr	83	12,740
3	1.6 TS 5dr	107	13,340
3	1.6 TS2 5dr	107	14,290
3	2.0 Sport 5dr	148	16,360
3	MPS	260	18,995
3	MPS sports aero kit	260	19,495
3	1.6 D S	89	12,920
3	1.6 D TS	107	14,830

Model	Derivative	BHP	UK price
3	1.6 D TS2	107	15,720
3	2.0 D TS2	141	16,750
3	2.0 D Sport	141	17,930
3	1.6 TS saloon	104	13,340
3	1.6 TS2 saloon	104	14,290
3	2.0 Sport saloon	148	16,360
3	1.6 D TS2 saloon	107	15,720
5	1.8 TS	113	14,530
5	1.8 TS2	113	15,380
5	2.0 TS2	143	15,880
5	2.0 Sport	143	16,680
5	2.0 Sport Nav	143	18,330
5	2.0 D TS	108	16,120
5	2.0 D TS2	108	16,970
5	2.0 D Sport	108	18,270
5	2.0 D Sport Nav	108	19,920
6	1.8 S 5dr	118	14,180
6	1.8 TS 5dr	118	15,180
6	2.0 TS 5dr	145	15,680
6	2.0 TS2 5dr	145	17,180
6	2.3 Sport 5dr	164	18,680
6	2.0 D S 5dr	119	15,270
6	2.0 D TS 5dr	119	16,270
6	2.0 D TS2 5dr	141	16,770
6	2.0 D TS2 5dr	141	18,270
6	2.0 D Sport 5dr	141	19,270
6	1.8 TS saloon	118	15,180
6	2.0 TS saloon	145	15,680
6	2.0 TS2 saloon	145	17,180
6	MPS saloon	256	24,100
6	2.0 D TS saloon	141	16,770
6	2.0 D TS2 saloon	141	18,270
6	2.0 S estate	145	15,680
6	2.0 TS estate	145	16,680
6	2.0 TS2 estate	145	18,180
6	2.0 D S estate	119	16,270
6	2.0 D TS estate	141	17,770
6	2.0 D TS2 estate	141	19,270
MX-5	1.8 coupe-cabriolet	125	18,580
MX-5	2.0 coupe-cabriolet	158	19,580
MX-5	2.0 Sport coupe-cabriolet	158	21,080
MX-5	1.8 roadster	125	15,730
MX-5	1.8 Icon roadster	125	16,825
MX-5	2.0 roadster	158	17,530
MX-5	2.0 Sport roadster	158	19,030
MX-5	2.0 Icon roadster	158	17,825
RX-8		189	21,500
RX-8		228	23,000
CX-7	2.3T	254	23,960

MERCEDES-BENZ

Model	Derivative	BHP	UK price
A	150 Classic 3dr	95	13,892
A	150 Classic 5dr	95	14,642
A	150 Classic SE 3dr	95	14,192
A	150 Classic SE 5dr	95	14,942
A	150 Elegance SE 3dr	95	15,742
A	150 Elegance SE 5dr	95	16,492
A	150 Avantgarde SE 3dr	95	15,937
A	150 Avantgarde SE 5dr	95	16,687
A	170 Classic 3dr	116	15,182
A	170 Classic 5dr	116	15,932
A	170 Classic SE 3dr	116	15,842
A	170 Classic SE 5dr	116	16,232
A	170 Elegance SE 3dr	116	17,032
A	170 Elegance SE 5dr	116	17,782
A	170 Avantgarde SE 3dr	116	17,227
A	170 Avantgarde SE 5dr	116	17,965
A	200 Classic 3dr	134	16,382
A	200 Classic 5dr	134	17,132
A	200 Classic SE 3dr	134	16,682
A	200 Classic SE 5dr	134	17,432
A	200 Elegance SE 3dr	134	18,232
A	200 Elegance SE 5dr	134	18,982
A	200 Avantgarde SE 3dr	134	18,427
A	200 Avantgarde SE 5dr	134	19,177
A	200 Turbo 3dr	190	21,027
A	200 Turbo 5dr	190	21,777
A	160 CDI Classic 3dr	82	14,647
A	160 CDI Classic 5dr	82	15,397
A	160 CDI Classic SE 3dr	82	14,947
A	160 CDI Classic SE 5dr	82	15,697
A	160 CDI Elegance SE 3dr	82	16,497
A	160 CDI Elegance SE 5dr	82	17,247
A	160 CDI Avantgarde SE 3dr	82	16,692
A	160 CDI Avantgarde SE 5dr	82	17,442
A	180 CDI Classic 3dr	108	15,967
A	180 CDI Classic 5dr	108	16,717
A	180 CDI Classic SE 3dr	108	16,267
A	180 CDI Classic SE 5dr	108	17,017
A	180 CDI Elegance SE 3dr	108	17,805
A	180 CDI Elegance SE 5dr	108	18,567
A	180 CDI Avantgarde SE 3dr	108	18,012
A	180 CDI Avantgarde SE 5dr	108	18,762
A	200 CDI Elegance SE 3dr	140	19,717
A	200 CDI Elegance SE 5dr	140	20,467
A	200 CDI Avantgarde SE 3dr	140	19,912
A	200 CDI Avantgarde SE 5dr	140	20,662
B	150	95	17,442
B	150 SE	95	18,422
B	170	116	18,732
B	170 SE	116	19,712
B	200 SE	134	20,982
B	200 Turbo	190	23,387
B	180 CDI	108	19,452
B	180 CDI SE	108	20,432
B	200 CDI SE	140	22,122
C	180 K SE Sportcoupé	143	19,672
C	180 K Evolution Panorama Sportcoupé	143	22,822

Model	Derivative	BHP	UK price
C	180 K Sport Sportcoupé	143	21,422
C	200 K SE Sportcoupé	163	21,072
C	200 K Evolution Panorama Sportcoupé	163	22,822
C	200 K Sport Sportcoupé	163	22,202
C	230 SE Sportcoupé	204	22,987
C	230 Evolution Panorama Sportcoupé	204	24,737
C	230 Sport Sportcoupé	204	24,117
C	350 SE Sportcoupé	268	25,757
C	350 Evolution Panorama Sportcoupé	268	27,507
C	350 Sport Sportcoupé	268	26,887
C	200 CDI SE Sportcoupé	122	20,752
C	200 CDI Evolution Panorama Sportcoupé	122	22,502
C	200 CDI Sport Sportcoupé	122	21,882
C	220 CDI SE Sportcoupé	150	21,997
C	220 CDI Evolution Panorama Sportcoupé	150	23,747
C	220 CDI Sport Sportcoupé	150	23,127
C	180 SE	154	22,937
C	180 Elegance	154	24,132
C	180 Sport	154	25,832
C	200 SE	181	24,117
C	200 Elegance	181	25,312
C	200 Sport	181	27,012
C	230 SE	201	26,382
C	230 Elegance	201	27,577
C	230 Sport	201	29,277
C	280 SE	228	28,182
C	280 Elegance	228	29,377
C	280 Sport	228	31,077
C	350 Elegance	268	33,877
C	350 Sport	268	35,577
C	200 CDI SE	134	24,107
C	200 CDI Elegance	134	25,302
C	200 CDI Sport	134	27,002
C	220 CDI SE	168	25,107
C	220 CDI Elegance	168	26,302
C	220 CDI Sport	168	28,002
C	320 CDI Elegance	224	31,612
C	320 CDI Sport	224	33,312
C	180 K Classic estate	143	22,962
C	180 K Classic SE estate	143	23,662
C	180 K Elegance SE estate	143	24,162
C	180 K Avantgarde SE estate	143	24,162
C	180 K Sport estate	143	24,792
C	200 K Classic estate	163	24,712
C	200 K Classic SE estate	163	25,412
C	200 K Elegance SE estate	163	25,912
C	200 K Avantgarde SE estate	163	25,912
C	200 K Sport estate	163	26,542
C	230 Classic estate	204	27,097
C	230 Classic SE estate	204	27,797
C	230 Elegance SE estate	204	28,297
C	230 Avantgarde SE estate	204	28,297
C	230 Sport estate	204	28,927
C	280 Classic estate	228	28,907
C	280 Classic SE estate	228	29,607
C	280 Elegance SE estate	228	30,107
C	280 Avantgarde SE estate	228	30,107
C	280 Sport estate	228	30,737
C	350 Elegance SE estate	268	34,782
C	350 Avantgarde SE estate	268	34,782
C	350 Sport estate	268	37,887
C	55 AMG estate	355	50,297
C	200 CDI Classic estate	122	24,852
C	200 CDI Classic SE estate	122	25,552
C	200 CDI Elegance SE estate	122	26,052
C	200 CDI Avantgarde SE estate	122	26,052
C	200 CDI Sport estate	122	26,682
C	220 CDI Classic estate	150	25,917
C	220 CDI Classic SE estate	150	26,617
C	220 CDI Elegance SE estate	150	27,117
C	220 CDI Avantgarde SE estate	150	27,117
C	220 CDI Sport estate	150	27,747
C	320 CDI Elegance SE estate	224	32,452
C	320 CDI Avantgarde SE estate	224	32,452
C	320 CDI Sport estate	224	35,557
E	200 K Classic	184	27,802
E	200 K Elegance	184	29,902
E	200 K Avantgarde	184	30,402
E	200 K Sport	184	31,372
E	280 Classic	231	32,397
E	280 Elegance	231	34,497
E	280 Avantgarde	231	34,497
E	280 Sport	231	35,967
E	350 Elegance	272	37,577
E	350 Avantgarde	272	38,077
E	350 Sport	272	39,047
E	500 Elegance	388	47,717
E	500 Avantgarde	388	48,217
E	500 Sport	388	49,187
E	63 AMG	503	67,597
E	220 CDI Classic	170	29,192
E	220 CDI Elegance	170	31,292
E	220 CDI Avantgarde	170	31,792
E	220 CDI Executive	170	28,515
E	280 CDI Classic	190	33,097
E	280 CDI Elegance	190	35,197
E	280 CDI Avantgarde	190	35,697
E	280 CDI Sport	190	36,667
E	320 CDI Elegance	224	37,247
E	320 CDI Avantgarde	224	37,747
E	320 CDI Sport	224	38,717
E	200 K Classic estate	184	29,602
E	200 K Elegance estate	184	31,702
E	200 K Avantgarde estate	184	32,202
E	200 K Sport estate	184	33,172
E	280 Classic estate	231	34,197
E	280 Elegance estate	231	36,297
E	280 Avantgarde estate	231	36,797
E	280 Sport estate	231	37,767
E	350 Elegance estate	272	39,377
E	350 Avantgarde estate	272	39,877
E	350 Sport estate	272	40,847
E	500 Elegance estate	388	49,217
E	500 Avantgarde estate	388	49,717
E	500 Sport estate	388	50,687
E	63 AMG estate	514	69,097
E	220 CDI Classic estate	170	31,032
E	220 CDI Elegance estate	170	33,132
E	220 CDI Avantgarde estate	170	33,632
E	280 CDI Classic estate	190	34,897
E	280 CDI Elegance estate	190	36,997
E	280 CDI Avantgarde estate	190	37,497
E	280 CDI Sport estate	190	38,467
E	320 CDI Elegance estate	224	39,047
E	320 CDI Avantgarde estate	224	39,547
E	320 CDI Sport estate	224	40,517
CLS	350	268	43,962
CLS	500	306	53,907
CLS	63 AMG	503	73,997
CLS	320 CDI	221	43,957
S	280	228	54317
S	350	268	56,867
S	350 L	268	60,867
S	500	382	69,917
S	500 L	382	73,917
S	600 L	510	104,600
S	63 L AMG	518	99,567
S	65 L AMG	604	147,965
S	320 CDI	232	55,022
S	320 L CDI	232	59,117
R	350 L	268	40,117
R	350 L SE	268	43,067
R	350 L Sport	268	43,067
R	500 L SE	382	51,637
R	500 L Sport	382	51,637
R	63 L AMG	510	74,115
R	280 CDI	188	36,517
R	280 CDI SE	188	39,467
R	280 CDI Sport	188	39,467
R	320 L CDI	221	40,117
R	320 L CDI SE	221	43,067
R	320 L CDI Sport	221	43,067
CLK	200 K Elegance	161	30,157
CLK	200 K Avantgarde	161	30,157
CLK	200 K Sport	161	32,657
CLK	280 Elegance	228	34,047
CLK	280 Avantgarde	228	34,047
CLK	280 Sport	228	36,547
CLK	350 Elegance	272	38,327
CLK	350 Avantgarde	272	38,327
CLK	350 Sport	272	40,827
CLK	500 Elegance	383	47,777
CLK	500 Avantgarde	383	47,777
CLK	500 Sport	383	50,277
CLK	63 AMG	474	66,317
CLK	220 CDI Elegance	150	30,792
CLK	220 CDI Avantgarde	150	30,792
CLK	220 CDI Sport	150	33,292
CLK	320 CDI Elegance	221	34,787
CLK	320 CDI Avantgarde	221	34,787
CLK	320 CDI Sport	221	37,287
CLK	200 K Elegance cabrio	181	33,757
CLK	200 K Avantgarde cabrio	181	33,757
CLK	200 K Sport cabrio	181	36,257
CLK	280 Elegance cabrio	228	37,647
CLK	280 Avantgarde cabrio	228	37,647
CLK	280 Sport cabrio	228	40,147
CLK	350 Elegance cabrio	272	41,927
CLK	350 Avantgarde cabrio	272	41,927
CLK	350 Sport cabrio	272	44,427
CLK	500 Elegance cabrio	383	51,327
CLK	500 Avantgarde cabrio	383	51,377
CLK	500 Sport cabrio	383	53,877
CLK	63 AMG cabrio	474	69,917
CL	500	388	79,652
CL	600	510	107,097
CL	63 AMG	518	103,552
CL	65 AMG	612	149,565
SLR		617	313,565
SLR	722	641	340,000
SLK	200 K	161	28,767
SLK	280	228	31,787
SLK	350	268	35,792
SLK	55 AMG	355	51,592
SL	350	272	63,782
SL	500	388	76,777
SL	600	517	102,117
SL	55 AMG	500	99,897
SL	65 AMG	612	150,097
ML	350	268	38,217
ML	350 SE	268	40,967
ML	350 Sport	268	40,967
ML	500 SE	302	50,532
ML	500 Sport	302	50,532
ML	63 AMG	503	75,147
ML	280 CDI	188	36,167
ML	280 CDI SE	188	38,917
ML	280 CDI Sport	188	38,917
ML	320 CDI	221	38,217
ML	320 CDI SE	221	40,967
ML	320 CDI Sport	221	40,967
ML	420 CDI SE	302	51,612
ML	420 CDI Sport	302	51,612
GL	500	383	66,522
GL	320 CDI	221	52,472
GL	420 CDI	302	63,872

Model	Derivative	BHP	UK price
Viano	3.5 Ambiente	228	34,517
Viano	3.5 Ambiente LWB	228	35,002
Viano	3.5 Ambiente XLWB	228	35,487
Viano	2.0 CDi Trend SWB	108	23,772
Viano	2.0 CDi Trend LWB	108	24,257
Viano	2.2 CDi Trend SWB	148	25,467
Viano	2.2 CDi Trend LWB	148	25,952
Viano	2.2 CDi Trend XLWB	148	26,437
Viano	2.2 CDi Ambiente SWB	148	30,062
Viano	2.2 CDi Ambiente LWB	148	30,547
Viano	2.2 CDi Ambiente XLWB	148	31,032
Viano	3.0 CDi Ambiente SWB	201	32,062
Viano	3.0 CDi Ambiente LWB	201	32,547
Viano	3.0 CDi Ambiente XLWB	201	33,032

MINI

Model	Derivative	BHP	UK price
Mini	One 1.4	94	11,625
Mini	Cooper 1.6	118	13,028
Mini	Cooper S 1.6T	170	16,025
Mini	Cooper S 1.6D	108	14,190
Mini	One cabrio	90	13,630
Mini	One Sidewalk cabrio	90	16,940
Mini	Cooper cabrio	115	14,960
Mini	Cooper Sidewalk cabrio	115	17,990
Mini	Cooper S cabrio	170	17,995
Mini	Cooper S Sidewalk cabrio	170	20,265
Mini	Cooper Clubman 1.6	118	14,235
Mini	Cooper S Clubman 1.6T	173	17,210
Mini	Cooper Clubman 1.6D	108	15,400

MITSUBISHI

Model	Derivative	BHP	UK price
i		57	9,084
Colt	1.1 CZ1 3dr	74	7,521
Colt	1.1 CZ1 5dr	74	8,021
Colt	1.3 CZ2 3dr	95	9,021
Colt	1.3 CZ2 5dr	95	9,521
Colt	1.5 CZ3 3dr	107	10,521
Colt	1.5 CZ3 5dr	107	11,021
Colt	1.5 CZT 3dr	147	13,026
Colt	1.5 DI-D CZ2 5dr	95	11,011
Colt	1.5 DI-D CZ3 3dr	95	11,011
Colt	CZC 1.5	107	14,026
Colt	CZC 1.5 Turbo	147	16,026
Lancer	1.6 Equippe saloon	96	10,026
Lancer	1.6 Elegance saloon	96	10,776
Lancer	2.0 Sport saloon	133	11,551
Lancer	1.6 Equippe estate	96	10,526
Lancer	1.6 Elegance estate	96	11,276
Lancer	2.0 Sport estate	133	12,051
Lancer	Evolution IX FQ-300	305	28,141
Lancer	Evolution IX FQ-320	326	30,141
Lancer	Evolution IX FQ-340	345	33,141
Lancer	Evolution IX FQ-360	366	35,641
Grandis	2.0 DI-D Classic	134	19,716
Grandis	2.0 DI-D Equippe	134	21,616
Grandis	2.0 DI-D Elegance	134	23,116
Grandis	2.0 DI-D Warrior	134	23,716
Outlander	2.0 DI-D Equippe	138	19,466
Outlander	2.0 DI-D Warrior	138	22,016
Outlander	2.0 DI-D Elegance	138	24,766
Shogun Sport	3.0 Equippe	168	20,134
Shogun Sport	2.5 TD Classic	98	17,129
Shogun Sport	2.5 TD Equippe	98	20,129
Shogun	3.2 DI-D Equippe 3dr	158	22,646
Shogun	3.2 DI-D Equippe 5dr	158	24,146
Shogun	3.2 DI-D Equippe 5dr	158	26,646
Shogun	3.2 DI-D Equippe auto 5dr	168	27,646
Shogun	3.2 DI-D Warrior auto 3dr	168	28,596
Shogun	3.2 DI-D Warrior auto 5dr	168	32,096
Shogun	3.2 DI-D Elegance 3dr	158	27,196
Shogun	3.2 DI-D Elegance auto 3dr	168	28,696
Shogun	3.2 DI-D Elegance 5dr	158	31,196
Shogun	3.2 DI-D Elegance auto 5dr	168	32,696
Shogun	3.2 DI-D Diamond auto 3dr	168	30,696
Shogun	3.2 DI-D Diamond auto 5dr	168	34,696

MORGAN

Model	Derivative	BHP	UK price
4/4	1.8 2str	125	24,323
Plus 4	2.0 2str	145	29,081
Plus 4	2.0 4str	145	32,018
Roadster	3.0 V6 2str	223	36,190
Roadster	3.0 V6 4str	223	39,127
Aero 8		325	62,500

NISSAN

Model	Derivative	BHP	UK price
Micra	1.2 Initia 3dr	79	7,495
Micra	1.2 Initia 5dr	79	8,145
Micra	1.2 Spirita 3dr	79	8,795
Micra	1.2 Spirita 5dr	79	9,445
Micra	1.2 Sport 3dr	79	9,895
Micra	1.2 Sport 5dr	79	10,545
Micra	1.4 Spirita 3dr	87	9,095
Micra	1.4 Spirita 5dr	87	9,745
Micra	1.4 Spirita (luxury pack) 3dr	87	10,295
Micra	1.4 Spirita (luxury pack) 5dr	87	10,945
Micra	1.4 Spirita (comfort pack) 3dr	87	10,295
Micra	1.4 Spirita (comfort pack) 5dr	87	10,945
Micra	1.4 Sport 3dr	87	10,195
Micra	1.4 Sport 5dr	87	10,845
Micra	1.4 Active Luxury 3dr	87	10,695
Micra	1.4 Active Luxury 5dr	87	11,345
Micra	1.6 Sport SR 3dr	108	11,345
Micra	1.6 Sport SR 5dr	108	12,195
Micra	1.6 Active Luxury 3dr	108	12,195
Micra	1.6 Active Luxury 5dr	108	12,845
Micra	1.5 dCi Initia 3dr	85	8,655
Micra	1.5 dCi Initia 5dr	85	9,305
Micra	1.5 dCi Spirita 3dr	85	9,955
Micra	1.5 dCi Spirita 5dr	85	10,605
Micra	1.5 dCi Spirita (luxury pack) 3dr	85	11,155
Micra	1.5 dCi Spirita (luxury pack) 5dr	85	11,805
Micra	1.5 dCi Spirita (comfort pack) 3dr	85	11,155
Micra	1.5 dCi Spirita (comfort pack) 5dr	85	11,805
Micra	1.5 dCi Sport 3dr	85	11,055
Micra	1.5 dCi Sport 5dr	85	11,705
Micra	1.5 dCi Active Luxury 3dr	85	11,855
Micra	1.5 dCi Active Luxury 5dr	85	12,505
Micra C+C	1.4 Urbis	87	13,500
Micra C+C	1.6 Sport	108	14,250
Micra C+C	1.6 Essenza	108	15,250
Micra C+C	1.6 Active Luxury	108	15,495
Note	1.4 Visia	87	9,990
Note	1.4 Acenta	87	11,240
Note	1.6 Visia	108	10,790
Note	1.6 Acenta	108	12,040
Note	1.6 Tekna	108	13,290
Note	1.5 dCi Visia	85	11,090
Note	1.5 dCi Acenta	85	12,340
Note	1.5 dCi Tekna	85	13,590
Qashqai	1.6 Visia 2WD	113	13,499
Qashqai	1.6 Acenta 2WD	113	14,999
Qashqai	1.6 Acenta sat-nav 2WD	113	16,349
Qashqai	1.6 Tekna 2WD	113	16,499
Qashqai	1.6 Tekna sat-nav 2WD	113	17,849
Qashqai	2.0 Visia 2WD	138	14,899
Qashqai	2.0 Acenta 2WD	138	16,399
Qashqai	2.0 Acenta sat-nav 2WD	138	17,749
Qashqai	2.0 Tekna 2WD	138	17,899
Qashqai	2.0 Tekna sat-nav 2WD	138	19,249
Qashqai	2.0 Visia 4WD	138	16,499
Qashqai	2.0 Acenta 4WD	138	17,999
Qashqai	2.0 Acenta sat-nav 4WD	138	19,349
Qashqai	2.0 Tekna 4WD	138	19,249
Qashqai	2.0 Tekna sat-nav 4WD	138	19,499
Qashqai	1.5 dCi Visia 2WD	105	14,649
Qashqai	1.5 dCi Acenta 2WD	105	16,149
Qashqai	1.5 dCi Acenta sat-nav 2WD	105	17,499
Qashqai	1.5 dCi Tekna 2WD	105	17,649
Qashqai	1.5 dCi Tekna sat-nav 2WD	105	18,999
Qashqai	2.0 dCi Visia 2WD	148	16,249
Qashqai	2.0 dCi Acenta 2WD	148	17,749
Qashqai	2.0 dCi Acenta sat-nav 2WD	148	19,099
Qashqai	2.0 dCi Tekna 2WD	148	19,249
Qashqai	2.0 dCi Tekna sat-nav 2WD	148	20,599
Qashqai	2.0 dCi Visia 4WD	148	17,849
Qashqai	2.0 dCi Acenta 4WD	148	19,349
Qashqai	2.0 dCi Acenta sat-nav 4WD	148	20,699
Qashqai	2.0 dCi Tekna 4WD	148	20,849
Qashqai	2.0 dCi Tekna sat-nav 4WD	148	22,199
350Z		309	26,795
350Z	GT	309	29,295
350Z	Roadster	309	28,295
350Z	GT Roadster	309	30,795
X-Trail	2.0 Trek	139	18,795
X-Trail	2.5 Sport	167	20,695
X-Trail	2.5 Sport Extreme	167	21,120
X-Trail	2.5 Sport Expedition	167	22,395
X-Trail	2.5 Sport Expedition Extreme	167	22,820
X-Trail	2.5 Aventura	167	22,695
X-Trail	2.5 Aventura Extreme	167	23,120
X-Trail	2.5 Aventura Explorer	167	24,395
X-Trail	2.5 Aventura Explorer Ext	167	24,820
X-Trail	2.0 dCi Trek	148	20,395
X-Trail	2.0 dCi Sport	148	21,495
X-Trail	2.0 dCi Sport Extreme	148	21,920
X-Trail	2.0 dCi Sport Expedition	148	23,195
X-Trail	2.0 dCi Sport Expedition Extreme	148	23,620
X-Trail	2.0 dCi Aventura	148	23,495
X-Trail	2.0 dCi Aventura Extreme	148	23,920
X-Trail	2.0 dCi Aventura Explorer	148	25,195
X-Trail	2.0 dCi Aventura Explorer Ext	171	22,495
X-Trail	2.0 dCi Sport	171	22,495
X-Trail	2.0 dCi Sport Extreme	171	22,920
X-Trail	2.0 dCi Sport Expedition	171	24,195
X-Trail	2.0 dCi Sport Expedition Extreme	171	24,620
X-Trail	2.0 dCi Aventura	171	24,495
X-Trail	2.0 dCi Aventura Extreme	171	24,920
X-Trail	2.0 dCi Aventura Explorer	171	26,195
X-Trail	2.0 dCi Aventura Explorer Ext	171	26,620
Murano	3.5	231	30,085
Patrol GR	3.0 TD Trek	160	24,395
Patrol GR	3.0 TD Aventura	160	28,395
Pathfinder	2.5 dCi Trek	171	23,395
Pathfinder	2.5 dCi Sport	171	25,995
Pathfinder	2.5 dCi Sport Tech Pack	171	27,995
Pathfinder	2.5 dCi Aventura	171	28,995

NOBLE

Model	Derivative	BHP	UK price
M400		425	55,995

PAGANI

Model	Derivative	BHP	UK price
Zonda	S	555	285,000
Zonda	F	594	390,000

PERODUA

Model	Derivative	BHP	UK price
Myvi	1.3 SXi	86	7799
Myvi	1.3 EZi auto	86	8499
Kelisa	1.0 EX	54	4812
Kelisa	1.0 GX SE	54	5,612
Kelisa	1.0 EZi SE auto	54	6,526
Kenari	1.0 GX SE	54	6,243
Kenari	1.0 EZi SE auto	54	7,057

PEUGEOT

Model	Derivative	BHP	UK price
107	1.0 Urban Lite 3dr	67	6,995
107	1.0 Urban Lite 5dr	67	7,345

Model	Derivative	BHP	UK price
107	1.0 Urban 3dr	67	7,440
107	1.0 Urban 5dr	67	7,795
107	1.0 Urban XS 3dr	67	8,352
1007	1.4 8v SE	75	11,770
1007	1.4 16v SE	111	12,270
1007	1.4 HDi SE	70	12,465
1007	1.6 HDi SE	110	13,400
Partner	2 1.6 HDi Escapade	90	11,895
206	1.4 Look 3dr	75	8,495
206	1.4 Look 5dr	75	8,995
206	1.4 Look A/C 3dr	75	8,995
206	1.4 Look A/C 5dr	75	9,595
206	1.6 Look Tip auto 3dr	110	10,522
206	1.6 Look Tip auto 5dr	110	11,122
206	1.4 HDi Look 3dr	68	9,692
206	1.4 HDi Look 5dr	68	10,292
207	1.4 Urban 3dr	75	9,095
207	1.4 Urban 5dr	75	9,695
207	1.4 S 3dr	75	9,575
207	1.4 S 5dr	75	10,175
207	1.4 S A/C 3dr	75	10,125
207	1.4 S A/C 5dr	75	10,175
207	1.4 S m:play 3dr	75	10,645
207	1.4 S m:play 5dr	75	11,245
207	1.4 S 16v 3dr	87	10,525
207	1.4 S 16v 5dr	87	11,125
207	1.4 Sport 3dr	87	11,225
207	1.4 Sport 5dr	87	11,825
207	1.4 VTi S 3dr	95	10,525
207	1.4 VTi S 5dr	95	11,125
207	1.4 VTi Sport 3dr	95	11,225
207	1.4 VTi Sport 5dr	95	11,825
207	1.4 VTi SE Premium 5dr	95	12,425
207	1.6 Sport 3dr	120	11,925
207	1.6 Sport 5dr	120	12,525
207	1.6 SE Premium 5dr	120	13,125
207	1.6T Sport XS 3dr	150	12,525
207	1.6T 150GT 3dr	150	14,475
207	1.6T 150GT 5dr	150	15,075
207	1.6T GTi 3dr	150	15,395
207	1.4 HDi Urban 3dr	70	9,995
207	1.4 HDi Urban 5dr	70	10,595
207	1.4 HDi S 3dr	70	10,475
207	1.4 HDi S 5dr	70	11,075
207	1.4 HDi S A/C 3dr	70	11,075
207	1.4 HDi S A/C 5dr	70	11,675
207	1.6 HDi S 3dr	90	11,595
207	1.6 HDi S 5dr	90	12,195
207	1.6 HDi SE Premium 5dr	90	13,495
207	1.6 HDi Sport 3dr	90	12,295
207	1.6 HDi Sport 5dr	90	12,895
207	1.6 HDi Sport 3dr	110	13,015
207	1.6 HDi Sport 5dr	110	13,615
207	1.6 HDi SE Premium 5dr	110	14,215
207	1.6 HDi GT 3dr	110	14,750
207	1.6 HDi GT 5dr	110	15,362
207	SW 1.4 VTi S	95	11,340
207	SW 1.4 VTi S A/C	95	11,875
207	SW 1.6 VTi S	120	12,575
207	SW 1.6 VTi Sport	120	13,275
207	SW 1.6 HDi S	90	12,945
207	SW 1.6 HDi Sport	90	13,645
207	CC 1.6 Sport	120	14,365
207	CC 1.6 GT	120	14,795
207	CC 1.6 THP GT	150	16,022
207	CC 1.6 HDi Sport	90	15,912
207	CC 1.6 HDi GT	110	17,112
307	1.4 X-Line 3dr	90	12,110
307	1.4 X-Line 5dr	90	12,710
307	1.4 S 3dr	90	12,865
307	1.4 S 5dr	90	13,465
307	1.6 S 3dr	110	13,465
307	1.6 S 5dr	110	14,065
307	1.6 Sport 3dr	110	14,715
307	1.6 Sport 5dr	110	15,315
307	2.0 Sport 5dr	140	16,615
307	1.6 HDi S 3dr	90	14,255
307	1.6 HDi S 5dr	90	14,855
307	1.6 HDi S 3dr	110	15,155
307	1.6 HDi S 5dr	110	15,755
307	1.6 HDi Sport 3dr	110	16,405
307	1.6 HDi Sport 5dr	110	17,005
307	2.0 HDi Sport 3dr	136	17,405
307	2.0 HDi Sport 5dr	136	18,005
307	1.6 S estate	110	14,665
307	1.6 HDi S estate	90	15,455
307	1.6 HDi S estate	110	16,355
307	SW 1.6 S	90	14,915
307	SW 1.6 SE	90	15,715
307	SW 1.6 HDi S	90	15,705
307	SW 1.6 HDi SE	90	16,505
307	SW 1.6 HDi S	110	16,605
307	SW 1.6 HDi SE	110	17,405
307	SW 2.0 HDi SE	136	18,405
307	CC 1.6 S	110	17,477
307	CC 1.6 Sport	110	18,877
307	CC 2.0 S	138	19,102
307	CC 2.0 Sport	138	20,502
307	CC 2.0 Sport	180	21,702
307	CC 2.0 HDi Sport	136	21,667
407	1.8 S	117	15,700
407	2.0 SE	138	17,390
407	2.2 Sport	163	19,350
407	1.6 HDi S	110	16,550
407	1.6 HDi SE	110	17,550
407	2.0 HDi S	136	17,455
407	2.0 HDi SE	136	18,455
407	2.0 HDi Sport	136	19,825
407	2.2 HDi Sport	170	21,305
407	2.7 V6 HDi Sport auto	205	23,635
407	SW 1.8 S	125	16,900
407	SW 2.0 SE	138	18,590
407	SW 2.2 Sport	163	20,540
407	SW 3.0 GT auto	211	25,735
407	SW 1.6 HDi S	110	17,750
407	SW 1.6 HDi SE	110	18,750
407	SW 2.0 HDi S	136	18,655
407	SW 2.0 HDi SE	136	19,655
407	SW 2.0 HDi Sport	136	21,005
407	SW 2.0 HDi GT	136	23,305
407	SW 2.2 HDi Sport	170	22,525
407	SW 2.2 HDi Sport XS	170	24,000
407	SW 2.2 HDi GT	170	24,805
407	SW 2.7 HDi Sport auto	205	24,930
407	SW 2.7 HDi GT auto	205	27,230
407	Coupé 2.2 Sport	163	19,530
407	Coupé 2.2 Sport multimedia	163	20,525
407	Coupé 3.0 V6 Sport	211	21,230
407	Coupé 3.0 V6 Sport multimedia	211	22,225
407	Coupé 2.0 HDi Sport	136	19,995
407	Coupé 2.0 HDi Sport multimedia	136	20,990
407	Coupé 2.7 HDi Sport	205	23,825
407	Coupé 2.7 HDi Sport multimedia	205	24,820
607	3.0 V6 Executive	211	29,142
607	2.0 HDi Executive	136	25,012
607	2.2 HDi Executive	170	26,512
807	2.0 S	140	19,662
807	2.0 SE	140	21,452
807	2.0 Executive	140	23,905
807	2.0 HDi S	120	21,117
807	2.0 HDi SE	120	22,907
807	2.0 HDi Executive	120	24,277
807	2.0 HDi SE	136	23,777
807	2.0 HDi Executive	136	25,117

PORSCHE

Model	Derivative	BHP	UK price
Boxster		241	33,170
Boxster	S	291	39,850
Cayman		245	36,220
Cayman	S	291	44,080
911	Carrera	321	60,010
911	Carrera 4	321	64,330
911	Carrera 4 Targa	325	70,320
911	Carrera S	350	67,860
911	Carrera 4S	350	71,980
911	Carrera 4S Targa	350	77,370
911	Carrera GT3	409	79,540
911	Carrera GT3 RS	409	94,280
911	Turbo	473	97,840
911	Carrera cabrio	321	67,860
911	Carrera 4 cabrio	321	71,980
911	Carrera S cabrio	350	74,910
911	Carrera 4S cabrio	350	79,040
911	Turbo cabrio	473	79,040
Cayenne	V6	290	37,100
Cayenne	S	385	46,610
Cayenne	Turbo	493	74,650

PROTON

Model	Derivative	BHP	UK price
Savvy	1.2 Street	75	5,995
Savvy	1.2 Style	75	6,995
Satria Neo	1.3 SX	94	7,995
Satria Neo	1.3 GSX	94	8,895
Satria Neo	1.6 GSX	94	9,595
Impian	1.6 GLS	102	10,595
Impian	1.6 GSX	102	11,395
Gen-2	1.3 GLS	74	8,895
Gen-2	1.6 GLS	110	9,595
Gen-2	1.6 GSX	110	10,595

RENAULT

Model	Derivative	BHP	UK price
Twingo	1.2 Dynamique	75	8,375
Twingo	1.2 TCE 100 GT	99	9,995
Kangoo	1.2 Authentique	75	10,175
Kangoo	1.2 Expression	75	10,825
Kangoo	1.6 Authentique auto	94	11,675
Kangoo	1.6 Expression	94	11,325
Kangoo	1.5 dCi Authentique	68	11,165
Kangoo	1.5 dCi Expression	68	11,815
Kangoo	1.5 dCi Expression	84	12,315
Clio Campus	1.2 3dr	60	7,995
Clio Campus	1.2 A/C 3dr	60	8,520
Clio Campus	1.2 5dr	60	8,695
Clio Campus	1.2 A/C 5dr	60	9,220
Clio Campus	1.2 Sport 3dr	75	8,925
Clio Campus	1.2 Sport A/C 3dr	75	9,450
Clio Campus	1.5 dCi 3dr	68	9,095
Clio Campus	1.5 dCi A/C 3dr	68	9,620
Clio Campus	1.5 dCi 5dr	68	9,765
Clio Campus	1.5 dCi A/C 5dr	68	10,290
Clio Campus	1.5 dCi Sport 3dr	68	9,795
Clio Campus	1.5 dCi Sport A/C 3dr	68	10,320
Clio	1.2 Freeway 3dr	75	7,485
Clio	1.2 Extreme 3dr	75	9,025
Clio	1.2 Authentique 5dr	75	9,455
Clio	1.2 Expression 3dr	75	9,840
Clio	1.2 Expression 5dr	75	10,510
Clio	1.2 Expression 3dr	98	10,540
Clio	1.2 Expression 5dr	98	11,210
Clio	1.2 Dynamique 3dr	98	10,840
Clio	1.2 Dynamique 5dr	98	11,510
Clio	1.2 Dynamique S 3dr	98	11,190
Clio	1.2 Dynamique S A/C 3dr	98	11,175
Clio	1.2 Dynamique SX 3dr	98	11,145
Clio	1.2 Dynamique SX A/C 3dr	98	11,980
Clio	1.2 Privilege 5dr	98	12,460

Model	Derivative	BHP	UK price
Clio	1.6 Expression 3dr auto	113	11,940
Clio	1.6 Expression 5dr auto	113	12,610
Clio	1.6 Dynamique 3dr auto	113	12,240
Clio	1.6 Dynamique 5dr auto	113	12,910
Clio	1.6 Dynamique S auto 3dr	113	12,590
Clio	1.6 Privilege auto 5dr	113	13,860
Clio	2.0 Dynamique S 3dr	113	13,090
Clio	Renaultsport 197	194	15,995
Clio	1.5 dCi Extreme 3dr	68	10,025
Clio	1.5 dCi Authentique 5dr	68	10,455
Clio	1.5 dCi Expression 3dr	68	10,840
Clio	1.5 dCi Expression 5dr	68	11,510
Clio	1.5 dCi Expression 5dr	85	11,340
Clio	1.5 dCi Expression 5dr	85	12,010
Clio	1.5 dCi Dynamique 3dr	85	11,640
Clio	1.5 dCi Dynamique 5dr	85	12,310
Clio	1.5 dCi Dynamique S 3dr	85	11,990
Clio	1.5 dCi Privilege 5dr	85	13,260
Clio	1.5 dCi Dynamique 5dr	105	13,560
Clio	1.5 dCi Dynamique S 3dr	105	13,240
Clio	1.5 dCi Dynamique SX 3dr	105	13,505
Clio	1.5 dCi Privilege 5dr	105	14,010
Clio	1.5 dCi Initiale 5dr	105	15,710
Modus	1.2 Authentique	75	9,075
Modus	1.2 Expression	75	9,825
Modus	1.2 TCE 100 Expression	99	10,525
Modus	1.2 TCE 100 Dynamique	99	11,170
Modus	1.4 Expression	97	10,325
Modus	1.6 Dynamique S auto	108	12,470
Modus	1.5 dCi Authentique	68	10,065
Modus	1.5 dCi Expression	68	10,815
Modus	1.5 dCi Expression	85	11,295
Modus	1.5 dCi Dynamique S	85	11,940
Modus	1.5 dCi Dynamique S	105	12,710
Mégane	1.4 Freeway 3dr	98	8,988
Mégane	1.4 Extreme 3dr	98	12,460
Mégane	1.4 Extreme 5dr	98	12,460
Mégane	1.4 Authentique 5dr	98	11,960
Mégane	1.4 Dynamique 3dr	98	13,260
Mégane	1.4 Dynamique 5dr	98	13,760
Mégane	1.4 Expression 5dr	98	13,260
Mégane	1.6 Authentique 5dr	109	12,460
Mégane	1.6 Extreme 3dr	109	12,460
Mégane	1.6 Extreme 5dr	109	12,960
Mégane	1.6 Dynamique 3dr	109	13,760
Mégane	1.6 Dynamique 5dr	109	14,260
Mégane	1.6 Dynamique S 5dr	109	15,260
Mégane	1.6 Expression 5dr	109	13,760
Mégane	2.0 Dynamique 3dr	136	14,760
Mégane	2.0 Dynamique 5dr	136	15,260
Mégane	2.0 Dynamique S 5dr	136	16,260
Mégane	2.0 Privilege 5dr	136	15,970
Mégane	2.0 T GT 3dr	165	16,460
Mégane	2.0 T GT 5dr	165	16,960
Mégane	Renaultsport 225 Cup 3dr	222	18,960
Mégane	Renaultsport 225 Lux 3dr	222	19,860
Mégane	Renaultsport 225 Lux 5dr	222	20,360
Mégane	1.5 dCi Extreme 3dr	85	12,730
Mégane	1.5 dCi Extreme 5dr	85	13,230
Mégane	1.5 dCi Expression 5dr	85	14,030
Mégane	1.5 dCi Dynamique 3dr	85	14,030
Mégane	1.5 dCi Dynamique 5dr	85	14,530
Mégane	1.5 dCi Expression 3dr	105	14,730
Mégane	1.5 dCi Dynamique 3dr	105	14,730
Mégane	1.5 dCi Dynamique 5dr	105	15,230
Mégane	1.5 dCi Dynamique S 5dr	105	16,230
Mégane	1.9 dCi Dynamique 3dr	128	15,950
Mégane	1.9 dCi Dynamique FAP 3dr	128	16,950
Mégane	1.9 dCi Dynamique 5dr	128	16,450
Mégane	1.9 dCi Dynamique FAP 5dr	128	17,450
Mégane	1.9 dCi Expression 5dr	128	15,950
Mégane	1.9 dCi Expression FAP 5dr	128	16,950
Mégane	1.9 dCi Dynamique S 5dr	128	17,450
Mégane	2.0 dCi Dynamique S 3dr	150	18,450
Mégane	2.0 dCi 150GT 3dr	150	17,450
Mégane	2.0 dCi 150GT 5dr	150	17,950
Mégane	2.0 dCi 175 Renaultsport 3dr	173	18,950
Mégane	2.0 dCi 175 Renaultsport 5dr	173	19,450
Mégane	2.0 dCi 175 Renaultsport Lux 3dr	173	20,350
Mégane	2.0 dCi 175 Renaultsport Lux 5dr	173	20,850
Mégane	1.4 Expression saloon	98	13,980
Mégane	1.4 Dynamique saloon	98	14,480
Mégane	1.6 Expression saloon	114	14,480
Mégane	1.6 Dynamique saloon	114	14,980
Mégane	1.6 Privilege saloon	114	15,980
Mégane	2.0 Dynamique saloon	134	15,980
Mégane	2.0 Privilege saloon	134	16,980
Mégane	1.5 dCi Expression saloon	85	14,770
Mégane	1.5 dCi Dynamique saloon	85	15,270
Mégane	1.5 dCi Dynamique saloon	105	15,470
Mégane	1.5 dCi Dynamique saloon	105	15,970
Mégane	1.5 dCi Privilege saloon	105	16,970
Mégane	1.9 dCi Expression saloon	128	16,670
Mégane	1.9 dCi Expression FAP saloon	128	17,670
Mégane	1.9 dCi Dynamique saloon	128	17,170
Mégane	1.9 dCi Dynamique FAP saloon	128	18,170
Mégane	1.9 dCi Privilege saloon	128	18,170
Mégane	1.9 dCi Privilege FAP saloon	128	19,170
Mégane	1.4 Expression estate	98	14,230
Mégane	1.4 Dynamique estate	98	14,730
Mégane	1.6 Expression estate	114	14,730
Mégane	1.6 Dynamique estate	114	15,230
Mégane	1.6 Dynamique S estate	114	16,230
Mégane	2.0 Dynamique estate	134	16,230
Mégane	2.0 Dynamique S estate	134	17,230
Mégane	1.5 dCi Expression estate	85	15,020
Mégane	1.5 dCi Dynamique estate	85	15,520
Mégane	1.5 dCi Expression estate	105	15,720
Mégane	1.5 dCi Dynamique estate	105	16220
Mégane	1.5 dCi Dynamique S estate	105	17220
Mégane	1.9 dCi Expression estate	128	16,920
Mégane	1.9 dCi Expression FAP estate	128	17,920
Mégane	1.9 dCi Dynamique estate	128	17,420
Mégane	1.9 dCi Dynamique FAP estate	128	18,420
Mégane	1.9 dCi Dynamique S estate	128	18,420
Mégane	1.9 dCi Dynamique S FAP estate	128	19,420
Mégane	2.0 dCi Dynamique estate	148	18,420
Mégane	2.0 dCi Dynamique S estate	148	19,420
Mégane	1.6 Extreme coupé-cabrio	115	17,840
Mégane	1.6 Dynamique coupé-cabrio	115	18,340
Mégane	1.6 Dynamique S coupé-cabrio	115	18,610
Mégane	1.6 Privilege coupé-cabrio	115	19,340
Mégane	2.0 Dynamique coupé-cabrio	136	19,340
Mégane	2.0 Dynamique S coupé-cabrio	136	19,610
Mégane	2.0 Privilege coupé-cabrio	136	20,340
Mégane	2.0 T Dynamique coupé-cabrio	165	20,540
Mégane	2.0 T Dynamique S coupé-cabrio	165	20,810
Mégane	2.0 T Privilege coupé-cabrio	165	21,540
Mégane	1.5 dCi Dynamique coupé-cabrio	105	19,330
Mégane	1.5 dCi Dynamique S coupé-cabrio	105	19,600
Mégane	1.5 dCi Privilege coupé-cabrio	105	20,330
Mégane	1.9 dCi Dynamique coupé-cabrio	128	20,530
Mégane	1.9 dCi Dynamique S coupé-cabrio	128	20,800
Mégane	1.9 dCi Privilege coupé-cabrio	128	21,530
Mégane	2.0 dCi Dynamique coupé-cabrio	148	21,530
Mégane	2.0 dCi Dynamique S coupé-cabrio	148	21,800
Mégane	2.0 dCi Privilege coupé-cabrio	148	22,530
Scénic	1.4 Authentique	97	13,945
Scénic	1.4 Extreme	97	14,445
Scénic	1.4 Expression	97	15,245
Scénic	1.6 Extreme	114	14,945
Scénic	1.6 Expression	114	15,745
Scénic	1.6 Dynamique	114	16,245
Scénic	1.6 Dynamique S	114	17,245
Scénic	1.6 Privilege	114	17,245
Scénic	2.0 Dynamique	134	17,245
Scénic	2.0 Dynamique S	134	18,245
Scénic	2.0 Privilege	134	18,245
Scénic	2.0 Conquest	134	17,945
Scénic	1.5 dCi Authentique	85	14,735
Scénic	1.5 dCi Extreme	85	15,235
Scénic	1.5 dCi Expression	85	16,035
Scénic	1.5 dCi Expression	85	16,535
Scénic	1.5 dCi Dynamique	104	16,735
Scénic	1.5 dCi Dynamique	104	17,235
Scénic	1.5 dCi Dynamique S	104	18,235
Scénic	1.5 dCi Privilege	104	18,235
Scénic	1.9 dCi Dynamique	128	18,435
Scénic	1.9 dCi Dynamique S	128	19,435
Scénic	1.9 dCi Privilege	128	19,435
Scénic	1.9 dCi Conquest	128	19,135
Scénic	2.0 dCi Dynamique	148	19,435
Scénic	2.0 dCi Dynamique S	148	20,435
Scénic	2.0 dCi Privilege	148	20,435
Grand Scénic	1.6 Extreme 5str	114	15,695
Grand Scénic	1.6 Expression 5str	114	16,495
Grand Scénic	1.6 Dynamique 5str	114	16,995
Grand Scénic	1.6 Dynamique S 5str	114	17,995
Grand Scénic	1.6 Privilege 5str	114	17,995
Grand Scénic	2.0 Dynamique 5str	134	17,995
Grand Scénic	2.0 Dynamique S 5str	134	18,995
Grand Scénic	2.0 Privilege 5str	134	18,995
Grand Scénic	1.5 dCi Extreme 5str	105	16,685
Grand Scénic	1.5 dCi Expression 5str	105	17,485
Grand Scénic	1.5 dCi Dynamique 5str	105	17,985
Grand Scénic	1.5 dCi Dynamique S 5str	105	18,985
Grand Scénic	1.5 dCi Privilege 5str	105	18,685
Grand Scénic	1.9 dCi Expression 5str	128	18,185
Grand Scénic	1.9 dCi Dynamique 5str	128	18,685
Grand Scénic	1.9 dCi Dynamique S 5str	128	20,185
Grand Scénic	1.9 dCi Privilege 5str	128	20,185
Grand Scénic	2.0 dCi Dynamique 5str	148	20,185
Grand Scénic	2.0 dCi Dynamique S 5str	148	21,185
Grand Scénic	2.0 dCi Privilege 5str	148	21,185
Grand Scénic	1.6 Extreme 7str	114	15,945
Grand Scénic	1.6 Expression 7str	114	16,745
Grand Scénic	1.6 Dynamique 7str	114	17,245
Grand Scénic	1.6 Dynamique S 7str	114	18,245
Grand Scénic	1.6 Privilege 7str	114	18,245
Grand Scénic	2.0 Dynamique 7str	134	18,245
Grand Scénic	2.0 Dynamique S 7str	134	18,245
Grand Scénic	2.0 Privilege 7str	134	19,245
Grand Scénic	1.5 dCi Extreme 7str	105	16,935
Grand Scénic	1.5 dCi Expression 7str	105	17,735
Grand Scénic	1.5 dCi Dynamique 7str	105	18,235
Grand Scénic	1.5 dCi Dynamique S 7str	105	19,235
Grand Scénic	1.5 dCi Privilege 7str	105	19,235
Grand Scénic	1.9 dCi Expression 7str	128	18,935
Grand Scénic	1.9 dCi Dynamique 7str	128	19,435
Grand Scénic	1.9 dCi Dynamique S 7str	128	20,435
Grand Scénic	1.9 dCi Privilege 7str	128	20,435
Grand Scénic	2.0 dCi Dynamique 7str	148	20,435
Grand Scénic	2.0 dCi Dynamique S 7str	148	21,435
Grand Scénic	2.0 dCi Privilege 7str	148	21,435
Laguna	2.0 Expression	138	15,990
Laguna	2.0 Dynamique	138	16,740
Laguna	2.0 Dynamique S	138	16,040
Laguna	2.0 Initiale	138	20,540
Laguna	2.0 T Dynamique auto	165	18,440
Laguna	2.0 T Dynamique S auto	165	19,440
Laguna	2.0 T Initiale auto	165	21,940
Laguna	1.5 dCi Expression	108	16,350
Laguna	1.5 dCi Dynamique	108	17,100
Laguna	2.0 dCi Dynamique	130	17,250
Laguna	2.0 dCi Dynamique	130	18,000
Laguna	2.0 dCi Expression	150	17,650

Model	Derivative	BHP	UK price
Laguna	2.0 dCi Dynamique	150	18,400
Laguna	2.0 dCi Dynamique S	150	19,700
Laguna	2.0 dCi Initiale	150	22,200
Laguna	2.0 Expression estate	138	16,940
Laguna	2.0 Dynamique estate	138	17,960
Laguna	2.0 Dynamique S estate	138	18,990
Laguna	2.0 Initiale estate	138	21,940
Laguna	2.0 T Dynamique auto estate	165	19,390
Laguna	2.0 T Dynamique S auto estate	165	20,390
Laguna	2.0 T Initiale auto estate	165	22,890
Laguna	1.5 dCi Expression estate	108	17,300
Laguna	1.5 dCi Dynamique estate	108	18,050
Laguna	2.0 dCi Expression estate	130	18,200
Laguna	2.0 dCi Dynamique estate	130	18,950
Laguna	2.0 dCi Expression estate	150	18,600
Laguna	2.0 dCi Dynamique estate	150	19,350
Laguna	2.0 dCi Dynamique S estate	150	20,650
Laguna	2.0 dCi Initiale estate	150	23,150
Espace	2.0 Tech Run	140	20,459
Espace	2.0 Team	140	18,595
Espace	2.0T Dynamique	165	22,405
Espace	2.0T Dynamique S	165	24,155
Espace	2.0 dCi Tech Run	129	22,825
Espace	2.0 dCi Team	129	21,020
Espace	2.0 dCi Dynamique	129	22,825
Espace	2.0 dCi Tech Run	148	23,750
Espace	2.0 dCi Team	148	21,945
Espace	2.0 dCi Dynamique	148	23,750
Espace	2.0 dCi Dynamique S	148	25,500
Espace	2.0 dCi Dynamique FAP	173	24,850
Espace	2.0 dCi Dynamique S FAP	173	26,500
Espace	2.2 dCi Dynamique FAP	137	26,995
Espace	2.2 dCi Dynamique S FAP	137	26,975
Grand Espace	2.0T Tech Run	168	23,605
Grand Espace	2.0T Team	168	21,800
Grand Espace	2.0T Dynamique	168	23,605
Grand Espace	2.0T Dynamique S	168	25,355
Grand Espace	3.5 V6 Initiale	245	33,285
Grand Espace	2.0 dCi Tech Run	148	23,145
Grand Espace	2.0 dCi Team	148	24,950
Grand Espace	2.0 dCi Dynamique	148	24,950
Grand Espace	2.0 dCi Dynamique S	148	26,700
Grand Espace	2.0 dCi Initiale	148	29,850
Grand Espace	2.0 dCi Dynamique	173	26,050
Grand Espace	2.0 dCi Dynamique S	173	27,800
Grand Espace	2.2 dCi Dynamique auto	137	28,175
Grand Espace	2.2 dCi Dynamique S auto	137	29,860
Grand Espace	3.0 dCi Dynamique	180	29,875
Grand Espace	3.0 dCi Initiale auto	180	33,300
ROLLS ROYCE			
Phantom		453	219,975
Phantom	LWB	453	260,500
Phantom		453	260,000
SAAB			
9-3	1.8i Airflow	122	18,575
9-3	1.8i Linear SE	122	20,585
9-3	1.8i Vector Sport	122	22,135
9-3	1.8t Airflow	150	20,050
9-3	1.8t Linear SE	150	22,060
9-3	1.8t Vector Sport	150	23,610
9-3	2.0t Vector Sport	175	24,800
9-3	2.0 T Aero	210	25,995
9-3	2.8 T V6 Aero	250	28,675
9-3	1.9 TiD Airflow	120	19,465
9-3	1.9 TiD Linear SE	120	21,475
9-3	1.9 TiD Vector Sport	120	23,025
9-3	1.9 TiD Airflow	150	20,520
9-3	1.9 TiD Linear SE	150	22,530
9-3	1.9 TiD Vector Sport	150	24,080
9-3	1.9 TiD 180 Aero	178	26,495
9-3	1.8i Airflow Sport Wagon	122	19,575
9-3	1.8i Linear SE Sport Wagon	122	21,585
9-3	1.8i Vector Sport Sport Wagon	122	23,135
9-3	1.8t Airflow Sport Wagon	150	21,050
9-3	1.8t Linear SE Sport Wagon	150	23,060
9-3	2.0t Vector Sport Sport Wagon	175	25,800
9-3	2.0 T Aero Sport Wagon	210	26,995
9-3	2.8 T V6 Aero Sport Wagon	250	29,675
9-3	1.9 TiD Airflow Sport Wagon	120	20,465
9-3	1.9 TiD Linear SE Sport Wagon	120	22,475
9-3	1.9 TiD Vector Sport Sport Wagon	120	24,025
9-3	1.9 TiD Airflow Sport Wagon	150	21,520
9-3	1.9 TiD Linear SE Sport Wagon	150	23,530
9-3	1.9 TiD Vector Sport Sport Wagon	150	25,080
9-3	1.9 TiD 180 Aero Sport Wagon	178	27,495
9-3	1.8t Linear SE cabrio	150	25,975
9-3	1.8t Vector Sport cabrio	150	28,540
9-3	2.0t Vector Sport cabrio	175	29,775
9-3	2.0 T Aero cabrio	210	32,030
9-3	2.8 T V6 Aero cabrio	247	34,495
9-3	1.9 TiD Linear SE cabrio	150	26,430
9-3	1.9 TiD Vector Sport cabrio	150	28,995
9-3	1.9 TiD Vector Sport cabrio	180	32,530
9-5	2.0t Linear SE	150	23,180
9-5	2.0t Vector Sport	150	25,475
9-5	2.0t Airflow	150	21,125
9-5	2.0t Airflow sat-nav	150	23,325
9-5	2.3t Linear SE	185	24,415
9-5	2.3t Vector Sport	185	26,710
9-5	2.3 HOT Aero	260	29,685
9-5	1.9 TiD Linear SE	150	23,600
9-5	1.9 TiD Vector Sport	150	25,895
9-5	1.9 TiD Airflow	150	21,545
9-5	1.9 TiD Airflow sat-nav	150	23,745
9-5	2.0t Linear SE estate	150	24,380
9-5	2.0t Vector Sport estate	150	26,675
9-5	2.0t Airflow estate	150	22,325
9-5	2.0t Airflow sat-nav estate	150	24,525
9-5	2.3t Linear SE estate	185	24,260
9-5	2.3t Vector Sport estate	185	27,910
9-5	2.3 HOT Aero estate	260	30,885
9-5	1.9 TiD Linear SE estate	150	24,800
9-5	1.9 TiD Vector Sport estate	150	27,095
9-5	1.9 TiD Airflow estate	150	22,745
9-5	1.9 TiD Airflow sat-nav estate	150	24,945
SEAT			
Ibiza	1.2 Reference 3dr	63	8,195
Ibiza	1.2 Reference 5dr	63	8,825
Ibiza	1.2 Reference Sport 3dr	63	8,695
Ibiza	1.2 Reference Sport 5dr	63	9,325
Ibiza	1.4 Stylance auto 3dr	74	10,150
Ibiza	1.4 Stylance auto 5dr	74	10,780
Ibiza	1.4 Stylance 3dr	84	9,395
Ibiza	1.4 Stylance 5dr	84	10,025
Ibiza	1.4 Sport 3dr	84	9,395
Ibiza	1.4 Sport 5dr	84	10,025
Ibiza	1.8 20VT FR 3dr	148	12,195
Ibiza	1.8 20VT FR 5dr	148	12,625
Ibiza	1.8 20VT Cupra	178	14,650
Ibiza	1.4 TDi Reference Sport 3dr	79	10,395
Ibiza	1.4 TDi Reference Sport 5dr	79	11,025
Ibiza	1.9 TDi Sport 3dr	99	10,995
Ibiza	1.9 TDi Sport 5dr	99	11,625
Ibiza	1.9 TDi FR 3dr	128	13,350
Ibiza	1.9 TDi FR 5dr	128	13,980
Ibiza	1.9 TDi Cupra	158	15,595
Leon	1.6 Essence	101	11,710
Leon	1.6 Reference	101	12,495
Leon	1.6 Stylance	101	13,695
Leon	2.0 TFSI FR 5dr	197	17,250
Leon	2.0 TFSI Cupra	237	19,695
Leon	1.9 TDi Reference	105	13,495
Leon	1.9 TDi Stylance	105	14,595
Leon	2.0 TDi Reference Sport	140	15,495
Leon	2.0 TDi Stylance	140	16,685
Leon	2.0 TDi FR	168	17,695
Altea	1.6 Essence	101	11,910
Altea	1.6 Reference	101	12,695
Altea	1.6 Reference Sport	101	12,995
Altea	2.0 FSI Stylance Tiptronic	147	16,822
Altea	2.0 TFSI FR	197	17,595
Altea	2.0 TFSI Freetrack 4	197	20,495
Altea	1.9 TDi Reference	103	13,695
Altea	1.9 TDi Reference Sport	103	13,995
Altea	1.9 TDi Stylance	103	14,695
Altea	2.0 TDi Stylance	138	16,695
Altea	2.0 TDi FR	168	17,800
Altea	2.0 TDi Freetrack 4	168	21,395
Altea	XL 1.6 Reference	101	13,250
Altea	XL 1.8T FSI Stylance	158	16,595
Altea	XL 2.0 FSI Stylance auto	148	17,495
Altea	XL 1.9 TDi Stylance	103	15,250
Altea	XL 2.0 TDi Stylance	138	17,195
Altea	XL 2.0 TDi Stylance	168	18,050
Toledo	1.6 Reference	101	12,910
Toledo	1.6 Stylance	101	13,910
Toledo	1.9 TDi Stylance	104	14,995
Toledo	2.0 TDi Stylance	138	16,995
Alhambra	2.0 Reference	113	16,422
Alhambra	1.9 TDi Stylance Tiptronic	113	21,860
Alhambra	2.0 TDi Reference	138	18,712
Alhambra	2.0 TDi Stylance	138	21,412
SKODA			
Fabia	1.2 Level 1	59	7,990
Fabia	1.2 Level 1	68	8,720
Fabia	1.2 Level 2	68	9,720
Fabia	1.4 Level 2	84	10,295
Fabia	1.4 Level 3	84	11,455
Fabia	1.6 Level 2	105	10,795
Fabia	1.6 Level 3	105	11,955
Fabia	1.4 TDI Level 1	68	9,825
Fabia	1.4 TDI Level 1	79	10,175
Fabia	1.4 TDI Level 2	79	11,175
Fabia	1.4 TDI Level 3	79	11,175
Fabia	1.9 TDI Level 2	103	11,855
Fabia	1.9 TDI Level 3	103	13,015
Fabia	1.2 Bohemia estate	64	8,295
Fabia	1.4 Bohemia estate	75	10,480
Fabia	1.4 TDI Bohemia estate	79	10,990
Fabia	1.9 TDI Bohemia estate	100	11,695
Roomster	1.2 Level 1	68	9950
Roomster	1.4 Level 1	85	10,510
Roomster	1.4 Level 2	85	11,510
Roomster	1.4 Level 3	85	12,510
Roomster	1.4 Scout	85	12,510
Roomster	1.6 Level 2	105	11,885
Roomster	1.6 Level 3	105	12,885
Roomster	1.6 Scout	105	12,885
Roomster	1.4 TDI Level 1	70	11,040
Roomster	1.4 TDI Level 2	80	12,470
Roomster	1.4 TDI Level 3	80	13,470
Roomster	1.4 TDI Scout	80	13,470
Roomster	1.9 TDI Level 2	105	13,070
Roomster	1.9 TDI Level 3	105	14,070
Roomster	1.9 TDI Scout	105	14,070
Octavia	1.4 Classic	75	11,020
Octavia	1.6 FSI Classic	115	12,115
Octavia	1.6 FSI Ambiente	115	13,125
Octavia	1.6 FSI Elegance	115	14,135
Octavia	2.0 FSI Ambiente	148	14,505
Octavia	2.0 FSI Sport	148	15,985

Model	Derivative	BHP	UK price
Octavia	2.0 FSI Elegance	148	15,515
Octavia	2.0 FSI L&K	148	16,280
Octavia	2.0 TFSI RS	197	17,725
Octavia	1.9 TDI Classic	105	13,605
Octavia	1.9 TDI Ambiente	105	14,615
Octavia	1.9 TDI Elegance	105	15,625
Octavia	2.0 TDI Ambiente	140	16,080
Octavia	2.0 TDI Sport	140	17,560
Octavia	2.0 TDI Elegance	140	17,090
Octavia	2.0 TDI L&K	140	19,855
Octavia	2.0 TDI RS	168	18,570
Octavia	1.6 FSI Classic estate	115	12,965
Octavia	1.6 FSI Ambiente estate	115	13,975
Octavia	1.6 FSI Elegance estate	115	14,985
Octavia	2.0 FSI Ambiente estate	148	15,395
Octavia	2.0 FSI Elegance estate	148	16,405
Octavia	2.0 FSI L&K estate	148	17,835
Octavia	2.0 FSI Scout estate 4x4	148	16,755
Octavia	2.0 FSI Scout estate 4x4	148	17,755
Octavia	2.0 TFSI RS estate	197	18,575
Octavia	1.9 TDI Classic estate	105	14,455
Octavia	1.9 TDI Ambiente estate	105	15,465
Octavia	1.9 TDI Elegance estate	105	16,475
Octavia	1.9 TDI estate 4x4	105	16,910
Octavia	2.0 TDI Ambiente estate	140	16,930
Octavia	2.0 TDI Elegance estate	140	17,940
Octavia	2.0 TDI L&K estate	140	20,705
Octavia	2.0 TDI 4x4 estate	168	18,690
Octavia	2.0 TDI 4x4 Scout estate	168	19,690
Octavia	2.0 TDI RS estate	168	19,420
Superb	2.0 Classic	114	13,955
Superb	1.8 T Classic	148	15,210
Superb	1.8 T Comfort	148	16,610
Superb	2.8 V6 Elegance	190	21,395
Superb	2.8 V6 L&K	190	22,195
Superb	1.9 TDI Classic	113	14,870
Superb	1.9 TDI Comfort	113	16,270
Superb	1.9 TDI Elegance	113	18,970
Superb	2.0 TDI Classic	140	16,010
Superb	2.0 TDI Comfort	140	17,410
Superb	2.0 TDI Elegance	140	20,135
Superb	2.0 TDI L&K	140	21,235
Superb	2.5 V6 TDI Classic	160	17,640
Superb	2.5 V6 TDI Comfort	160	19,040
Superb	2.5 V6 TDI Elegance	160	21,740

SMART

Model	Derivative	BHP	UK price
Fortwo	Pure Coupé	50	6,782
Fortwo	Pure Coupé	61	7,137
Fortwo	Pulse Coupé	61	8,037
Fortwo	Passion Coupé	61	8,237
Fortwo	Coupé Brabus	74	12,797
Fortwo	Pure cabrio	61	8,937
Fortwo	Pulse cabrio	61	9,837
Fortwo	Passion cabrio	61	10,037
Fortwo	cabrio Brabus	74	14,642

SPYKER

Model	Derivative	BHP	UK price
C8		400	185,000

SSANGYONG

Model	Derivative	BHP	UK price
Rexton	II 270 SE	163	22592
Rexton	II 270 SE 7str	163	23092
Rexton	II 270 SX	163	24592
Rexton	II 270 SX 7str	163	25092
Kyron	2.0 S 2WD	141	16,995
Kyron	2.0 S 4WD	141	18017
Kyron	2.0 SE 4WD	141	19017
Kyron	2.0 SX 4WD	141	22,517
Rodius	S	163	14,997
Rodius	SE	163	15,997
Rodius	SX	163	21592

SUBARU

Model	Derivative	BHP	UK price
Impreza	2.0 RX saloon	158	16252
Impreza	2.0 WRX saloon	227	20097
Impreza	2.0 WRX SL saloon	227	21597
Impreza	2.0 WRX STi Type UK saloon	276	26597
Impreza	1.5R estate	104	12,522
Impreza	2.0RX estate	157	16,752
Impreza	2.5 WRX	227	21,097
Impreza	2.5 WRX SL	276	22,597
Legacy	2.0R	163	18,022
Legacy	2.0REn	163	21,277
Legacy	3.0R spec. B	241	28,597
Legacy	2.0R estate	163	19,022
Legacy	2.0RE estate	163	20,422
Legacy	2.0REn estate	163	22,422
Legacy	3.0R spec. B estate	241	29,597
Outback	2.5i S	162	21,652
Outback	2.5i SE	162	23,952
Outback	2.5i SEn	162	25,352
Outback	3.0R	241	28,597
Outback	3.0Rn	241	29,997
Forester	2.0 X	156	17,677
Forester	2.0 XC	156	19,702
Forester	2.0 XEn	156	21,977
Forester	2.5 XT	208	22,252
Forester	2.5 XTEn	208	25,252
B9 Tribeca	3.0 S5	242	29,097
B9 Tribeca	3.0 SE5	242	32,097
B9 Tribeca	3.0 SE7	242	34,097

SUZUKI

Model	Derivative	BHP	UK price
Wagon R+	1.2 GL	79	8,149
Swift	1.3 GL 3dr	91	7,999
Swift	1.3 GL 5dr	91	8,299
Swift	1.5 GLX 3dr	101	8,899
Swift	1.5 GLX 5dr	101	9,199
Swift	1.6 Sport	123	11,699
Swift	1.3 DDIS	68	9,999
Ignis	1.3 GL	83	7,699
Ignis	1.5 GLX auto	99	8,999
Ignis	1.5 4GRIP GLX	99	9,699
SX4	1.6 GL	106	9,999
SX4	1.6 GLX	106	10,999
SX4	1.6 4GRIP	106	12,999
SX4	1.9 DDIS	120	12,799
Liana	1.6 GL saloon	105	9,999
Liana	1.6 GLX saloon	105	10,999
Liana	1.6 GL 5dr	102	9,999
Liana	1.6 GLX 5dr	102	10,999
Jimny	JLX	84	9,999
Jimny	JLX+	84	10,499
Grand Vitara	1.6 VVT	105	12,875
Grand Vitara	1.6 VVT+	105	13,475
Grand Vitara	2.0	138	15,675
Grand Vitara	1.9 DDiS 3dr	127	14,299
Grand Vitara	1.9 DDiS 5dr	127	17,025

TATA

Model	Derivative	BHP	UK price
Safari	2.0 TDi	89	13,995
Safari	2.0 TDi EX	89	14,995

TOYOTA

Model	Derivative	BHP	UK price
Aygo	1.0 VVT-i 3dr	67	6,845
Aygo	1.0 VVT-i 5dr	67	7,095
Aygo	1.0 VVT-i+ 3dr	67	7,345
Aygo	1.0 VVT-i+ 5dr	67	7,595
Aygo	1.0 VVT-i Black 3dr	67	7,995
Aygo	1.0 VVT-i Black 5dr	67	8,245
Aygo	1.0 VVT-i Blue 3dr	67	7,995
Aygo	1.0 VVT-i Blue 5dr	67	8,245
Yaris	1.0 T2 3dr	67	8,810
Yaris	1.0 T2 5dr	67	9,310
Yaris	1.0 T3 3dr	67	9,995
Yaris	1.0 T3 5dr	67	10,495
Yaris	1.3 T3 3dr	86	10,495
Yaris	1.3 T3 5dr	86	10,995
Yaris	1.3 T-Spirit 3dr	86	11,345
Yaris	1.3 T-Spirit 5dr	86	11,845
Yaris	1.3 SR 3dr	86	10,795
Yaris	1.3 SR 5dr	86	11,295
Yaris	1.8 SR 3dr	131	13,075
Yaris	1.8 SR 5dr	131	13,575
Yaris	1.4 D-4D T2 3dr	89	10,260
Yaris	1.4 D-4D T2 5dr	89	10,760
Yaris	1.4 D-4D T3 3dr	89	11,265
Yaris	1.4 D-4D T3 5dr	89	11,945
Yaris	1.4 D-4D T-Spirit 3dr	89	12,295
Yaris	1.4 D-4D T-Spirit 5dr	89	12,795
Yaris	1.4 D-4D SR 3dr	89	13,075
Yaris	1.4 D-4D SR 5dr	89	13,575
Auris	1.4 T2 3dr	95	12,095
Auris	1.4 T2 5dr	95	12,595
Auris	1.4 T3 3dr	95	13,095
Auris	1.4 T3 5dr	95	13,595
Auris	1.6 T3 3dr	122	13,595
Auris	1.6 T3 5dr	122	14,095
Auris	1.6 TR 3dr	122	12,595
Auris	1.6 TR 5dr	122	13,095
Auris	1.6 T-Spirit 5dr	122	14,995
Auris	1.4 D-4D T2 3dr	89	13,195
Auris	1.4 D-4D T2 5dr	89	13,695
Auris	1.4 D-4D T3 3dr	89	14,195
Auris	1.4 D-4D T3 5dr	89	14,645
Auris	2.0 D-4D T3 3dr	124	15,195
Auris	2.0 D-4D T3 5dr	124	15,695
Auris	2.0 D-4D TR 3dr	124	14,195
Auris	2.0 D-4D TR 5dr	124	14,695
Auris	2.0 D-4D T-Spirit 5dr	124	16,595
Auris	2.2 D-4D T180 3dr	175	18,395
Auris	2.2 D-4D T180 5dr	175	18,895
Avensis	1.8 T2	127	15,595
Avensis	1.8 T3-S	127	17,095
Avensis	1.8 T3-X	127	17,495
Avensis	1.8 TR	127	17,095
Avensis	2.0 T4	145	19,595
Avensis	2.0 T-Spirit	145	21,095
Avensis	2.0 D-4D T2	124	16,245
Avensis	2.0 D-4D T3-S	124	17,745
Avensis	2.0 D-4D T3-X	124	17,745
Avensis	2.0 D-4D TR	124	18,145
Avensis	2.2 D-4D T3-S	148	18,245
Avensis	2.2 D-4D T3-X	148	18,245
Avensis	2.2 D-4D TR	148	18,645
Avensis	2.2 D-4D T4	148	19,595
Avensis	2.2 D-4D T-Spirit	148	21,095
Avensis	2.2 D-4D T180	148	21,595
Avensis	1.8 T2 saloon	127	15,595
Avensis	1.8 T3-S saloon	127	17,095
Avensis	1.8 T3-X saloon	127	17,095
Avensis	1.8 TR saloon	127	17,495
Avensis	2.0 T4 saloon	145	19,595
Avensis	2.0 T-Spirit saloon	145	21,095
Avensis	2.0 D-4D T2 saloon	124	16,245
Avensis	2.0 D-4D T3-S saloon	124	17,745
Avensis	2.0 D-4D T3-X saloon	124	17,745
Avensis	2.0 D-4D TR saloon	124	18,145
Avensis	2.2 D-4D T3-S saloon	148	18,245
Avensis	2.2 D-4D T3-X saloon	148	18,245
Avensis	2.2 D-4D TR saloon	148	18,645
Avensis	2.2 D-4D T4 saloon	148	19,595
Avensis	2.2 D-4D T-Spirit saloon	148	21,095
Avensis	2.2 D-4D T180 saloon	175	22,595
Avensis	1.8 T3-S estate	127	18,095

Model	Derivative	BHP	UK price
Avensis	1.8 T3-X estate	127	18,095
Avensis	1.8 TR estate	127	18,495
Avensis	2.0 T4 estate	145	20,595
Avensis	2.0 T-Spirit estate	145	22,095
Avensis	2.0 D-4D T2 estate	124	17,245
Avensis	2.0 D-4D T3-S estate	124	18,745
Avensis	2.0 D-4D T3-X estate	124	18,745
Avensis	2.0 D-4D TR estate	124	19,145
Avensis	2.2 D-4D T3-S estate	148	19,245
Avensis	2.2 D-4D T3-X estate	148	19,245
Avensis	2.2 D-4D TR estate	148	19,645
Avensis	2.2 D-4D T4 estate	148	20,595
Avensis	2.2 D-4D T-Spirit estate	148	22,095
Avensis	2.2 D-4D T180 estate	148	22,595
Verso	1.6 T2	109	14,445
Verso	1.8 T2	127	16,395
Verso	1.8 T3	127	17,295
Verso	1.8 T-Spirit	127	19,295
Verso	1.8 SR	127	16,995
Verso	2.2 D-4D T2	134	16,395
Verso	2.2 D-4D T3	134	18,395
Verso	2.2 D-4D T-Spirit	134	20,395
Verso	2.2 D-4D T180	175	21,245
Prius	T3	76	17,777
Prius	T4	76	18,577
Prius	T-Spirit	76	20,677
RAV4	2.0 XT3	150	19,095
RAV4	2.0 XT-R	150	19,995
RAV4	2.0 XT4	150	21,595
RAV4	2.0 XT5	150	24,595
RAV4	2.2 D-4D XT3	134	20,345
RAV4	2.2 D-4D XT-R	134	21,245
RAV4	2.2 D-4D XT4	134	22,845
RAV4	2.2 D-4D XT5	134	25,845
RAV4	2.2 D-4D T180	175	27,045
Land Cruiser	4.0 V6 LC4	245	34,595
Land Cruiser	4.0 V6 LC5	245	38,495
Land Cruiser	3.0 D-4D LC3 3d	164	27,595
Land Cruiser	3.0 D-4D LC3 5d	164	29,095
Land Cruiser	3.0 D-4D LC4 5d	164	32,895
Land Cruiser	3.0 D-4D LC5 5d	164	36,795
Land Cruiser	3.0 D-4D Invincible 5d	164	38,495
Amazon	4.7	235	50,930
Amazon	4.2 D-4D	201	48,245
TVR (DEFUNCT AS THIS BOOK WENT TO PRESS)			
Tuscan	3.6 Targa	350	39,850
Tuscan	4.0 Targa S	400	49,995
Tuscan	3.6 convertible	350	41,950
Tuscan	4.0 convertible	400	51,995
Tamora	3.6	350	36,425
T400	4.0	400	70,193
T400	4.0 440	440	75,193
Sagaris	4.0	400	49,350
VAUXHALL			
Agila	1.0 Expression	59	6,625
Agila	1.2 Enjoy	79	8,745
Agila	1.2 Design	79	9,025
Corsa	1.0 Expression 3dr	60	7,495
Corsa	1.0 Life 3dr	60	8,600
Corsa	1.0 Life 5dr	60	9,250
Corsa	1.2 Life 3dr	79	9,000
Corsa	1.2 Life 5dr	79	9,650
Corsa	1.2 Club 3dr	79	9,400
Corsa	1.2 Club 5dr	79	10,050
Corsa	1.2 Design 3dr	79	11,050
Corsa	1.2 Design 5dr	79	11,700
Corsa	1.2 SXi 3dr	79	10,300
Corsa	1.2 SXi 5dr	79	10,950
Corsa	1.4 Club 3dr	89	9,990
Corsa	1.4 Club 5dr	89	10,640
Corsa	1.4 Design 3dr	89	11,550
Corsa	1.4 Design 5dr	89	12,200
Corsa	1.4 SXi 3dr	89	10,800
Corsa	1.4 SXi 5dr	89	11,450
Corsa	1.6 VXR	189	15,625
Corsa	1.3 CDTi Life 3dr	74	9,810
Corsa	1.3 CDTi Life 5dr	74	10,460
Corsa	1.3 CDTi Club 3dr	74	10,210
Corsa	1.3 CDTi Club 5dr	74	10,860
Corsa	1.3 CDTi SXi 3dr	90	11,490
Corsa	1.3 CDTi SXi 5dr	90	12,140
Corsa	1.3 CDTi Design 3dr	90	12,240
Corsa	1.3 CDTi Design 5dr	90	12,890
Corsa	1.7 CDTi SXi 3dr	123	12,640
Corsa	1.7 CDTi SXi 5dr	123	13,290
Corsa	1.7 CDTi Design 3dr	123	13,390
Corsa	1.7 CDTi Design 5dr	123	14,040
Tigra	1.4	90	13,995
Tigra	1.4 Sport	90	15,195
Tigra	1.4 Twinport Exclusive	88	15,195
Tigra	1.8 Sport	125	16,025
Tigra	1.8 Exclusive	123	16,025
Tigra	1.3 CDTi	69	15,035
Tigra	1.3 CDTi Sport	69	16,185
Meriva	1.4 Expression	89	10,495
Meriva	1.4 Life	89	11,695
Meriva	1.4 Club	89	13,445
Meriva	1.4 Design	89	13,650
Meriva	1.6 Life	111	12,395
Meriva	1.6 Club	111	14,145
Meriva	1.6 Design	111	14,350
Meriva	1.8 Club	123	14,870
Meriva	1.8 Design	123	15,075
Meriva	1.8 VXR	178	16,570
Meriva	1.3 CDTi Expression	74	11,275
Meriva	1.3 CDTi Life	74	12,980
Meriva	1.3 CDTi Club	74	14,730
Meriva	1.7 CDTi Life	99	13,730
Meriva	1.7 CDTi Club	99	15,480
Meriva	1.7 CDTi Design	99	15,685
Astra	1.4 Expression	90	11,560
Astra	1.4 Life	90	12,915
Astra	1.4 Club	90	13,915
Astra	1.4 SXi	90	14,415
Astra	1.6 Life	105	13,565
Astra	1.6 Club	105	14,565
Astra	1.6 Design	113	15,415
Astra	1.6 Elite	113	16,465
Astra	1.6 SXi	113	15,065
Astra	1.6T Design	178	18,550
Astra	1.6T SRi	178	18,250
Astra	1.8 Life	125	14,115
Astra	1.8 Club	125	15,115
Astra	1.8 Design	125	15,965
Astra	1.8 Elite	125	17,015
Astra	1.8 SRi	125	16,300
Astra	1.3 CDTi Life	89	14,500
Astra	1.3 CDTi Club	89	15,500
Astra	1.7 CDTi Life	99	15,350
Astra	1.7 CDTi Club	99	15,850
Astra	1.7 CDTi Design	99	16,700
Astra	1.7 CDTi Elite	99	17,750
Astra	1.7 CDTi SXi	99	16,350
Astra	1.7 CDTi SRi	99	17,050
Astra	1.9 CDTi Design	120	17,555
Astra	1.9 CDTi Elite	120	18,605
Astra	1.9 CDTi SRi	120	17,605
Astra	1.9 CDTi Design	149	18,405
Astra	1.9 CDTi SRi	149	18,105
Astra	1.4 Life estate	90	13,665
Astra	1.4 Club estate	90	14,665
Astra	1.4 SXi estate	90	15,165
Astra	1.6 Life estate	105	14,315
Astra	1.6 Club estate	105	15,315
Astra	1.6 Design estate	105	16,165
Astra	1.6 SXi estate	105	15,815
Astra	1.6T Design estate	178	19,300
Astra	1.6T SRi estate	178	19,000
Astra	1.8 Life estate	125	14,850
Astra	1.8 Club estate	125	15,850
Astra	1.8 Design estate	125	16,700
Astra	1.8 SRi estate	125	17,050
Astra	1.3 CDTi Life estate	89	15,250
Astra	1.3 CDTi Club estate	89	16,250
Astra	1.7 CDTi Life estate	99	16,100
Astra	1.7 CDTi Club estate	99	16,600
Astra	1.7 CDTi Design estate	99	17,450
Astra	1.7 CDTi SXi estate	99	17,100
Astra	1.7 CDTi SRi estate	99	17,800
Astra	1.9 CDTi Design estate	120	18,305
Astra	1.9 CDTi SRi estate	120	18,355
Astra	1.9 CDTi Design estate	150	19,155
Astra	1.9 CDTi SRi estate	150	18,855
Astra	1.4 SXi Sporthatch	90	14,415
Astra	1.6 Design Sporthatch	105	15,415
Astra	1.6 SXi Sporthatch	105	15,065
Astra	1.6T Design Sporthatch	178	18,550
Astra	1.6T SRi Sporthatch	178	18,250
Astra	1.8 Design Sporthatch	125	15,965
Astra	1.8 SRi Sporthatch	125	16,300
Astra	VXR	237	19,185
Astra	1.7 CDTi Design Sporthatch	99	16,700
Astra	1.7 CDTi SXi Sporthatch	99	16,350
Astra	1.7 CDTi SRi Sporthatch	99	17,050
Astra	1.9 CDTi Design Sporthatch	120	17,555
Astra	1.9 CDTi SRi Sporthatch	120	17,605
Astra	1.9 CDTi Design Sporthatch	149	18,405
Astra	1.9 CDTi SRi Sporthatch	149	18,105
Astra	TwinTop 1.6	105	17,195
Astra	TwinTop 1.6 Sport	103	17,995
Astra	TwinTop 1.8	138	17,695
Astra	TwinTop 1.8 Sport	138	18,495
Astra	TwinTop 1.8 Design	138	19,195
Astra	TwinTop 2.0T Design	197	21,325
Astra	TwinTop 1.9 CDTi Sport	148	20,465
Astra	TwinTop 1.9 CDTi Design	148	21,165
Zafira	1.6 Expression	104	12,995
Zafira	1.6 Life	104	14,800
Zafira	1.6 Club	104	15,525
Zafira	1.8 Life	138	16,025
Zafira	1.8 Club	138	16,750
Zafira	1.8 Design	138	17,950
Zafira	1.8 SRi	138	18,150
Zafira	1.8 Elite	138	17,950
Zafira	2.2 Life	146	17,175
Zafira	2.2 Club	146	17,900
Zafira	2.2 Design	146	19,350
Zafira	2.2 SRi	146	18,900
Zafira	2.2 Elite	146	19,350
Zafira	2.0 T Design	197	20,895
Zafira	2.0 T SRi	197	20,445
Zafira	2.0 T Elite	197	20,895
Zafira	VXR	237	22,145
Zafira	1.9 CDTi Life	118	17,290
Zafira	1.9 CDTi Club	118	18,015
Zafira	1.9 CDTi Design	118	19,215
Zafira	1.9 CDTi SRi	118	19,415
Zafira	1.9 CDTi Elite	118	19,215
Zafira	1.9 CDTi Design	148	20,340
Zafira	1.9 CDTi SRi	148	19,890
Zafira	1.9 CDTi Elite	148	20,340
Vectra	1.8 Exclusive	138	14,885
Vectra	1.8 Design	120	17,935
Vectra	1.8 SRi	120	17,210
Vectra	2.0T SRi	173	18,250

398

Model	Derivative	BHP	UK price
Vectra	2.2 Design	154	18,535
Vectra	2.2 Elite	154	20,850
Vectra	2.2 SRi	154	17,810
Vectra	2.8T Elite	227	23,910
Vectra	VXR	252	24,505
Vectra	1.9 CDTi Life	120	17,760
Vectra	1.9 CDTi Club	120	17,480
Vectra	1.9 CDTi Exclusive	120	15,860
Vectra	1.9 CDTi Design	120	19,410
Vectra	1.9 CDTi SRi	120	18,685
Vectra	1.9 CDTi Life	150	18,260
Vectra	1.9 CDTi Exclusive	150	16,360
Vectra	1.9 CDTi Design	150	19,910
Vectra	1.9 CDTi Elite	150	22,260
Vectra	1.9 CDTi SRi	150	19,185
Vectra	3.0 CDTi Elite	174	25,325
Vectra	3.0 CDTi SRi	174	22,250
Vectra	1.8 Life saloon	120	16,582
Vectra	1.8 Design saloon	120	17,935
Vectra	2.2 Design saloon	154	18,535
Vectra	1.9 CDTi Life saloon	120	17,760
Vectra	1.9 CDTi Design saloon	120	19,410
Vectra	1.9 CDTi Life saloon	150	18,260
Vectra	1.9 CDTi Design saloon	150	19,910
Vectra	1.8 Life estate	138	17,400
Vectra	1.8 Exclusive estate	138	16,000
Vectra	1.8 Design estate	138	19,050
Vectra	1.8 SRi estate	138	18,325
Vectra	2.0 T SRi estate	173	19,365
Vectra	2.2 Design estate	154	19,690
Vectra	2.2 Elite estate	154	22,040
Vectra	2.2 SRi estate	154	18,965
Vectra	2.8 T Elite estate	227	25,485
Vectra	VXR estate	252	25,620
Vectra	1.9 CDTi Life estate	120	19,225
Vectra	1.9 CDTi Exclusive estate	120	17,325
Vectra	1.9 CDTi Design estate	120	20,875
Vectra	1.9 CDTi SRi estate	120	20,150
Vectra	1.9 CDTi Life estate	150	19,725
Vectra	1.9 CDTi Exclusive estate	150	17,825
Vectra	1.9 CDTi Design estate	150	21,375
Vectra	1.9 CDTi Elite estate	150	23,725
Vectra	1.9 CDTi SRi estate	150	20,650
Vectra	3.0 CDTi Elite estate	174	26,440
Vectra	3.0 CDTi Elite estate	174	23,365
Signum	1.8 Elegance	138	19,045
Signum	1.8 Exclusive	138	18,200
Signum	2.0T Elegance	173	20,270
Signum	2.0T Design	173	20,975
Signum	2.0T Elite	173	23,425
Signum	2.2 Elegance	154	19,685
Signum	2.2 Exclusive	154	18,840
Signum	2.2 Design	154	20,375
Signum	2.2 Elite	154	22,825
Signum	2.8T Design	227	23,175
Signum	2.8T Elite	227	25,685
Signum	1.9 CDTi Elegance	120	20,870
Signum	1.9 CDTi Exclusive	120	20,025
Signum	1.9 CDTi Design	120	21,560
Signum	1.9 CDTi Elegance	150	21,370
Signum	1.9 CDTi Exclusive	150	20,525
Signum	1.9 CDTi Design	150	22,060
Signum	1.9 CDTi Elite	150	24,510
Signum	3.0 CDTi Design	174	24,775
Signum	3.0 CDTi Elite	174	27,225
Antara	2.4 E	138	19,995
Antara	2.0 CDTi E	148	21095
Antara	2.0 CDTi S	148	22620
Antara	2.0 CDTi SE	148	26320
VXR8	6.0	414	35105
VOLKSWAGEN			
Fox	1.2	54	6,602
Fox	1.2 Urban	54	7,202
Fox	1.4	74	7,422
Fox	1.4 Urban	74	8,022
Polo	1.2 E 3dr	59	7,612
Polo	1.2 E 5dr	59	8,212
Polo	1.2 S 3dr	59	9,222
Polo	1.2 S 5dr	59	9,822
Polo	1.2 E 3dr	69	8,227
Polo	1.2 E 5dr	69	8,827
Polo	1.2 S 3dr	69	9,622
Polo	1.2 S 5dr	69	10,222
Polo	1.4 S 3dr	79	9,932
Polo	1.4 S 5dr	79	10,532
Polo	1.4 SE 3dr	79	10,642
Polo	1.4 SE 5dr	79	11,242
Polo	1.4 Dune	74	12,832
Polo	1.6 Sport 3dr	104	12,697
Polo	1.6 Sport 5dr	104	13,297
Polo	GTI 3dr	150	15,022
Polo	GTI 5dr	150	15,622
Polo	1.4 TDI S 3dr	69	10,687
Polo	1.4 TDI S 5dr	69	11,287
Polo	1.4 TDI SE 3dr	79	11,717
Polo	1.4 TDI SE 5dr	79	12,317
Polo	1.4 TDI Bluemotion 1 3dr	79	11,995
Polo	1.4 TDI Bluemotion 1 5dr	79	12,595
Polo	1.4 TDI Bluemotion 2 3dr	79	12,845
Polo	1.4 TDI Bluemotion 2 5dr	79	13,445
Polo	1.4 TDI Dune	70	13,667
Polo	1.9 TDI Sport 3dr	99	13,652
Polo	1.9 TDI Sport 5dr	99	14,252
Golf	1.4 S 3dr	79	12,127
Golf	1.4 S 5dr	79	12,627
Golf	1.4 TSI Sport 3dr	138	17,422
Golf	1.4 TSI Sport 5dr	138	17,922
Golf	1.4 TSI Sport 3dr	168	18,522
Golf	1.4 TSI Sport 5dr	168	19,022
Golf	1.6 FSI S 3dr	113	14,027
Golf	1.6 FSI S 5dr	113	14,527
Golf	1.6 FSI Match 5dr	113	15,162
Golf	2.0 FSI GTI 3dr	197	20,607
Golf	2.0 FSI GTI 5dr	197	21,107
Golf	R32 3dr	250	24,597
Golf	R32 5dr	250	25,097
Golf	2.0 SDI S 3dr	74	12,811
Golf	2.0 SDI S 5dr	74	13,317
Golf	1.9 TDI S 3dr	104	14,327
Golf	1.9 TDI S 5dr	104	15,427
Golf	1.9 TDI Match 5dr	104	16,067
Golf	1.9 TDI Sport 3dr	104	16,025
Golf	1.9 TDI Sport 5dr	104	16,525
Golf	2.0 TDI GT 3dr	138	18,387
Golf	2.0 TDI GT 5dr	138	18,887
Golf	2.0 TDI Sport 4Motion 5dr	138	19,067
Golf	2.0 TDI DPF GT Sport 3dr	168	19,512
Golf	2.0 TDI DPF GT Sport 5dr	168	20,012
Golf	1.6 S estate	100	14347
Golf	1.6 SE estate	100	15632
Golf	1.9 TDI S estate	104	15572
Golf	1.9 TDI SE estate	104	16952
Golf	2.0 TDI SE estate	138	17862
Golf	2.0 TDI Sportline estate	138	18637
Golf Plus	1.4 Luna	79	13,162
Golf Plus	1.4 TSI Sport	138	17,442
Golf Plus	1.6 FSI Luna	113	15,177
Golf Plus	1.6 FSI SE	113	16,022
Golf Plus	1.9 TDI Luna	89	15,012
Golf Plus	1.9 TDI Luna	105	16,027
Golf Plus	1.9 TDI SE	105	16,877
Golf Plus	1.9 TDI Dune	105	18,495
Golf Plus	2.0 TDI Sport	138	18,757
Touran	1.4 TSI SE	138	18,262
Touran	1.6 S	101	14,777
Touran	1.6 SE	89	15,742
Touran	1.9 TDI S	104	16,292
Touran	1.9 TDI DPF S	104	16,740
Touran	1.9 TDI SE	104	17,982
Touran	1.9 TDI DPF SE	104	18,432
Touran	2.0 TDI SE	138	19,307
Touran	2.0 TDI DPF SE	138	19,757
Touran	2.0 TDI Sport	138	21,077
Touran	2.0 TDI DPF Sport	138	21,527
Touran	2.0 TDI Sport	168	22,277
Jetta	1.4 TSI SE	138	16,502
Jetta	1.4 TSI Sport	168	18,092
Jetta	1.6 FSI S	113	14,802
Jetta	1.6 FSI SE	113	15,792
Jetta	2.0 TFSI Sport	197	19,007
Jetta	1.9 TDI S	103	15,507
Jetta	1.9 TDI SE	103	16,472
Jetta	2.0 TDI SE	138	17,682
Jetta	2.0 TDI Sport	138	18,172
New Beetle	1.4 Luna	74	11,547
New Beetle	1.6 Luna	102	12,487
New Beetle	2.0	115	14,947
New Beetle	1.8 T	150	16,167
New Beetle	1.9 TDI	99	14,907
New Beetle	1.4 Luna cabrio	74	14,372
New Beetle	1.6 Luna cabrio	102	15,787
New Beetle	2.0 cabrio	115	13,812
New Beetle	1.8 T cabrio	150	19,682
New Beetle	1.9 TDI cabrio	100	18,787
New Beetle	1.9 TDI cabrio	113	19,722
Eos	1.6 FSI	113	21,142
Eos	2.0 FSI	148	22,087
Eos	2.0 FSI Sport	148	23,667
Eos	2.0 TFSI Sport	197	25,767
Eos	2.0 TFSI Individual	197	28,427
Eos	3.2 V6 FSI Sport DSG	247	29,527
Eos	3.2 V6 FSI Individual DSG	247	21,702
Eos	2.0 TDI	138	22,647
Eos	2.0 TDI Sport	138	24,747
Eos	2.0 TDI Individual	138	15,522
Passat	1.6 FSI S	113	16,692
Passat	2.0 FSI S	150	18,267
Passat	2.0 FSI SE	150	21,107
Passat	2.0 TFSI Sport	197	26,147
Passat	3.2 4Motion	249	16,332
Passat	1.9 TDI S	104	17,637
Passat	1.9 TDI SE	104	17,662
Passat	2.0 TDI S	138	18,967
Passat	2.0 TDI SE	138	20,217
Passat	2.0 TDI SE 4MOTION	138	20,407
Passat	2.0 TDI Sport	138	21,657
Passat	2.0 TDI Sport 4MOTION	138	21,212
Passat	2.0 TDI Sport	168	21,937
Passat	2.0 TDI SEL	168	16,642
Passat	1.6 FSI S estate	113	18,077
Passat	2.0 FSI S estate	150	19,367
Passat	2.0 FSI SE estate	150	22,207
Passat	2.0 TFSI Sport estate	197	27,247
Passat	3.2 4Motion estate	249	17,472
Passat	1.9 TDI S estate	104	18,762
Passat	1.9 TDI SE estate	104	18,777
Passat	2.0 TDI S estate	138	20,067
Passat	2.0 TDI SE estate	138	21,317
Passat	2.0 TDI SE estate 4MOTION	138	21,507
Passat	2.0 TDI Sport estate	138	22,757
Passat	2.0 TDI Sport 4MOTION estate	168	22,337
Passat	2.0 TDI Sport estate	168	23,062
Passat	2.0 TDI SEL estate	168	
Phaeton	3.2 V6 4Motion LWB	238	46,902
Phaeton	4.2 V8 4Motion LWB	330	56,042
Phaeton	6.0 W12 4Motion LWB	444	73,272

Model	Derivative	BHP	UK price
Phaeton	3.0 V6 TDI 4Motion	222	37,995
Phaeton	3.0 V6 TDI 4Motion LWB	222	40,265
Touareg	3.6 V6 SE	276	36,532
Touareg	3.6 V6 Altitude	276	39,302
Touareg	2.5 TDI	172	29,562
Touareg	2.5 TDI SE	172	32,947
Touareg	2.5 TDI Altitude	172	35,712
Touareg	3.0 V6 TDI	222	32,322
Touareg	3.0 V6 TDI SE	222	35,707
Touareg	3.0 V6 TDI Altitude	222	38,472
Touareg	5.0 V10 TDI SE	309	54,867
Touareg	5.0 V10 TDI Altitude	309	57,632
Sharan	2.0 S	115	25,005
Sharan	2.0 SE	115	18,152
Sharan	1.8 T Sport	150	19,547
Sharan	1.9 TDI S	113	23,457
Sharan	1.9 TDI SE	113	19,707
Sharan	2.0 TDI S	138	20,867
Sharan	2.0 TDI SE	138	20,457
Sharan	2.0 TDI Sport	138	21,617
			24,162

Model	Derivative	BHP	UK price
VOLVO			
C30	1.6 S	99	14,750
C30	1.6 SE	99	16,250
C30	1.6 SE Sport	99	18,995
C30	1.8 S	124	15,995
C30	1.8 SE	124	17,495
C30	1.8 SE Sport	124	18,995
C30	1.8 SE Lux	124	18,995
C30	2.0 S	143	16,995
C30	2.0 SE	143	18,495
C30	2.0 SE Sport	143	19,995
C30	2.0 SE Lux	143	19,995
C30	2.4 S	168	17,995
C30	2.4 SE	168	19,495
C30	2.4 SE Sport	168	20,995
C30	2.4 SE Lux	168	20,995
C30	T5 SE	220	21,495
C30	T5 SE Sport	220	22,995
C30	T5 SE Lux	220	22,995
C30	1.6 D S	108	16,795
C30	1.6 D SE	108	18,295
C30	2.0 D S	134	17,795
C30	2.0 D SE	134	19,295
C30	2.0 D SE Sport	134	20,795
C30	2.0 D SE Lux	134	20,795
C30	D5 Geartronic SE	180	22,295
C30	D5 Geartronic SE Sport	180	23,795
C30	D5 Geartronic SE Lux	180	23,795
S40	1.6 S	99	13,750
S40	1.8 S	123	15,995
S40	1.8 SE	123	17,495
S40	1.8 Sport	123	17,645
S40	2.0 SE	143	18,495
S40	2.0 Sport	143	18,645
S40	2.0 SE Sport	143	19,695
S40	2.0 SE Lux	143	19,995
S40	2.4 SE	168	19,495
S40	2.4 SE Lux	168	20,995
S40	T5 Sport	227	21,645
S40	T5 SE Sport	227	22,695
S40	T5 SE Lux	227	22,995
S40	1.6 D S	108	16,795
S40	1.6 D SE	108	18,295
S40	2.0 D S	134	17,795
S40	2.0 D Sport	134	19,445
S40	2.0 D SE	134	19,295
S40	2.0 D SE Sport	134	20,495
S40	2.0 D SE Lux	134	20,795
S40	D5 Sport	178	22,445
S40	D5 SE	178	22,295
S40	D5 SE Sport	178	23,495
S40	D5 SE Lux	178	23,795
V50	1.6 S	99	15,995
V50	1.8 S	123	17,345
V50	1.8 Sport	123	18,995
V50	1.8 SE	123	18,845
V50	2.0 Sport	143	19,995
V50	2.0 SE	143	19,845
V50	2.0 SE Sport	143	21,045
V50	2.0 SE Lux	143	22,245
V50	2.4 SE	168	20,845
V50	2.4 SE Lux	168	23,345
V50	T5 SE Lux	217	22,995
V50	T5 SE Sport	217	24,345
V50	1.6 D S	108	18,145
V50	1.6 D SE	108	19,645
V50	2.0 D S	134	19,145
V50	2.0 D Sport	134	20,795
V50	2.0 D SE	134	20,645
V50	2.0 D SE Sport	134	21,845
V50	2.0 D SE Lux	134	22,145
V50	D5 Sport	178	23,795
V50	D5 SE	178	23,645
V50	D5 SE Sport	178	24,845
V50	D5 SE Lux	178	25,145
S60	2.0T S	177	19,995
S60	2.0T Sport	177	21,495
S60	2.0T SE	177	21,745
S60	2.0T SE Sport	177	22,995
S60	2.0T SE Lux	177	23,995
S60	2.5T S	210	22,840
S60	2.5T Sport	210	24,340
S60	2.5T SE	210	24,590
S60	2.5T SE Sport	210	25,840
S60	2.5T SE Lux	210	26,840

Model	Derivative	BHP	UK price
S60	T5 Sport	260	26,425
S60	T5 SE	250	26,675
S60	T5 SE Sport	260	27,925
S60	T5 SE Lux	250	28,925
S60	2.4D S	163	22,395
S60	2.4D Sport	163	23,895
S60	2.4D SE	163	24,145
S60	2.4D SE Sport	163	25,395
S60	2.4D SE Lux	163	26,395
S60	D5 S	185	23,270
S60	D5 Sport	185	24,470
S60	D5 SE	185	25,020
S60	D5 SE Sport	185	26,270
S60	D5 SE Lux	185	27,270
V70	2.5T SE	197	26,495
V70	2.5T SE Sport	197	29,345
V70	2.5T SE Lux	197	29,245
V70	3.2 SE	235	30,600
V70	3.2 SE Sport	235	33,450
V70	3.2 SE Lux	235	33,350
V70	3.0 T6 AWD SE	281	35,430
V70	3.0 T6 AWD SE Sport	281	38,280
V70	3.0 T6 AWD SE Lux	281	38,180
V70	2.4D SE	161	26,995
V70	2.4D SE Sport	161	29,845
V70	2.4D SE Lux	161	30,745
V70	D5 SE	182	27,995
V70	D5 SE Sport	182	30,845
V70	D5 SE Lux	182	30,745
XC70	3.2 SE	235	33,600
XC70	3.2 SE Sport	235	35,700
XC70	3.2 SE Lux	235	36,200
XC70	D5 SE	182	31,035
XC70	D5 SE Sport	182	33,135
XC70	D5 SE Lux	182	33,635
C70	2.4 S	170	25,750
C70	2.4 Sport	170	26,500
C70	2.4 SE	170	27,750
C70	2.4 SE Lux	170	29,975
C70	T5 Sport	217	29,775
C70	T5 SE	217	31,025
C70	T5 SE Lux	217	33,250
C70	2.0D S	134	26,000
C70	D5 Sport	178	29,695
C70	D5 SE	178	30,945
C70	D5 SE Lux	178	33,170
S80	2.5T SE	197	24,995
S80	2.5T SE Sport	197	27,845
S80	2.5T SE Lux	197	27,495
S80	3.2 SE	235	28,995
S80	3.2 SE Sport	235	31,845
S80	3.2 SE Lux	235	31,495
S80	3.2 Executive	235	39,995
S80	3.2 AWD SE	235	30,130
S80	3.2 AWD SE Sport	235	32,630
S80	3.2 AWD SE Lux	235	32,980
S80	3.2 AWD Executive	235	40,995
S80	4.4 SE	311	36,995
S80	4.4 SE Sport	311	39,845
S80	4.4 SE Lux	311	39,495
S80	4.4 Executive	311	47,995
S80	2.4D SE	161	25,495
S80	2.4D SE Sport	161	28,345
S80	2.4D SE Lux	161	27,995
S80	D5 SE	182	26,495
S80	D5 SE Sport	182	29,345
S80	D5 SE Lux	182	29,245
S80	D5 Executive	182	38,515
S80	D5 AWD SE	182	27,630
S80	D5 AWD SE Sport	182	30,480
S80	D5 AWD SE Lux	182	30,380
S80	D5 AWD Executive	182	39,650
XC90	3.2 SE	235	36,435
XC90	3.2 SE Sport	235	38,385
XC90	3.2 SE Lux	235	38,535
XC90	3.2 Executive	235	46,525
XC90	4.4 SE	311	44,330
XC90	4.4 SE Sport	311	46,055
XC90	4.4 SE Lux	311	46,430
XC90	4.4 Executive	311	54,420
XC90	D5 S	182	32,845
XC90	D5 SE	182	35,345
XC90	D5 SE Sport	182	37,295
XC90	D5 SE Lux	182	37,445
XC90	D5 Executive	182	46,780

Model	Derivative	BHP	UK price
WESTFIELD			
XTR2	1.3	178	27,950
XTR4	1.8	192	29,995
Sport	1800	120	15,999
Sport	1800	155	16,999
Sport	2000	192	19,950
Mega Roadster	Megabusa	178	22,999
Seight	3.9 V8	200	24,999